Corporate Governance

Corporate Governance

FOURTH EDITION

Christine A. Mallin

OXFORD
UNIVERSITY PRESS

OXFORD

UNIVERSITY PRESS

Great Clarendon Street, Oxford OX2 6DP,
United Kingdom

Oxford University Press is a department of the University of Oxford.
It furthers the University's objective of excellence in research, scholarship,
and education by publishing worldwide. Oxford is a registered trade mark of
Oxford University Press in the UK and in certain other countries

First Edition Published 2004
Second Edition Published 2007
Third Edition Published 2010

Impression: 1

British Library Cataloguing in Publication Data
Data available

ISBN 978-0-19-964466-7

Printed in Great Britain by
Ashford Colour Press Ltd, Gosport, Hampshire

To: Mum and Dad

Preface

Corporate governance is an area that has grown rapidly in the past few years. The global financial crisis, corporate scandals and collapses, and public concern over the apparent lack of effective boards and perceived excessive executive remuneration packages have all contributed to an explosion of interest in this area. The corporate and investment sectors, as well as public, voluntary, and non-profit organizations, are all placing much more emphasis on good governance. More and more universities, both in the UK and internationally, are offering corporate governance courses on undergraduate or postgraduate degree programmes. Some universities have dedicated taught masters in corporate governance and/or PhD students specializing in this as their area of research.

Corporate governance is now an integral part of everyday business life and this book provides insights into its importance not just in the UK, but also globally, including the USA, Europe, Asia, South Africa, Latin America, Egypt, India, and Australia. The book is designed to provide an understanding of the development of corporate governance over the past two decades and to illustrate the importance of corporate governance to the firm, to directors, shareholders, and other stakeholders, and to the wider business community. It also seeks to shed light on why there are continuing incidences of corporate scandals, to what extent these are a corporate governance failure, and in which ways corporate governance—and the behaviour of those involved in ensuring good governance in their business—may be improved in the future.

CAM
May 2012

Acknowledgements

I would like to thank everyone who has encouraged and supported me in writing this book.

First, thanks go to those who have encouraged me to research and write about corporate governance. In the early 1990s, Sir Adrian Cadbury inspired me to undertake research in the field of corporate governance and has continued to do so. Other leading figures who have influenced me with their contributions to the development of corporate governance include Robert (Bob) A.G. Monks, Nell Minow, Jonathan Charkham, Steve Davis, and Professor Bob Tricker, to name but a few.

Thank you to everyone at Oxford University Press who has contributed to the publication of this book but especially to Kirsty Reade for her enthusiasm, expertise, and helpful advice. Thanks also go to the anonymous reviewers who constructively reviewed earlier drafts of the book and gave many helpful comments.

A heartfelt thanks to family and friends who have encouraged me to write this book, and have always been there for me, especially to: Paul; Rita, Bernard, and Christopher; Pam and Tom; Liz; Alice, Yu-Loon, and Thorsten; Ioana, Costin, and Mara; and Jane. Also a special thank you to Ben. Finally, to Merlin and Harry ('the two magicians') for their patience, devotion, and sense of fun at all times.

Source Acknowledgements

The author and publisher wish to thank the following for kind permission to use copyright material: The Association of British Insurers (ABI) for extracts from various ABI Guidelines 2001–2008; the Australian Stock Exchange for extracts from the *Principles of Good Corporate Governance and Best Practice Recommendations, ASX Corporate Governance Council* (2003), and *Corporate Governance Principles and Recommendations* (2007); the Basel Committee on Banking Supervision for extracts from *Enhancing Corporate Governance for Banking Organisations* (2006) [please note: in this book the English spelling 'Basle' has been used]; the Budapest Stock Exchange for extracts from the *Corporate Governance Recommendations* (2004); the China Securities Regulatory Commission for extracts from the *Code of Corporate Governance for Listed Companies in China* (2001); the Conference Board for extracts from the *Commission on Public Trust and Private Enterprise Findings and Recommendations*, Parts 1, 2, and 3 (2002, 2003); the Copenhagen Stock Exchange for extracts from the Nørby Commission's *Recommendations for Good Corporate Governance in Denmark* (2001); the Czech Securities Commission for extracts from the *Revised Corporate Governance Code* (2001); Ethical Investment Research Service for details of socially responsible investment strategies; the Internal Market Directorate General of the European Communities 2002, for Gregory, H.J. and Simmelkjaer, R.T. (2002) *Comparative Study of Corporate Governance Codes Relevant to the European Union and its Member States;* the Financial Reporting Council for extracts from the *Combined Code on Corporate Governance* (2006); Gee Publishing Ltd. for extracts from the *Report of the Committee on the Financial Aspects of Corporate Governance* (1992); the German Commission for extracts from the *German Corporate Governance Code* (2002); Hermes Pensions Management Limited for extracts from *The Hermes Principles* (2002) and the *Hermes Corporate Governance Principles* (2006); International Financial Services London for the extract from *Sovereign Wealth Funds* (2009); the UK Institute of Directors for extracts from *Standards for the Board* (2006); the South African Institute of Directors for extracts from the King Report on Corporate Governance (2002); the Investment Management Association for extracts from the *Responsibilities of Institutional Shareholders and Agents—A Statement of Principles* (2002 and 2005); the Japan Corporate Governance Forum for extracts from the *Revised Corporate Governance Principles*; Maciej Dzierzanowski and Piotr Tamowicz of the Gdansk Institute for Market Economics for extracts from the *Corporate Governance Code for Polish Listed Companies* (2002); the High Pay Commission for extracts from *Cheques with Balances: why tackling high pay is in the national interest* (2011); the Monetary Authority of Singapore for extracts from *Code of Corporate Governance* (2012); ecoDa for extracts from *Corporate Governance Guidance and Principles for Unlisted Companies in Europe* (2010); the Financial Reporting Council for extracts from the *UK Corporate Governance Code* (2010); TheCityUK/SWF Institute for extracts from *Sovereign Wealth Funds 2011* (2012); UK Sustainable Investment and Finance Association (UKSIF) (UKSIF) for extracts from *Focused on the Future: Celebrating ten years of responsible investment disclosure by UK occupational pension funds* (2010); the *Financial Times* for Sullivan, R. (2012) 'Squeezed Charities Seek Better Investment', 22 April. Crown copyright material is reproduced under Class

Licence Number C01P0000148 with the permission of the Controller of HMSO and the Queen's printer for Scotland. The author and publisher also wish to thank the *Financial Times* for: Armstrong, P. and Spellman, J.D. (2009) 'Integrity is Key to Gaining Good Governance', 2 February; Jacob, R. (2012) 'Kwok Brothers Row Escalates After Arrests', 13 May; Sullivan, R. (2012) 'Institutions Wary of Full Disclosure on How They Vote', 29 April; Sullivan, R. (2012) 'Managers "Talk More than Walk" on SRI', 1 April; Smith, A. (2011) 'Increase in Overseas Directors in UK', 27 November; Davoudi, S. (2012) 'Trinity Mirror Investors Rebel Over Pay', 10 May; Sanderson, R. (2012) 'Italy Groups' Cross-holdings in Spotlight', 26 April; Belton, C. (2012) 'Investors Wary Over Rusal Stand-off', 14 March; Cookson, R. (2012) 'Auditor Quits Chinese Group Boshiwa', 15 March; and Crabtree, J. (2012) 'TCI Fund Clashes with Indian Deference', 15 March.

Every effort has been made to trace all copyright holders, but if any have been inadvertently overlooked the publishers will be pleased to make the necessary arrangements at the first opportunity.

Contents

List of Examples and Case Studies

List of Figures

List of Tables

List of Abbreviations

ABI	Association of British Insurers
ACGA	Asian Corporate Governance Association
AFG	L'Association Française de la Gestion Financière
AFL-CIO	The American Federation of Labor and Congress of Industrial Organizations
AITC	Association of Investment Trust Companies
APEC	Asia-Pacific Economic Co-operation
ASX	Australian Stock Exchange
ASIC	Australian Securities and Investments Commission
BIS	Department for Business, Innovation & Skills
BVCA	British Private Equity and Venture Capital Association
CACG	Commonwealth Association for Corporate Governance
CalPERS	California Public Employees' Retirement System
CEO	Chief executive officer
CEPS	Centre for European Policy Studies
CFO	Chief financial officer
CLERP	Corporate Law Economic Reform Program
CLR	Company Law Review
CR	Corporate responsibility
CSR	Corporate social responsibility
CSRC	China Securities Regulatory Commission
Defra	Department for Environment, Food, and Rural Affairs
DVCA	Danish Venture Capital and Private Equity Association
ecoDa	European Confederation of Directors' Associations
EFAMA	European Fund and Asset Management Association
EIRIS	Ethical Investment Research Service
FESE	Federation of European Securities Exchanges
FRC	Financial Reporting Council
FSA	Financial Services Authority
FTSE	Financial Times Stock Exchange
ICGN	International Corporate Governance Network
IIC	Institutional Investor Committee
ILO	International Labour Organization
IMA	Investment Management Association
IMF	International Monetary Fund

IoD	Institute of Directors
ISC	Institutional Shareholders' Committee
IWG	International Working Group of Sovereign Wealth Funds
KPI	Key performance indicator
MOF	Ministry of Finance
NAPF	National Association of Pension Funds
NCVO	National Council for Voluntary Organisations
NEST	National Employment Savings Trust
NGO	Non-governmental organization
NHS	National Health Service
OECD	Organisation for Economic Co-operation and Development
OPSI	Office of Public Sector Information
PBOC	People's Bank of China
PIRC	Pensions Investment Research Consultants
PSPD	People's Solidarity for Participatory Democracy
QCA	Quoted Companies Alliance
RREV	Research recommendations electronic voting
SE	Societas Europaea
SETC	State Economic and Trade Commission
SID	Senior independent director
SRI	Socially responsible investment
SVWG	Shareholder Voting Working Group
SWF	Sovereign wealth fund
UKSIF	UK Sustainable Investment and Finance Association
UNPRI	United Nations Principles of Responsible Investment

Glossary

Agency theory One party (the principal) delegates work to another party (the agent). In a corporate scenario, the principal is the shareholder and the agent the directors/managers. Agency theory relates to the costs involved in this principal-agent relationship, including the costs of aligning the two sets of interests.

Audit The examination by an independent external auditor to determine whether the annual report and accounts have been appropriately prepared and give a true and fair view.

Audit committee A subcommittee of the board that is generally comprised of independent non-executive directors. It is the role of the audit committee to review the scope and outcome of the audit, and to try to ensure that the objectivity of the auditors is maintained.

Auditor rotation The audit firm is changed after a number of years in order to help ensure that the independence of the external auditor is retained. There are disparate views on the effectiveness of auditor rotation.

Bank-oriented system Banks play a key role in the funding of some companies and so may be able to exercise some control via the board structure, depending on the governance system.

Board diversity Gender, ethnicity, and other characteristics considered to make the board more diverse.

Board evaluation Boards should be evaluated annually to determine whether they have met the objectives set. The board as a whole, the board subcommittees, and individual directors should each be assessed.

Board subcommittees The board of directors may delegate various duties in specific areas to specialized committees, such as the audit committee, remuneration committee, and nomination committee.

Chairman Responsible for the running of the board and chairing board meetings.

Chief executive officer Responsible for the running of the company.

Civil law Tends to be prescriptive and based on specific rules. Generally gives less protection to minority shareholders.

Co-determination The right of employees to be kept informed of the company's activities and to participate in decisions that may affect the workers.

Common law Based on legal principles supplemented by case law. Generally gives better protection to minority shareholders.

Comply or explain A company should comply with the appropriate corporate governance code but, if it cannot comply with any particular aspect of it, then it should explain why it is unable to do so.

Controlling shareholders Those who have control of the company, although this may be indirectly through their holdings in other entities, and not directly.

Corporate social responsibility Voluntary actions that a company may take in relation to the management of social, environmental, and ethical issues.

Directors' remuneration Can encompass various elements, including base salary, bonus, stock options, stock grants, pension, and other benefits.

Directors' share options Directors may be given the right to purchase shares at a specified price over a specified time period.

Dual board A dual board system consists of a supervisory board and an executive board of management.

Fiduciary duty This is an obligation to act in the best interests of another party, for example, directors have a fiduciary duty to act in the best interests of the shareholders.

Inclusive approach The company considers the interests of all of its stakeholders.

Independent directors Directors who have no relationships with the business, or its directors and management, or other circumstances, which could affect their judgement.

Information asymmetries Different parties may have access to different levels of information, which may mean that some have a more complete or more accurate picture than others.

Insider system Ownership of shares is concentrated in individuals or a group of individuals, such as families or holding companies.

Institutional investors   Generally large investors, such as pension funds, insurance companies, and mutual funds.

Internal controls   Policies, procedures, and other measures in an organization that are designed to ensure that the assets are safeguarded, that systems operate as intended, that information can be produced in a timely and accurate manner, and that the business operates effectively and efficiently.

Market-oriented system   The influence of banks does not tend to be prevalent and does not impact on the company's board structure.

Minority rights   The rights of shareholders who own smaller stakes in a company. They should have the same rights as larger shareholders but often this is not the case.

Minority shareholders   Shareholders who have smaller holdings of shares.

Nominated advisor   A firm or company that acts as an advisor to a company coming to/on the Alternative Investment Market.

Nomination committee   A subcommittee of the board and should generally comprise independent non-executive directors. Its role is to make recommendations to the board on all new board appointments.

Non-executive director   These are not full-time employees of the company (unlike most executive directors). As far as possible they should be independent and capable of exercising independent judgement in board decision-making.

Outsider system   There is dispersed ownership of shares and hence individuals, or groups of individuals, do not tend to have direct control.

Private equity   A private equity fund is broadly defined as one that invests in equity which is not traded publicly on a stock exchange.

Proxy vote   The casting of shareholders' votes by shareholders, often by mail, fax, or electronic means.

Remuneration committee   A subcommittee of the board and should generally comprise independent non-executive directors. Its role is to make recommendations to the board on executive directors' remuneration.

Risk assessment   An assessment of the overall risk that a company may be exposed to. Overall risk can include many different types of risk, including financial risk, operating risk, and reputation risk.

Say on pay   Shareholder vote on the remuneration packages of executive directors, may be binding or non-binding on the company.

Shareholder value   The value of the firm after deducting current and future claims.

Socially responsible investment   Involves considering the ethical, social, and environmental performance of companies selected for investment as well as their financial performance.

Sovereign wealth fund   A fund, often very large and influential, which is owned by a government.

Stakeholder theory   This theory takes into account the views of a wider stakeholder group and not just the shareholders.

Stakeholders   Any individual or group on which the activities of the company have an impact, including the employees, customers, and local community.

Supervisory board   In a dual board system the supervisory board oversees the direction of the business, whilst the management board is responsible for the running of the business.

Transaction cost economics   Views the firm itself as a governance structure, which in turn can help align the interests of directors and shareholders.

Unitary board   A unitary board of directors is characterized by one single board comprising of both executive and non-executive directors.

Introduction

Businesses around the world need to be able to attract funding from investors in order to expand and grow. Before investors decide to invest their funds in a particular business, they will want to be as sure as they can be that the business is financially sound and will continue to be so in the foreseeable future. Investors therefore need to have confidence that the business is being well managed and will continue to be profitable.

In order to have this assurance, investors look to the published annual report and accounts of the business, and to other information releases that the company might make. They expect that the annual report and accounts will represent a true picture of the company's present position; after all, the annual report and accounts are subject to an annual audit whereby an independent external auditor examines the business' records and transactions, and certifies that the annual report and accounts have been prepared in accordance with accepted accounting standards and give a 'true and fair view' of the business' activities. However, although the annual report may give a reasonably accurate picture of the business' activities and financial position at that point in time, there are many facets of the business that are not effectively reflected in the annual report and accounts.

There have been a number of high-profile corporate collapses that have arisen despite the fact that the annual report and accounts seemed fine. These corporate collapses have had an adverse effect on many people: shareholders who have seen their financial investment reduced to nothing; employees who have lost their jobs and, in many cases, the security of their company pension, which has also evaporated overnight; suppliers of goods or services to the failed companies; and the economic impact on the local and international communities in which the failed companies operated. In essence, corporate collapses affect us all. Why have such collapses occurred? What might be done to prevent such collapses happening again? How can investor confidence be restored?

The answers to these questions are all linked to corporate governance: a lack of effective corporate governance meant that such collapses could occur; good corporate governance can help prevent such collapses happening again and restore investor confidence.

To illustrate why corporate failures might occur, despite the companies seeming healthy, it is helpful to review a few examples from recent years, each of which has sent shock waves through stock markets around the world.

Barings Bank

The downfall in 1995 of one of England's oldest established banks was brought about by the actions of one man, Nick Leeson, whose actions have been immortalized in the film

Rogue Trader. Nick Leeson was a clever, if unconventional, trader with a gift for sensing the way that stock market prices would move in the Far Eastern markets. In 1993 he was based in Singapore and made more than £10 million, about 10 per cent of Barings' total profit that year. He was highly thought of at that time.

However, his run of good luck was not to last and, when a severe earthquake in Japan affected the stock market adversely, he incurred huge losses of Barings' money. He requested more funds from Barings' head office in London, which were sent to him, but unfortunately he suffered further losses. The losses were so great (£850 million) that Barings Bank collapsed and was eventually bought for £1 by ING, the Dutch banking and insurance group.

Barings Bank has been criticized for its lack of effective internal controls at that time, which left Nick Leeson able to cover up the losses that he was making for quite a number of months. The case also illustrates the importance of having effective supervision, by experienced staff with a good understanding of the processes and procedures, of staff who are able to expose the company to such financial disaster. The collapse of Barings Bank sent ripples through financial markets across the world as the importance of effective internal controls and appropriate monitoring was reinforced.

Enron

Enron was ranked in the USA's Fortune top ten list of companies, based on its turnover in 2000. Its published accounts for the year ending 31 December 2000 showed a seemingly healthy profit of US$979 million and there was nothing obvious to alert shareholders to the impending disaster that was going to unfold over the next year or so, making Enron the largest bankruptcy in US history.

Enron's difficulties related to its activities in the energy market and the setting-up of a series of 'special purpose entities' (SPEs). Enron used the SPEs to conceal large losses from the market by giving the appearance that key exposures were hedged (covered) by third parties. However, the SPEs were really nothing more than an extension of Enron itself and so Enron's risks were not covered. Some of the SPEs were used to transfer funds to some of Enron's directors. In October 2001 Enron declared a non-recurring loss of US$1 billion and also had to disclose a US$1.2 billion write-off against shareholders' funds. Later in October Enron disclosed another accounting problem, which reduced its value by over US$0.5 million. It looked as though a takeover might be on the cards from a rival, Dynegy, but in November, announcements by Enron of further debts led to the takeover bid falling through. In December 2001 Enron filed for bankruptcy.

In retrospect, it seems that the directors were not questioned closely enough about the use of the SPEs and their accounting treatment. What has become clear is that there was some concern amongst Enron's auditors (Andersen) about the SPEs and Enron's activities. Unfortunately, Andersen failed to question the directors hard enough and Andersen's own fate was sealed when some of its employees shredded paperwork relating to Enron, thus obliterating vital evidence and contributing to the demise of Andersen, which has itself been taken over by various rivals.

Lawsuits were brought against the directors of Enron and whilst it was notable that some directors were able to settle the lawsuits by paying hugely significant sums of money personally, others received hefty jail sentences. In 2006 Jeffrey Skilling, former Enron Chief Executive, was found guilty of fraud and conspiracy and sentenced to more than twenty-four years in prison. In April 2012 the Supreme Court rejected his appeal, although his sentence may be shortened. Kenneth Lay, also a former Chairman and Chief Executive of Enron, was similarly found guilty of fraud and conspiracy although he died in 2006, no doubt taking to the grave many of the details of what went on at Enron.

Interestingly, one of the employees at Enron, Sherron Watkins, had made her concerns known to Andrew Fastow, the Chief Finance Officer, and to the firm's auditors, Arthur Andersen, about some of the accounting transactions taking place at Enron as early as 1996. However, no notice was apparently taken of her concerns and she moved to work in a different area of the company. In 2001 she was again back in the finance department and became aware that an extensive fraud was taking place with SPEs being used as vehicles to hide Enron's growing losses. She then expressed her concerns more openly and became the whistle-blower to one of the most infamous corporate scandals of all time.

The Enron case highlights the overriding need for integrity in business: for the directors to act with integrity and honesty, and for the external audit firm to be able to ask searching questions of the directors without holding back for fear of offending a lucrative client. This latter situation is exacerbated when auditors receive large fees for non-audit services that may well exceed the audit fee itself, thus endangering the independence of the auditors. Enron also highlights the need for independent non-executive directors who are experienced enough to be able to ask searching questions in board and committee meetings to try to ensure that the business is operated appropriately.

Parmalat

Parmalat, an Italian company specializing in long-life milk, was founded by Calisto Tanzi. It seemed to be a marvellous success story although, as it expanded by acquiring more companies, its debt increased and, in late 2003, Parmalat had difficulty making a bond payment despite the fact that it was supposed to have a large cash reserve. After various investigations had been carried out, it transpired that the large cash reserves were non-existent and Parmalat went into administration. With debts estimated at £10 billion, Parmalat has also earned itself the name of 'Europe's Enron'.

Calisto Tanzi was a central figure in one of Europe's largest fraud trials started during 2005. He was accused of providing false accounting information and misleading the Italian stock-market regulator. In December 2008 after a trial lasting more than three years, he was found guilty on a number of counts, including falsifying accounts, and misleading investors and regulators. He was given a ten-year sentence.

Satyam

Satyam Computer Services was India's fourth largest information technology group by revenue. In early 2009 its Chairman, B. Ramalinga Raju, wrote to the Board and confessed to having manipulated many of the figures in the company's annual financial statements over a number of years, resulting in overstated profits and non-existent assets. The case has been called 'India's Enron' and has undermined confidence in Indian companies, with the Bombay Stock Exchange suffering a significant fall in share prices. The Securities and Exchange Board of India (SEBI) moved quickly to make it mandatory for controlling shareholders to declare whether they have pledged any shares to lenders as this was one of the contributory factors in this case. Satyam was sold in 2009 to Tech Mahindra and was later renamed Mahindra Satyam. In March 2012 Tech Mahindra announced plans to combine with Mahindra Satyam; the combined group is expected to drop the Satyam name. The combined group will still face legal charges brought by shareholders in relation to the Satyam scandal.

Royal Bank of Scotland (RBS)

In 2008 the RBS together with a number of other large UK banks was caught up in the toxic asset scandal that saw mortgage-backed securities tumble in value, along with a concomitant fall in the value of banks' shares. The Bank of England had long feared that big bonuses linked to short-term performance measures encouraged excessive risk-taking by traders who were in a win–win situation: they were rewarded if they succeeded but, if they failed and lost money for the bank, they did not have to pay the money back. It would have been more prudent to use at least some longer term performance measures.

Much criticism has also been laid at the door of Sir Fred Goodwin, the former Chief Executive of RBS, who had followed an aggressive acquisitions policy during 2008, including purchasing part of ABN Amro at what turned out to be an overly generous price. The excessive remuneration packages of the executive directors of the banks—for what is now seen as underperformance and a lack of consideration of all the appropriate risks—have angered investors, the public and the government alike. So much so, that there have been calls for a cap on directors' pay, especially bonuses, and the huge pension pot of the now retired Sir Fred Goodwin has caused an outcry, especially now that UK taxpayers effectively own the vast majority of shares in RBS, the result of a government bailout. Furthermore, in early 2012 Sir Fred Goodwin was stripped of his knighthood—awarded in 2004 for his services to banking—as he was the dominant decision-maker in RBS in 2008 when decisions were made that contributed significantly to RBS's problems and to the financial crisis.

The Financial Services Authority (FSA) report (2011) into the failure of the RBS highlighted a number of factors that contributed to RBS's failure and also stated that 'the multiple poor decisions that RBS made suggest, moreover, that there are likely to have been underlying deficiencies in RBS management, governance and culture which made it prone to make poor decisions'.

Clearly the story of the UK's banks—and indeed the US banks where the default rates on subprime mortgages began to rise in 2006—have received much attention. As further events have come to light, there have been more corporate governance implications. These have included the key questions relating to what the remuneration committees were doing to approve apparently excessive executive director remuneration packages; why boards of directors were not more aware of the risks, or if they were aware of them, why didn't they take more notice of them; whether the board composition was appropriate in terms of skills, knowledge and experience; and what lessons can be learnt for the future.

Securency

Securency, a Reserve Bank of Australia (RBA) subsidiary which produces and supplies polymer banknotes, has been the subject of allegations of bribery and corruption. The allegations centred on Securency's payment of commissions to foreign middlemen, who it is believed would then attempt to bribe central banking officials in countries throughout Asia, Latin America and Africa to replace their paper notes with Securency's polymer banknotes. The allegations were made by a Securency insider who witnessed much of this behaviour first-hand. KPMG Forensics prepared an audit report that showed impropriety on the part of Securency's officials, and in April 2012 the RBA fired two top executives of Securency, the former Managing Director and the former Director of Commercial Services.

China Forestry

China Forestry is a company engaged in the management of forests, and the harvesting and sales of timber logs. In 2008 and 2009 it had attracted investments from private equity firms including the USA's Carlyle Group and Switzerland-based Partners Group. Subsequently, China Forestry's auditors informed the board of irregularities in the books which led to a suspension in the trading of the company's shares. It transpired that China Forestry's former management team provided the auditor with false bank statements, as well as inconsistent insurance-policy documentation and falsified logging permits. Most of the group's sales from 2010 were conducted in cash and Mr Li Han Chun, the former Chief Executive Officer, kept more than one set of books, meaning that movements in cash could be concealed from the board. China Forestry reported a loss for 2010 of 2.71 billion yuan after drastically lowering the value of its plantation holdings, which are the company's chief asset.

Mr Li Han Chun was arrested by Chinese authorities on allegations that he embezzled 30 million yuan from the company, and other senior staff including the chief financial officer left the company. China Forestry subsequently proposed a number of changes, including improved centralized financial reporting and new management to oversee it.

Olympus Corporation

Olympus is a long-established Japanese manufacturer of optics and reprography products. In April 2011 Michael Woodford became its President and CEO, replacing Tsuyoshi Kikukawa, who became Chairman. Woodford became suspicious about various transactions that had taken place, including in relation to the acquisition of UK medical equipment maker Gyrus, and confronted the board about them. He was removed from office after questioning the transactions. He subsequently passed on information to the British Serious Fraud Office and requested police protection. It transpired that substantial fees were paid to middlemen in merger and acquisition transactions. It also seemed that some of the assets of the business were overvalued in the accounts. Later in 2011 the company admitted that the money had been used to cover up losses on investments dating back to the 1990s and that the company's accounting practices had not been appropriate.

In February 2012 a number of Olympus executives were arrested, including the ex-President, Tsuyoshi Kikukawa, the auditor, Hideo Yamada, and the Executive Vice-President Hisashi Mori, together with the former bankers, Akio Nakagawa and Nobumasa Yokoo and two others, suspected of having helped the board to hide significant losses.

The Olympus scandal shocked Japan and is seen as something of a litmus test of corporate governance in the country, in the sense of whether it will lead to improved corporate governance practices—for example, in the way that new directors are nominated to try to ensure independence—or whether it will stay as a reflection of the old ways where companies such as Olympus retain a high level of cross-holdings with their financial institutions.

These examples of high-profile corporate collapses and scandals in the UK, USA, Europe, Australia, China, Japan and India have had, and continue to have, international implications, and would seem to illustrate a number of shortcomings in the way that the companies were run and managed:

- Barings appears to highlight the lack of effective internal controls and the folly of trusting one employee without adequate supervision and understanding of his activities.
- Enron appears to highlight a basic need to ensure, as far as possible, that directors are people of integrity and act honestly; that external auditors must be able to ask searching questions unfettered by the need to consider the potential loss of large audit/accounting fees; and the contribution that might be made by independent directors on boards and committees who question intelligently and insightfully.
- Parmalat appears to highlight some of the weaknesses that may exist in family-owned firms where members of the family take a dominant role across the board structure as a whole. In Parmalat's case, the board lacked independence as, of the thirteen directors, only three were independent. This had a knock-on effect on the composition of the various board committees where independent directors were a minority rather than a majority. There was also a lack of timely disclosure of information.
- Satyam Computer Services appears to highlight the risks associated both with a powerful chairman who was able to falsify accounts over a period of time, seemingly without raising the suspicions of the auditors or anyone in the company. It also highlights the effects of a lack of appropriate disclosure requirements so that controlling shareholders did not need to disclose information that could have an adverse effect on minority shareholders.
- RBS appears to highlight what can happen when the risks associated with the business' activities are not fully taken into account. It would have been difficult to envisage the particular circumstances that led to the global financial crisis but nonetheless, the board should be aware of the implications should the worst arise. The case also illustrates that remuneration committees need to be more aware of the effects of the structuring of performance-related bonus measures. The case also illustrates once more that sometimes a board finds it difficult to question, and limit, the activities of a powerful chief executive.
- Securency appears to highlight a lack of ethical behaviour by some of the key directors. Given the recent tighter controls on bribery and corruption, it is particularly likely that firms that make payments as bribes to try to gain business will be brought to account in

the current global regulatory environment. Such firms risk incurring both financial losses and reputational damage, and therefore directors should be instilling an ethical culture, and also facilitating whistle-blowing.

- China Forestry appears to highlight the risks associated with dishonest individuals who are in a position to manipulate the accounting figures and provide inaccurate paperwork to apparently back these up. This case serves to illustrate the importance of appropriate internal controls and segregation of duties in the handling of, and accounting for, the company's transactions.

- Olympus appears to highlight the risks associated with collusion between key executives, the auditor, and bankers. A lack of independent directors and a negative attitude towards whistle-blowing served to compound the problems that arose at Olympus.

This brings us back to our original questions about corporate failures such as those mentioned earlier. Why have such collapses occurred? What might be done to prevent such collapses happening again? How can investor confidence be restored? The answers to these questions are all linked to corporate governance.

Corporate governance is an area that has grown very rapidly in the last decade, particularly since the collapse of Enron in 2001 and the subsequent financial problems of other companies in various countries. As already mentioned, emerging financial scandals will continue to ensure that there is a sharp focus on corporate governance issues, especially relating to transparency and disclosure, control and accountability, and to the most appropriate form of board structure that may be capable of preventing such scandals occurring in future. Not surprisingly, there has been a significant interest shown by governments in trying to ensure that such collapses do not happen again because these lead to a lack of confidence in financial markets. In order to realize why corporate governance has become so important, it is essential to have an understanding of what corporate governance actually is and how it may improve corporate accountability.

A fairly narrow definition of corporate governance is given by Shleifer and Vishny (1997): 'Corporate governance deals with the ways in which suppliers of finance to corporations assure themselves of getting a return on their investment'. A broader definition is provided by the Organisation for Economic Co-operation and Development (OECD) (1999), which describes corporate governance as: 'a set of relationships between a company's board, its shareholders and other stakeholders. It also provides the structure through which the objectives of the company are set, and the means of attaining those objectives, and monitoring performance, are determined'. Similarly, Sir Adrian Cadbury (1999) said: 'Corporate governance is concerned with holding the balance between economic and social goals and between individual and communal goals . . . the aim is to align as nearly as possible the interests of individuals, corporations and society'. These definitions serve to illustrate that corporate governance is concerned with both the shareholders and the internal aspects of the company, such as internal control, and the external aspects, such as an organization's relationship with its shareholders and other stakeholders. Corporate governance is also seen as an essential mechanism helping the company to attain its corporate objectives and monitoring performance is a key element in achieving these objectives.

It can be seen that corporate governance is important for a number of reasons, and is fundamental to well-managed companies and to ensuring that they operate at optimum efficiency. Some of the important features of corporate governance are as follows:

- it helps to ensure that an adequate and appropriate system of controls operates within a company and hence assets may be safeguarded;
- it prevents any single individual having too powerful an influence;
- it is concerned with the relationship between a company's management, the board of directors, shareholders, and other stakeholders;
- it aims to ensure that the company is managed in the best interests of the shareholders and the other stakeholders;
- it tries to encourage both transparency and accountability, which investors are increasingly looking for in both corporate management and corporate performance.

The first feature refers to the internal control system of a company whereby there are appropriate and adequate controls to ensure that transactions are properly recorded and that assets cannot be misappropriated. Each year a company has an annual audit and a key part of the auditor's job is to assess whether the internal controls in a business are operating properly. Of course, the auditor has to exercise a certain degree of judgement regarding the assurances given by the directors, the directors being ultimately responsible for the implementation of an appropriate internal control system in the company. The directors are also responsible for ensuring that there are risk assessment procedures in place to identify the risks that companies face in today's business environment, including, for example, exposures to movements in foreign exchange and risks associated with business competition.

As well as being fundamental to investor confidence, good corporate governance is essential to attracting new investment, particularly for developing countries where good corporate governance is often seen as a means of attracting foreign direct investment at more favourable rates. As the emphasis on corporate governance has grown during the last decade, we have seen a sea change in many countries around the world. Developed and developing countries alike have introduced corporate governance codes by which companies are expected to abide. The codes emphasize the importance of transparency, accountability, internal controls, board composition and structure, independent directors, and performance-related executive pay. There is much emphasis on the rights of shareholders and an expectation that shareholders, especially institutional investors, will take a more proactive role in the companies in which they own shares and actually start to act more as owners rather than playing a passive shareholder role. Corporate governance is an exciting area, fast developing to accommodate the needs of a changing business environment where investor expectations are higher than ever before; the cost to companies that ignore the benefits of good corporate governance can be high and, ultimately, can mean the collapse of the company.

The global financial crisis—which started in 2006, rippled into 2007, exploded in 2008, and from which the aftershock is still being felt and no doubt will be for years to come—has already led to statements about corporate governance in times of financial crisis and the lessons that can be learnt. The International Corporate Governance Network (ICGN) issued a Statement on the Global Financial Crisis in November 2008, and stated 'corporate governance failings were not the only cause but they were significant, above all because boards failed to understand and manage risk and tolerated perverse incentives. Enhanced governance structures should therefore be integral to an overall solution aimed at restoring confidence to markets and protecting us from future crises'. The ICGN describe the crisis as a 'collective problem with many and varied causes' and the statement is therefore aimed at all concerned, 'including financial institutions and their boards, regulatory and policy makers and, of course, shareholders themselves'. The statement advocates strengthening shareholder rights; strengthening boards; fair and transparent markets; accounting standards (set without political interference); remuneration (having a 'say on pay'; encouraging boards to ensure that their policies do not foster excessive risk-raking; incentives aligned with medium- and long-term strategy and no payments for failure); and credit-rating agencies (there should be more competition in this market). A second statement by the ICGN in March 2009 reiterates the ICGN's view about 'the role that corporate governance can and should play in restoring trust in global capital markets'.

Similarly, the OECD issued a report in February 2009 *Corporate Governance Lessons from the Financial Crisis*. The report states that 'the financial crisis can be to an important extent attributed to failures and weaknesses in corporate governance arrangements. When they were put to a test, corporate governance routines did not serve their purpose to safeguard against excessive risk taking in a number of financial services companies'. The report highlights failures in risk management systems; lack of information about risk exposures reaching the board; lack of monitoring by boards of risk management; lack of disclosure relating to risks and their management; inadequate accounting standards and regulatory requirements in some areas; and remuneration systems not being related to the strategy and longer term interests of the company. The report concludes that the adequacy of the OECD corporate governance principles will be re-examined to determine whether additional guidance and/or clarification is needed.

Clarke (2010) highlights that 'the prolonged systemic crisis in international financial markets commencing in 2007 was also a crisis in corporate governance and regulation. The apparent ascendency of Anglo-American markets and governance institutions was profoundly questioned by the scale and contagion of the global financial crisis.' Clarke's words will resonate with many who wonder what went wrong with corporate governance; how could we have had so many developments over the years in terms of regulation, self-regulation, codes of best practice, guidelines and so on, and yet still suffered financial scandal and collapse on such a scale? Part of the answer lies in the fact that at the root of so many problems has been a lack of ethical behaviour, a lack of consideration for others who would be affected by these actions, and a consummate greed for money, power, or both. Ultimately, it is individual integrity, and then the board as a collective of individuals acting with integrity that will help shape ethical corporate behaviour in the future.

Nonetheless, the International Finance Corporation (IFC) (2010) points out that the global financial crisis also demonstrated the crucial importance of corporate governance and a strong board of directors to aid companies in managing the impact of unexpected events and that good corporate governance makes companies more resilient to unforeseen changes in the environment in which they operate.

This text seeks to chart the development of corporate governance over the last two decades and to illustrate the importance of corporate governance to the company itself, to directors, shareholders and other stakeholders, and to the wider business community. The text is structured in four major parts. Part One contains two chapters that chart the development of corporate governance and look at the various theoretical aspects, including the frameworks within which corporate governance might be developed, and the development of corporate governance codes in various countries. A section on the governance of non-governmental organizations (NGOs), the public sector, non-profit organizations and charities is included to reflect the increased interest in governance in these organizations.

Part Two contains four chapters, the first of which, Chapter 4, looks at the role of shareholders and stakeholders, identifies the various stakeholder groups, and discusses their role in companies and in corporate governance. The text recognizes that corporate ownership across the world varies and that the family-owned firm is the dominant form of business in many countries: Chapter 5 is devoted solely to family-owned firms and their governance. Chapter 6 looks at the role of institutional investors in corporate governance; institutional investors are the predominant type of owner in the UK and the USA. Also in Chapter 6 is a discussion of the roles of private equity investors and sovereign wealth funds. Chapter 7 is devoted to socially responsible investment, or ethical investment, because it is an area that is attracting increasing interest in many countries and in which institutional investors in particular are taking much more of an interest.

Part Three concentrates on various aspects of directors and board structure: Chapter 8 examines the role of directors, their duties, their responsibilities, and looks at the important areas of boards and board subcommittees. Non-executive directors (outsiders), emphasized in many of the corporate governance codes as being a key element of good corporate governance, are discussed in detail. Board diversity is also discussed in some depth in the light of the growing emphasis on this area. Chapter 9 looks at directors' performance and remuneration. It reviews the background to the debate on directors' remuneration and looks at the ways in which directors' performance and remuneration may be effectively linked. The 'say on pay' is examined as a mechanism through which investors can express their views on executive remuneration.

The text is designed to appeal to a global audience and Part Four is devoted to corporate governance development in various continents around the world: Chapter 10 looks at corporate governance in mainland Europe, incorporating Continental European countries; Chapter 11, corporate governance in the Central and Eastern European countries; Chapter 12, corporate governance in South East Asia, including the addition of Singapore in this edition; Chapter 13, corporate governance in a number of other countries, including South Africa, Egypt, India, and Brazil. Chapter 14 provides some concluding comments on these developments in corporate governance, the evolution of the various shareholder and stakeholder groups, and the potential future developments in corporate governance.

At the start of each chapter, there are learning objectives that identify the key objectives of the chapter, and at the end of each chapter, there is a useful summary of the key points raised. There are short discussion questions and mini case studies to illustrate the key issues raised in various chapters, and references to appropriate publications and websites for each chapter.

An important feature of the book is the accompanying **Online Resource Centre (ORC)**, which contains additional useful material such as student learning tools incorporating questions and web links, additional examples and mini case studies, and lecturers' material, including PowerPoint slides and updates (on an annual basis) of significant new material. A new resource is the book's corporate governance blog at http://corporategovernanceoup. wordpress.com where topical postings are made on a regular basis.

References

Cadbury, Sir Adrian (1999), *Corporate Governance Overview*, World Bank Report, Washington DC.

Clarke, T. (2010), 'Recurring Crises in Anglo-American Corporate Governance', *Contributions to Political Economy*, Vol. 29, Issue 1, pp. 9–32.

FSA (2011), *The Failure of the Royal Bank of Scotland*, FSA Board Report, London.

ICGN (2008), *Statement on the Global Financial Crisis*, ICGN, London.

—— (2009), *Second Statement on the Global Financial Crisis*, ICGN, London.

IFC (2010), *Navigating Through Crises, A Handbook for Boards*, IFC, Washington DC.

OECD (1999), *Principles of Corporate Governance*, OECD, Paris.

—— (2009), *Corporate Governance Lessons from the Financial Crisis*, OECD, Paris.

Shleifer, A. and Vishny, R. (1997), 'A Survey of Corporate Governance', *Journal of Finance*, Vol. LII, No. 2.

For further links to useful sources of information visit the Online Resource Centre **www.oxfordtextbooks.co.uk/orc/mallin4e/**

Part 1

Developments in Corporate Governance

2

Theoretical Aspects of Corporate Governance

⊙ **Learning Objectives**

- To understand the various main theories that underlie the development of corporate governance

- To be aware of the impact of the form of legal system, capital market, and ownership structure on the development of corporate governance

Introduction

Corporate governance has only relatively recently come to prominence in the business world; the term 'corporate governance' and its everyday usage in the financial press is a new phenomenon of the last twenty years or so. However, the theories underlying the development of corporate governance, and the areas it encompasses, date from much earlier and are drawn from a variety of disciplines including finance, economics, accounting, law, management, and organizational behaviour.

It must be remembered that the development of corporate governance is a global occurrence and, as such, is a complex area, including legal, cultural, ownership, and other structural differences. Therefore some theories may be more appropriate and relevant to some countries than others, or more relevant at different times depending on what stage an individual country, or group of countries, is at. The stage of development may refer to the evolution of the economy, corporate structure, or ownership groups, all of which affect how corporate governance will develop and be accommodated within its own country setting. An aspect of particular importance is whether the company itself operates within a shareholder framework, focusing primarily on the maintenance or enhancement of shareholder value as its main objective, or whether it takes a broader stakeholder approach, emphasizing the interests of diverse groups, such as employees, providers of credit, suppliers, customers, and the local community.

Theories associated with the development of corporate governance

Given that many disciplines have influenced the development of corporate governance, the theories that have fed into it are quite varied. Table 2.1 gives a summary of some of the theories that may be associated with the development of corporate governance.

The main theories that have affected the development of corporate governance are now discussed in more detail. For a comprehensive exposition of theories underlying the development

Table 2.1 Summary of theories affecting corporate governance development

Theory name	Summary
Agency	Agency theory identifies the agency relationship where one party (the principal) delegates work to another party (the agent). In the context of a corporation, the owners are the principal and the directors are the agent.
Transaction cost economics	Transaction cost economics views the firm itself as a governance structure. The choice of an appropriate governance structure can help align the interests of directors and shareholders.
Stakeholder	Stakeholder theory takes account of a wider group of constituents rather than focusing on shareholders. Where there is an emphasis on stakeholders, the governance structure of the company may provide for some direct representation of the stakeholder groups.
Stewardship	Directors are regarded as the stewards of the company's assets and will be predisposed to act in the best interests of the shareholders.
Class hegemony	Directors view themselves as an elite at the top of the company and will recruit/promote to new director appointments taking into account how well new appointments might fit into that elite.
Managerial hegemony	Management of a company, with its knowledge of day-to-day operations, may effectively dominate the directors and hence weaken the influence of the directors.
Path dependence	Path dependence may be structure driven and rule driven; corporate structures depend on the structures with which an economy started.
Resource dependence	Directors are able to connect the company to the resources needed to achieve corporate objectives.
Institutional	The institutional environment influences societal beliefs and practices that impact on various 'actors' within society.
Political	Political theory has a significant influence on different ownership and governance structures.
Network governance	A structure of network governance allows for superior risk management.

of corporate governance, Clarke (2004) is well worth reading. Coffee (2006) also adds new dimensions with his seminal book on gatekeepers whom he defines as 'the professional agents of the board and the shareholders, who inform and advise them: auditors, attorneys, securities analysts, credit-rating agencies and investment bankers'. He states that 'only if the board's agents properly advise and warn it, can the board function properly'.

Agency theory

A significant body of work has built up in this area within the context of the principal–agent framework. The work of Jensen and Meckling (1976) in particular, and of Fama and Jensen

(1983), are important. Agency theory identifies the agency relationship where one party (the principal) delegates work to another party (the agent). The agency relationship can have a number of disadvantages relating to the opportunism or self-interest of the agent: for example, the agent may not act in the best interests of the principal, or the agent may act only partially in the best interests of the principal. There can be a number of dimensions to this, including, for example, the agent misusing his/her power for pecuniary or other advantage, and the agent not taking appropriate risks in pursuance of the principal's interests because he/she (the agent) view those risks as not being appropriate (he/she and the principal may have different attitudes to risk). There is also the problem of information asymmetry whereby the principal and the agent have access to different levels of information; in practice, this means that the principal is at a disadvantage because the agent will have more information.

In the context of corporations and issues of corporate control, agency theory views corporate governance mechanisms, especially the board of directors, as being an essential monitoring device to try to ensure that any problems that may be brought about by the principal–agent relationship are minimized. Blair (1996) states:

> Managers are supposed to be the 'agents' of a corporation's 'owners', but managers must be monitored and institutional arrangements must provide some checks and balances to make sure they do not abuse their power. The costs resulting from managers misusing their position, as well as the costs of monitoring and disciplining them to try to prevent abuse, have been called 'agency costs'.

Much of agency theory as related to corporations is set in the context of the separation of ownership and control as described in the work of Berle and Means (1932). In this context, the agents are the managers and the principals are the shareholders, and this is the most commonly cited agency relationship in the corporate governance context. However, it is useful to be aware that the agency relationship can also cover various other relationships, including those of company and creditor, and of employer and employee.

Separation of ownership and control

The potential problems of the separation of ownership and control were identified in the eighteenth century by Smith (1838): 'the directors of such companies [joint stock companies] however being the managers rather of other people's money than of their own, it cannot well be expected that they should watch over it with the same anxious vigilance [as if it were their own]'. Almost a century later, the work of Berle and Means (1932) is often cited as providing one of the fundamental explanations of investor and corporate relationships. Berle and Means' work highlighted that, as countries industrialized and developed their markets, the ownership and control of corporations became separated. This was particularly the case in the USA and the UK where the legal systems have fostered good protection of minority shareholders and hence there has been encouragement for more diversified shareholder bases.

However, in many countries, especially where there is a code of civil law as opposed to common law, the protection of minority shareholders is not effective and so there has been less impetus for a broad shareholder base. The common law system builds on England's medieval laws whilst the civil law system is based on Roman law. A succinct comparison of the two legal systems is provided by Wessel (2001), who states that 'common-law countries—including the US and other former British colonies—rely on independent judges and juries and legal principles supplemented by precedent-setting case law, which results in greater flexibility', whilst 'in civil-law countries—which include much of Latin America—judges often are life-long civil servants who administer legal codes packed with specific rules, which hobbles them in their ability to cope with change'. In countries with a civil law system, there is therefore more codification but weaker protection of rights, hence there is less encouragement to invest.

In other words, the relationship between ownership and control outlined by Berle and Means is largely applicable to the USA and the UK but not to many other countries. This was highlighted by La Porta *et al.* (1999) who found that the most common form of ownership around the globe is the family firm or controlling shareholders, rather than a broad share-holder base (family firms and their corporate governance implications are discussed in more detail in Chapter 5).

However, the influence of Berle and Means' work cannot be underestimated: it has coloured thinking about the way companies are owned, managed, and controlled for over seventy years, and represents the reality in many US and UK companies. Monks (2001) states: 'The tendency during this period [the twentieth century] has been the dilution of the controlling blocks of shares to the present situation of institutional and widely dispersed ownership—ownership without power.'

In the last few years, there has been increasing pressure on shareholders, and particularly on institutional shareholders who own shares on behalf of the 'man in the street', to act more as owners and not just as holders of shares. The drive for more effective shareholders, who act as owners, has come about because there have been numerous instances of corporate excesses and abuses, such as perceived overpayment of directors for poor performance, corporate collapses, and scandals, which have resulted in corporate pension funds being wiped out, and shareholders losing their investment. The call for improved transparency and disclosure, embodied in corporate governance codes and in International Accounting Standards (IASs), should improve the information asymmetry situation so that investors are better informed about the company's activities and strategies.

Once shareholders do begin to act like owners again, then they will be able to exercise a more direct influence on companies and their boards, so that boards will be more account-able for their actions and, in that sense, the power of ownership will be returned to the owners (the shareholders). Useem (1996) highlights, however, that institutional investors will ultimately become accountable to 'the millions of ultimate owners . . . who may come to question the policies of the new powers that be. Then the questions may expand from whether the professional money managers are achieving maximum private return to whether they are fostering maximum public good. Their demands for downsizing and single-minded focus on shareholder benefits—whatever the costs—may come to constitute a new target of ownership challenge'.

Transaction cost economics (TCE)

TCE, as expounded by the work of Williamson (1975, 1984), is often viewed as closely related to agency theory. TCE views the firm as a governance structure whereas agency theory views the firm as a nexus of contracts. Essentially, the latter means that there is a connected group or series of contracts amongst the various players, arising because it is seemingly impossible to have a contract that perfectly aligns the interests of principal and agent in a corporate control situation.

In the earlier discussion of agency theory, the importance of the separation of ownership and control of a firm was emphasized. As firms have grown in size, whether caused by the desire to achieve economies of scale, by technological advances, or by the fact that natural monopolies have evolved, they have increasingly required more capital, which has needed to be raised from the capital markets and a wider shareholder base has been established. The problems of the separation of ownership and control, and the resultant corporate governance issues have thus arisen. Coase (1937) examines the rationale for firms' existence in the context of a framework of the efficiencies of internal, as opposed to external, contracting. He states:

> the operation of a market costs something and by forming an organisation and allowing some authority (an 'entrepreneur') to direct the resources, certain marketing costs are saved. The entrepreneur has to carry out his function at less cost, taking into account the fact that he may get factors of production at a lower price than the market transactions which he supersedes.

In other words, there are certain economic benefits to the firm itself to undertake transactions internally rather than externally. In its turn, a firm becomes larger the more transactions it undertakes and will expand up to the point where it becomes cheaper or more efficient for the transaction to be undertaken externally. Coase therefore posits that firms may become less efficient the larger they become; equally, he states that 'all changes which improve managerial technique will tend to increase the size of the firm'.

Williamson (1984) builds on the earlier work of Coase, and provides a justification for the growth of large firms and conglomerates, which essentially provide their own internal capital market. He states that the costs of any misaligned actions may be reduced by 'judicious choice of governance structure rather than merely realigning incentives and pricing them out'.

Hart (1995) states that there are a number of costs to writing a contract between principal and agent, which include the cost of thinking about and providing for all the different eventualities that may occur during the course of the contract, the cost of negotiating with others, and the costs of writing the contract in an appropriate way so that it is, for example, legally enforceable. These costs tend to mean that contracts are apt to be incomplete in some way and so contracts will tend to be revisited as and when any omissions or required changes come to light. Hart indicates that, 'in a world of incomplete contracts (where agency problems are also present), governance structure does have a role. Governance structure can be seen as a mechanism for making decisions that have not been specified in the initial contract'.

Stiles and Taylor (2001) point out that 'both theories [TCE and agency] are concerned with managerial discretion, and both assume that managers are given to opportunism (self-interest seeking) and moral hazard, and that managers operate under bounded rationality . . . [and] both agency theory and TCE regard the board of directors as an instrument of control'. In this context, 'bounded rationality' means that managers will tend to satisfice rather than maximize profit (this, of course, not being in the best interests of shareholders).

Stakeholder theory

In juxtaposition to agency theory is stakeholder theory. Stakeholder theory takes account of a wider group of constituents rather than focusing on shareholders. A consequence of focusing on shareholders is that the maintenance or enhancement of shareholder value is paramount, whereas when a wider stakeholder group—such as employees, providers of credit, customers, suppliers, government, and the local community—is taken into account, the overriding focus on shareholder value becomes less self-evident. Nonetheless, many companies do strive to maximize shareholder value whilst at the same time trying to take into account the interests of the wider stakeholder group. One rationale for effectively privileging shareholders over other stakeholders is that they are the recipients of the residual free cash flow (being the profits remaining once other stakeholders, such as loan creditors, have been paid). This means that the shareholders have a vested interest in trying to ensure that resources are used to maximum effect, which in turn should be to the benefit of society as a whole.

Shareholders and stakeholders may favour different corporate governance structures and also monitoring mechanisms. We can, for example, see differences in the corporate governance structures and monitoring mechanisms of the so-called Anglo-American model, with its emphasis on shareholder value and a board comprised totally of executive and non-executive directors elected by shareholders, compared to the German model, whereby certain stakeholder groups, such as employees, have a right enshrined in law for their representatives to sit on the supervisory board alongside the directors. Chapter 4 is devoted to shareholders and stakeholders, and discusses various aspects in more detail.

An interesting development is that put forward by Jensen (2001), who states that traditional stakeholder theory argues that the managers of a firm should take account of the interests of all stakeholders in a firm but, because the theorists refuse to say how the trade-offs against the interests of each of these stakeholder groups might be made, there are no defined measurable objectives and this leaves managers unaccountable for their actions. Jensen therefore advocates enlightened value maximization, which he says is identical to enlightened stakeholder theory: 'Enlightened value maximization utilizes much of the structure of stakeholder theory but accepts maximization of the long-run value of the firm as the criterion for making the requisite trade-offs among its stakeholders . . . and therefore solves the problems that arise from multiple objectives that accompany traditional stakeholder theory'.

Stewardship theory

Stewardship theory draws on the assumptions underlying agency theory and TCE. The work of Donaldson and Davis (1991) cautioned against accepting agency theory as a given and introduced an alternative approach to corporate governance: stewardship theory.

The thrust of Donaldson and Davis' paper was that agency theory,

> emphasises the control of managerial 'opportunism' by having a board chair independent of the CEO and using incentives to bind CEO interests to those of shareholders. Stewardship theory stresses the beneficial consequences on shareholder returns of facilitative authority structures which unify command by having roles of CEO and chair held by the same person . . .

The safeguarding of returns to shareholders may be along the track, not of placing management under greater control by owners, but of empowering managers to take autonomous executive action.

Other theoretical perspectives

Managerial hegemony and class hegemony theories highlight the potential for a gap between what boards are expected to do and what they actually do in practice. Mace (1971) points out that managers may circumvent control away from the board by various means, including information asymmetry and elite networks. Huse (2007) made a significant contribution to the thinking on how research into boards and board behaviour might be carried out by applying lessons from the behavioural theory of the firm.

Resource dependence theory views the board of directors as 'the lynch pin between a company and the resources it needs to achieve its objectives' (Tricker, 2009, 2012).

Path dependence theory identifies two sources of path dependence: structure driven and rule driven, pointing out that corporate structures depend on the structures with which the economy started: 'Initial ownership structures can affect both the identity of the rules that would be efficient and the interest group politics that can determine which rules would actually be chosen' (Bebchuk and Roe, 1999).

Institutional theory looks at the institutional environment, its influence on societal beliefs and practices which impact on various 'actors' within society (Scott, 1987).

Political theory is identified as having a deep influence on different ownership and governance structures (Roe, 2003).

Network governance building on the work of Jones *et al.* (1997), Turnbull advocated the adoption of network governance as a logical way to extend the science of cybernetics to organizations. Pirson and Turnbull (2011) argue that companies should have a structure of network governance and suggest 'increasing board level information processing and decision-making capabilities by including multiple boards for different stakeholders to create a division of power and labor' which would allow superior risk management.

Whilst Table 2.1 gives a summary of a range of theories that may be associated with the development of corporate governance, Figure 2.1 illustrates the main theories that have traditionally been seen as the key influences on the development of corporate governance: agency theory, transaction cost economics, stakeholder theory and stewardship theory.

The theories in context

The approach taken in this book is to assume a public corporation business form (that is, a publicly quoted company), unless specifically stated otherwise. Therefore, the theories discussed earlier should be viewed in the light of this type of business form. In the UK this type of business form generally has a dispersed shareholder base, although there is a

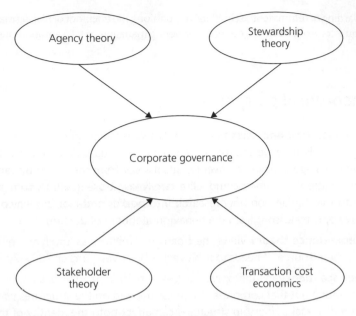

Figure 2.1 Main theories influencing the development of corporate governance

concentration of shareholdings amongst the institutional investors, such as the pension funds and insurance companies. Agency theory, together with the work of Berle and Means, seems particularly relevant in this context.

The theories that have affected the development of corporate governance should also be viewed in conjunction with the legal system and capital market development, as well as the ownership structure. For example, countries like the UK and the USA have a common law system that tends to give good protection of shareholder rights, whilst civil law countries, such as France, tend to have less effective legal protection for shareholder rights, and more emphasis may be given to the rights of certain stakeholder groups.

However, it is clear that companies cannot operate in isolation without having regard to the effect of their actions on the various stakeholder groups. To this end, companies need to be able to attract and retain equity investment, and be accountable to their shareholders, whilst at the same time giving real consideration to the interests of their wider stakeholder constituencies.

Convergence

There are a number of views as to where corporate governance systems are converging or are likely to converge. Roe (2003) states: 'That corporate governance structures around the world have differed is hardly contested. The very fact that many people talk today, at the beginning of the twenty-first century, about corporate convergence due to globalization tells us that people believe that corporate structures have sharply varied'. He goes on to discuss the influence of political forces that may impact in different ways, at different times, and in different countries, and he states 'a democratic polity does not easily accept powerful pro-shareholder institutions'. He illustrates this with the example of the USA where traditionally there have been limits on the power of pro-shareholder institutions, for example, not encouraging hostile takeovers; whilst in Europe, employees have comparatively good job protection. He sums up: 'If one fails to understand these political impulses, one cannot fully understand the world's, or any single nation's, corporate governance institutions'.

Aguilera and Jackson (2003) highlight that 'institutional change tends to occur in a slow, piecemeal fashion, rather than as a big bang. Where international pressures may lead to similar changes in one institutional domain, these effects may be mediated by the wider configuration of national institutions. This explains why internationalization has not led to quick convergence on national corporate governance models.'

Branson (2004) and Guillén (2004) argue against convergence occurring on economic, legal, and cultural grounds. For example, the family-owned firm is the dominant form of business around the globe and not the publicly owned corporation on which US and UK corporate governance is premised, hence we can see that one size is unlikely to fit all and that there will likely continue to be some divergence. There does, however, seem to be convergence on the core aspects of corporate governance, such as transparency, disclosure, and the important contribution that independent non-executive directors can make.

Conclusions

Corporate governance is a relatively new area and its development has been affected by theories from a number of disciplines, including finance, economics, accounting, law, management, and organizational behaviour. The main theory that has affected its development, and that provides a theoretical framework within which it most naturally seems to rest, is agency theory. However, stakeholder theory is coming more into play as companies increasingly become aware that they cannot operate in isolation and that, as well as considering their shareholders, they need also to have regard to a wider stakeholder constituency. Nonetheless it is fair to say that corporate governance is still seeking its theoretical foundations and, as Tricker (2009) states, 'corporate governance, as yet, does not have a single widely accepted theoretical base nor a commonly accepted paradigm . . . the subject lacks a conceptual framework that adequately reflects the reality of corporate governance'.

Future developments in the theory of corporate governance need to take account of a multitude of parts that make up the whole labyrinth of corporate governance: different business forms, different legal and cultural characteristics, and, of course, different 'actors' (directors, shareholders and various stakeholders). The interaction of these different actors, and the effects both from, and on, the environment in which they operate, means that corporate governance is of its nature a complex and evolving system.

Summary

- Corporate governance is a relatively new area and its development has been affected by theories from a number of disciplines, including finance, economics, accounting, law, management, and organizational behaviour.

- Agency theory has probably affected the development of the corporate governance framework the most. It identifies the agency relationship where one party (the principal) delegates work to another party (the agent). In the context of a corporation, the owners are the principal and the directors are the agent.

- Stakeholder theory takes account of a wider group of constituents rather than focusing on shareholders. Where there is an emphasis on stakeholders, then the governance structure of the company may provide for some direct representation of the stakeholder groups.

- The development of corporate governance is a global occurrence and, as such, is a complex area, including legal, cultural, ownership, and other structural differences. Therefore some theories may be more appropriate and relevant to some countries than others.

Questions

The discussion questions to follow cover the key learning points of this chapter. Reading of some of the additional reference material will enhance the depth of the students' knowledge and understanding of these areas.

1. Critically discuss the main theories that have influenced the development of corporate governance.

2. Do you think that different theories are more appropriate to different types of ownership structure?

3. What are the main problems that may arise in a principal – agent relationship and how might these be dealt with?

4. What links might there be between a country's legal system and capital market developments, and the impact of the theories underlying corporate governance?

5. Critically discuss the potential impact of the global financial crisis on the likelihood of convergence of corporate governance systems.

6. 'Stakeholders can, and should, be principals enabling them to further their interests in the same way as shareholders.' Critically discuss this statement.

References

Aguilera, R. and Jackson, G. (2003), 'The Cross-National Diversity of Corporate Governance: Dimensions and Determinants', *Academy of Management Review*, Vol. 28, No. 3, pp. 447–65.

Bebchuk, L.A. and Roe, M.J. (1999), 'A Theory of Path Dependence in Corporate Ownership and Governance', *Stanford Law Review*, Vol. 52.

Berle, A.A. and Means, G.C. (1932), *The Modern Corporation and Private Property*, Macmillan, New York.

Blair, M. (1996), *Ownership and Control: Rethinking Corporate Governance for the Twenty-first Century*, Brookings Institution, Washington.

Branson, D.M. (2004), 'The Very Uncertain Prospects of "Global" Convergence in Corporate Governance' in *Theories of Corporate Governance*, T. Clarke (ed.), Routledge, London.

Charkham, J. and Simpson, A. (1999), *Fair Shares: The Future of Shareholder Power and Responsibility*, Oxford University Press, Oxford.

Clarke, T. (2004), *Theories of Corporate Governance*, Routledge, London.

Coase, R.H. (1937), 'The Nature of the Firm', *Economica* IV, 13–16.

Coffee, J.C. (2006), *Gatekeepers, the Professions and Corporate Governance*, Oxford University Press, Oxford.

Donaldson, L. and Davis, J.H. (1991), 'Stewardship Theory or Agency Theory: CEO Governance and Shareholder Returns', *Australian Journal of Management*, Vol. 16, No. 1.

Fama, E.F. and Jensen, M. (1983), 'Separation of Ownership and Control', *Journal of Law and Economics* 26.

Gordon, J.N. and Roe, M. J. (2004), *Convergence and Persistence in Corporate Governance*, Cambridge University Press, Cambridge.

Guillén, M.F. (2004), 'Corporate Governance and Globalization: Is There Convergence Across Countries' in *Theories of Corporate Governance*, T. Clarke (ed.), Routledge, London.

Hart, O. (1995), 'Corporate Governance: Some Theory and Implications', *The Economic Journal* 105.

Huse, M. (2007), *Boards, Governance and Value Creation: The Human Side of Corporate Governance*, Cambridge University Press, Cambridge.

Jensen, M. (2001), 'Value Maximization, Stakeholder Theory, and the Corporate Objective Function', *Journal of Applied Corporate Finance*, Vol. 14, No. 3.

—— and Meckling, W. (1976), 'Theory of the Firm: Managerial Behaviour, Agency Costs and Ownership Structure', *Journal of Financial Economics* 3.

Jones, C., Hesterly, W.S., and Borgatti, S.P. (1997), 'A General Theory of Network Governance: Exchange Conditions and Social Mechanisms', *Academy of Management Review*, Vol. 22. No. 4, pp. 911–45.

La Porta, R., Lopez-de-Silanes, F., Shleifer, A., and Vishny, R. (1999), 'Corporate Ownership Around the World', *Journal of Finance* 54.

Mace, M. (1971), *Directors: Myth and Reality*, Harvard University Press, Cambridge, MA.

Monks, R.A.G. (2001), *The New Global Investors*, Capstone Publishing, Oxford.

Pirson, M. and Turnbull, S. (2011), 'Corporate Governance, Risk Management, and the Financial Crisis: An Information Processing View', *Corporate Governance: An International Review*, Vol. 19, Issue 5, pp. 459–70.

Roe, M.R. (2003), *Political Determinants of Corporate Governance*, Oxford University Press, Oxford.

Scott, W.R. (1987), 'The Adolescence of Institutional Theory', *Administrative Science Quarterly* 32, pp. 493–511.

Smith, A. (1838), *The Wealth of Nations*, Ward Lock, London.

Stiles, P. and Taylor, B. (2001), *Boards at Work: How Directors View Their Roles and Responsibilities*, Oxford University Press, Oxford.

Tricker, B. (2009, 2012), *Corporate Governance, Principles, Policies and Practices*, Oxford University Press, Oxford.

Useem, M. (1996), *Investor Capitalism: How Money Managers Are Changing the Face of Corporate America*, Basic Books, New York.

Wessel, D. (2001), 'Capital: The Legal DNA of Good Economies', *Wall Street Journal*, 6 September 2001.

Williamson, O.E. (1975), *Markets and Hierarchies*, Free Press, New York.

—— (1984), 'Corporate Governance', *Yale Law Journal* Vol. 93.

Useful websites

http://blog.thecorporatelibrary.com Contains many useful and topical articles/references for the study of corporate governance (renamed the GMI blog).

http://leadership.wharton.upenn.edu/governance/readings/index.shtml Contains references to key academic articles in a number of corporate governance areas.

 For further links to useful sources of information visit the Online Resource Centre **www.oxfordtextbooks.co.uk/orc/mallin4e/**

Development of Corporate Governance Codes

Learning Objectives

- To understand the key factors affecting the development of corporate governance codes
- To be aware of the main developments in corporate governance codes
- To have an awareness of the corporate governance codes that have been most influential globally
- To critically assess the characteristics of corporate governance codes and the mode of operation

The growth in corporate governance codes

During the last decade, each year has seen the introduction, or revision, of a corporate governance code in a number of countries. These countries have encompassed a variety of legal backgrounds (for example, common law in the UK, civil law in France), cultural and political contexts (for example, democracy in Australia, communism in China), business forms (for example, public corporations compared to family-owned firms), and share ownership (institutional investor-dominated in the UK and USA, state ownership in China). However, in each of the countries, the introduction of corporate governance codes has generally been motivated by a desire for more transparency and accountability, and a desire to increase investor confidence (of both potential and existing investors) in the stock market as a whole. The development of the codes has often been driven by a financial scandal, corporate collapse, or similar crisis.

The corporate governance codes and guidelines have been issued by a variety of bodies ranging from committees (appointed by government departments and usually including prominent respected figures from business and industry, representatives from the invest-ment community, representatives from professional bodies, and academics), through to stock exchange bodies, various investor representative groups, and professional bodies, such as those representing directors or company secretaries.

As regards compliance with the various codes, compliance is generally on a voluntary disclosure basis, whilst some codes (such as the UK Corporate Governance Code (2010)) are on a 'comply or explain basis': that is, either a company has to comply fully with the code and state that it has done so, or it explains why it has not.

In this chapter, the development of corporate governance in the UK is covered in some detail, particularly in relation to the Cadbury Report (1992), which has influenced the development of many corporate governance codes globally. Similarly, the Organisation for Economic Co-operation and Development (OECD) Principles are reviewed in detail as these have also formed the cornerstone of many corporate governance codes. The impact of various other international organizations on corporate governance developments, including the World Bank, Global Corporate Governance Forum (GCGF), International Corporate Governance Network (ICGN), and Commonwealth Association for Corporate Governance (CACG), are discussed. Recent developments in the EU, which have implications both for existing and potential member countries' corporate governance, are covered. There is also a brief overview of the Basle Committee recommendations for corporate governance in banking organizations.

Corporate collapses in the USA have had a significant impact on confidence in financial markets across the world and corporate governance developments in the USA are discussed in some detail.

In addition, a section on the governance of non-governmental organizations (NGOs), the public sector, non-profit organizations, and charities is included, as there is an increased focus on the governance of these organizations. The adoption of good governance should enable them to spend public money wisely and to strengthen their position.

The impact of the global financial crisis has had ramifications for corporate governance internationally, as countries seek to restore confidence in their financial markets and, in particular, in banks and other financial institutions.

Corporate governance in the UK

The UK has a well-developed market with a diverse shareholder base, including institutional investors, financial institutions, and individuals. The UK illustrates well the problems that may be associated with the separation of the ownership and control of corporations, and hence has many of the associated agency problems discussed in Chapter 2. These agency problems, including misuse of corporate assets by directors and a lack of effective control over, and accountability of, directors' actions, contributed to a number of financial scandals in the UK.

As in other countries, the development of corporate governance in the UK was initially driven by corporate collapses and financial scandals. The UK's Combined Code (1998) embodied the findings of a trilogy of reports: the Cadbury Report (1992), the Greenbury Report (1995), and the Hampel Report (1998). Brief mention is made of each of these three at this point to set the context, whilst a detailed review of the Cadbury Report (1992) is given subsequently in this chapter because it has influenced the development of many codes across the world. Reference is made to relevant sections of various codes in appropriate subsequent chapters.

Figure 3.1 illustrates the development of corporate governance in the UK. The centre oval represents the UK Corporate Governance Code, and the UK Stewardship Code, both published in 2010 by the Financial Reporting Council (FRC). Around the centre oval, we can see the various influences since 1998 (the original Combined Code, published in 1998, encompassed the Cadbury, Greenbury, and Hampel reports recommendations). These influences can be split into four broad areas. First, there are reports that have looked at specific areas of corporate governance:

- the Turnbull Report on internal controls;
- Myners Report on institutional investment;
- Higgs Review of the role and effectiveness of non-executive directors;
- Tyson Report on the recruitment and development of non-executive directors;
- the Smith Review of audit committees;
- the Davies Report on board diversity.

Secondly, there has been the influence of institutional investors and their representative groups; of particular note here is the work of the Institutional Shareholders' Committee (ISC) as their statement on the responsibilities of institutional shareholders formed the body of the first UK Stewardship Code (2010). Thirdly, influences affecting the regulatory framework within which corporate governance in the UK operates have included the UK company law review, the Walker Review for HM Treasury and the Financial Services Authority Review. Fourthly, there have been what might be termed 'external influences' such as the EU review of company law, the EU Corporate Governance Framework and the US Sarbanes–Oxley Act. Each of these is now discussed in turn.

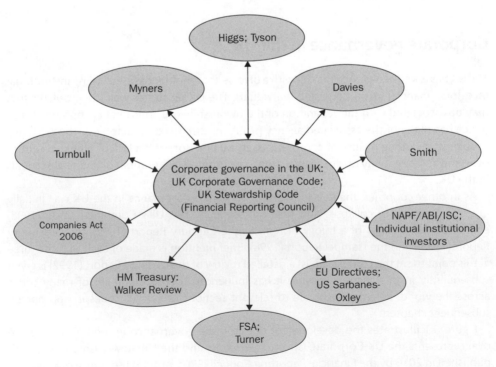

Figure 3.1 Development of corporate governance in the UK

Cadbury Report (1992)

Following various financial scandals and collapses (Coloroll and Polly Peck, to name but two) and a perceived general lack of confidence in the financial reporting of many UK companies, the FRC, the London Stock Exchange, and the accountancy profession established the Committee on the Financial Aspects of Corporate Governance in May 1991. After the Committee was set up, the scandals at Bank of Credit and Commerce International (BCCI) and Maxwell (which respectively involved maintaining secret files for fraudulent purposes and using secret loans to try to disguise financial collapse) occurred, and as a result, the Committee interpreted its remit more widely and looked beyond the financial aspects to corporate governance as a whole. The Committee was chaired by Sir Adrian Cadbury and, when the Committee reported in December 1992, the report became widely known as 'the Cadbury Report'.

The recommendations covered: the operation of the main board; the establishment, composition, and operation of key board committees; the importance of, and contribution that can be made by, non-executive directors; and the reporting and control mechanisms of a business. The Cadbury Report recommended a Code of Best Practice with which the boards of all listed companies registered in the UK should comply, and utilized a 'comply or explain' mechanism. This mechanism means that a company should comply with the code but, if it cannot comply with any particular aspect of it, then it should explain why it is unable to do so. This disclosure gives investors detailed information about any instances of non-compliance and enables them to decide whether the company's non-compliance is justified.

Greenbury Report (1995)

The Greenbury Committee was set up in response to concerns about both the size of directors' remuneration packages, and their inconsistent and incomplete disclosure in companies' annual reports. It made, in 1995, comprehensive recommendations regarding disclosure of directors' remuneration packages. There has been much discussion about how much disclosure there should be of directors' remuneration and how useful detailed disclosures might be. Whilst the work of the Greenbury Committee focused on the directors of public limited companies, it hoped that both smaller listed companies and unlisted companies would find its recommendations useful.

Central to the Greenbury Report recommendations were strengthening accountability and enhancing the performance of directors. These two aims were to be achieved by (i) the presence of a remuneration committee comprised of independent non-executive directors who would report fully to the shareholders each year about the company's executive remuneration policy, including full disclosure of the elements in the remuneration of individual directors; and (ii) the adoption of performance measures linking rewards to the performance of both the company and individual directors, so that the interests of directors and shareholders were more closely aligned.

Since that time (1995), disclosure of directors' remuneration has become quite prolific in UK company accounts. The main elements of directors' remuneration are considered further in Chapter 9.

Hampel Report (1998)

The Hampel Committee was set up in 1995 to review the implementation of the Cadbury and Greenbury Committee recommendations. The Hampel Committee reported in 1998. The Hampel Report said: 'We endorse the overwhelming majority of the findings of the two earlier committees'. There has been much discussion about the extent to which a company should consider the interests of various stakeholders, such as employees, customers, suppliers, providers of credit, the local community, etc., as well as the interests of its shareholders. The Hampel Report stated that 'the directors as a board are responsible *for relations with* stakeholders; but they are accountable *to* the shareholders' [emphasis in original]. However, the report does also state that 'directors can meet their legal duties to shareholders, and can pursue the objective of long-term shareholder value successfully, only by developing and sustaining these stakeholder relationships'.

The Hampel Report, like its precursors, also emphasized the important role that institutional investors have to play in the companies in which they invest (investee companies). It is highly desirable that companies and institutional investors engage in dialogue and that institutional investors make considered use of their shares; in other words, institutional investors should consider carefully the resolutions on which they have a right to vote and reach a decision based on careful thought, rather than engage in 'box ticking'.

Combined Code (1998)

The Combined Code drew together the recommendations of the Cadbury, Greenbury, and Hampel reports. It has two sections, one aimed at companies and another aimed at institutional investors. The Combined Code operates on the 'comply or explain' basis mentioned earlier. In relation to the internal controls of the business, the Combined Code states that 'the board should maintain a sound system of internal control to safeguard shareholders' investment and the company's assets' and that 'the directors should, at least annually, conduct a review of the effectiveness of the group's system of internal control and should report to shareholders that they have done so. The review should cover all controls, including financial, operational, and compliance controls and risk management' (Part D.2.1). The Turnbull Report issued in 1999 gave directors guidance on carrying out this review.

Turnbull (1999)

The Turnbull Committee, chaired by Nigel Turnbull, was established by the Institute of Chartered Accountants in England and Wales (ICAEW) to provide guidance on the implementation of the internal control requirements of the Combined Code. The Turnbull Report confirms that it is the responsibility of the board of directors to ensure that the company has a sound system of internal control, and that the controls are working as they should. The board should assess the effectiveness of internal controls and report on them in the annual report. Of course, a company is subject to new risks both from the outside environment and as a result of decisions that the board makes about corporate strategy and objectives. In the managing of risk, boards will need to take into account the existing internal control system in the company and also whether any changes are required to ensure that new risks are adequately and effectively managed.

Myners (2001, 2008)

The Myners Report on Institutional Investment, issued in 2001 by HM Treasury, concentrated more on the trusteeship aspects of institutional investors and the legal requirements for trustees, with the aim of raising the standards and promoting greater shareholder activism. For example, the Myners Report expects that institutional investors should be more proactive, especially in the stance they take with underperforming companies. Some institutional investors have already shown more of a willingness to engage actively with companies to try to ensure that shareholder value is not lost by underperforming companies.

In 2007 the National Association of Pension Funds (NAPF) published the results of its review of the extent to which pension fund trustees were complying with the principles. The report stated 'the recommendations set out in this report provide a framework for developing further the Principles so that they remain relevant for the world in which pension fund trustees operate today'. Subsequently, HM Treasury published Updating the Myners Principles: A Response to Consultation in 2008. There are six principles identified: effective decision-making, clear objectives, risk and liabilities, performance assessment, responsible ownership, transparency, and reporting. The report emphasized greater industry ownership of the principles and places the onus on trustees to report on their own practices.

Higgs (2003)

The Higgs Review, chaired by Derek Higgs, reported in January 2003 on the role and effectiveness of non-executive directors. Higgs offered support for the Combined Code whilst making some additional recommendations. These recommendations included: stating the number of meetings of the board and its main committees in the annual report, together with the attendance records of individual directors; that a chief executive director should not also become chairman of the same company; non-executive directors should meet as a group at least once a year without executive directors being present, and the annual report should indicate whether such meetings have occurred. Higgs also recommended that chairmen and chief executives should consider implementing executive development programmes to train and develop suitable individuals in their companies for future director roles; the board should inform shareholders as to why they believe a certain individual should be appointed to a non-executive directorship and how they may meet the requirements of the role; there should be a comprehensive induction programme for new non-executive directors, and resources should be available for ongoing development of directors; the performance of the board, its committees and its individual members, should be evaluated at least once a year, the annual report should state whether these reviews are being held and how they are conducted. Higgs went on to recommend that a full-time executive director should not hold more than one non-executive directorship or become chairman of a major company; and that no one non-executive director should sit on all three principal board committees (audit, remuneration, nomination). There was substantial opposition to some of the recommendations but they nonetheless helped to inform the Combined Code. Good practice suggestions from the Higgs Report were published in 2006.

Following a recommendation in Chapter 10 of the Higgs Review, a group led by Professor Laura Tyson, looked at how companies might utilize broader pools of talent with varied skills and experience, and different perspectives to enhance board effectiveness. The Tyson Report was published in 2003.

Smith (2003)

The Smith Review of audit committees, a group appointed by the FRC, reported in January 2003. The review made clear the important role of the audit committee: 'While all directors have a duty to act in the interests of the company, the audit committee has a particular role, acting independently from the executive, to ensure that the interests of shareholders are properly protected in relation to financial reporting and internal control' (para. 1.5). The review defined the audit committee's role in terms of a high-level overview; it needs to satisfy itself that there is an appropriate system of controls in place but it does not undertake the monitoring itself.

Combined Code (2003)

The revised Combined Code, published in July 2003, incorporated the substance of the Higgs and Smith reviews. However, rather than stating that no one non-executive director should sit on all three board committees, the Combined Code stated that 'undue reliance' should not be placed on particular individuals. The Combined Code also clarified the roles of the chairman and the senior independent director (SID), emphasizing the chairman's role in providing leadership to the non-executive directors and in communicating shareholders' views to the board; it also provided for a 'formal and rigorous annual evaluation' of the board's, the committees', and the individual directors' performance. At least half the board in larger listed companies were to be independent non-executive directors.

Revised Turnbull Guidance (2005)

In 2005 revised guidance on the Turnbull Report (1999) was published. There were few substantive changes but boards were encouraged to review their application of the guidance on a continuing basis and to look on the internal control statement as an opportunity to communicate to their shareholders how they manage risk and internal control. They should notify shareholders, in the annual report, of how any 'significant failings or weaknesses' in the effectiveness of the internal control system have been dealt with.

Combined Code (2006)

An updated version of the Combined Code was issued in June 2006. There were three main changes made:

- to allow the company chairman to serve on (but not to chair) the remuneration committee where he is considered independent on appointment as chairman;
- to provide a 'vote withheld' option on proxy appointment forms to enable a shareholder to indicate that they wish to withhold their vote;
- to recommend that companies publish on their website the details of proxies lodged at general meetings where votes were taken on a show of hands.

Combined Code (2008)

The findings of the FRC Review of the Impact of the Combined Code were published in December 2007. The overall findings indicated that the Combined Code (2006) had general support and that the FRC would concentrate on improving the practical application of the Combined Code.

In June 2008, the FRC published a new edition of the Combined Code which introduced two changes. These changes were (i) to remove the restriction on an individual chairing more than one FTSE 100 company; and (ii) for listed companies outside the FTSE 350, to allow the company chairman to sit on the audit committee where he or she was considered independent on appointment.

The Combined Code (2008) took effect at the same time as new FSA Rules implementing EU requirements relating to corporate governance statements and audit committees.

Revised Smith Guidance (2008)

A new edition of the guidance was issued in October 2008. The main changes to the guidance as detailed on the FRC website are:

audit committees are encouraged to consider the need to include the risk of the withdrawal of their auditor from the market in their risk evaluation and planning; companies are encouraged to include in the audit committee's report information on the appointment, reappointment or removal of the auditor, including supporting information on tendering frequency, the tenure of the incumbent auditor and any contractual obligations that acted to restrict the committee's choice of auditor; a small number of detailed changes have been made to the section dealing with the independence of the auditor, to bring the guidance in line with the Auditing Practices Board's [APB's] Ethical Standards [for Auditors (2004, revised 2008)] for auditors, which have been issued since the guidance was first published in 2003; and an appendix has been added containing guidance on the factors to be considered if a group is contemplating employing firms from more than one network to undertake the audit.

Walker Review (2009)

Following on from the financial crisis, an independent review of the governance of banks and other financial institutions was carried out by Sir David Walker. The Walker Review published its final recommendations in November 2009. The thirty-nine recommendations comprised:

- five relating to board size, composition and qualification (including improvements to director training and induction);
- eight relating to the functioning of the board and evaluation of performance (including several recommendations relating to the role of the Chair);
- nine relating to the role of institutional shareholders' communication and engagement (emphasizing the development and regulatory sponsorship of a Stewardship Code);
- five relating to the governance of risk (emphasizing the role of the risk committee);

● twelve relating to remuneration (including the role of the board remuneration committee; disclosure of executive remuneration; and the Code of Conduct for executive remuneration consultants written by the Remuneration Consultants Group (RCG)).

Some of the recommendations were to be taken forward by the FRC through amendments to the Combined Code, whilst others were to be taken forward by the FSA.

UK Corporate Governance Code (2010)

In the summer of 2009 the FRC published a progress report on the effectiveness of the Combined Code. They subsequently consulted on the issues raised in the progress report, and then published a report on their findings and also indicated what action they proposed to take. A further consultation followed and an updated corporate governance code for UK companies, incorporating some of the Walker recommendations, was issued in May 2010. Formerly known as 'the Combined Code', the newly issued UK Corporate Governance Code (hereafter 'the Code') retained the 'comply or explain' approach.

The FRC identified six main changes which were as follows. First, to improve risk management, the company's business model should be explained and the board should be responsible for the nature and extent of significant risks it is willing to take. Secondly, performance-related pay should be aligned to the long-term interests of the company and to its risk policy and systems. Thirdly, all directors of FTSE 350 companies should be put forward for re-election every year as a way of increasing their accountability. Fourthly, new principles on the leadership of the chairman, the responsibility of the non-executive directors to provide constructive challenge, and the time commitment expected of all directors will help to encourage appropriate debate in the boardroom. Fifthly, new principles on the composition and selection of the board, including the need to appoint members on merit, against objective criteria, and with due regard for the benefits of diversity, including gender diversity should encourage boards to be well balanced and avoid 'group think'. And finally, the chairman should hold regular development reviews with each director and FTSE 350 companies should have externally facilitated board effectiveness reviews at least every three years. These latter measures should help enhance the board's performance and awareness of its strengths and weaknesses.

Guidance Notes on Implementation of the UK Corporate Governance Code

The FRC has published a series of guidance notes to assist companies in applying the principles of the Code.

In 2010 the FRC published the *Guidance on Board Effectiveness*, which relates primarily to Sections A and B of the Code on the leadership and effectiveness of the board. The guidance was developed by the Institute of Chartered Secretaries and Administrators (ICSA) on the FRC's behalf, and replaces 'Suggestions for Good Practice from the Higgs Report' (known as 'the Higgs Guidance'), which has been withdrawn.

In addition, three guidance notes have been issued in relation to Section C of the Code. Guidance on the requirement in Section C.1.3 of the Code to report on whether the business is a going concern, and other related regulatory requirements is given in *Going Concern and*

Liquidity Risk: Guidance for Directors of UK Companies. Meanwhile *Internal Control: Revised Guidance for Directors* (known as 'the Turnbull Guidance') provides guidance to companies on how to apply the section of the Code dealing with risk management and internal control (Section C.2); and *Guidance on Audit Committees* (formerly known as 'the Smith Guidance'), provides guidance on Section C.3 of the Code, which deals with the audit committee and the engagement of the external auditor.

Stewardship Code (2010)

When the Code was first published, it included in Schedule C some engagement principles for institutional investors. However, Schedule C has now been deleted as it has been superseded by the *UK Stewardship Code* (hereafter 'the Stewardship Code'). The Stewardship Code is seen as complementary to the Code and 'aims to enhance the quality of engagement between institutional investors and companies to help improve long-term returns to shareholders and the efficient exercise of governance responsibilities'. The Stewardship Code builds largely on the ISC's work on the responsibilities of institutional shareholders (discussed in detail in Chapter 6) by essentially setting out the best practice engagement, including dialogue and voting of shares, for institutional investors in their investee companies. This should help build a much stronger link between the investment process and corporate governance. The Stewardship Code is to be applied on a 'comply or explain' basis.

Davies Report (2011, 2012)

Concerned by the lack of progress with the representation of women on UK boards, the UK's Coalition Government invited Lord Davies to review the situation, to identify the barriers that were preventing more women from reaching the boardroom, and to make recommendations as to how this situation might be redressed. Lord Davies' report, *Women on Boards*, was published in February 2011 and reviewed the current situation on UK boards (FTSE 350) and considered the business case for having gender-diverse boards.

A number of recommendations were made including that the Chairmen of FTSE 350 companies should state the percentage of women that they aim to have on their boards in 2013 and 2015, and that FTSE 100 companies should aim for a minimum 25 per cent women in the boardroom by 2015 although many might achieve a higher figure. Quoted companies should disclose annually the proportion of women on the board, women in senior executive positions, and female employees in the organizations as a whole. Furthermore, Lord Davies recommended that the FRC amend the Code to require listed companies to establish a policy on boardroom diversity, including measurable objectives for implementing the policy, and disclose a summary of the policy and the progress made towards achieving the objectives each year. It was also recommended that executive search firms should draw up a voluntary code of conduct addressing gender diversity and best practice covering the relevant search criteria and processes in relation to FTSE 350 board appointments.

Early in 2012 a follow-up report was published which indicated that over the year since the original report was published, the biggest ever reported increase in the percentage of women on boards was evidenced.

UK Corporate Governance Code (2012)

In May 2011 the FRC began consulting on possible amendments to the Code that would require companies to publish their policy on boardroom diversity and report against it annually, as recommended by Lord Davies in his *Women on Boards* report published in February 2011 (see earlier discussion), and to consider the board's diversity, amongst other factors, when assessing its effectiveness. In October 2011 the FRC announced that these changes would be implemented in a revised version of the Code which will be issued in 2012 and will apply to financial years beginning on or after 1 October 2012.

The changes affect two sections of the Code. First, in relation to Section B.2.4, where it is proposed that the work of the nomination committee should be described in a separate section of the annual report, including the process used in relation to board appointments. This section should include a description of 'the board's policy on diversity, including gender, any measurable objectives that it has set for implementing the policy, and progress on achieving the objectives. An explanation should be given if neither an external search consultancy nor open advertising has been used in the appointment of a chairman or a non-executive director.' Secondly, in relation to Section B6, where 'the evaluation of the board should consider the balance of skills, experience, independence and knowledge of the company on the board, its diversity, including gender, how the board works together as a unit, and other factors relevant to its effectiveness'.

Subsequently, in September 2011 the FRC announced that it intended to consult on proposed further changes to the Code in relation to audit committees and audit retendering. It is possible that further changes may be proposed as a consequence of the Sharman Panel of Inquiry into 'going concern' and the Department for Business, Innovation & Skills (BIS) consultation on narrative reporting; the outcomes of both of these being available in 2012. Should any changes be agreed as a result, they would also be incorporated into the revised Code that will apply from 1 October 2012.

In December 2011 the FRC reported on the impact and implementation of the UK Corporate Governance and Stewardship Codes. The FRC highlighted that any changes made in 2012 will be specifically targeted at strengthening the current framework rather than changing it, and that their aim will then be to leave both codes unchanged for a further two years.

'Comply or Explain'

As mentioned earlier, the Code operates on a 'comply or explain' basis. In February 2012, the FRC reported on discussions it arranged between companies and investors with the aim of comparing notes between these two groups on their perceptions of the 'explain' part of 'comply or explain'. The report found that the two groups believed that a great strength of the Code was that the principles were expressed in general, rather than very specific, terms which allowed some latitude in their implementation. Therefore, companies could still comply with the Code, even if they deviated from one or more of its provisions, by making a full explanation of why they had not complied with a particular aspect. The report concluded that 'used properly, the Code-based "comply or explain" approach can deliver greater transparency and confidence than formal regulation which is purely a matter of compliance'. The discussions were also timely in the context of some scepticism in the EU about the effectiveness of the 'comply or explain' approach and whether it is taken seriously by investors and companies. Such discussions could result in a more prescriptive and inherently less flexible approach giving more power to regulators and less to shareholders. Hence it was helpful to be able to demonstrate the strengths of the 'comply or explain' approach.

Institutional investors and their representative groups

Large institutional investors—mainly insurance companies and pension funds—usually belong to one of two representative bodies that act as a professional group 'voice' for their views: the Association of British Insurers (ABI) and the National Association of Pension Funds (NAPF). Both the ABI and the NAPF have best practice corporate governance guidelines that encompass the recommendations of the UK Corporate Governance Code. They monitor the corporate governance activities of companies and provide advice to members.

Some large institutional investors are very active in their own right in terms of their corporate governance activities. Hermes is a case in point, and it has published the Hermes Principles, which detail how it perceives its relationship with the companies in which it invests (investee companies), what its expectations are of investee companies, and what investee companies can expect from Hermes.

Whilst the role and influence of institutional investors is covered in detail in Chapter 6, mention should be made here of the work of the ISC, whose *Code on the Responsibilities of Institutional Investors* formed the basis for the *UK Stewardship Code* (2010). The ISC was renamed in the summer of 2011, as the Institutional Investor Committee (IIC) whose members are the NAPF, the ABI and the Investment Management Association (IMA).

Companies Act 2006

In the UK the corporate law had been in need of a thorough review for some years and the Modern Company Law Review culminated in July 2002 in the publication of outline proposals for extensive modernization of company law, including various aspects of corporate governance. These proposals included: statutory codification of directors' common law duties; enhanced company reporting and audit requirements, including a requirement that economically significant companies produce an annual Operating and Financial Review (OFR); disclosure on corporate websites of information relating to the annual report and accounts, and disclosure relating to voting.

The government published the Company Law Reform Bill in November 2005, and the Companies Act 2006 was enacted in late 2006. The Act updates previous Companies' Acts legislation, but does not completely replace them, and it contains some significant new provisions that will impact on various constituents, including directors, shareholders, auditors, and company secretaries. The Act draws on the findings of the Company Law Review proposals.

The main features of the Companies Act 2006 are as follows:

- directors' duties are codified;
- companies can make greater use of electronic communications for communicating with shareholders;

- directors can file service addresses on public record rather than their private home addresses;
- shareholders can agree limitations on directors' liability;
- simpler model Articles of Association for private companies, to reflect the way in which small companies operate;
- private companies are not required to have a company secretary;
- private companies do not need to hold an annual general meeting unless they agree to do so;
- the requirement for an OFR has not been reinstated, rather companies are encouraged to produce a high quality business review;
- nominee shareholders can elect to receive information in hard copy form or electronically if they wish to do so;
- shareholders will receive more timely information;
- enhanced proxy rights will make it easier for shareholders to appoint others to attend and vote at general meetings;
- shareholders of quoted companies may have a shareholder proposal (resolution) circulated at the company's expense if received by the financial year end;
- whilst there has been significant encouragement over a number of years to encourage institutional investors to disclose how they use their votes, the Act provides a power that could be used to require institutional investors to disclose how they have voted.

Overall there seems to be an increasing burden for quoted companies, whilst on the other hand the burden seems to have been reduced for private companies. In terms of the rights of shareholders, these are enhanced in a number of ways, including greater use of electronic communications, more information, enhanced proxy rights, and provision regarding the circulation of shareholder proposals at the company's expense. Equally, there is a corres-ponding emphasis on shareholders' responsibilities with encouragement for institutional shareholders to be more active and to disclose how they have voted.

Financial Services Authority (FSA)

In September 2002, the FSA launched a review of the listing regime with the main aim being to assess the existing rules and identify which should be retained and which changed. The areas covered by the review were: corporate governance; continuing obligations (encompassing corporate communication, and shareholders' rights and obligations); financial information; and the sponsor regime.

The FSA Review took place against the background of potentially significant changes in both the EU and UK regulatory environments, and although some changes were made, there was much continuity in the proposals introduced in 2005.

Following the global banking crisis, Lord Adair Turner, Chairman of the FSA, was asked by the Chancellor of the Exchequer to carry out a review and make recommendations for reforming UK and international approaches to the way banks are regulated. The Turner

Review was published in the spring of 2009. Issues highlighted include remuneration policies designed to avoid incentives for undue risk-taking; whether changes in governance structure are needed to increase the independence of risk management functions; and consideration of the skill and time commitment required for non-executive directors of large complex banks to effectively perform their role.

In 2010 the UK Government decided that it would be appropriate for the FSA to undergo some internal restructuring. The FSA has therefore been streamlining its operations in the wake of the financial crisis so that it can perform more effective regulation of banks and the financial markets. The changes include combining the retail and wholesale supervision units into a single division and creating standalone risk and international units.

Financial Reporting Council (FRC)

The FRC has six operating bodies: the Accounting Standards Board (ASB), the APB, the Board for Actuarial Standards (BAS), the Professional Oversight Board, the Financial Reporting Review Panel (FRRP), and the Accountancy and Actuarial Discipline Board (AADB).

The importance placed on corporate governance is evidenced by the fact that, in March 2004, the FRC set up a new committee to lead its work on corporate governance.

Overall, the FRC is responsible for promoting high standards of corporate governance. It aims to do so by:

- maintaining an effective UK Corporate Governance Code and promoting its widespread application;
- ensuring that related guidance, such as that on internal control, is current and relevant;
- influencing EU and global corporate governance developments;
- helping to promote boardroom professionalism and diversity;
- encouraging constructive interaction between company boards and institutional shareholders.

The FRC has carried out several consultative reviews of the Combined Code which led to the amended Combined Code in 2006 and 2008; whilst the review in 2009 culminated in the issue of the UK Corporate Governance Code in 2010. The latest reviews have taken place in 2011 and 2012. The frequency of the reviews are both an indicator of the FRC's responsibility for corporate governance of UK companies, which involves leading public debate in the area, and its response to the global financial crisis, which has, in turn, affected confidence in aspects of corporate governance.

'External' influences

The report of the EU High-Level Group of Company Law Experts had implications for company law across Europe, including the UK, and, together with other pronouncements such as the High-Level Group on Financial Supervision in the EU (2009) and the Green Paper on Corporate Governance in Europe (2011), is later discussed in more detail in the context of an international development. The impact of legislation in the USA, including the Sarbanes–Oxley Act (2002), has also made its influence felt in the UK, and is also discussed in detail later.

Influential corporate governance codes

Corporate governance codes and guidelines for various countries around the world will be looked at in more detail in some of the later chapters, whilst in this chapter codes and guidelines that have had a fundamental influence on the development of corporate governance more generally will be examined. It is always slightly contentious to try to state which corporate governance codes have had the most influence on the development of corporate governance codes in other countries, but the following codes and principles have undoubtedly had a key impact on the development of corporate governance globally.

Cadbury Report (1992)

The Cadbury Report recommended a Code of Best Practice with which the boards of all listed companies registered in the UK should comply, and utilized a 'comply or explain' mechanism. Whilst the Code of Best Practice is aimed at the directors of listed companies registered in the UK, the Committee also exhorted other companies to try to meet its requirements. The main recommendations of the Code are shown in Box 3.1.

The recommendations—covering the operation of the main board, the establishment, composition, and operation of key board committees; the importance of, and contribution that can be made by, non-executive directors; and the reporting and control mechanisms of a business—had a fundamental impact on the development of corporate governance not just in the UK, but on the content of codes across the world, amongst countries as diverse as India and Russia.

Today the recommendations of the Cadbury Report and subsequent UK reports on corporate governance are embodied in the UK Corporate Governance Code. Various sections of the Code are referred to in appropriate chapters and the full text of the UK Corporate Governance Code (2010) is available for download from the FRC website at: <http://www.frc.org.uk/documents/pagemanager/Corporate_Governance/UK%20Corp%20Gov%20Code%20June%202010.pdf>

Box 3.1 The Code of Best Practice

1. The Board of Directors

    1.1 The board should meet regularly, retain full and effective control over the company, and monitor the executive management.

    1.2 There should be a clearly accepted division of responsibilities at the head of a company, which will ensure a balance of power and authority, such that no one individual has unfettered powers of decision. Where the chairman is also the chief executive, it is essential that there should be a strong and independent element on the board, with a recognized senior member.

    1.3 The board should include non-executive directors of sufficient calibre and number for their views to carry significant weight in the board's decisions.

1.4 The board should have a formal schedule of matters specifically reserved to it for decision to ensure that the direction and control of the company is firmly in its hands.

1.5 There should be an agreed procedure for directors in the furtherance of their duties to take independent professional advice if necessary, at the company's expense.

1.6 All directors should have access to the advice and services of the company secretary, who is responsible to the board for ensuring that board procedures are followed and that applicable rules and regulations are complied with. Any question of the removal of the company secretary should be a matter for the board as a whole.

2. Non-executive Directors

2.1 Non-executive directors should bring an independent judgement to bear on issues of strategy, performance, resources, including key appointments, and standards of conduct.

2.2 The majority should be independent of management and free from any business or other relationship which could materially interfere with the exercise of their independent judgement, apart from their fees and shareholding. Their fees should reflect the time which they commit to the company.

2.3 Non-executive directors should be appointed for specified terms and reappointment should not be automatic.

2.4 Non-executive directors should be selected through a formal process and both this process and their appointment should be a matter for the board as a whole.

3. Executive Directors

3.1 Directors' service contracts should not exceed three years without shareholders' approval.

3.2 There should be full and clear disclosure of directors' total emoluments and those of the chairman and highest paid UK director, including pension contributions and stock options. Separate figures should be given for salary and performance-related elements and the basis on which performance is measured should be explained.

3.3 Executive directors' pay should be subject to the recommendations of a remuneration committee made up wholly or mainly of non-executive directors.

4. Reporting and Controls

4.1 It is the board's duty to present a balanced and understandable assessment of the company's position.

4.2 The board should ensure that an objective and professional relationship is maintained with the auditors.

4.3 The board should establish an audit committee of at least three non-executive directors with written terms of reference which deal clearly with its authority and duties.

4.4 The directors should explain their responsibility for preparing the accounts next to a statement by the auditors about their reporting responsibilities.

4.5 The directors should report on the effectiveness of the company's system of internal control.

4.6 The directors should report that the business is a going concern, with supporting assumptions or qualifications as necessary.

Source: Cadbury Code (1992)

OECD Principles of Corporate Governance (1999) as revised (2004)

The OECD published its *Principles of Corporate Governance* in 1999, following a request from the OECD Council to develop corporate governance standards and guidelines. Prior to producing the Principles, the OECD consulted the national governments of member states, the private sector, and various international organizations, including the World Bank.

The OECD recognizes that 'one size does not fit all', that is, that there is no single model of corporate governance that is applicable to all countries. However, the Principles represent certain common characteristics that are fundamental to good corporate governance. The OECD Principles were reviewed and revised in 2004. The revised Principles are shown in Box 3.2.

The OECD Principles focus on publicly traded companies but, as in the Cadbury Report, there is an encouragement for other business forms, such as privately held or state-owned enterprises, to utilize the Principles to improve corporate governance.

The OECD Principles are non-binding but, nonetheless, their value as key elements of good corporate governance has been recognized and they have been incorporated into codes in many different countries. For example, the Committee on Corporate Governance in Greece produced its *Principles on Corporate Governance in Greece* in 1999, which reflected the OECD Principles, whilst the China Securities Regulatory Commission published its *Code of Corporate Governance for Listed Companies in China* in 2001, which also drew substantially on the OECD Principles.

In 2006 the OECD published its *Methodology for Assessing Implementation of the OECD Principles of Corporate Governance*. This was followed in 2008 by the publication *Using the OECD Principles of Corporate Governance: A Boardroom Perspective* which gives guidance on how the principles have been put into practice in different companies using real life examples.

In 2009 the OECD launched an action plan to address weaknesses in corporate governance related to the financial crisis with the aim of developing a set of recommendations for improving board practices, risk management, governance of the remuneration process, and the exercise of shareholder rights. In 2010 *Corporate Governance and the Financial Crisis: Conclusions and Emerging Good Practices to Enhance Implementation of the Principles* was published. The OECD's Corporate Governance Committee noted that the ability of the board to effectively oversee executive remuneration—including both the amount and also the way in which remuneration is aligned with the company's longer term interests—appears to be a key challenge in practice and remains one of the central elements of the corporate governance debate in a number of countries. The OECD underlines the importance of boards being able to treat remuneration and risk alignment as an iterative process, recognizing the links between the two, and disclosing in a remuneration report the specific mechanisms that link compensation to the longer term interests of the company. The capacity of a firm's governance structure to produce such a balanced incentive system is critical and therefore ways to enhance governance structures have received more emphasis recently including the role of independent non-executive directors and the 'say on pay', whereby shareholders may have either a binding or non-binding vote on executive pay.

Box 3.2 OECD Principles of Corporate Governance (2004)

Principle	Narrative
I. Ensuring the basis for an effective corporate governance framework	The corporate governance framework should promote transparent and efficient markets, be consistent with the rule of law, and clearly articulate the division of responsibilities among different supervisory, regulatory, and enforcement authorities.
II. The rights of shareholders and key ownership functions	The corporate governance framework should protect and facilitate the exercise of shareholders' rights.
III. The equitable treatment of shareholders	The corporate governance framework should ensure the equitable treatment of all shareholders, including minority and foreign shareholders. All shareholders should have the opportunity to obtain effective redress for violation of their rights.
IV. The role of stakeholders in corporate governance	The corporate governance framework should recognize the rights of stakeholders established by law or through mutual agreements and encourage active co-operation between corporations and stakeholders in creating wealth, jobs, and the sustainability of financially sound enterprises.
V. Disclosure and transparency	The corporate governance framework should ensure that timely and accurate disclosure is made on all material matters regarding the corporation, including the financial situation, performance, ownership, and governance of the company.
VI. The responsibilities of the board	The corporate governance framework should ensure the strategic guidance of the company, the effective monitoring of management by the board, and the board's accountability to the company and the shareholders.

Source: Principles of Corporate Governance (OECD, 2004)

Subsequently, in 2011 the OECD published *Board Practices, Incentives and Governing Risks* in which it looked at how effectively boards manage to align executive and board remuneration with the longer term interests of their companies as this was one of the key failures highlighted by the financial crisis. The OECD highlights that 'aligning incentives seems to be far more problematic in companies and jurisdictions with a dispersed shareholding structure since, where dominant or controlling shareholders exist, they seem to act as a moderating force on remuneration outcomes'.

World Bank

The World Bank's corporate governance activities focus on the rights of shareholders, the equitable treatment of shareholders, the treatment of stakeholders, disclosure and transparency, and the duties of board members. Clearly, the OECD Principles are very much in evidence in this approach.

The World Bank utilizes the OECD Principles to prepare country corporate governance assessments that detail and assess the corporate governance institutional frameworks and practices in individual countries. These assessments may then be used to support policy dialogue, strategic work and operations, and to aid in determining the level of technical assistance needed in given countries in relation to their corporate governance development.

In addition, the International Monetary Fund (IMF) produces reports on the observance of standards and codes that summarize the extent to which countries observe internationally recognized standards and codes. Sections on corporate governance, accounting, and auditing are included in these reports.

Global Corporate Governance Forum (GCGF)

The GCGF is at the heart of corporate governance co-operation between the OECD and the World Bank. It is, as its name suggests, an international initiative aimed at bringing together leading groups in governance, including banks, organizations, country groupings, the private sector, and professional standard-setting bodies. The GCGF's mandate is 'to promote the private sector as an engine of growth, reduce the vulnerability of developing and emerging markets to financial crisis, and provide incentives for corporations to invest and perform efficiently in a transparent, sustainable, and socially responsible manner'.

The GCGF's work programme includes information dissemination events at national and regional levels, whereby interested parties are brought together to discuss the issues, identify priorities for reform, and to develop action plans and initiatives to achieve them. Toolkits published by the GCGF relate to various topics, including director training and board leadership, whilst it also has a series of focus publications looking at topical issues in corporate governance relevant to developing countries.

International Corporate Governance Network (ICGN)

The ICGN was founded in 1995. Its membership encompasses major institutional investors, investor representative groups, companies, financial intermediaries, academics, and others with an interest in the development of global corporate governance practices. Its objective is to facilitate international dialogue on corporate governance issues.

In 1999 the ICGN issued its *Statement on Global Corporate Governance Principles*, which comprised three main areas. First is a statement on the OECD Principles, which the ICGN views as 'a remarkable convergence on corporate governance common ground among diverse interests, practices, and cultures', and which it sees as the minimum acceptable standard for companies and investors around the world. Secondly, the ICGN statement discusses its approach to the OECD Principles, a 'working kit' statement of corporate governance criteria that encompasses ten areas: the corporate objective, communications and reporting, voting rights, corporate boards, corporate remuneration policies, strategic focus, operating performance, shareholder returns, corporate citizenship, and corporate governance implementation. Thirdly, the ICGN statement amplifies the OECD Principles, emphasizing or interpreting each principle as appropriate. For example, in relation to 'The Rights of Shareholders', the ICGN amplification includes the statement that 'major strategic modifications to the core business(es) of a corporation should not be made without prior shareholder approval of the proposed modification'.

Following the revision of the OECD Principles (2004), the ICGN reviewed its global corporate governance principles and published revised principles in 2005. Again building on the OECD Principles, the ICGN revised principles also identify some additional principles of particular concern to the ICGN and its members. The ICGN Principles cover eight areas: corporate objective, shareholder returns; disclosure and transparency; audit; shareholders' ownership, responsibilities, and voting rights and remedies; corporate boards; corporate remuneration policies; corporate citizenship, stakeholder relations and the ethical conduct of business; and corporate governance implementation.

A further revision of the ICGN Principles was made in 2009. The ICGN stated: 'The aim of these Principles is to assert standards of corporate governance to which we believe that all companies should aspire. . . . The Principles are intended to be of general application around the world, irrespective of legislative background or listing rules.' The Principles cover the corporate objective; corporate boards; corporate culture; risk management; remuneration; audit; disclosure and transparency; shareholder rights; and shareholder responsibilities.

Commonwealth Association for Corporate Governance (CACG)

The CACG has produced some useful guidelines and principles of guidelines. The guidelines cover fifteen principles detailing the board's role and responsibilities. These cover areas such as leadership, board appointments, strategy and values, company performance, compliance, communication, accountability to shareholders, relationships with stakeholders, balance of power, internal procedures, board performance assessment, management appointments and development, technology, risk management, and an annual review of future solvency.

EU and corporate governance

The EU High-Level Group of Company Law Experts, comprised of a group of lawyers, was established in late 2001 by the EU to provide independent advice for modernizing company law in Europe. The group was headed by Jaap Winter, hence the report produced by the group is sometimes referred to as 'the Winter Report' (2002). In relation to corporate governance issues, the group made the following recommendations for listed companies.

- EU law should require companies to publish an annual corporate governance statement in their accounts and on their websites. Companies would need to state their compliance with their national corporate governance code, on a 'comply or explain' basis.

- The nomination and remuneration of directors, and the audit of accounts, should be decided upon by non-executive or supervisory directors, the majority of whom are independent.

- Companies should disclose in their annual corporate governance statement who their independent directors are, why they are independent, what their qualifications are to serve on the board, and their other directorships.

- The remuneration of individual directors should be disclosed in detail.

- Share option schemes would require the prior approval of the shareholders.

- In relation to (annual) general meetings, companies should be required to publish all relevant material on their website, and should offer facilities for electronic voting.

- Companies should inform shareholders of the procedure for asking questions at general meetings, and also of the process for submitting shareholder resolutions (proposals).

Frits Bolkestein, the European Commissioner for Internal Market and Services promised an action plan to take forward the recommendations of the group, with the aim of providing a comprehensive, dynamic, and flexible framework for corporate governance in Europe. There are clear implications for all members of the EU. As far as the UK is concerned, the group's recommendations are generally similar to those of the UK Company Law Review (now embodied in the Companies Act 2006) and do not pose any problems.

In 2006 the European Commission organized a public hearing on future priorities for the Action Plan on 'Modernizing Company Law and Enhancing Corporate Governance in the EU'. These priorities included shareholders' rights and obligations, internal control, and the modernization and simplification of European company law. Also in 2006 amendments to the fourth and seventh Company Law Directives were issued with the aim of enhancing confidence in financial statements and annual reports. These amendments prescribe that, inter alia, listed companies must now publish a separate corporate governance statement in the annual report, and board members are to take collective responsibility for the annual report and accounts. The Directive on statutory audit of annual and consolidated accounts clarifies the duties of auditors; a key provision requires listed companies to have audit committees with at least one member of the audit committee being independent and competent in accounting/auditing.

In June 2007 the Commission published an external study on proportionality between capital and control in EU listed companies. Proportionality is the relationship between capital and control ('one share, one vote'). The study, carried out by Institutional Shareholder Services Europe (ISS Europe), the European Corporate Governance Institute (ECGI), and the law firm Shearman & Sterling LLP, found that

> on the basis of the academic research available, there is no conclusive evidence of a causal link between deviations from the proportionality principle and either the economic performance of listed companies or their governance. However, there is some evidence that investors perceive these mechanisms negatively and consider more transparency would be helpful in making investment decisions.

In 2007 the Directive on the exercise of shareholder rights was issued. This Directive recommended that shareholders have timely access to information, and that there should be the facility to vote at a distance, that is, without having to be physically present at the meeting to vote. The practice of share-blocking, which required shareholders to deposit shares at a specified institution for a period of time around the company's annual general meeting, which then meant that the shares could not be traded during that time, is abolished. These changes all facilitate the shareholders' ability to exercise their votes and enhance cross-border voting practices.

Following on from the global financial crisis, the High-Level Group on Financial Supervision in the EU, chaired by Jacques de Larosiere, published its report in February 2009. It highlighted failures in corporate governance as one of the most important failures of the crisis, and made recommendations regarding compensation incentives and internal risk management. Importantly, the report advocated the creation of a European Systemic Risk Council (ESRC). The ESRC was subsequently established in December 2010 and is responsible for the macro-prudential oversight of the financial system within the EU to help prevent and mitigate systemic risks to financial stability.

In 2011 the EU issued the Green Paper on the EU Corporate Governance Framework which launched a public consultation on possible ways forward to improve existing corporate governance mechanisms. The Green Paper contains three chapters: boards, shareholders and the 'comply or explain' principle. The objective of the Green Paper is to have a broad debate on the issues raised. The consultation period ended in July 2011 with the final report expected in 2012.

Basle Committee

The Basle Committee (1999) guidelines related to enhancing corporate governance in banking organizations. The guidelines have been influential in the development of corporate governance practices in banks across the world. Sound governance can be practised regardless of the form of a banking organization.

In 2006 the Basle Committee issued new guidance comprising eight sound corporate governance principles.

- Principle 1—board members should be qualified for their positions, have a clear understanding of their role in corporate governance, and be able to exercise sound judgement about the affairs of the bank.
- Principle 2—the board of directors should approve and oversee the bank's strategic objectives and corporate values that are communicated throughout the banking organization.
- Principle 3—the board of directors should set and enforce clear lines of responsibility and accountability throughout the organization.
- Principle 4—the board should ensure that there is appropriate oversight by senior management consistent with board policy.
- Principle 5—the board and senior management should effectively utilize the work conducted by the internal audit function, external auditors, and internal control functions.

- Principle 6—the board should ensure that compensation policies and practices are consistent with the bank's corporate culture, long-term objectives and strategy, and control environment.
- Principle 7—the bank should be governed in a transparent manner.
- Principle 8—the board and senior management should understand the bank's operational structure, including where the bank operates in jurisdictions, or through structures, that impede transparency (i.e. 'know your structure').

Source: *Enhancing Corporate Governance for Banking Organisations* (Basle Committee on Banking Supervision, 2006).

However, following on from various corporate governance failures and lapses that came to light in subsequent years, the Committee revisited the 2006 guidance. Taking into account the lessons learned during the financial crisis, the Committee reviewed and revised the Principles and reaffirmed their continued relevance and the critical importance of their adoption by banks and supervisors. The Committee issued its *Principles for Enhancing Corporate Governance* (2010) and identified some key areas—board practices; senior management; risk management and internal controls; compensation; complex or opaque corporate structures; and disclosure and transparency—which it believed should be the areas of greatest focus and lists fourteen Principles in relation to these, as follows.

A. Board practices—the Committee identified four Principles relating to:

- the board's overall responsibilities; which it discussed under three main headings: the responsibilities of the board; corporate values and code of conduct; and oversight of senior management;
- board qualifications; which it discussed under the headings of qualifications; training; and composition;
- board's own practices and structure; which it discussed under the headings of the organization and functioning of the board; the role of the chair; board committees (audit committee; risk committee and other committees); conflicts of interest; and controlling shareholders;
- group structures, which it discussed under the headings of board of parent company; and board of regulated subsidiary.

B. Senior management—the Committee identified one Principle in this area which is that the senior management, under direction of the board, should ensure that the bank's activities are consistent with the business strategy, risk tolerance/appetite and policies approved by the board.

C. Risk management and internal controls—the Committee identified four Principles relating to risk management versus internal controls; chief risk officer or equivalent; the scope of responsibilities, stature and independence of the risk management function; resources; qualifications; and risk methodologies and activities.

D. Compensation—the Committee identified two Principles relating to the board being actively involved in the design, implementation, monitoring and review of the compensation system; and compensation being appropriately linked to, and aligned with, the various risks of the firm.

E. Complex or opaque corporate structure—the Committee identified two Principles for this area, relating to the board and senior management being aware of the business and its risks, i.e. 'know your structure'; and the board being aware of, and mitigating against, risks arising when special purpose or related structures are used, or when operating in a less transparent jurisdiction.

F. Disclosure and transparency—the Committee identified one Principle here, being that the bank's governance should be 'adequately transparent to its shareholders, depositors, other relevant stakeholders and market participants'.

The Committee also included a section in the *Principles for Enhancing Corporate Governance* (2010) on the role of supervisors and emphasized the importance of supervisors regularly evaluating the bank's corporate governance policies and practices as well as its implementation of the Committee's Principles.

US corporate governance

Like the UK, the USA has a well-developed market with a diverse shareholder base, including institutional investors, financial institutions, and individuals. It also has many of the agency problems associated with the separation of corporate ownership from corporate control.

The USA is somewhat unusual in not having had a definitive corporate governance code in the same way that many other countries do. Rather, there have been various state and federal developments over a number of years, although the passage of Sarbanes–Oxley (2002), the New York Stock Exchange (NYSE) Corporate Governance Rules (2003), and subsequent developments have signalled national developments in corporate governance. Some idiosyncratic features of the USA include: the Delaware General Corporation Law, which essentially gives companies incorporated in Delaware certain advantages; and the Employee Retirement Income Security Act 1974 (ERISA), which mandates private pension funds to vote their shares. Each of these is now dealt with in more detail.

Delaware corporate law

Over the years Delaware has built up a body of corporate case law that has become the norm in corporate America. The Delaware approach has been seen as 'company friendly' and indeed the majority of US companies listed on the NYSE are registered in Delaware in order to be able to take advantage of the more flexible non-prescriptive approach. The emphasis is on giving boards of directors the authority to pursue corporate strategy and objectives whilst at the same time operating within the concept of fiduciary duty (usually this would mean acting in the best interests of the shareholders, who are the ultimate beneficiaries of the company). In addition, there are certain statutory requirements that need to be abided by, such as protection of minority interests. However, on balance, the Delaware law is less procedural than other state law in the USA and hence Delaware is an attractive state in which to register a company.

Employee Retirement Income Security Act 1974 (ERISA)

ERISA established federal statutory duties of loyalty and prudence for trustees and managers of private pension funds. ERISA has been interpreted as effectively mandating private pension funds to vote their shares, and this includes not just shares held in the USA (domestic shares), but shares held overseas too. It is recommended that a cost-benefit analysis be carried out before purchasing overseas shareholdings to ensure that it will be viable (cost-effective) to vote the overseas shares. Whilst public pension funds are not covered by ERISA, as private pension funds are mandated to vote, there is an expectation that public pension funds will also vote, and this has been the case in practice.

Sarbanes–Oxley Act 2002

Following directly from the financial scandals of Enron, Worldcom, and Global Crossing, in which it was perceived that the close relationship between companies and their external auditors was largely to blame, the US Congress agreed reforms together with changes to the NYSE Listing Rules that have had a significant impact not just in the USA but around the world. The changes are embodied in the Accounting Industry Reform Act 2002, widely known as the 'Sarbanes–Oxley Act'.

Initially, one of the most publicized aspects of the Sarbanes–Oxley Act was the requirement for chief executive officers (CEOs) and chief finance officers to certify that quarterly and annual reports filed on forms 10-Q, 10-K, and 20-F are fully compliant with applicable securities laws and present a fair picture of the financial situation of the company. The penalties for making this certification when aware that the information does not comply with the requirements are severe: up to US$1 million fine or imprisonment of up to ten years, or both.

The Sarbanes–Oxley Act seeks to strengthen (external) auditor independence and also to strengthen the company's audit committee. Listed companies, for example, must have an audit committee comprised only of independent members, and must also disclose whether they have at least one 'audit committee financial expert' on their audit committee. The 'audit committee financial expert' should be named and the company should state whether the expert is independent of management (for listed companies, the audit committee should comprise only independent members).

The Act establishes a new regulatory body for auditors of US listed firms—the Public Company Accounting Oversight Board (PCAOB)—with which all auditors of US listed companies have to register, including non-US audit firms. Correspondingly, the Securities Exchange Commission (SEC) has issued separate rules that encompass the prohibition of some non-audit services to audit clients, mandatory rotation of audit partners, and auditors' reports on the effectiveness of internal controls. The SEC implementation of the Sarbanes–Oxley Act prohibits nine non-audit services that might impair auditor independence. In many cases, these effectively prohibit the audit firm from either auditing accounting services provided by the audit firm's staff or providing help with systems that will then be audited by the audit firm. These nine areas cover:

- book-keeping or other services related to the accounting records or financial statements of the audited company;
- financial information systems design and implementation;

- appraisal or valuation services, fairness opinions, or contribution-in-kind reports (where the firm provides its opinion on the adequacy of consideration in a transaction);

- actuarial services;

- internal audit outsourcing services;

- management functions/human resources (an auditor should not be a director, officer, or employee of an audit client, or perform any executive role for the audit client, such as supervisory, decision-making, or monitoring);

- broker or dealer, investment advisor, or investment banking services;

- legal services or expert services unrelated to the audit;

- any other service that the PCAOB decides is not permitted.

Interestingly, taxation services may be provided by the auditor to the audit client and certain other services may also be provided with the prior approval of the audit committee (these include non-audit services that do not amount to more than 5 per cent of the total paid by the company to its auditor). Companies are required to disclose in their annual report the fees paid to the 'independent accountant' for each of audit, audit-related, tax, and other services.

There are also requirements relating to the rotation of audit partners such that the lead audit partner should rotate every five years, and is then subject to a five-year period during which he/she cannot be the audit partner for that company. Similarly, other partners involved in the audit, but not acting as the lead partner, are subject to a seven-year rotation followed by a two-year bar. Any member of the audit team is barred for one year from accepting employment in certain specified positions in a company that he or she has audited.

The auditor is required to report to the audit committee various information, which includes all critical accounting policies and practices, and alternative accounting treatments.

The Sarbanes–Oxley Act provides for far-reaching reform and has caused much disquiet outside the USA because the Act applies equally to US and non-US firms with a US listing. However, some of the provisions of the Sarbanes–Oxley Act are in direct conflict with provisions in the law/practice of other countries. In reality, this has led to some companies delisting from the NYSE and has deterred other non-US firms from applying to be listed on the NYSE.

Commission on Public Trust and Private Enterprise 2003

The Commission on Public Trust and Private Enterprise was formed by the Conference Board, an influential US-based non-profit-making organization, to look at the circumstances that gave rise to corporate scandals, which resulted in a loss of confidence in the US markets. The Commission's work focused on three main areas: executive compensation, corporate governance, and auditing and accounting. The Commission issued its report on executive compensation in 2002 and this is covered in Chapter 9; the second report, being on corporate governance, and auditing and accounting, was issued in early 2003.

The Commission listed nine principles relating to corporate governance, which cover the following areas:

- relationship of the board and management;
- fulfilling the board's responsibilities;

- director qualifications;
- role of the nominating/governance committee;
- board evaluation;
- ethics oversight;
- hiring special investigative counsel;
- shareowner involvement;
- long-term share ownership.

In relation to the board, the Commission recommends that careful thought should be given to separating the roles of chairman and CEO. This is an interesting development because the roles of chairman and CEO have traditionally tended to be combined in US companies. By splitting these roles, as in the UK, the US corporations would achieve the separation of the running of the board of directors (chairman) from the executive running of the business (chief executive). The Commission states that the chairman should be an independent director but, where he/she is not, then a lead independent director can be appointed. If companies choose not to separate the two roles, then a presiding director should be appointed. An important aspect of the lead independent director's role is to act as a liaison between the CEO and the other independent directors, whilst the presiding director would, in addition, take on some of the activities usually carried out by the chairman.

The Commission emphasizes the importance of a substantial majority of independent directors, with appropriate backgrounds, knowledge, and skills to enable them to take an active role in the company and to be satisfied with the company's management, legal, and ethical compliance. The independent directors should be nominated by the nominating/governance committee, whose role would also include stating the requirements for the training of directors. The evaluation of boards via a tiered approach, which would analyse board performance, subcommittee performance, and individual performance, is recommended.

The concept of an ethical culture is something that should be developed at board level and applied across the company. The Commission believes 'that ethical conduct, including adherence to the law's requirements, is vital to a corporation's sustainability and long-term success'.

Special investigative counsel should be appointed by the board (and not management) where it seems that an independent investigation is 'reasonably likely' to implicate company executives.

The Commission tries to encourage shareholders to be more active and behave as owners, and suggests that companies should allow shareholder nominations for board seats. If investors wish to put forward candidates to challenge the board nominations, they generally have to circulate the details to shareholders themselves at a cost of upwards of US$250,000, an amount that is sufficient to deter most investors. However, given the Commission's recommendation and a growing tide of large institutional investors who wished to change the situation, the SEC subsequently issued *Facilitating Shareholder Director Nominations* in August 2010, which laid down detailed guidance on shareholder nominations.

Long-term share ownership, as opposed to a short-term focus, should be encouraged by the company executives adopting and communicating to investors 'a strategy specifically designed to attract investors known to pursue long-term holding investment strategies'. This should encourage a more committed, longer term shareholder base. The other side of the coin is that the Commission suggests that institutional investors should have remuneration policies that align portfolio managers' interests with the long term rather than the short term.

In relation to audit and accounting, the Commission states seven principles:

- Principle 1—the enhanced role of the audit committee.
- Principle 2—audit committee education.
- Principle 3—improving internal controls and internal auditing.
- Principle 4—auditor rotation.
- Principle 5—professional advisors for the audit committee.
- Principle 6—services performed by accounting firms.
- Principle 7—the business model of accounting firms.

The Commission views the seven principles as strengthening the reforms begun by the Sarbanes–Oxley Act and the NYSE, and hopes that they will help to restore public confidence in audit firms, audited financial statements, and hence in the market generally.

The Commission emphasizes that the audit committee should be comprised of independent members with appropriate knowledge and experience. The wider remit of the audit committee includes being responsible for the appointment, remuneration, and oversight of the work of the auditors, with the outside (external) auditors reporting directly to the audit committee. In its turn, the board should review the independence and qualifications of the audit committee members to ensure that they are appropriate. Audit committee members should have an induction to the work of the audit committee and thereafter follow a continuing education programme. It is recommended that all companies should have an internal audit function, with the internal auditor having reporting responsibility to the audit committee via a direct line of communication.

In addition to this, the Commission recommends rotation of outside audit firms, for example, when the audit firm has been employed by the company for more than ten years, or when a former audit firm partner or manager is employed by the company, or significant non-audit services are provided by the company. Audit committees may retain independent professional advisers (for example, those with no ties to management or the audit firm). Accounting firms should limit their services to audit services and closely related services that do not put the auditor 'in an advocacy position'. Finally, the Commission recommends that the 'Big Four' accounting firms should look at their business model, strategies, and focus to ensure that quality auditing is their top priority.

NYSE Corporate Governance Rules (2003)

In November 2003 the Securities and Exchange Commission approved new rules on corporate governance proposed and adopted by the NYSE and the Nasdaq Stock Market. The new rules mean a significant strengthening of corporate governance standards for listed companies and are designed to enable the directors, officers, and employees to operate more effectively. The new rules should also enable shareholders to monitor the companies better in terms of their performance, and hopefully to reduce the incidences of corporate scandals or collapses.

The NYSE rules require that the majority of directors are independent and give detailed guidance on who would be classed as independent. Non-management directors should meet at regularly scheduled executive sessions without management being present. A nominating/corporate governance committee, a compensation committee, and an audit committee should each be established and be comprised entirely of independent directors. All committees should have charters detailing their purpose and there should be an annual evaluation of each committee. An internal audit function should be established in each company.

Companies should adopt corporate governance guidelines and disclose these on their websites together with the charters of the various board committees. Companies should also adopt a code of business conduct and ethics.

The CEO is required to certify to the NYSE each year that he/she is not aware of any violation by the company of the NYSE's corporate governance listing standards. A public reprimand letter could be issued to any company that violates an NYSE listing standard.

These new rules should restore investor confidence in companies, and in the stock market generally, by significantly strengthening corporate governance structures and notions of ethical behaviour in companies.

Emergency Economic Stabilization Act (2008)

The Emergency Economic Stabilization Act was passed by the US Congress in 2008. It authorized the US Treasury Secretary to establish a Troubled Asset Relief Program (TARP) so that the US government could purchase up to US$700 billion of mortgage-backed and other troubled assets from financial institutions. Those financial institutions involved in the TARP are required to meet certain corporate governance standards, which include the requirement for companies to eliminate compensation structures that encourage unnecessary and excessive risks being taken by executives; a provision for claw-back of any bonus or incentive-based compensation paid to senior executive officers where it is subsequently proven that the criteria, for example statement of earnings, were inaccurate; and a prohibition of certain types of 'golden parachute' payments (sometimes called 'golden goodbyes').

NACD Key Agreed Principles to Strengthen Corporate Governance for US Publicly Traded Companies (2008)

The National Association of Corporate Directors issued its *Key Agreed Principles to Strengthen Corporate Governance for US Publicly Traded Companies (2008)* with the aim of encouraging thoughtful governance rather than a 'tick box' approach. The Principles are as follows:

- Principle 1—board responsibility for governance.
- Principle 2—corporate governance transparency.
- Principle 3—director competency and commitment.
- Principle 4—board accountability and objectivity.
- Principle 5—independent board leadership.

- Principle 6—integrity, ethics, and responsibility.
- Principle 7—attention to information, agenda, and strategy.
- Principle 8—protection against board entrenchment.
- Principle 9—shareholder input in director selection.
- Principle 10—shareholder communications.

The Business Roundtable has also expressed its support for these Principles, which 'provide a framework for board leadership and oversight in the especially critical areas of strategic planning, risk oversight, executive compensation, and transparency'.

Dodd-Frank Wall Street Reform and Consumer Protection Act (2010)

In July 2010 the USA passed the Dodd-Frank Wall Street Reform and Consumer Protection Act that amended US requirements relating to executive compensation practices in a number of respects. From mid-2011 the SEC required listed companies compensation committee members to be independent directors. There are new 'say on pay' provisions such that the Act requires that, at least once every three years, there is a shareholder advisory vote to approve the company's executive compensation, as well as to approve 'golden parachute' compensation arrangements. Whilst the 'say on pay' is at least once every three years, it may occur every year.

New York Stock Exchange (NYSE) Commission on Corporate Governance (2010)

The NYSE Commission on Corporate Governance was established in 2009 to examine core governance principles that could achieve broad consensus from amongst various market participants. The Commission reported in September 2010 with ten principles, as follows:

Principle 1—The board's fundamental objective should be to build long-term sustainable growth in shareholder value for the corporation, and the board is accountable to shareholders for its performance in achieving this objective.

Principle 2—While the board's responsibility for corporate governance has long been established, the critical role of management in establishing proper corporate governance has not been sufficiently recognized. The Commission believes that a key aspect of successful governance depends upon successful management of the company, as management has primary responsibility for creating an environment in which a culture of performance with integrity can flourish.

Principle 3—Shareholders have the right, a responsibility, and a long-term economic interest to vote their shares in a thoughtful manner, in recognition of the fact that voting decisions influence director behaviour, corporate governance, and conduct, and that voting decisions are one of the primary means of communicating with companies on issues of concern.

Principle 4—Good corporate governance should be integrated with the company's business strategy and objectives and should not be viewed simply as a compliance obligation separate from the company's long-term business prospects.

Principle 5—Legislation and agency rule-making are important to establish the basic tenets of corporate governance and ensure the efficiency of our markets. Beyond these fundamental principles, however, the Commission has a preference for market-based governance solutions whenever possible.

Principle 6—Good corporate governance includes transparency for corporations and investors, sound disclosure policies and communication beyond disclosure through dialogue and engagement as necessary and appropriate.

Principle 7—While independence and objectivity are necessary attributes of board members, companies must also strike the right balance between the appointment of independent and non-independent directors to ensure that there is an appropriate range and mix of expertise, diversity, and knowledge on the board.

Principle 8—The Commission recognizes the influence that proxy advisory firms have on the market, and believes that such firms should be held to appropriate standards of transparency and accountability. The Commission commends the SEC for its issuance of the Concept Release on the US Proxy System, which includes inviting comments on how such firms should be regulated.

Principle 9—The SEC should work with the NYSE and other exchanges to ease the burden of proxy voting and communication while encouraging greater participation by individual investors in the proxy voting process.

Principle 10—The SEC and/or the NYSE should consider a wide range of views to determine the impact of major corporate governance reforms on corporate performance over the last decade. The SEC and/or the NYSE should also periodically assess the impact of major corporate governance reforms on the promotion of sustainable, long-term corporate growth and sustained profitability.

Source: NYSE Commission on Corporate Governance (2010)

Non-Governmental Organizations (NGOs), public sector, non-profit organizations, and charities

As mentioned earlier there is an increased focus on the governance of NGOs, the public sector, non-profit organizations, and charities. Such organizations may play a key role in providing social services, provision of healthcare and education, as well as raising funds for a variety of charitable causes.

Nolan (1996), in the context of local public spending bodies, made two general recommendations: (i) 'the principles of good practice on appointments, training, openness, codes of conduct and conflicts of interest, set out here and in our first report, should be adopted with suitable modifications across the sectors covered in this report', and (ii) 'Local public spending bodies should institute codes of practice on whistleblowing, appropriate to their circumstances, which would enable concerns to be raised confidentially inside and, if necessary, outside the organization'.

Cornforth (2003) highlighted the fact that,

> as the importance of quangos and voluntary organizations in delivering public services has grown, they have come under increased public scrutiny. In particular, paralleling developments in the private sector, the governance of these organizations has been questioned. Serious concerns have been raised both about the democratic legitimacy of governing boards and their effectiveness, for example, the ability of what are often lay board members to effectively supervise senior managers, ensure probity and protect the interests of relevant stakeholders and the public.

Given the concerns about the governance of these organizations, there is therefore a growing emphasis on the appointment of trustees who are experienced and capable; boards which have appropriate oversight; and the appointment of non-executive directors who both understand and can contribute to the strengthening of standards. Moreover, these organizations are not immune to the recent global financial crisis and now, more than ever, it is time to strengthen their governance.

In 2005 the Independent Commission for Good Governance in Public Services, chaired by Sir Alan Langlands, produced the *Good Governance Standard for Public Services*. The Standard presents six principles of good governance that are common to all public service organizations and are intended to help all those with an interest in public governance to assess good governance practice. It is intended for use by all organizations and partnerships that work for the public, using public money. Most of these are public sector organizations but some are non-public organizations. The six principles are:

- Principle 1—Good governance means focusing on the organization's purpose and on outcomes for citizens and service users.
- Principle 2—Good governance means performing effectively in clearly defined functions and roles.
- Principle 3—Good governance means promoting values for the whole organization and demonstrating the values of good governance through behaviour.
- Principle 4—Good governance means taking informed, transparent decisions and managing risk.
- Principle 5—Good governance means developing the capacity and capability of the governing body to be effective.
- Principle 6—Good governance means engaging stakeholders and making accountability real.

In 2007 the Standard was reviewed and it was found that the principles of the Standard were 'clearly standing the test of time and are being widely applied across public services'.

The National Council for Voluntary Organisations (NCVO) is a registered charity and is the largest umbrella body for the voluntary and community sector in England. In June 2005 it published *Good Governance: A Code for the Voluntary and Community Sector*. In October

2010, the NCVO published the second edition of the code. The code is based on an 'apply or explain' approach; the NCVO anticipate that the 'apply or explain' principle will be adopted. If one good governance characteristic appears not to be valid in a particular setting, then an alternative may be sought, but organizations should be prepared to give reasons for that decision. The six principles of good governance have been designed to be valid for the entire voluntary and community sector. The code states that an effective board will provide good governance and leadership by understanding their role, ensuring delivery of organizational purpose, working effectively both as individuals and as a team, exercising effective control, behaving with integrity, and being open and accountable.

The Charity Commission for England and Wales is established by law as the regulator and registrar of charities in England and Wales. Their aim is to provide the best possible regulation of these charities in order to increase charities' efficiency and effectiveness and public confidence and trust in them. The Charities Commission has on its website a set of model governing documents which are helpful to those wishing to establish a charity. The documents include memorandum and articles, information about boards of trustees, and the trustee role, a growing area in governance. The Charities Commission has also published 'Protecting charities from harm' which is an online toolkit that aims to give trustees the knowledge and tools they need to manage risks and protect their charity from harm and abuse. The guidance covers charities and terrorism; due diligence, monitoring, and verification of the end use of funds; fraud and financial crime; raising, storing, and moving funds; and bribery, corruption, and facilitation payments.

In the UK the National Health Service (NHS) is comprised of various types of trust, including, inter alia, acute trusts (hospitals) and primary care trusts. For these trusts, non-executive director appointments are made by the Appointments Commission. However, there are also foundation trusts which have more independence. These are regulated by Monitor which is the independent regulator of NHS foundation trusts. It is independent of central government, is directly accountable to Parliament, and was established in January 2004 to authorize and regulate NHS foundation trusts. Monitor has developed a non-executive director development programme to help ensure that non-executive directors are aware of their role and duties in this area and have a good understanding of the health sector. NHS Direct has adopted the 'Codes of Conduct and Accountability' from the Department of Health, and all members of the Board are required to act in accordance with the Codes. In addition, the Board of Directors have adopted the public service values detailed within the Nolan report.

Whilst the codes and guidelines on NGOs, the public sector, non-profit organizations, and charities discussed earlier relate to the UK, there are similar developments in many countries around the world, all seeking to ensure that these types of organizations in their country are governed to best effect, to ensure appropriate use of funds, effective management, and to help maintain confidence in them.

Conclusions

Corporate governance is very much an evolving area. In recent years its development has been driven by the need to restore investor confidence in capital markets. Investors and governments alike have been proactive in seeking reforms that will ensure that corporate boards are more accountable, that qualified independent non-executive (outside) directors can play a key role, that audit committees are able to operate effectively, and that external audit firms are able to perform their audits properly and appropriately. These measures will also help ensure that the rights of shareholders are protected.

However, the recent global financial crisis has highlighted that, despite all the developments in corporate governance codes across the world, there are still evident deficiencies. For example, powerful individuals are still able to exercise too much power without appropriate restraint; boards of directors have not taken adequate account of the risks their business may be subject to, independent non-executive directors may not have had the skills and experience to question effectively the use of complex instruments, which subsequently became 'toxic assets'; executive directors' compensation has seemingly often not been linked to appropriate performance measures; and generous remuneration packages and hefty pension pots have caused concern amongst government, investors, and the public alike.

Many of the codes operate using a 'comply or explain' basis and, as we have seen, this means either that a company has to comply fully with the code and state that it has done so, or that it explains why it has not complied fully. Investors will therefore be able to determine to what extent a company has or has not complied, and to assess the company's stated reasons for non-compliance. Investor pressure would tend to be the most immediate response to non-compliance, and such instances may lead investors—particularly those who can exert significant influence on the company, for example, because of the size of their shareholding—to seek further information/assurance from the directors. There has been some discussion about whether 'apply or explain' might be a more appropriate wording than 'comply or explain' as it may be that some companies comply only with those principles which they consider cost-effective, or which they wish to comply with, and then they explain why they don't comply with the other principles. It is fair to say that 'apply or explain' carries with it more of an expectation that companies will apply the principles and therefore that the incidences of 'explain' will be fewer.

We have seen the influence of the Cadbury Code and the OECD Principles on the development of corporate governance codes in many countries. We have discussed the roles of several international bodies—such as the World Bank, the GCGF, the ICGN, and the CACG—in the development of corporate governance globally. The report of the EU High-Level Group of Company Law Experts and the subsequent corporate governance reforms have had implications for company law and corporate governance across Europe. The impact of legislation in the USA, the Sarbanes–Oxley Act, and further developments in US corporate governance, especially in the light of the meltdown in the financial markets, have been highlighted. The growth and importance of governance for NGOs, the public sector, non-profit organizations, and charities has also been discussed.

Whilst one can argue that a single model of corporate governance is not suitable for all countries—and certainly the stage of development of the country, its cultural traditions, legal structure, and ownership structure make it unlikely that one model would be appropriate for all countries at any given time—we have seen that there are common core principles that have been influential in the setting of codes across the globe. Whilst there should be flexibility in individual countries, it would seem that there is also a recognition of the key elements of good corporate governance in an international dimension. The latest global financial crisis has led to calls for action to be taken on a global basis, encouraging countries to cooperate and work together more to try to restore confidence in shattered markets.

Summary

- The development of corporate governance has been driven, to a large extent, by the desire for more transparency and accountability to help restore investor confidence in the world's stock markets after the damage caused by financial scandals and corporate collapses.

- The Cadbury Code and the OECD Principles, in particular, have each played a major role in the development of corporate governance codes around the world.

- The Cadbury Code's main recommendations include the establishment of key board committees (audit and remuneration), with a nomination committee suggested as an appropriate way to ensure a transparent appointments process; the appointment of at least three independent non-executive (outside) directors; and the separation of roles of chairman and CEO.

- The Cadbury Code utilizes a best practice 'comply or explain' approach in contrast to a mandatory or legislative approach.

- The OECD Principles encompass five main areas: the rights of shareholders, the equitable treatment of shareholders, the role of stakeholders in corporate governance, disclosure and transparency, and the responsibilities of the board.

- Following a few years after the publication of the Cadbury Report, the Greenbury Report on disclosure of directors' remuneration, and the Hampel Report, which reviewed the implementation of the Cadbury and Greenbury recommendations, were published. In 2003 the Combined Code was revised to take into account the Higgs and Smith reviews. The Combined Code was further revised in 2006, 2008, and 2009, the last revision culminating in the UK Corporate Governance Code (2010); the UK Stewardship Code was also issued in 2010. The UK Companies Law has also been through a major update with the enactment of the Companies Act 2006.

- A number of influential organizations have issued corporate governance guidelines/statements or have been instrumental in the implementation of better corporate governance globally. These organizations include the World Bank, the GCGF, the CACG, and the ICGN.

- The EU High-Level Group of Company Law Experts reported in 2002, making various corporate governance recommendations for listed companies. Amongst their recommendations were that companies should be required to publish an annual corporate governance statement in their accounts and on their websites, and that there should be detailed disclosure of individual directors' remuneration. These recommendations have been enacted across Europe, although some countries provide more basic information whilst others disclose over and above the EU recommendations. The Green Paper on the EU Corporate Governance Framework discusses boards, shareholders, and the 'comply or explain' principle.

- The USA has a number of interesting features, including the Delaware General Corporation Law, which gives companies incorporated in Delaware certain advantages, and ERISA, which mandates private pension funds to vote their shares.

- The US Sarbanes–Oxley Act is far reaching, encompassing not only US firms but non-US firms with a US listing. The Act seeks to strengthen auditor independence and also establishes a new regulatory body for auditors for US-listed firms—the Public Company Accounting Oversight Board—with which all auditors of US-listed companies, including non-US audit firms, have to register.

- The Commission on Public Trust and Private Enterprise was formed by the Conference Board and its reports published 2002 and 2003 have focused on executive compensation, corporate governance, and auditing and accounting.

- The US introduced the Emergency Economic Stabilization Act (2008) which authorized the establishment of TARP. Whilst the corporate governance recommendations in the Emergency Economic Stabilization Act applied only to participating financial institutions, the Dodd-Frank Wall Street Reform and Consumer Protection Act (2010) introduced the 'say on pay' and other remuneration-related provisions more widely. The NYSE Commission on Corporate Governance (2010) introduced further corporate governance principles.

- There is an increased focus on the governance of NGOs, the public sector, non-profit organizations, and charities reflecting the fact that these organizations need to be seen to have effective boards and to utilize public funds in an appropriate way.

Questions

The discussion questions to follow cover the key learning points of this chapter. Reading of some of the additional reference material will enhance the depth of the students' knowledge and understanding of these areas.

1. What have been the main influences on the development of corporate governance codes and guidelines? What might be the shortcomings in the implementation of corporate governance codes and guidelines?

2. Critically discuss whether it would be desirable to have one model of corporate governance applicable to all countries.

3. What are the advantages and disadvantages of a 'comply or explain' model of corporate governance? How does this compare to a mandatory model?

4. In what ways might the OECD Principles of Corporate Governance help improve shareholders' rights?

5. In what ways might the legal and cultural context of a country impact on the development of the corporate governance model in a given country?

6. Why is good governance important in NGOs, the public sector, non-profit organizations, and charities? How might it best be achieved?

References

APB (2004), *Ethical Standards for Auditors*, FRC, London.

APB (2008), *Revised Ethical Standards for Auditors*, FRC, London.

Basle Committee on Banking Supervision (1999), *Enhancing Corporate Governance for Banking*

Organisations, Bank for International Settlements, Basle.

—— (2006), *Enhancing Corporate Governance for Banking Organisations*, Bank for International Settlements, Basle.

—— (2010), *Principles for Enhancing Corporate Governance*, Bank for International Settlements, Basle.

Cadbury, Sir Adrian (1992), *Report of the Committee on the Financial Aspects of Corporate Governance*, Gee & Co. Ltd, London.

Capital Market Commission, Athens (1999), 'Principles on Corporate Governance in Greece: Recommendations for its Competitive Transformation', Capital Market Commission, Athens.

China Securities Regulatory Commission (2001), 'Code of Corporate Governance for Listed Companies in China', China Securities Regulatory Commission, State Economic Trade Commission, Beijing.

Combined Code (1998), *Combined Code, Principles of Corporate Governance*, Gee & Co. Ltd, London.

——(2003), *The Combined Code on Corporate Governance*, FRC, London.

——(2006), *The Combined Code on Corporate Governance*, FRC, London.

——(2008), *The Combined Code on Corporate Governance*, FRC, London.

Conference Board (2003), *Commission on Public Trust and Private Enterprise Findings and Recommendations Part 2: Corporate Governance and Part 3: Audit and Accounting*, Conference Board, New York.

Cornforth, C. (2003), *The Governance of Public and Non-Profit Organisations, What do boards do?* Routledge, London.

Davies E.M. (2011), *Women on Boards*, BIS, London.

——(2012), *Women on Boards, One Year On*, BIS, London.

de Larosiere, J. (2009), *High-Level Group on Financial Supervision in the EU*, EU Brussels.

Dodd-Frank Wall Street Reform and Consumer Protection Act (2010), US Congress, Washington DC.

Employee Retirement Income Security Act (1974), Department of Labor, Washington DC.

Emergency Economic Stabilization Act (2008), US Congress, Washington DC.

EU (2011), Green Paper The EU Corporate Governance Framework, European Commission, Brussels.

FRC (2007), *Review of the Impact of the Combined Code*, FRC, London.

——(2010), *Guidance on Board Effectiveness*, FRC, London.

——(2010), *UK Corporate Governance Code*, FRC, London.

——(2010), *UK Stewardship Code*, FRC, London.

——(2011), *Developments in Corporate Governance 2011: The impact and implementation of the UK Corporate Governance and Stewardship Codes*, FRC, London.

——(2012), *What Constitutes An Explanation Under 'Comply or Explain'? Report of Discussions Between Companies and Investors*, FRC, London.

Greenbury, Sir Richard (1995), *Directors' Remuneration*, Gee & Co. Ltd., London.

Hampel, Sir Ronnie (1998), *Committee on Corporate Governance: Final Report*, Gee & Co. Ltd., London.

HM Treasury (2008), *Updating the Myners Principles: A Response to Consultation*, Her Majesty's Treasury, London.

Higgs, D. (2003), *Review of the Role and Effectiveness of Non-Executive Directors*, Department of Trade and Industry, London.

ICGN (1999), *Statement on Global Corporate Governance Principles*, ICGN, London.

——(2005), *Statement on Global Corporate Governance Principles*, ICGN, London.

——(2009), *ICGN Global Corporate Governance Principles (Revised) 2009*, ICGN, London.

ISS, ECGI and Shearman & Sterling (2007), *Report on the Proportionality Principle in the European Union*, EU, Brussels.

Langlands, Sir A. (2005), *Good Governance Standard for Public Services*, The Independent Commission for Good Governance in Public Services, Office for Public Management and the Chartered Institute of Public Finance and Accountancy in partnership with the Joseph Rowntree Foundation, London.

Myners Report (2001), *Myners Report on Institutional Investment*, HM Treasury, London.

National Association of Corporate Directors (NACD) (2008), *Key Agreed Principles to Strengthen Corporate Governance for U.S. Publicly Traded Companies*, NACD, Washington DC.

NAPF (2007), *Institutional Investment in the UK: Six Years On*, NAPF, London.

NCVO (2005), *Good Governance: A Code for the Voluntary and Community Sector*, published by NCVO on behalf of the *National Hub of Expertise in Governance*, London.

——(2010), *Good Governance: A Code for the Voluntary and Community Sector*, published by NCVO on behalf of the National Hub of Expertise in Governance, London.

Nolan, Lord (1996), *Standards in Public Life: Local Public Spending Bodies, Second Report of the Committee May 1996*, HMSO, London.

NYSE (2003), 'Final NYSE Corporate Governance Rules', New York.

NYSE (2010), *Report of the New York Stock Exchange Commission on Corporate Governance*, New York.

OECD (1999), *Principles of Corporate Governance*, OECD, Paris.

——(2004), *Principles of Corporate Governance*, OECD, Paris.

——(2006), *Methodology for Assessing Implementation of the OECD Principles of Corporate Governance*, OECD, Paris.

——(2008), *Using the OECD Principles of Corporate Governance: A Boardroom Perspective*, OECD, Paris.

——(2010), *Corporate Governance and the Financial Crisis: Conclusions and Emerging Good Practices to Enhance Implementation of the Principles*, OECD, Paris.

——(2011), *Board Practices, Incentives and Governing Risks*, OECD, Paris.

Sarbanes–Oxley Act (2002), US Legislature.

SEC (2010), *Facilitating Shareholder Director Nominations*, Release No. 33-9136 (25 August 2010), SEC, Washington DC.

Smith, Sir Robert (2003), *Audit Committees Combined Code Guidance*, FRC, London.

——(2008), *Guidance on Audit Committees*, FRC, London.

Turnbull, N. (1999), *Internal Control: Guidance for Directors on the Combined Code*, Institute of Chartered Accountants in England and Wales, London.

——(2005), *Internal Control: Revised Guidance for Directors on the Combined Code*, FRC, London.

Turner, A. (2009), *The Turner Review—A Regulatory Response to the Global Banking Crisis*, Financial Services Authority, London.

Tyson, L. (2003), *The Tyson Report on the Recruitment and Development of Non-Executive Directors*, London Business School, London.

Walker, D. (2009), *A Review of Corporate Governance in UK Banks and Other Financial Industry Entities, Final Recommendations*, HM Treasury, London.

Winter, J. (2002), Report of the High-Level Group of Company Law Experts on a Modern Regulatory Framework for Company Law in Europe, European Commission, Brussels.

Useful websites

www.accaglobal.com The website of the Association of Chartered Certified Accountants gives information about corporate governance and their related activities.

www.bis.gov.uk/ The website of the Department for Business, Innovation & Skills (created in June 2009 from the merger of the Department for Business, Enterprise and Regulatory Reform and the Department for Innovation, Universities and Skills) contains information the Department's activities.

www.bis.gov.uk/shareholderexecutive The website of the Shareholder Executive which was created in September 2003 to improve the government's performance as a shareholder in businesses.

www.bis.org The website of the Bank for International Settlements contains information about central banks and other agencies and has the full text of the Basle Committee corporate governance recommendations.

www.charity-commission.gov.uk/ The website of the Charity Commission for England and Wales.

www.conference-board.org/ The Conference Board website gives details of their corporate governance activities and publications.

www.ecgi.org The European Corporate Governance Institute website has details of global corporate governance developments. Corporate governance codes for countries around the world are listed and in most cases can be downloaded.

www.frc.org.uk/ The Financial Reporting Council's website contains details of its activities and those of its operating bodies.

www.fsa.gov.uk The Financial Services Authority website contains information about various regulatory aspects, including corporate governance, of capital markets.

www.hm-treasury.gov.uk The website of Her Majesty's Treasury.

www.icaew.com The website of the Institute of Chartered Accountants in England and Wales provides updates on corporate governance issues.

www.icgn.org This website contains information about corporate governance developments and guidelines issued by the International Corporate Governance Network.

www.icsa.org.uk This website of the Institute of Chartered Secretaries and Administrators contains useful information about various aspects of corporate governance.

www.legislation.gov.uk/ This website brings together the legislative content previously held on the OPSI website and revised legislation from the Statute Law Database to provide a single legislation service.

www.monitor-nhsft.gov.uk/ The website of Monitor which is the independent regulator of NHS foundation trusts.

www.ncvo-vol.org.uk/ The website of the National Council for Voluntary Organisations.

www.oecd.org The OECD website contains useful information relating to corporate governance for both member and non-member states.

www.opm.co.uk/ The website of the Office for Public Management.

www.ukfi.gov.uk/ The website of UK Financial Investments Ltd which was established in November 2008 to manage the government's investments in financial institutions including the Royal Bank of Scotland, Lloyds TSB/Halifax Bank of Scotland (Lloyds Banking Group), Northern Rock and Bradford & Bingley.

www.worldbank.org The World Bank website has information about various corporate governance developments.

 For further links to useful sources of information visit the Online Resource Centre **www.oxfordtextbooks.co.uk/orc/mallin4e/**

 **FT Clippings**

FT: Squeezed charities seek better investment

By Ruth Sullivan

April 22, 2012

The UK government's proposed cap on tax relief for charitable donations is likely to push charities to sweat their investments more as they struggle to survive in a tough economic climate — meeting demands on services amid falling donations.

"The tax relief cap is another blow to the sector at a time when costs are rising and both donations and public sector funding sources are under severe pressure," says Jane Tully, head of policy at the Charity Finance Group.

"Cutting funding will hit their bottom line and charities will have to make their assets work harder," she adds.

A report on UK charities, published last week and carried out by PwC, Charity Finance Group and the Institute of Fundraising*, shows nearly a quarter (23 per cent) of the 355 respondents plan to focus on better investment of their funds in the next 12 months, although they did not explain how they would do this. Around one in 10 (11 per cent) say investments are their most important source of income.

James Pike, head of JO Hambro Investment Management Charity Investment Committee, expects to see "more pressure on asset managers to deliver better returns this year".

In particular, charities will be anxious to discuss whether they are following the right strategy to gain the best returns, he says.

A rise in the number of charities keen to review their investment strategies recently triggered a headcount increase in JOHIM's charity team, from nine to 10.

The investment manager, which manages portfolios for 95 charities, expects the number to grow further this year. "Charities want to discuss their investment strategy and whether they

are heading in the right direction," Mr Pike adds.

Many charities are concerned their past strategy is too cautious to boost returns sufficiently, and are pondering whether taking on more risk would be a good way to boost returns. Few asset managers advocate this, pointing out the downside of increasing exposure to riskier or more illiquid assets such as hedge funds and property.

Much depends on the size, activity and cash flow of the individual charity.

Richard Maitland, head of charities at Sarasin & Partners, says: "Some charities need to up returns and are prepared to take more risk but it is down to individual trustees and they know fund managers might get a risky portfolio wrong. There is a need to balance market risk with the possibility of better returns." James Bevan, chief investment officer at CCLA Investment Management, a specialist manager for charities, faith organisations and local authorities, points to an ongoing strategy shift among charities from cash to other asset classes as "the cost of staying in cash is too high", he says.

"The onset of low interest rates has been driving charities to see how much they really need to hold in cash for reserves or operational needs," says Mr Bevan. Some of this has gone into equities, he adds, although the average UK charity allocation to equities has fallen from 70-80 per cent to about 65 per cent in the past few years.

Not all investment houses agree that charities will try to get more out of their assets following the furore over capping tax relief on donations. "The implication is that charities are not sweating them enough now. Most [of the trustees] that we look after are doing this already," says Mr Maitland.

However, he is ready to admit charities have not seen good returns in the past 10 years with the typical (Sarasin) portfolio split of 70 per cent in equities, 17.5 per cent in bonds, 7.5 per cent in property and the rest in alternative investments.

Yet in spite of poor returns, which Mr Maitland largely puts down to market conditions, he recommends little change to the asset mix, cautioning against taking more risk.

He expects market volatility to subside over the next five years, and says charities that maintain a high equity weighting should see real returns of about 4 per cent a year, after taking out inflation (2.5 per cent) and management fees (about 0.5 per cent).

For Mr Maitland, the game is one of patient waiting to pick up market gains rather than rushing to change strategy.

As charities are forced to reduce overall costs, they are also likely to put pressure on asset managers to cut fees. Cathy Pharoah, professor of charity funding at Cass Business School, says: "Charities will be looking carefully at costs and the bigger ones, in particular, are likely to use their clout to negotiate fees downwards." This has already been happening to some extent following the financial crisis but some fund managers expect fee negotiating to intensify this year.

A large number of charities are also considering dipping into their reserves, with 73 per cent open to such a course of action this year, according to the PwC report. A fifth of charities are also considering a merger as a means of survival, up from 12 per cent a year ago.

The outlook for charities is far from bright and at a time when investments are more critical than ever to their survival and success, the uncertainty triggered by recent tax announcements is "just adding another nail in the coffin", says Mr Pike.

Managing charities in the new normal. A perfect storm?

© 2012 *The Financial Times Ltd.*

Part 2

Owners and Stakeholders

4 Shareholders and Stakeholders

Learning Objectives

- To understand the difference between shareholders and stakeholders
- To be aware of the various different stakeholder groups
- To have an overview of the way that shareholders and stakeholders are provided for in various corporate governance codes and guidelines
- To understand the roles that shareholders and stakeholders can play in companies and the development of corporate governance

Shareholders and stakeholders

The term 'stakeholder' can encompass a wide range of interests: it refers to any individual or group on which the activities of the company have an impact. Shareholders can be viewed as a stakeholder group but, for the purposes of this discussion, we will view shareholders as being distinct from other stakeholder groups. Why? First, shareholders invest their money to provide risk capital for the company and, secondly, in many legal jurisdictions, shareholders' rights are enshrined in law whereas those of the wider group of stakeholders are not. Of course, this varies from jurisdiction to jurisdiction, with creditors' rights strongly protected in some countries, and employee rights' strongly protected in others.

As highlighted in Chapter 2 in the discussion of stakeholder theory, one rationale for effectively privileging shareholders over other stakeholders is that they are the recipients of the residual free cash flow (being the profits remaining once other stakeholders, such as loan creditors, have been paid). This means that the shareholders have a vested interest in trying to ensure that resources are used to maximum effect, which in turn should be to the benefit of society as a whole.

The simplest definition of a shareholder seems straightforward enough: an individual, institution, firm, or other entity that owns shares in a company. Of course, the reality of the situation can be much more complicated with beneficial owners and cross-holdings making the chain of ownership complex. Shareholders' rights are generally protected by law, although the extent and effectiveness of this protection varies from country to country. However, the definition of a stakeholder is much less clear and along with this lack of clarity comes an opaqueness regarding the role of stakeholders and the protection of their rights.

There are various stakeholder groups that may have an interest in a company's performance and activities. Stakeholders include: employees, suppliers, customers, banks, and other creditors; the government; various 'interest' groups, for example, environmental groups; indeed anyone on whom the activities of the company may have an impact. Figure 4.1 illustrates the various groups whose interests the company may need to take into account.

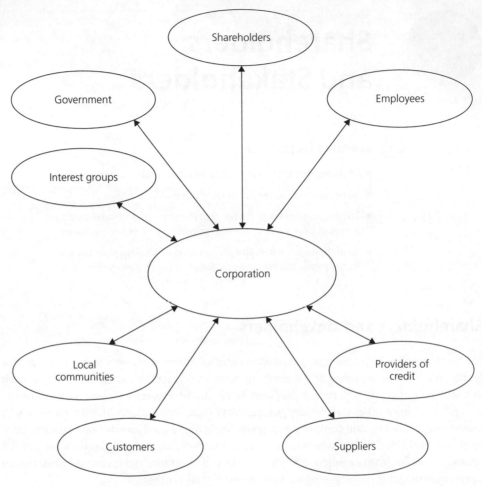

Figure 4.1 The corporation and its stakeholders

Stakeholder groups

There are various stakeholder groups: some directly related to the company, such as employees, providers of credit, suppliers and customers; others more indirectly related to the company, such as the local communities of the towns or cities in which it operates; environmental groups; and the government. Looking at each of these in turn, we can clarify the interest that each group might have as a stakeholder.

Employees

The employees of a company have an interest in the company because it provides their livelihood in the present day and, at some future point, employees will often also be in receipt of a pension provided by the company's pension scheme. In terms of present-day employment, employees will be concerned with their pay and working conditions, and how the company's strategy will impact on these. Of course, the long-term growth and prosperity of the company is important for the longer term view of the employees, particularly as concerns pension benefits in the future.

Most companies include, in their annual report and accounts, a statement or report to the employees stating in what ways they are looking after the employees' interests. The report will usually mention training programmes, working conditions, and equal opportunities. Many companies have employee share schemes that give the employees the opportunity to own shares in the company, and feel more of a part of it; the theory being that the better the company performs (through employees' efforts, etc.), the more the employees themselves will benefit as their shares increase in price.

Companies need also to consider and work with the employees' trade unions, recognizing that a good relationship with the unions is desirable. The trade unions may, amongst other things, act as a conduit for company employee information dissemination, or be helpful when trying to ascertain the employees' views. Increasingly, trade unions are exerting their influence, via the pension funds, pressing for change by use of their voting rights.

Companies need also to consider and comply with employee legislation, whether related to equal opportunities, health and safety at work, or any other aspect. Companies should also have in place appropriate whistle-blowing procedures for helping to ensure that if employees feel that there is inappropriate behaviour in the company, they can 'blow the whistle' on these activities whilst minimizing the risk of adverse consequences for themselves as a result of this action.

Providers of credit

Providers of credit include banks and other financial institutions. Providers of credit want to be confident that the companies to which they lend are going to be able to repay their debts. They will seek assurance from the annual report and accounts, and from various management accounts and forecasts that companies produce. It is in the company's best interests to maintain the confidence of providers of finance to ensure that no calls are made for repayment of funds, that they are willing to lend to the company in the future, and that the company is able to borrow at the best possible rate.

Suppliers

Suppliers have an interest in the companies that they supply on two grounds. First, having supplied the company with goods or services, they want to be sure that they will be paid for these and in a timely fashion. Secondly, they will be interested in the continuance of the company because they will wish to have a sustainable outlet for their goods and services.

Sometimes, suppliers will be supplying specialized equipment or services and, if the company it supplies has financial difficulties, then this can have a severe impact on the supplier as well. Of course, on an ongoing basis, suppliers of goods and services will also like to be paid on time because otherwise they will have problems with their own cash flow and meeting their own costs, such as labour and materials, incurred in supplying the company in the first place. So, ideally, the companies supplied will treat their suppliers with understanding and ensure that they settle their debts on time. In practice, many large companies will make their suppliers wait for payment, occasionally for such a length of time that the supplier either ends up with severe financial difficulties or refuses to supply the company in future.

Customers

A company's customers will want to try to make sure that they can buy the same product time and again from the company. The company itself will presumably be building up its customer loyalty through various marketing exercises, and customers themselves will get used to a familiar product that they will want to buy in the future. Sometimes, a product bought from one company will become part of a product made by the customer, and again it will be important for the customer to be assured that they can continue to buy and incorporate that product into their own production.

Increasingly, customers are also more aware of social, environmental, and ethical aspects of corporate behaviour and will try to ensure that the company supplying them is acting in a corporately socially responsible manner.

Local communities

Local communities have a number of interests in the companies that operate in their region. First, the companies will be employing large numbers of local people and it will be in the interest of sustained employment levels that companies in the locality operate in an efficient way. Should the company's fortunes start to decline, then unemployment might rise and may lead to part of the workforce moving away from the area to seek jobs elsewhere. This, in turn, would have an effect on local schools, as the number of pupils declined, and the housing market would be hit too, as demand for housing in the area declined. However, local communities will also be concerned that companies in the area act in an environmentally friendly way because the last thing they want is pollution in local rivers, in the soil, or in the atmosphere more generally. It is therefore in the local community's interest that companies in their locality continue to thrive, but do so in a way that takes account of local and national concerns.

Environmental groups

Environmental groups will seek to ensure that companies operate to both national and international environmental standards such as the *Ceres Principles* and the *Global Reporting Initiative Sustainability Guidelines* (these are discussed in more detail in Chapter 7). Increasingly, environmental issues are viewed as part of the mainstream rather than being at the periphery as a 'wish list'. The recognition that an environmentally responsible company should also, in the longer term, be as profitable, if not more so, as one that does not act in an environmentally responsible way is in many ways self-evident. An environmentally responsible company will not subject its workers to potentially hazardous processes without adequate protection (which unfortunately does still happen despite the best endeavours of health and safety regulations); will not pollute the environment; and will, where possible, use recyclable materials or engage in a recycling process. Ultimately, all of these things will benefit society at large and the company itself.

Government

The government has an interest in companies for several diverse reasons. First, as with the local and environmental groups—although not always with such commitment—it will try to make sure that companies act in a socially responsible way, taking account of social, ethical, and environmental considerations. Secondly, it will analyse corporate trends for purposes such as employment levels, monetary policy, and market supply and demand of goods and services. Lastly, but not least, it will be looking at various aspects to do with fiscal policy, such as capital allowances, incentives for investing in various industries or various parts of the country, and, of course, the taxation raised from companies.

Guidance on shareholders' and stakeholders' interests

There are a variety of codes, principles, and guidelines that include a discussion of the role of shareholders' and stakeholders' interests in a company and how the corporate governance system might accommodate these interests. This section looks at some of the most influential of these publications.

Organisation for Economic Co-operation and Development (OECD)

There are two main OECD publications that give some thought to this area. First, there is the OECD (1998) report on *Corporate Governance: Improving Competitiveness and Access to Capital in Global Markets* by the Business Sector Advisory Group on Corporate Governance. This report recognizes that the companies' central mission is long-term enhancement of shareholder value, but that companies operate in the larger society, and that there may be different societal pressures and expectations that may impact on the financial objective to some extent, so that non-financial objectives may need to be addressed as well.

The OECD *Principles of Corporate Governance* (1999), revised in 2004, include as one of the principles, the role of stakeholders in corporate governance. The Principles (2004) state that 'the corporate governance framework should recognize the rights of stakeholders established by law or through mutual agreements and encourage active co-operation between corporations and stakeholders in creating wealth, jobs, and the sustainability of financially sound enterprises'. This really highlights two aspects: first, that the rights of stakeholders will depend to a large extent on the legal provision for stakeholders in any given country (one would expect that stakeholders would have a right of redress for any violation of their rights); secondly, that stakeholders do have a role to play in the long-term future of businesses, that the corporate governance framework should 'permit performance-enhancing mechanisms for stakeholder participation', and that stakeholders should have access to relevant information in order to participate effectively.

The OECD publication *Using the OECD Principles of Corporate Governance: A Boardroom Perspective* (2008) detailed real-life examples of the ways in which the Principles (2004) have been put into action in the boardroom by business leaders. In the context of stakeholders—which, as we have discussed, encompass many different groups—one example in relation to employees is that site visits by the board and direct communication with employees are beneficial; whilst another example, this time in the context of social responsibility and philanthropy, is that the board should consult with shareholders, employees, and other appropriate stakeholders regarding their philanthropic agenda.

The Royal Society of Arts (RSA) and Tomorrow's Company

The RSA in the UK is a multidisciplinary independent body that has commissioned reports in various areas, including one called the *Tomorrow's Company Report* (2005), which was led by Mark Goyder. The report advocated an inclusive approach for business in its relationship with various stakeholder groups. The inclusive approach recognizes that there is an interdependence between the employees, investors, customers, and suppliers, which increasingly means that the business needs to take a long-term view rather than having the short-term focus on increasing shareholder value that many businesses are perceived as having.

There was significant demand from businesses involved in the RSA Inquiry for an organization to carry forward its work and Tomorrow's Company is now well established as 'a not-for-profit research and agenda-setting organisation committed to creating a future for business which makes equal sense to staff, shareholders and society'. The organization has expanded its horizons and joined with other business and non-governmental organizations (NGO) leaders around the globe to publish *Tomorrow's Global Company: Challenges and Choices* (2007) which advocates that companies should work with governments, NGOs, and others to create stronger frameworks of law and regulation for the world's markets. The report argues that 'stronger frameworks are needed to enable companies to create wealth and shareholder value at the same time as delivering practical solutions to global issues such as climate change, persistent poverty and human rights abuses'.

In 2008 the RSA published *Tomorrow's Investor*, by Rowland Manthorpe, which highlighted 'the looming pensions crisis, exacerbated by the financial crisis, is one of the most pressing problems society faces. The issues are well known: a population in which not enough people are saving; where saving is declining; where investors are being let down by their representatives.' The report also looks at ways in which transparency and accountability might be improved, and investor engagement made more effective. It argues that pension funds should 'take more advantage of the resources at their disposal by utilising new methods of social engagement'.

In December 2010 *Tomorrow's Investor: Building the Consensus for a People's Pension in Britain* by David Pitt-Watson was published by RSA Projects. The report finds that the system of occupational and private pensions in the UK is not fit for purpose. It details how the UK has ended up in such a poor position, and the key questions that pension policymakers now need to address to help build an effective pensions architecture.

Hampel (1998)

The Hampel Committee was established in the UK in 1995 following the recommendations of the Cadbury (1992) and Greenbury (1995) committees that a new committee should review the implementation of their findings. Whilst recognizing that 'good governance ensures that constituencies (stakeholders) with a relevant interest in the company's business are fully taken into account', the Hampel Report (1998) stated quite clearly that the objective of all listed companies is the 'preservation and the greatest practicable enhancement over time of their shareholders' investment'.

The report took the view that whilst management should develop appropriate relationships with its various stakeholder groups, it should have regard to the overall objective of the company: to preserve and enhance shareholder value over time. The report also highlighted the practical point that 'directors as a board are responsible *for relations with* stakeholders; but they are accountable *to* shareholders' [emphasis in original]. This is a fundamental point because, if it were not so, then it would be very difficult to identify exactly to which stakeholder groups directors might be responsible and the extent of their responsibilities.

Hermes Principles (2002, 2006, 2010)

Hermes is one of the largest institutional investors in the UK with several million people depending on Hermes' investments to generate their retirement income. Hermes has long been one of the most active institutional investors in corporate governance and, in 2002, it published *The Hermes Principles*. In introducing the Principles, Hermes state:

> Hermes' overriding requirement is that companies be run in the long-term interest of shareholders. Companies adhering to this principle will not only benefit their shareholders, but also we would argue, the wider economy in which the company and its shareholders participate. We believe a company run in the long-term interest of shareholders will need to manage effectively relationships with its employees, suppliers and customers, to behave ethically and have regard for the environment and society as a whole.

In 2006 Hermes introduced its *Hermes Corporate Governance Principles*, which form the basis of its engagement with the companies in which it, or its clients, invest. These Principles have two parts: the Global Principles and the Regional Principles. The former are based on the *International Corporate Governance Network's Global Corporate Governance Principles*, whilst the latter explain which corporate governance codes or guidance, produced by local market participants or regulators, are supported by Hermes. In 2010 Hermes published *The Hermes Responsible Ownership Principles* detailing what they expect of listed companies and what listed companies can expect from them.

EU Accounts Modernization Directive

The EU Accounts Modernization Directive was intended to produce more comparability across the financial reporting of its member states. By its provisions, companies in various countries in the EU are subject to common standards of both the level of disclosure and content of disclosures. The Directive applied to all medium and large EU companies and, effective from 1 April 2005, the Directive required additional material to be included in the Director's Report to provide an enhanced review of a company's business. The Directive states that

> the review must, to the extent necessary for an understanding of the development, performance or position of the business of the company, include:
>
> a. analysis using financial key performance indicators, and
>
> b. where appropriate, analysis using other key performance indicators, including information relating to environmental matters and employee matters.

Companies Act (2006)

The *Companies Act* (2006) was published in November 2006. There are several significant provisions in relation to shareholders and stakeholders that it is appropriate to mention in this chapter.

First, in relation to directors' duties, the Companies Act (2006) draws on the concept of 'enlightened shareholder value'. In the Department of Trade and Industry consultative Company Law Reform (2005) document which preceded the Companies Act (2006), in relation to directors' duties, it said:

> The statement of duties will be drafted in a way which reflects modern business needs and wider expectations of responsible business behaviour. The CLR [Company Law Review] proposed that the basic goal for directors should be the success of the company for the benefit of its members as a whole; but that, to reach this goal, directors would need to take a properly balanced view of the implications of decisions over time and foster effective relationships with employees, customers and suppliers, and in the community more widely. The Government strongly agrees that this approach, which the CLR called 'enlightened shareholder value', is most likely to drive long-term company performance and maximise overall competitiveness and wealth and welfare for all. It will therefore be reflected in the statement of directors' duties.

In the Companies Act (2006), it is made clear that a director's duty is to

> act in the way he considers, in good faith, would be most likely to promote the success of the company for the benefit of its members as a whole and, in doing so have regard (amongst other matters) to:
>
> a. the likely consequences of any decision in the long term,
>
> b. the interests of the company's employees,
>
> c. the need to foster the company's business relationships with suppliers, customers and others,
>
> d. the impact of the company's operations on the community and the environment,
>
> e. the desirability of the company maintaining a reputation for high standards of business conduct, and
>
> f. the need to act fairly as between members of the company. (Part 10, Chapter 2, section 172.)

Clearly, there is a significant emphasis being given here for directors to have regard to wider stakeholder interests as well as to the shareholders. Unless the company is classified as a small company, the Directors' Report must contain a business review that would comply with the aforementioned EU Accounts Modernization Directive as well as the Companies Act 2006. The Companies Act states that the business review must contain a fair review of the company's business, and a description of the principal risks and uncertainties facing the company.

> The business review must, to the extent necessary for an understanding of the development, performance or position of the company's business, include:
>
> a. the main trends and factors likely to affect the future development, performance and position of the company's business; and

b. information about—

   i. environmental matters (including the impact of the company's business on the environment),

   ii. the company's employees, and

   iii. social and community issues, including information about any policies of the company in relation to those matters and the effectiveness of those policies;

The review must, to the extent necessary for an understanding of the development, performance or position of the company's business, include—

a. analysis using financial key performance indicators, and

b. where appropriate, analysis using other key performance indicators, including information relating to environmental matters and employee matters.

'Key performance indicators' means factors by reference to which the development, performance or position of the company's business can be measured effectively. (Part 15, Chapter 5, section 417.)

In January 2006 the Department for Environment, Food, and Rural Affairs (Defra) issued voluntary guidance on environmental key performance indicators (KPIs) that companies might include in their disclosures about environmental reporting. The KPIs might also provide appropriate information for the business review.

King Report (2002, 2009)

The King Report (2002) is a comprehensive document that provides guidelines for corporate governance in South Africa. It builds on the earlier King Report published in 1994, which stated that there should be an integrated approach to corporate governance and took into account the interests of various stakeholder groups. King (2002) states that the inclusive approach is fundamental to the operation of business in South Africa. The company should define its purpose, decide on the values by which the company's day-to-day activities will be carried on, and identify its stakeholders; all of these aspects should be taken into account when the company develops its strategies for achieving corporate objectives. The King Report was updated in 2009. The King Report (2002, 2009) is covered in more detail in Chapter 13 but it is mentioned here as a good example of a code that emphasizes the inclusive approach and the importance of considering the interests of stakeholders.

Roles of shareholders and stakeholders

In reality, the involvement of shareholders and stakeholders will depend on national laws and customs, and also the individual company's approach. However, even in countries where companies traditionally have not been profit-oriented (such as state-owned enterprises) as those countries now seek to develop their capital markets and raise external finance, the shareholders' interests will likely tend to rise to the top of the corporate agenda. However, it is of fundamental importance that stakeholders' interests cannot, and should not, be ignored.

As can be seen from the codes/principles discussed above, whilst recognizing that companies need to take into account the views of stakeholders, in the UK, the prima facie purpose of a company is the maintenance or enhancement of long-term shareholder value. In the UK neither the legal nor the corporate governance systems make any provision for employee representation on the board, nor for representation of other stakeholder groups such as providers of finance, and there has been consistent opposition to representation of stakeholder groups on corporate boards. However, the UK has employee share schemes so employees can be involved in that way, although, of course, they do not have the same type of input as if they were represented on the board.

In the UK and the USA the emphasis is on the relationship between the shareholders (owners) and the directors (managers). In contrast, the German and French corporate governance systems, which view companies as more of a partnership between capital and labour, provide for employee representation at board level, whilst banks (providers of finance) may also be represented on the supervisory board. However, it is interesting to note that one downside of employee representation on the board is that decisions, which may be in the best interests of the company as a whole but not of the workforce, may not get made, so may lead to sub-optimal decision-making. Whilst the German and French corporate governance systems are dealt with in detail in Chapter 10, it is useful at this point to highlight the different approach to stakeholders and the impact that this may have on the company.

Another important point is that if the directors of a company were held to be responsible to shareholders and the various stakeholders groups alike, then what would be the corporate objective? How could the board function effectively if there were a multiplicity of different objectives, no one of which took priority over the others? At present in many countries, the enhancement of shareholder wealth is the overriding criterion, but if it were not, what would be? This could actually lead to quite a dangerous situation where directors and managers were not really accountable.

Given that all companies operate within a wider society, the interests of shareholders and stakeholders are often intertwined. Also, the distinction between shareholders and stakeholders is often not clear-cut. For example, Charkham and Simpson (1999) point out that, in the UK, shareholders are often drawn from other stakeholder groups: 'Pension funds are the largest group of shareholders, yet their assets are drawn from the savings of half the workforce and invested to provide retirement income when this group becomes pensioners.' Similar statements can be made about the insurance companies, and also about individual shareholders who may also be customers of the companies in which they invest, for example, utilities.

Significantly, Goergen et al. (2010a) point out that 'understandings of corporate governance that are concerned only with the rights of owners and shareholders and the relationship between them and the management of the business are inevitably limited. Organizations are complex bodies and have many other parties involved, including regulators, customers, suppliers, and local citizens'. Goergen et al. (2010b) point out that 'in the UK it is still controversial to regard stakeholders as "actors" within the landscape of corporate governance' but that 'shareholders, employees, stakeholders and gatekeepers are all part of the complex social ecosystem surrounding the corporation'. They advocate using the principles of complexity theory to analyse the complex behaviour between the multiple stakeholders within the corporate governance social ecosystem.

Harper Ho (2010) urges 'a vision of the corporation and its purpose that transcends the shareholder-stakeholder divide'. Under this 'enlightened shareholder value' approach, attention is given to corporate stakeholders, including the environment, employees, and local communities, as these groups are now being seen as critical to generating long-term shareholder wealth and to effective risk management.

Finally, Lan and Heracleous (2010) in an innovative proposal drawing from legal theory, redefine agency theory along three key dimensions, 'redefining the principal from shareholders to the corporation, redefining the status of the board from shareholders' agents to autonomous fiduciaries, and redefining the role of the board from monitors to mediating hierarchs'. Furthermore, they state that 'our redefined agency theory may be seen as more applicable and palatable to countries other than those in the Anglo-Saxon world, such as China, Germany, Japan, and Russia, that are more stakeholder oriented and where shareholders are not always treated as primary. Even so, as we have shown, the legal systems in the Anglo-Saxon world also support this approach'.

Conclusions

Companies operate in a wider society not within a defined corporate vacuum. Therefore, companies should take account of the views of various stakeholders in addition to those of shareholders. Whilst the corporate objective is generally to maintain or enhance shareholder value, the impact of the company's activities on its other stakeholders must be taken into account when deciding the strategy to be developed for achieving the corporate objective.

By taking account of the views and interests of its stakeholders, the company should be able to achieve its objectives with integrity and help to achieve sustainability of its long-term operations.

Summary

- Shareholders are the providers of capital. Often, the corporate objective is expressed in terms of maximizing shareholder value.

- Stakeholders include employees, providers of credit, customers, suppliers, local communities, government, environmental and social groups; in fact, any group on which the company's activities may have an impact.

- Most corporate governance codes and guidelines tend to perceive the prima facie objective of the company as the maximization of shareholder wealth. However, there is also the understanding that the achievement of this objective should have regard to the interests of various stakeholder groups.

- Stakeholders can make their views known to the company and, in some countries, may have representation on the company's decision-making bodies (such as the supervisory board in Germany). However, in the UK and many other countries, it is the shareholders who can hold the board of directors accountable for their actions.

Questions

The discussion questions to follow cover the key learning points of this chapter. Reading of some of the additional reference material will enhance the depth of the students' knowledge and understanding of these areas.

1. What stakeholder groups might directors of a company have to take into consideration, and how might the stakeholders' interests impact on the company?

2. In what ways might stakeholders' interests conflict with each other?

3. What role do you believe stakeholders should play in corporate governance?

4. Critically contrast the roles of shareholders and stakeholders.

5. 'A company's long-term success is dependent on its stakeholders, therefore it can no more fail to take stakeholders' interests into consideration than it can those of its shareholders.' Critically discuss this statement.

6. What corporate governance mechanisms might help with representing the views of stakeholders?

References

Cadbury, Sir Adrian (2002), *Corporate Governance and Chairmanship: A Personal View*, Oxford University Press, Oxford.

Charkham, J. and Simpson, A. (1999), *Fair Shares: The Future of Shareholder Power and Responsibility*, Oxford University Press, Oxford.

Companies Act (2006), Her Majesty's Stationery Office, London.

Defra (2006), *Environmental Key Performance Indicators, Reporting Guidelines for UK Business*, Defra/Trucost, London.

Goergen M., Brewster C., and Wood, G. (2010a), 'Corporate Governance: Nonequity Stakeholders', in H. Kent Baker and R. Anderson (eds), *Corporate Governance, A Synthesis of Theory, Research and Practice*, The Robert W. Kolb Series in Finance, John Wiley & Sons Inc., New Jersey.

——, Mallin C., Mitleton-Kelly E., Al-Hawamdeh A., and Chui H-Y. (2010b), *Corporate Governance and Complexity Theory*, Edward Elgar Publishing Ltd, Cheltenham.

Greenbury, Sir Richard (1995), *Directors' Remuneration*, Gee & Co. Ltd, London.

Hampel, Sir Ronnie (1998), *Committee on Corporate Governance: Final Report*, Gee & Co. Ltd, London.

Harper Ho, V.E. (2010), '"Enlightened Shareholder Value": Corporate Governance Beyond the Shareholder-Stakeholder Divide', *Journal of Corporation Law*, Vol. 36, No. 1, p. 59–112.

Hermes (2002), *The Hermes Principles*, Hermes Pensions Management Ltd, London.

—— (2006), *Hermes Corporate Governance Principles*, Hermes Pensions Management Ltd, London.

—— (2010), *The Hermes Responsible Ownership Principles*, Hermes Pensions Management Ltd, London.

King, M. (1994), *King Report on Corporate Governance for South Africa—1994*, King Committee on Corporate Governance, Institute of Directors in Southern Africa, Parktown, South Africa.

—— (2002), *King Report on Corporate Governance for South Africa – 2002*, King Committee on Corporate Governance, Institute of Directors in Southern Africa, Parktown, South Africa.

—— (2009), *King Code of Governance for South Africa 2009*, King Committee on Corporate Governance, Institute of Directors in Southern Africa, Parktown, South Africa.

Lan, L.L. and Heracleous, L. (2010), 'Rethinking Agency Theory: The View from Law', *Academy of Management Review*, Vol. 35, No.2, pp. 294–314.

Manthorpe, R. (2008), *Tomorrow's Investor* (2008), RSA, London.

OECD (1998), *Corporate Governance: Improving Competitiveness and Access to Capital in Global Markets*, A report to the OECD by the Business Sector Advisory Group on Corporate Governance, OECD, Paris.

—— (1999), *Principles of Corporate Governance*, OECD, Paris.

—— (2004), *Principles of Corporate Governance*, OECD, Paris.

—— (2008), *Using the OECD Principles of Corporate Governance: A Boardroom Perspective*, OECD, Paris.

Pitt-Watson, D. (2010), *Tomorrow's Investor: Building the Consensus for a People's Pension in Britain*, RSA, London.

Tomorrow's Company Report (2005), RSA, London.

Tomorrow's Global Company: Challenges and Choices (2007), Tomorrow's Company, London.

Useful websites

http://blog.thecorporatelibrary.com/ The website of the Corporate Library, which has comprehensive information about various aspects of corporate governance including shareholders and stakeholders (renamed the GMI blog).

www.bsr.org/ This is the website of the Business for Social Responsibility, a global non-profit organization that promotes corporate success in ways that respect ethical values, people, communities, and the environment.

www.defra.gov.uk The website of the Department for Environment, Food and Rural Affairs, which contains various publications relating to the environment, sustainability, and related matters.

www.bis.gov.uk/ The website of the Department for Business, Innovation & Skills (created in June 2009 from the merger of the Department for Business, Enterprise and Regulatory Reform, and the Department for Innovation, Universities and Skills) contains information about the Department's activities.

www.legislation.gov.uk/ This website brings together the legislative content previously held on the OPSI website and revised legislation from the Statute Law Database to provide a single legislation service.

www.parliament.uk/ The website of the UK Parliament covers parliamentary debates in the House of Commons and House of Lords and has a wide range of publications.

http://www.thersa.org/ The website of the Royal Society of Arts, a charity that encourages the development of a principled, prosperous society.

www.tomorrowscompany.com The website of Tomorrow's Company contains various publications produced to help achieve Tomorrow's Company's objectives.

 For further links to useful sources of information visit the Online Resource Centre **www.oxfordtextbooks.co.uk/orc/mallin4e/**

 FT Clippings

FT: Integrity is key to gaining good governance

By Philip Armstrong and James D. Spellman

Financial Times 2 February 2009

Recent failures in risk management and poor decisions on credit exposures, setting in motion the global financial implosion, are some of many issues triggering questions about the efficacy of corporate governance.

Entire businesses lacked parental supervision, with rogue wunderkids recklessly gambling away capital.

There are questions, too, about the shareholders and their poor exercise of power, if not impotence, in influencing board composition, conduct and decisions. Management proposals generally pass and uncontested directors receive most of the votes. Yes, activism has risen, but the evidence suggests that investor activism alone has not improved companies' long-term operating or share price performance. Worse still, where were the regulators?

There is much blame to go round, particularly with share prices in free fall. The annual meetings during proxy season this year promise to be street brawls. Meanwhile, new laws seem certain in Europe and the US to give investors a 'say on executive pay', impose tougher requirements to ensure transparency in board decisions and strengthen investors' ability to force changes in policies that entrenched boards had rubber-stamped.

Best practice dictates that effective boards provide strategic vision, monitor management and act transparently to ensure full accountability to shareholders. Directors must have a well-articulated view of the business, market conditions and main performance metrics.

Fiduciary obligations include identifying and monitoring risks, with incentives that reward prudence. Internal controls must ensure that financial and operational reports are based on accurate, truthful information – not Enron-like hocus pocus.

Sound corporate governance practices inspire investor and lender confidence, spur domestic and foreign investment and improve corporate competitiveness. Well-governed companies worldwide perform better than poorly governed ones. Capital costs are lower, a company's valuation is higher and operational performance improves.

As we see now, when trust deteriorates in a board and the company it governs, investors run in panic from the falling knives.

Despite the justifiable scepticism, it is only through corporate governance – abiding by the letter and the spirit of a regime in which the interests of the owners are a director's reliable compass – that trust and confidence can be restored.

So, where to go from here? It starts with shareholders. They own the company. Only when all shareholders act as owners will companies be better managed. Financial literacy must, then, be part of the solution to restore trust and rebuild capital markets.

Boards need to communicate better and engage shareholders, rather than seeing them as nuisances. Too often, directors cringe when they hear the peasants are up in arms, dismissing them as the fringe to ignore. We can expect regulators to require that more information flow to investors, but meaningful change will come only when shareholders are perceived as worthy peers. There is wisdom in the crowd: the many outsmart the lone few.

Director training should also be stepped up. What we have heard from institutes of directors worldwide is that directors lack knowledge in a number of areas: their functions and obligations; what constitutes good corporate governance; the value of accountability through a rigorous audit process; and the leadership responsibilities to ensure investors' interests are paramount in decision-making. Directors are often unfamiliar with a business's financial nuances and the associated risks.

Well-trained directors understand the value of an early warning system, value competence above cameraderie and demand better information to help them spot trouble early. They work to protect the board's independence and its distance from day-to-day management. Skilful, detached navigation builds trust with management internally and investors, vendors, customers and other stakeholders externally. In the end, though, it is all about character. Integrity drives how we behave. Character cannot be instilled by regulation or law. It is built by meeting life with honesty and courage, learning through successes and failures.

FT: Benefit corporations: Companies obliged to do good

By Sarah Murray

April 23, 2012

Greyston Bakery, a business based in Yonkers, New York, that aims to transform lives and renew urban communities, says: "We don't hire people to bake brownies. We bake brownies to hire people." But the bakery's slogan is more than an aspiration – the company is legally bound to pursue this mission. Greyston Bakery is a benefit corporation, a new kind of business entity that under US law is required to generate social and environmental benefits as well as profits.

Only a few companies are so far incorporated under the new rules, but some believe the model could bring about big changes in the way business is done and unlock billions of dollars in socially focused investment capital.

Under legislation now passed in seven US states, registered benefit corporations must work to create positive social and environmental impact, expand their fiduciary duty to consider the interests of workers, the community and the environment and report publicly every year on their social and environmental performance using a credible third-party standard.

"These are for-profit companies," says Andrew Kassoy, co-founder of B Lab, a US non-profit group that worked to introduce and support the new legislation. "But those things now become part of the fiduciary duty of these companies." This constitutes a significant divergence from the traditional model in which corporate officers and directors have a legal duty to maximise shareholder value, which generally means profit.

"Anything you do that costs money and deviates from that leaves you open to a lawsuit," says Andrew Greenblatt, a New York University professor and founder of Vendorboon, a social venture that negotiates vendor discounts for its members.

For companies wanting to use market forces to solve some of the world's biggest problems, benefit corporation legislation is a powerful tool. The law means officers and directors are legally protected when it comes to making decisions that balance profit making with social or environmental goals. One example of how this protection can come into play is when companies face takeover bids.

Under traditional incorporation law, a company would find it hard to resist a bid if it was in shareholders' financial interests to make the sale – even if the buyer was not driven by social, environmental or ethical values. A benefit corporation could turn down such an offer.

Chid Liberty is founder of Liberty Justice, a for-profit fair-trade-certified company with a garment factory in Liberia that was established to employ women. He comments: "Often people go into business thinking they'll do good, but sometimes they get pushed up against the wall and need to make tough decisions." The ability to base business decisions on a wide range of factors is one of the reasons Mr Liberty is re-registering his company in one of the US states that will allow it to become a registered benefit corporation. "We wanted to make sure that if, say, a large Chinese buyer that didn't agree with our ethics came in, we had legal grounds to say no, because it doesn't fit with our organisational structure," says Mr Liberty.

The legislation also provides certainty for the growing number of investors who want to use their money to generate social and environmental benefits as well as financial returns.

These include socially responsible investors as well as a growing group of investors putting their money into impact investments, which JPMorgan has called "an emerging asset class", estimating the size of the market opportunity at between $400bn and $1tn.

The legal structure of benefit corporations means these investors can be sure that their investee companies will adhere to their social and environmental goals as they grow, rather than being tempted to switch to pure profit making when the business takes off.

"What this new law does is give investors the accountability to make officers and directors keep their promise to make the world a better place," says Prof Greenblatt. "And that unlocks intermediaries such as fund managers, who can raise money from people who want to invest in those kinds of things." Of course, the emphasis on social and environmental good does not mean benefit corporations can let profits slip. "On a daily basis, you're definitely struggling with the things any company struggles with," says Mr Liberty. "The only difference is that you are not only looking at this from the perspective of a typical financial analysis but also at what the impact is socially." Benefit corporation legislation exists only in the US at present. However, other countries – including Chile – are looking at the possibility of introducing similar corporate/structures. Meanwhile, in the US, several more states are considering introducing benefit corporation legislation in the near future.

This comes as no surprise. For cash-strapped governments looking to the private sector to play a bigger role in addressing issues such as poverty and climate change, benefit corporation legislation offers a cost-effective policy tool.

"There's a lot of interest," says Mr Kassoy at B Lab. "Policy makers see this as a development opportunity. All they have to do is change the law – they don't have to spend a lot of money. It's a no brainer."

5 Family-owned Firms

 Learning Objectives

- To be aware of the predominance of family-owned firms in many countries around the world
- To understand the evolution of governance structures in family-owned firms
- To realize the benefits that good corporate governance may bring to family-owned firms
- To understand the problems that may be faced by family-owned firms in implementing good corporate governance

Introduction

The dominant form of business around the world is the family-owned business. In many instances, the family-owned business takes the form of a small family business whilst in other cases, it is a large business interest employing hundreds, or even thousands, of staff. The family-owned business can encompass sole traders, partnerships, private companies, and public companies. In fact, family ownership is prevalent not only amongst privately held firms but also in publicly traded firms in many countries across the globe. However, whatever the size of the business, it can benefit from having a good governance structure. Firms with effective governance structures will tend to have a more focused view of the business, be willing to take into account, and benefit from, the views of 'outsiders' (that is, non-family members), and be in a better position to evolve and grow into the future.

Ownership structures around the world

La Porta *et al.* (1999) analysed the ownership structure in a number of countries and found that the family-owned firm is quite common. Analyzing a sample of large firms in 27 countries, La Porta *et al.* used as one of their criteria a 10 per cent chain definition of control. This means that they analysed the shareholdings to see if there were 'chains' of ownership: for example, if company B held shares in company C, who then held company B's shares. On this 10 per cent chain definition of control, only 24 per cent of the large companies are widely held, compared to 35 per cent that are family-controlled, and 20 per cent state-controlled. Overall, they show that:

1) Controlling shareholders often have control rights in excess of their cash flow rights. 2) This is true of families, who are so often the controlling shareholders. 3) Controlling families

participate in the management of the firms they own. 4) Banks do not exercise much control over firms as shareholders . . . 5) Other large shareholders are usually not there to monitor the controlling shareholders. Family control of firms appears to be common, significant, and typically unchallenged by other equity holders.

La Porta *et al.*'s paper made an important contribution to our understanding of the prevalence of family-owned/controlled firms in many countries across the world.

A key influence on the type of ownership and control structure is the legal system. Traditionally, common law legal systems, such as in the UK and USA, have better protection of minority shareholders' rights than do civil law systems, such as those of France, Germany, and Russia. Often, if the legal environment does not have good protection of shareholders' rights, then this discourages a diverse shareholder base whilst being more conducive to family-owned firms where a relatively small group of individuals can retain ownership, power, and control. For example, in the UK and USA, where the rights of minority shareholders are well protected by the legal system, there are many more companies with diversified shareholder bases, and family-controlled businesses are much less common.

However, research by Franks *et al.* (2004 and 2005) highlighted that, in the UK in the first half of the twentieth century, there was an absence of minority investor protection as we know it today, and yet there still occurred a move from family ownership to a more dispersed share ownership. This was attributable to the issuance of shares through acquisitions and mergers, although families tried to retain control of the board by holding a majority of the seats. Franks *et al.* (2004) state,

> the rise of hostile takeovers and institutional shareholders made it increasingly difficult for families to maintain control without challenge. Potential targets attempted to protect themselves through dual class shares and strategic share blocks but these were dismantled in response to opposition by institutional shareholders and the London Stock Exchange (LSE). The result was a regulated market in corporate control and a capital market that looked very different from its European counterparts. Thus, while acquisitions facilitated the growth of family controlled firms in the first half of the century, they also diluted their ownership and ultimately their control in the second half.

In many countries, including European countries such as France, many Asian countries, and South American countries, the legal protection of minority shareholders is today still either non-existent or ineffective, and so families often retain control in companies because non-family investors will not find the businesses an attractive investment when their rights are not protected.

However, many countries are recognizing that, as the business grows and needs external finance to pursue its expansion, then non-family investors will only be attracted to the business if there is protection of their rights, both in the context of the country's legal framework and also in the corporate governance of the individual companies in which they invest. This is leading to increasing pressure both for legal reforms to protect shareholders' rights and for corporate governance reforms within the individual companies. However, balanced against the pressures for reform are the often very powerful voices of family shareholders with controlling interests, who may not wish to see reform to give better protection to minority interests because this would effectively dilute their control.

Family-owned firms and governance

When a family-owned business is relatively small, the family members themselves will be able to manage and direct it. One advantage of a family-owned firm is that there should be less chance of the type of agency problems discussed in Chapter 2. This is because, rather than being split, ownership and control are still one and the same, and so the problems of information asymmetry and opportunistic behaviour should (in theory, at least) be lessened. As a result of this overlap of ownership and control, one would hope for higher levels of trust and hence less monitoring of management activity should be necessary. However, problems may still occur and especially in terms of potential for minority shareholder oppression, which may be more acute in family-owned firms. Morck and Yeung (2003) point out some of the potential agency costs in family-owned firms:

> In family business group firms, the concern is that managers may act for the controlling family, but not for shareholders in general. These agency issues are: the use of pyramidal groups to separate ownership from control, the entrenchment of controlling families, and non-arm's-length transactions (aka 'tunnelling') between related companies that are detrimental to public investors.

In some countries remedies such as formal shareholder agreements, in which the nature of each shareholder's participation in the company is recorded, may be utilized as a mechanism to help resolve the potential oppression of minorities. Furthermore, the European Commission's Shareholder Rights Directive, adopted in 2007, is designed to help strengthen the role of shareholders by ensuring that they have relevant information in a timely manner and are able to vote in an informed way. Although the Directive is aimed at listed companies, and so likely primarily to affect institutional investors, Member States are free to extend to non-listed companies some or all of the provisions of the proposed Directive.

Another advantage of family-owned firms may be their ability to be less driven by the short-term demands of the market. Of course, they still ultimately need to be able to make a profit, but they may have more flexibility as to when and how they do so.

However, even when a family business is still relatively small, there may be tensions and divisions within the family as different members may wish to take different courses of action that will affect the day-to-day way the business operates and its longer term development. In the same way, as different generations of a family will have diverse views on various aspects of life, so they will in the business context as well. Similarly, as siblings may argue about various things, so are they likely to differ in their views of who should hold power within the business and how the business should develop. Even in the early stages of a family firm, it is wise to have some sort of forum where the views of family members regarding the business and its development can be expressed. One such mechanism is the family meeting or assembly, where family members can meet, often on a formal pre-arranged basis, to express their views. As time goes by and the family expands by marriage and new generations, then the establishment of a family council may be advisable. Neubauer and Lank (1998) suggest that a family council may be advisable once there are more than thirty to forty family members.

When a business is at the stage where family relationships are impeding its efficient operation and development, or even if family members just realize that they are no longer managing the business as effectively as they might, then it is definitely time to develop a more

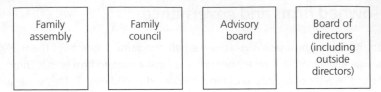

Figure 5.1 Possible stages in a family firm's governance

formal governance structure. There may be an intermediate stage where the family is advised by an advisory board, although this would not provide the same benefits to the family firm as a defined board structure with independent non-executive directors. Figure 5.1 illustrates the possible stages in a family firm's governance development.

Cadbury (2000) states that establishing a board of directors in a family firm is a means of progressing from an organization based on family relationships to one that is based primarily on business relationships. The structure of a family firm in its formative years is likely to be informal and to owe more to past history than to present needs. Once the firm has moved beyond the stage where authority is vested in the founders, it becomes necessary to clarify responsibilities and the process for taking decisions.

The advantages of a formal governance structure are several. First of all, there is a defined structure with defined channels for decision-making and clear lines of responsibility. Secondly, the board can tackle areas that may be sensitive from a family viewpoint but which nonetheless need to be dealt with: succession planning is a case in point, i.e. deciding who would be best to fill key roles in the business should the existing incumbents move on, retire, or die. Succession planning is important too in the context of raising external equity because, once a family business starts to seek external equity investment, then shareholders will usually want to know that succession planning is in place. The third advantage of a formal governance structure is also one in which external shareholders would take a keen interest: the appointment of non-executive directors. It may be that the family firm, depending on its size, appoints just one, or maybe two, non-executive directors. The key point about the non-executive director appointments is that the persons appointed should be independent; it is this trait that will make their contribution to the family firm a significant one. Of course, the independent non-executive directors should be appointed on the basis of the knowledge and experience that they can bring to the family firm: their business experience, or a particular knowledge or functional specialism of relevance to the firm, which will enable them to 'add value' and contribute to the strategic development of the family firm.

Cadbury (2000) sums up the three requisites for family firms to manage successfully the impacts of growth: 'They need to be able to recruit and retain the very best people for the business, they need to be able to develop a culture of trust and transparency, and they need to define logical and efficient organisational structures'. A good governance system will help family firms to achieve these requisites.

In the context of succession planning, Bennedsen *et al.* (2007), in a study of family firms in Denmark, report that their empirical results demonstrate that professional, non-family chief executive officers (CEOs) provide extremely valuable services to the organizations they head. On the other hand, they report that family CEO underperformance is particularly large in fast-growing industries, industries with a highly skilled labour force, and relatively large firms.

Bammens and Voordeckers (2009), in a study of family firms in Belgium, find that 'contrary to traditional agency wisdom, family firm boards devote substantial attention to controlling the management team . . . those family firms that employ trust and control in a complementary manner will be most effective'. Bammens *et al.* (2011) provide an interesting discussion on boards of directors in family businesses and the literature relating thereto.

Bennedsen *et al.* (2010) make the point that 'family firms are unique because the governance of these firms is determined by the governance of the family behind the family firm'. The International Finance Corporation (IFC) (2011) point out that 'family members' duty is not only limited to the governance of their company, they are also responsible for the governance of the family and its relationship with the business. Setting up a solid family governance system early in the lifecycle of the family will help anticipate and resolve potential conflicts among family members about issues. This will make it possible for family members to concentrate on other key issues such as growing the business.'

Franks *et al.* (2011) find that 'family firms evolve into widely held companies as they age only in countries with strong investor protection, well-developed financial markets and active markets for corporate control. In countries with weak investor protection, less developed financial markets and inactive markets for corporate control, family control is very persistent over time. This happens for both private and public firms'.

Smaller quoted companies

In the UK many firms with family control will be smaller quoted companies, either on the main market or on the UK's Alternative Investment Market (AIM), which can be seen as a way for smaller firms to obtain market recognition and access to external sources of finance, often before moving on to the main market.

The UK Corporate Governance Code 2010 forms part of the UK Listing Authority's Rules and is applicable to all UK listed companies. This means that there should be no distinction between the governance standards expected of larger and smaller companies. The UK Corporate Governance Code encourages smaller companies to adopt the Code's approach. However, in relation to smaller companies (those outside the FTSE 350), it states that they should have at least two independent non-executive directors (rather than half the board being independent non-executive directors, which is the requirement for larger companies); and also for listed companies outside the FTSE 350, it allows the company chairman to sit on, but not chair, the audit committee where he/she was considered independent on appointment.

The Quoted Companies Alliance (QCA), formerly the City Group for Smaller Companies (CISCO), is an association representing the interests of smaller companies and their advisors. The QCA fully embraces the principles of corporate governance contained in the UK Corporate Governance Code and advocates that these principles should be adopted by all public quoted companies in so far as it is practicable for their size. Over the years, the QCA has published guidance on corporate governance as follows: the QCA *Guidance for Smaller Companies* (2001), updated in 2004, urged smaller companies to comply with the Combined Code as far as they were able, but where they were unable to comply fully, then they should explain why they were unable to comply. The QCA Corporate Governance Committee

(2005, updated in 2007) published a corporate governance guide for AIM companies to help smaller companies seeking to develop their governance, or to meet the expectations of institutional investors. The 2007 QCA Guidelines have been superseded by a new publication, *Corporate Governance Guidelines for Smaller Quoted Companies* (the QCA Guidelines) published in September 2010. The QCA Guidelines take into account the UK Corporate Governance Code 2010.

The underlying theme behind the QCA Guidelines (2010) is that trust and transparency between an AIM company's board and its shareholders will reduce the need for more regulation. The QCA Guidelines promulgate four key elements to effective corporate governance: the chairman's responsibility for corporate governance, the board acting together as a team, the adoption of best practice corporate governance processes, and non-executive directors being truly independent. The independence of a board member should be defined according to the individual's approach to the role and his/her ability to behave independently and appropriately, rather than an absence of connections.

There has been relatively little research into aspects of corporate governance in small companies, with a few exceptions being Collier (1997) on audit committees in smaller listed companies, and Mallin and Ow-Yong (1998a, 1998b) on corporate governance in AIM companies and corporate governance in small companies on the main market. Mallin and Ow-Yong (2008) carried out a further study of corporate governance in AIM companies and highlighted a concern that 'with the rapid expansion of AIM and the increasing number of overseas companies, from countries whose culture of good governance may be weaker than that of the UK, a damaging financial scandal or collapse is only a matter of time'. They recommended that

> the role of the NOMAD [stet] [nominated advisor] be re-examined; the admission of overseas companies to AIM should be more closely scrutinized; small boards which may not be able to institute all the features of 'good' corporate governance should consider increasing the number of directors on their board, subject to resource constraints; and the regulatory authorities should monitor more closely the governance of AIM companies which have yet to start trading.

Mendoza (2008) analysed how AIM's regulatory regime has contributed to the success of low-cost listing stock exchanges. However, he argued that NOMADs as AIM's regulators may be questioned on the grounds that these entities are paid by the firms they counsel. On the other hand, he argues that it is in the NOMADs' interest to avoid any damage to their reputation which might then impact on their future business. He draws a number of conclusions about the future continued success of AIM including that the LSE should remain vigilant in overseeing the NOMADs and their client firms.

Mallin and Ow-Yong (2011a) highlighted potential shortcomings on AIM which might have ethical and governance implications but felt that, in general, the 'lighter touch' on corporate governance for AIM companies seems to be working quite well, with directors' own sense of best practice and investor expectation usually helping to ensure that appropriate governance practices are adopted. However, they conclude that 'potential ethical issues, whether relating to corporate governance shortcomings or due diligence pre or post listing, can largely be overcome by the more rigorous processes and reviews established recently by the LSE, and especially the monitoring mechanism of regular reviews of NOMADs'.

Another strand of the literature concentrates on firm-level characteristics that may serve to differentiate large and small firms. Larger firms tend to be more complex, whereas smaller firms adopt simpler systems and structures; smaller firms tend to have more concentrated leadership, whilst in a larger firm control may be more diffuse, or more subject to question by a larger board (Fama and Jensen 1983; Begley and Boyd 1987). In terms of the impact on corporate governance structures, it can be expected that in general, small and medium-sized firms will have simpler corporate governance structures than large firms—this may include: combining various of the key committees (audit, remuneration, nomination); a smaller number of non-executive directors (NEDs); a combined chair/CEO; longer contractual terms for directors due to the more difficult labour market for director appointments into small and medium-sized companies.

Mallin and Ow-Yong (2011b) examine the relationship between company, and ownership characteristics and the disclosure level of compliance with QCA recommendations on corporate governance in AIM companies. They find that compliance increases with company size, board size, the proportion of independent non-executive directors, the presence of turnover revenue, and being formerly listed on the Main Market. They find no evidence that ownership structure or the type of NOMAD is related to disclosure of compliance with QCA guidelines.

The role and importance of NEDs was emphasized in the Cadbury Report (1992) and in the Code of Best Practice it is stated that NEDs 'should bring an independent judgement to bear on issues of strategy, performance, resources, including key appointments, and standards of conduct' (para. 2.1). Similarly, the Hampel Report (1998) stated: 'Some smaller companies have claimed that they cannot find a sufficient number of independent non-executive directors of suitable calibre. This is a real difficulty, but the need for a robust independent voice on the board is as strong in smaller companies as in large ones' (para. 3.10). The importance of the NED selection process is also emphasized: they 'should be selected through a formal process and both this process and their appointment should be a matter for the board as a whole' (para. 2.4).

From Table 5.1, it can be seen that the areas where potential difficulties are most likely to arise tend to be those relating to the appointment of directors, particularly non-executive directors, which has implications for board structure. These differences arise partly because of the difficulties of attracting and retaining suitable non-executive directors in small companies.

Mallin and Ow-Yong (1998b) found that the most important attribute for small businesses when recruiting non-executive directors was their business skills and experience. Overall, the inference could be made that the ability to 'add value' to the business is the most important factor influencing NED appointments, which is in line with a study by Collier (1997). Similarly,

Table 5.1 Areas of the UK Corporate Governance Code that may prove difficult for smaller companies

UK Corporate Governance Code recommendations	Potential difficulty
Minimum two independent NEDs	Recruiting and remunerating independent NEDs
Split roles of chair/CEO	May not be enough directors to split the roles
Audit committee comprised of two NEDs	Audit committee may include executive directors
NEDs should be appointed for specific terms	NEDs often appointed for term

the Hampel Committee (1998) stated 'particularly in smaller companies, non-executive directors may contribute valuable expertise not otherwise available to management' (para. 3.8). However, many small companies do not have a nomination committee, and therefore non-executive director appointments are often made by the whole board. Interestingly, Mallin and Ow-Yong (2008) found that the factor that was considered to be most influential when making non-executive director appointments was considered to be 'objectivity and integrity' followed by 'relevant business skills and experience'. This perhaps highlights the impact of various corporate scandals and collapses in bringing to the fore the importance of these characteristics of objectivity and integrity.

In terms of the adoption of board committees, small companies tend to have adopted audit and remuneration committees fairly widely but not nomination committees. In some smaller companies, the committees may carry out combined roles where, for example, the remuneration and nomination committees are combined into one; often the board as a whole will carry out the function of the nomination committee rather than trying to establish a separate committee from a small pool of non-executive directors.

A word of caution should be sounded though in relation to quoted companies where there is still a large block of family ownership (or indeed any other form of controlling share-holder). Charkham and Simpson (1999) point out:

> The controlling shareholders' role as guardians is potentially compromised by their interest as managers. Caution is needed. The boards may be superb and they may therefore be fortunate enough to participate in a wonderful success, but such businesses can decline at an alarming rate so that the option of escape through what is frequently an illiquid market anyway may be unattractive.

The points made are twofold: first, that despite a good governance structure on paper, in practice, controlling shareholders may effectively be able to disenfranchise the minority shareholders; secondly, that in a family-owned business, or other business with a controlling shareholder, the option to sell one's shares may not be either attractive or viable at a given point in time.

Unlisted companies

European Confederation of Directors' Associations (ecoDa) Corporate Governance Guidance and Principles for Unlisted Companies in Europe 2010

In 2010 ecoDa issued the *Corporate Governance Guidance and Principles for Unlisted Companies in Europe*. The financial crisis highlighted the importance of good corporate governance including for unlisted enterprises many of which 'are owned and controlled by single individuals or coalitions of company insiders (e.g. a family). In many cases, owners continue to play a significant direct role in management. Good governance in this context is not a question of protecting the interests of absentee shareholders. Rather, it is concerned with establishing a framework of company processes and attitudes that add value to the business and help ensure its long-term continuity and success.'

The ecoDa Principles follow a phased approach with phase 1 principles, which represent a core framework of basic governance principles, applying to all unlisted companies, whatever their size; whilst phase 2 principles are those that are relevant to larger or more complex unlisted companies, or those with significant external funding. EcoDa highlights that the most important of the phase 2 principles is appointing independent directors to the board as 'it normally signals an irreversible step towards good governance and is likely to exert an immediate effect over the culture of boardroom behaviour'.

Phase 1 principles: Corporate governance principles applicable to all unlisted companies

- Principle 1—Shareholders should establish an appropriate constitutional and governance framework for the company.

- Principle 2—Every company should strive to establish an effective board, which is collectively responsible for the long-term success of the company, including the definition of the corporate strategy. However, an interim step on the road to an effective (and independent) board may be the creation of an advisory board.

- Principle 3—The size and composition of the board should reflect the scale and complexity of the company's activities.

- Principle 4—The board should meet sufficiently regularly to discharge its duties, and be supplied in a timely manner with appropriate information.

- Principle 5—Levels of remuneration should be sufficient to attract, retain, and motivate executives and non-executives of the quality required to run the company successfully.

- Principle 6—The board is responsible for risk oversight and should maintain a sound system of internal control to safeguard shareholders' investment and the company's assets.

- Principle 7—There should be a dialogue between the board and the shareholders based on the mutual understanding of objectives. The board as a whole has responsibility for ensuring that a satisfactory dialogue with shareholders takes place. The board should not forget that all shareholders have to be treated equally.

- Principle 8—All directors should receive induction on joining the board and should regularly update and refresh their skills and knowledge.

- Principle 9—Family-controlled companies should establish family governance mechanisms that promote coordination and mutual understanding amongst family members, as well as organize the relationship between family governance and corporate governance.

Phase 2 principles: Corporate governance principles applicable to large and/or more complex unlisted companies

- Principle 10—There should be a clear division of responsibilities at the head of the company between the running of the board and the running of the company's business. No one individual should have unfettered powers of decision.

- Principle 11—Board structures vary according to national regulatory requirements and business norms. However, all boards should contain directors with a sufficient mix of competencies and experiences. No single person (or small group of individuals) should dominate the board's decision-making.

- Principle 12—The board should establish appropriate board committees in order to allow a more effective discharge of its duties.

- Principle 13—The board should undertake a periodic appraisal of its own performance and that of each individual director.

- Principle 14—The board should present a balanced and understandable assessment of the company's position and prospects for external stakeholders, and establish a suitable programme of stakeholder engagement.

EcoDa states that 'the implementation of phase 2 principles is likely to increase the formality of governance arrangements. However, this is invariably a necessary step in larger or more complex enterprises in order to provide the necessary reassurance to owners or external creditors regarding the longer-term sustainability of the enterprise'.

Overall, the Principles provide a governance road map for family owners or founder-entrepreneurs as they look ahead to the life cycle of the business.

Corporate Governance Guidance and Principles for Unlisted Companies in the UK 2010

The ecoDa guidance discussed above has been adapted by the UK Institute of Directors for the UK business environment. The *Corporate Governance Guidance and Principles for Unlisted Companies in the UK* 2010 is based on the ecoDa guidance discussed in detail above and so the principles will not be outlined again here.

The rationale for this guidance in the UK is that the vast majority of the UK's 2.6 million registered companies are small or medium-sized enterprises or start-up companies which remain under the ownership and control of the founder or founding family. The Institute of Directors 'is convinced that appropriate corporate governance practices can contribute to the success of UK companies of all types and sizes, including those that are unlisted or privately held. . . . Unlisted companies—such as founder and family-owned businesses—can utilize this stepwise framework to ensure their long-term sustainability, to bring external parties to their boards, to attract funds, and to solve issues between shareholders and other stakeholders'.

Conclusions

In many countries, family-owned firms are prevalent. Corporate governance is of relevance to family-owned firms, which can encompass a number of business forms, including private and publicly quoted companies, for a number of reasons. Corporate governance structures can help the company to develop successfully; they can provide the means for defined lines of decision-making and accountability, enable the family firm to benefit from the contribution of independent non-executive directors, and help ensure a more transparent and fair approach to the way the business is organized and managed. Family-owned firms may face difficulties in initially finding appropriate independent non-executive directors, but the benefits that such directors can bring is worth the time and financial investment that the family-owned firm will need to make.

Summary

- Family ownership of firms is the prevalent form of ownership in many countries around the globe.

- The legal system of a country tends to influence the type of ownership that develops, so that in common law countries with good protection for minority shareholders' rights, the shareholder base is more diverse, whereas in civil law countries with poor protection for minority shareholders' rights, there tends to be more family ownership and control.

- The governance structure of a family firm may develop in various stages, such as starting with a family assembly, then a family council, advisory board, and, finally, a defined board structure with independent non-executive directors.

- The advantages to the family firm of a sound governance structure are that it can provide a mechanism for defined lines of decision-making and accountability, enable the family firm to benefit from the contribution of independent non-executive directors, and help ensure a more transparent and fair approach to the way the business is organized and managed.

- The ecoDa *Corporate Governance Guidance and Principles for Unlisted Companies in Europe* 2010 provides a phased framework of corporate governance guidance for unlisted companies.

Example: Cadbury Plc, UK

This is an example of a family firm that grew over time, developed an appropriate governance structure, and became an international business.

Today, Cadbury is a household name in homes across the world. It was founded in the first part of the nineteenth century when John Cadbury decided to establish a business based on the manufacture and marketing of cocoa. His two sons joined the firm in 1861 and, over the years, more family members joined, and subsequently the firm became a private limited liability company, Cadbury Brothers Ltd. A board of directors was formed consisting of members of the family.

Non-family directors were first appointed to the firm in 1943, and in 1962, the firm became a publicly quoted company with the family members still being the majority on the board and holding a controlling interest (50 per cent plus) in the shares. Cadbury merged with Schweppes in the late 1960s, and over the next 40 years, Cadbury Schweppes developed a diverse shareholder base and a board of directors appointed from the wider business community. The direct family involvement, via either large shareholdings or board membership, therefore declined over the years. In the spring of 2007, Cadbury Schweppes revealed plans to split its business into two separate entities: one focusing on its main chocolate and confectionery market; the other on its US drinks business. The demerger took effect in May 2008 so that Cadbury Schweppes Plc became Cadbury Plc (focusing on the former market) and Dr Pepper Snapple Group Inc. (focusing on the US drinks business).

In 2009 Kraft launched a hostile takeover bid for Cadbury. Cadbury decided to fight to retain its independence but the firm's shareholders eventually accepted Kraft's hostile takeover and accepted a bid of £11.5 billion in January 2010.

Kraft's purchase was hugely controversial given that Cadbury is viewed as a great British institution. Unfortunately, once the sale went through, Kraft closed Cadbury's Somerdale factory near Bristol, with a loss of 400 jobs. In 2011 Kraft announced that another 200 jobs were being cut through voluntary redundancies and redeployment, though it has also announced a £50 million investment in the business. In 2012 a twist to the tale is that the great-granddaughter of the founder of Cadbury has decided to set up her own chocolate business.

Example: Hutchison Whampoa, Hong Kong

This is an example of an international company where there is controlling ownership by a family via a pyramid shareholding.

Hutchison Whampoa is a multinational conglomerate with five core businesses, including ports and related services, property and hotels, telecommunications, retail and manufacturing, energy, and infrastructure. It ranks as one of the most valuable companies in Hong Kong and a large proportion of it is controlled by Cheung Kong Holdings in which the Li Ka Shing family has a significant interest, which means that the family has significant influence over both companies, one through direct ownership, the other via an indirect, or pyramid, shareholding.

Hutchison Whampoa has, for many years, been the recipient of various awards and accolades. In 2005 it was voted the best-managed company in Hong Kong in a poll of institutional investors and equity analysts carried out for the Finance Asia annual awards. In the same poll, it was voted Asia's Best Conglomerate and its Chief Finance Officer (CFO) received the 'Best CFO Award' in Hong Kong. The Hong Kong Institute of Certified Public Accountants awarded its 'Significant Improvement Award' in the Hang Seng Index Category to Hutchison Whampoa in 2005 for its 'very clear and positive approach to upgrading its corporate governance practice'. Whilst having a controlling family interest, Hutchison Whampoa is committed to good corporate governance and to its wider shareholder base. In 2008 it was recognized by Corporate Governance Asia as one of 'The Best of Asia', that is one of 'Asia's Best Companies for Corporate Governance'. More recently in 2011, its awards included the following: Asiamoney 'Best Managed Company Awards: Hong Kong—Large-cap Corporate of the Year in Hong Kong'; and Corporate Governance Asia 'Asia's Best CFO (Mr Frank Sixt)', 'Asia's Best CSR' and 'Best Investor Relations by Hong Kong Company'. So far in 2012 it has been awarded the Hong Kong Council of Social Service '5 Years Plus Caring Company Award 2011/12'.

Mini case study   Fiat, Italy

This is a good example of a firm where the founding family still has significant influence through a complex shareholding structure.

Fabbrica Italiana Automobili Torino, better known as Fiat, was founded in 1899 by a group of investors including Giovanni Agnelli. Fiat automobiles were immediately popular not just in Italy but internationally too. Fiat expanded rapidly in the 1950s and, in 1966, the founder's grandson, also Giovanni Agnelli, became the company's Chairman. As well as cars, Fiat's business empire included commercial vehicles, agricultural, and construction equipment, insurance, aviation, the press, electric power, and natural gas distribution. In past years, it has achieved enormous financial success.

More than 90 per cent of Italian-registered companies are family owned, with many companies being run by Italian families who wield great power. Traditionally, control has been achieved, often with the minimum of capital outlay, through a complex structure involving a series of holding companies. In the case of Fiat, control by the Agnelli family is via pyramids (indirect holdings) and voting trusts particularly Ifi (a financial holding company) in which the Agnelli family has control of all the votes.

By 2002 Fiat had significant financial problems with losses of US$1.2 billion in that year. General Motors, which had acquired a 20 per cent shareholding in Fiat at a cost of US$2.4 billion, was asked to invest further in Fiat but was reluctant to do so. In 2003 the group restructured its core business area by again focusing manufacturing and service activities on the traditional motor vehicle sector.

In 2003 Umberto Agnelli died, and in 2004, Luca Cordero di Montezemolo was nominated as Chairman. Also in 2004 Sergio Marchionne was appointed as Chief Executive of Fiat and this marked a turning point in the company's fortunes. An astute and experienced businessman, Mr Marchionne oversaw changes to various areas of the Fiat business. At the beginning of 2005 Fiat announced the creation of Fiat Powertrain Technologies, a new industrial unit designed to integrate the groups' innovation capabilities and expertise in engines and transmissions. In February 2005 the boards of directors of Fiat and General Motors met to approve a contract to terminate the master agreement and related joint ventures between the two companies. The Chairman of Fiat, Luca Cordero di Montezemolo, said:

> We are delighted to have been able to conclude this agreement with General Motors. While highly beneficial to both Fiat and GM since 2000, the arrangements had become too confining for the development of Fiat Auto in today's market environment. We now have all the necessary freedom to develop strategic growth alternatives for Fiat Auto, while retaining a base on which to build a much more constructive relationship with GM in the future.

There were also important changes to Fiat's corporate governance structure in June 2005, with Fiat extending its board of directors to 15 members, so that the board comprised a majority of independent non-executive directors. At the same time, Fiat strengthened its independence requirements for directors. In its press release, it stated:

> After a thorough review of current international practice on this issue, the Company has adopted a set of criteria which are designed to ensure that the independence qualification is held to the highest possible standard. As an example, directors who have served on the Board for more than nine years, even though not consecutively, are deemed not to be independent. Furthermore, board members who are executive directors of other companies on whose board[s] sit executive board members of Fiat are also deemed not to be independent.

In January 2006 Fiat announced another significant strategic change with the signing of an agreement to cooperate on dealer networks with Tata Motors Ltd, which meant that Fiat cars could be distributed via the Tata network in India. Late in January 2006 Fiat announced that it had seen its first positive quarterly trading profit after 17 successive quarters of losses.

With the revision of Italian corporate governance provisions, the Fiat Group adopted and abides by the Corporate Governance Code of Italian Listed Companies issued in March 2006. Fiat provides information regarding how it meets the individual principles and criteria of the Corporate Governance Code by providing a reprise of the individual principles and criteria, and then summarizing how each of these is implemented at Fiat.

2006 saw the strengthening of Fiat's presence in Europe and the gaining of access into markets, including China, India, and Russia. In 2007 Sergio Marchionne announced the 2007–10 plan geared towards growth. In 2009 he unveiled his plan to put Fiat at the heart of the car-making industry globally by forging an alliance with the giant troubled US car manufacturers Chrysler and General Motors (Opel, the European arm). In June 2009 Fiat and Chrysler announced that they had finalized a global strategic partnership to begin immediately. The ultimate success of the alliance will depend on many factors and will likely have implications for the workforces in the various countries affected, including Germany and the UK.

In December 2011 Fiat made a groundbreaking deal with the Italian trade unions, which gives it more flexibility in labour contracts in exchange for a rise in wages. By early 2012 Fiat and Chrysler together were selling more than four million cars. Fiat adheres to the new Corporate Governance Code for Italian Listed Companies issued in December 2011. Its Corporate Governance Report is divided into four sections: a description of the governance structure; information on the ownership structure; an analysis of the implementation of the Code and a description of the principal characteristics of the system of risk management and internal control over financial reporting, in addition to the principal governance practices implemented; and a summary tables and corporate governance documents for the Fiat Group, as well as a side-by-side comparison showing the principles of the Code and how they have been implemented.

Questions

The discussion questions to follow cover the key learning points of this chapter. Reading of some of the additional reference material will enhance the depth of the students' knowledge and understanding of these areas.

1. What are the key factors affecting the ownership structure of businesses in different countries, and how might these impact on the development of a business?
2. What are the advantages and disadvantages of a family-owned firm?
3. How might the corporate governance structure in a family firm develop?
4. Critically discuss the value of a board, including the contribution to the family firm that may be made by independent non-executive directors.
5. 'The need for a professional business approach is arguably even greater in a family than in a non-family firm' (Sir Adrian Cadbury, 2000). Critically discuss this statement.
6. What advantages would a good governance structure bring to a family-owned firm?

References

Bammens, Y. and Voordeckers, W. (2009), 'The Board's Control Tasks in Family Firms', in *The Value Creating Board*, M. Huse (ed.), Routledge, London.

——— and Van Gils A. (2011) 'Boards of Directors in Family Businesses: A Literature Review and Research Agenda', *International Journal of Management Reviews*, Vol.13, Issue 2, pp. 134–52.

Begley, T.M. and Boyd, D.P. (1987), 'Psychological Characteristics Associated with Performance in Entrepreneurial Firms and Smaller Businesses', *Journal of Business Venturing*, Vol. 2, No. 1.

Bennedsen, M., Nielsen, K.M., Perez-Gonzalez, F., and Wolfenzon, D. (2007), 'Inside the Family Firm: The Role of Families in Succession Decisions and Performance', *Quarterly Journal of Economics*, 122(2), pp. 647–91.

——, Pérez-González F., and Wolfenzon, D. (2010), 'The Governance of Family Firms', in H. Kent Baker and R. Anderson (eds), *Corporate Governance, A Synthesis of Theory, Research and Practice*, The Robert W. Kolb Series in Finance, John Wiley & Sons Inc., New Jersey.

Cadbury, Sir Adrian (1992), *Report of the Committee on the Financial Aspects of Corporate Governance*, Gee & Co. Ltd, London.

—— (2000), *Family Firms and their Governance: Creating Tomorrow's Company from Today's*, Egon Zehnder International, London.

Charkham, J. and Simpson, A. (1999), *Fair Shares: The Future of Shareholder Power and Responsibility*, Oxford University Press, Oxford.

Collier, P. (1997), 'Audit Committees in Smaller Listed Companies' in *Corporate Governance: Responsibilities, Risks and Remuneration*, K. Keasey and M. Wright (eds), John Wiley & Sons, London.

Combined Code (2008), *The Combined Code on Corporate Governance*, Financial Reporting Council, London.

ecoDa (2010), *ecoDa Corporate Governance Guidance and Principles for Unlisted Companies in Europe*, ecoDa, Brussels.

Fama, E.F. and Jensen, M.C. (1983), 'Separation of Ownership and Control', *Journal of Law and Economics*, Vol. 26.

Franks, J.R., Mayer, C., and Rossi, S. (2004), 'Spending Less Time with the Family: The Decline of Family Ownership in the UK', ECGI—*Finance Working Paper No.35/2004*.

Franks, J.R., Mayer, C., and Rossi, S. (2005), 'Ownership: Evolution and Regulation', ECGI—*Finance Working Paper No.09/2003*.

Franks, J. R., Mayer, C., Volpin, P. F., and Wagner, H. F. (2011), 'The Life Cycle of Family Ownership: International Evidence' (September 2, 2011). Paris December 2011 Finance Meeting EUROFIDAI—AFFI. Available at SSRN: http://ssrn.com/abstract=1102475 or http://dx.doi.org/10.2139/ssrn.1102475

Hampel, Sir Ronnie (1998), *Committee on Corporate Governance: Final Report*, Gee & Co. Ltd., London.

Institute of Directors (2010) *Corporate Governance Guidance and Principles for Unlisted Companies in the UK*, Institute of Directors, London.

IFC (2011) *IFC Family Business Governance Handbook*, IFC, Washington DC.

La Porta, R., Lopez-de-Silanes, F., Shleifer, A., and Vishny, R. (1999), 'Corporate Ownership Around the World', *Journal of Finance*, Vol. 54.

Mallin, C.A. and Ow-Yong, K. (1998a), 'Corporate Governance in Small Companies: the Alternative Investment Market', *Corporate Governance An International Review*, September 1998.

——— (1998b), *Corporate Governance in Small Companies on the Main Market*, ICAEW Research Board, ICAEW, London.

——— (2008), *Corporate Governance in Alternative Investment Market (AIM) Companies*, Institute of Chartered Accountants of Scotland, Edinburgh.

——— (2011a), 'The UK Alternative Investment Market–Ethical Dimensions' *Journal of Business Ethics*, Vol. 95, Issue 2 (2011), pp. 223–39.

—— (2011b), 'Factors Influencing Corporate Governance Disclosures in Alternative Investment Market (AIM) Companies', *European Journal of Finance*, available at Vol. 18(16), 515–33.

Mendoza, J.M. (2008), 'Securities Regulation in Low-Tier Listing Venues: The Rise of the Alternative Investment Market', *Fordham Journal of Corporate & Financial Law*, X111, 257–328.

Morck, R. and Yeung, B. (2003), 'Agency Problems in Large Family Business Groups', *Entrepreneurship: Theory and Practice*, Summer, Vol. 27, No. 4.

Neubauer, F. and Lank, A.G. (1998), *The Family Business: Its Governance for Sustainability*, Macmillan, Basingstoke.

QCA (2001), *Guidance for Smaller Companies*, QCA, London.

—— (2005), *Corporate Governance Guidelines for AIM Companies*, QCA, London.

—— (2007), *Corporate Governance Guidelines for AIM Companies*, QCA, London.

—— (2010) *Corporate Governance Guidelines for Smaller Quoted Companies*, QCA, London.

Useful websites

http://rru.worldbank.org The website of the Rapid Response Unit of the World Bank has matters of interest to a range of companies and countries.

www.ecgi.org The website of the European Corporate Governance Institute has details of recent research into family-owned firms and their governance.

www.ecoda.org The website of The European Confederation of Directors' Associations where information can be found about their activities relating to representing the views of company directors from EU Member States to corporate governance policy-makers at EU level.

www.fbn-i.org The Family Business Network website has items of interest to family businesses.

www.financeasia.com The website of FinanceAsia has information relating to various matters, including corporate governance, of particular interest to firms and investors in Asia.

www.ifb.org.uk The website of the Institute for Family Business, with an emphasis on the UK, has items of interest to family businesses.

www.iod.com The website of the Institute of Directors where information can be found about its activities in support of business including corporate governance.

www.theqca.com The website of the Quoted Companies Alliance has items of particular interest to companies outside the UK's FTSE 350.

 For further links to useful sources of information visit the Online Resource Centre **www.oxfordtextbooks.co.uk/orc/mallin4e/**

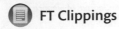 FT Clippings

FT: Kwok brothers row escalates after arrests

By Rahul Jacob in Hong Kong

May 13, 2012

When Walter Kwok lost a court battle in May 2008 to prevent his removal as chief executive by the board of Sun Hung Kai Properties, Hong Kong's largest property developer, he suggested a cease in hostilities.

His two younger brothers, Thomas and Raymond, had wanted him demoted, claiming he suffered from bipolar disorder. Walter, 61, then wrote a letter to the board of the family-owned company that said: "We three are brothers. Why should we keep fighting each other?" The desire for peace between him and his two younger siblings proved brief. In 2010 Walter's share of the family trust, which owns the 42 per cent family stake in the company with a market capitalisation of $30bn, was transferred to his family by his mother.

On May 3, however, when Hong Kong's Independent Commission Against Corruption arrested Walter before releasing him on bail, the brothers might have had reason to unite. Just weeks earlier, Thomas, 60, and Raymond, 58, had themselves been arrested and released on bail under Hong Kong's prevention of bribery ordinance that also included the arrest of a former head of the civil service, Rafael Hui.

The arrests sent shockwaves up the more than 100 floors of the gleaming ICC Tower that is owned by Sun Hung Kai and dominates Hong Kong's skyline today. The investigation is likely to come to a climax in the next few weeks, if and when the brothers are charged. But few expect a truce between Walter and his younger brothers.

It is not clear whether Walter was a source of information for the investigation. Mr Kwok's representative refused to comment. In 2008, one of the issues of contention involved enquiries launched by Walter into "why construction contracts were frequently awarded by SHKP to a select number of contractors".

His brothers in turn alleged he unilaterally made decisions, especially in the company's business in mainland China, without informing them or the board. Walter denies being bipolar. This pattern of "he says, they say" is likely to escalate if Hong Kong's anti-corruption agency bring charges against Thomas and Raymond in the next few weeks.

Raymond and Thomas, whose properties include a bizarre theme park that is a replica of Noah's Ark, have denied any wrongdoing. On April 3, days after they were released on bail, Thomas, who is a co-chairman of the company with Raymond, said, "Don't worry. Here at SHKP it's business as usual." The stock market has been less sanguine; Sun Hung Kai has lost a fifth of its value since March 29. Rafael Hui, who was arrested on the same day as the younger Kwoks, happens to be a long-time friend of the Kwoks who worked briefly for the company before he was elevated to Hong Kong's chief secretary, the city's second most powerful official, between 2005 and 2007.

Mr Hui, 64, made his way up the colonial civil service before leaving to head the territory's provident fund company. He then worked for the Kwoks before returning to the government as political appointee in 2005. One retired senior government official, who Mr Hui worked with closely for a number of years, says: "Rafael told me that the Kwoks' mother looked to him to give the brothers advice." Ronny Tong, a local legislator, recalls Mr Hui lobbying him and other legislators when he was working for the Kwoks before he was reappointed to the government as head of the civil service in 2005.

Mr Hui was allegedly the beneficiary of large unsecured loans and the rent-free use of a flat in a luxury development owned by Sun Hung Kai, according to reports published in the Chinese language press in Hong Kong.

Mr Hui has not publicly made any statements since his release on bail and the Kwoks have not commented on the details of the case. Under the city's bribery ordinance, the ICAC would have to link charges of corruption to "some official duty Hui performed or chose not to perform," says Mr Tong, the legislator and former chairman of the bar association in Hong Kong. "The linkage could be fairly tenuous." At an ICAC conference this month, its director Timothy Tong said there had been a shift towards public officials using and abusing public office to obtain a private benefit.

The comment captured the public mood. In the past few months, Hong Kong has been witness to outrage over revelations of an illegal basement of more than 2000 sq ft in the home of Henry Tang that derailed his campaign to become the city's top official in July and trips by the city's current de facto mayor, Donald Tsang, to Phuket on a tycoon's plane.

For both the ICAC and the Kwoks, however, this tussle could be damaging.

Mr Tong may be in tune with the public mood in Hong Kong, but the ICAC is under the microscope as well. "It is inappropriate to arrest, release the news to the public and then sit back and not charge anyone forthwith," says a lawyer, who is likely to represent one of the defendants.

Only two of the Kwok brothers' 10 children work in the company and they are in their twenties and are regarded as too inexperienced to take over the company if Raymond and Thomas are charged.

"Of course, if the Kwoks are charged, acquisitions and major decisions will be affected," says analyst Sylvia Wong of UOB Kay Hian, dismissing the business-as-usual line of the brothers. "Come on, it's a family-run company."

FT: Beyond the family boardroom

By Andrew Hill

March 11, 2012

When Cristina Stenbeck chairs meetings of Investment AB Kinnevik's board she wields a gavel that dates from the early days of the 75-year-old Swedish holding company. She is watched over by three portraits, including one of her father, Jan, with one of his basset hounds.

History, family and family history are three threads that run through the 34-year-old's stewardship of a global business with investments ranging from packaging to telecoms to microfinance.

"There is a real respect and regard for our heritage," she says, sitting in her offices off London's Piccadilly. But while Ms Stenbeck led last year's 75th anniversary celebrations and oversaw production of a short film about the group, she insists that, far from looking back over her shoulder, she is moving the group forwards in her own way, with her own style.

It was Jan Stenbeck's sudden death, aged 59, nearly 10 years ago that thrust his then 24-year-old daughter into the role of de facto steward of the family's interests and eventual successor as chairman of the group. Her father, himself the son of the founder, had prepared her for the job. Informal chats about the importance of their business legacy started when she was six, at the family home on Long Island, New York. "I joined the board at 19, and I think I always expressed interest in the businesses, and certainly in his role in building them," she says, in the measured tone of a Swede and the accent of an American.

But the fact she had to take up the reins so soon came as a shock – to her, and to investors in the separately listed, Kinnevik-controlled companies Mr Stenbeck had formed and chaired.

"There were lots of people who had great expectations. They'd signed up for a 59-year-old serial entrepreneur who had been breaking monopolies and building over 200 business since the '80s, and they got 24-year-old me. So, of course, there was a disconnect in terms of what certain individuals wanted to do and where they wanted to take their businesses," she says.

Disconnect understates it. The shares of the companies did not collapse, but there was speculation about the stability of the web of interests and cross-holdings Mr Stenbeck had assembled, and fears of infighting among his favourites. Ms Stenbeck initially had no formal role other than one directorship. The Swedish press dubbed her "Queen Cristina" but held her lack of experience—two years working at Polo Ralph Lauren in New York—against her.

But Hans-Holger Albrecht, who has worked for group companies under both Stenbecks since 1997 and now runs Modern Times Group, a Kinnevik-controlled broadcaster, says she knew "what was good for the owner and major shareholder: that was quite impressive from the first moment".

Ms Stenbeck says "the importance of active ownership" is one clear message, learnt from her father, that she will pass on to her children. "The lesson is to step forward and take responsibility for our significant ownership. That's all. Not to put it in the hands of lawyers and others." Another lesson is to "surround yourself with smart people, who are willing to give you time and to give the businesses their expertise". Mia Brunell Livfors, Kinnevik's chief executive, runs the group day-to-day, but Ms

Stenbeck—who speaks for 35.1 per cent of the votes and 9.1 per cent of the capital through a private Luxembourg vehicle—describes herself as "very hands-on". Having stepped up to chair the holding company in 2007, she exercises her influence through the portfolio companies' boards and nomination committees, on which the largest investors in Swedish companies sit. Some families delegate that duty, but not the Stenbecks: "I do it myself because I think it's a great way to recruit outside people . . . who understand what it is we're looking for, the importance of cultural fit, competence, that kind of thing." With a fortune estimated by The Sunday Times at £350m and a comfortable life in the UK with her British husband and family, could she not just sit back, like many third-generation heirs? She responds politely, but firmly: "I could. I could maybe just be a board director. I could sit on the [boards of] family businesses. But I don't. There's lots to do."

Kinnevik-controlled companies are pressing forward in emerging markets—both digital and geographic. The group holds a stake in Groupon, the online discount company, directly and through quarter-owned Rocket Internet, which is incubating other online companies. Meanwhile, she says the group has a long-term vision for Millicom, the mobile phone company it controls, and microfinance and media units in high-growth regions such as Africa, Latin America and Russia. She uses her privileged position as "the owner" to open doors for group companies to discuss regulation with heads of state—she recently brokered a meeting with Colombia's president—or to pave the way for deals with oligarchs. She is plainly happy that the old accusation of inexperience no longer stands up: "That's shown itself to be less of an issue with age and the performances of the businesses." Kinnevik, like its chairman, is now a more mature, more international group than it was 10 years ago—with all the regulatory responsibilities that entails. Ms Stenbeck has made the once-opaque group structure more transparent, while keeping a low profile herself. She bridles at the suggestion she was treated as heir to the throne and indeed, her style—courteous and self-assured but unassuming—is far from regal. In the boardroom, too, she says she is "very open and straightforward . . . I have lots of conversations". Fellow directors agree.

As for being compared with her father, she quite likes that, though recognises differences in their approaches. Mr Stenbeck founded all the businesses with the exception of Kinnevik and famously courted controversy, for instance by challenging the Swedish TV monopoly by broadcasting from the UK. "There is the difference between [a] founder-entrepreneur, and the next generation…But in terms of my personal engagement, it's very much the same. It's knowing the people that run the businesses, it's knowing the entrepreneurs out in the markets and it's spending time looking at the risks but also the rewards." The strongest charge against Ms Stenbeck these days may be that she is not adventurous enough. Maintaining an average annual total return of 20 per cent for shareholders over the past 30 years is harder as the group gets bigger. Dividends continue to increase, but the shares have returned 5 per cent annually over the past five years and Kinnevik suffers the curse of all holding companies: the stock trades at a wide discount to the value of its underlying investments. She agrees she must communicate more to investors how Kinnevik is taking cash from telecoms and investing it in e-commerce, just as Mr Stenbeck once took cash from the forestry, pulp and paper business to seed longer-term bets on telecoms. To some degree, she too is leading the group into the unknown. Does she sometimes feel a need to ask her father's permission? Ms Stenbeck recalls how last year, she and fellow directors of Tele2, the Kinnevik-controlled telecoms

group, met in the holding company's boardroom in Stockholm to discuss a potential €460m investment in Kazakhstan—arguably more ambitious than anything her father attempted. When the panelling was folded back for the slide presentation, she could see only one portrait: her father and his faithful hound. "I just caught his eye, and the dog's eye, [and thought] 'Definitely, we're going to go'." Were they endorsing the decision? She laughs: "I didn't look long enough to figure that out."

The CV

- Born:1977 in New York
- Nationality: Swedish/American
- Education: 2000 Bachelor of Science, Georgetown University
- Employment: 2000-02 Polo Ralph Lauren Corporation, New York
- 1997 Member of the board of directors at Invik and Co
- 2003 Joins the board of various Kinnevik-controlled companies
- 2003-07 Vice-chairman of Investment AB Kinnevik
- 2007 Becomes chairman
- Other appointments:
- Chairman of Playing for Change Foundation, a group-wide campaign to promote social entrepreneurship and innovation through identifying and supporting talented youth in key strategic markets such as Sweden, Ghana and Russia
- Board of Stenbeck Foundation
- Board of Trustees of St. Andrew's School, Delaware, US
- Founder's Council of Blue Marine Foundation
- Family: lives in London with husband and three daughters
- Interests: supporter of charities including the Eve Appeal, the Prince's Foundation and Great Ormond Street children's hospital

The Role of Institutional Investors in Corporate Governance

Learning Objectives

- To appreciate who institutional investors are
- To understand the growing influence of institutional investors and why they are increasingly interested in corporate governance
- To realize the importance of institutional investors' relationships with their investee companies and the role of stewardship
- To be aware of the 'tools of governance' that institutional investors have available to them
- To be able to assess the potential impact of 'good' corporate governance on corporate performance

Introduction

The potential influence of large shareholders was identified back in the 1930s when Berle and Means (1932) highlighted the separation of the owners (shareholders) from the control of the business, 'control' being in the hands of the directors. This separation of ownership and control leads to the problems associated with agency theory, so that the managers of the business may not act in the best interests of the owners. Throughout the twentieth century, the pattern of ownership continued to change and, in the USA and UK in particular, individual share ownership has declined and institutional share ownership has increased. Over eighty years later, institutional investors own large portions of equity in many companies across the world, and the key role played by institutional investors in corporate governance cannot be underestimated. With the internationalization of cross-border portfolios, and the financial crises that have occurred in many parts of the world, it is perhaps not surprising that institutional investors increasingly look more carefully at the corporate governance of companies. After all, corporate governance goes hand in hand with increased transparency and accountability. In this chapter, the rise of the institutional investors and their role in corporate governance is examined.

Growth of institutional share ownership

In the UK the level of share ownership by individuals has decreased over the last forty years, whilst ownership by institutional investors has increased. These institutional investors have traditionally comprised mainly pension funds and insurance companies, although newer types of investor, including hedge funds (included in the 'Other financial institutions' category below) are now gaining more foothold. The nature of the changing composition of the UK shareholder base is summarized in Table 6.1.

In 1963 individual investors owned 54 per cent of shares in the UK. The proportion of shares owned by this group fell steadily until, by 1989, it had dropped to just under 21 per cent. Since 1989 there have been a few factors that should have encouraged individual share ownership. First, there were the large privatization issues that occurred in the UK in the early 1990s, and, in more recent years, the demutualization of some of the large building societies. However, by 2010, the percentage had dropped to 11.5 per cent.

In contrast to the individual investors' level of share ownership, the ownership of shares by the insurance companies and the pension funds increased dramatically over the same period to 13.4 per cent and 12.8 per cent respectively in 2008. However, the latest ONS (2012) survey of share ownership, which gives statistics as at the end of December 2010, shows that the relative percentages owned by these two groups have fallen to their lowest level since the share ownership survey began in 1963, with 8.6 per cent and 5.1 per cent for insurance companies and pension funds respectively. This might reflect insurance companies switching from UK equities to alternative investments, whilst pension fund managers have broadened their portfolios attempting to obtain higher returns and to spread risk. However, it is important to note that the ONS have changed their methodology for their 2012 survey—for example, by updating the sector analysis for pooled nominee accounts—and this has had a large impact on the results, and they caution that this should be taken into account when making comparisons with earlier years. Nonetheless, insurance companies and pension funds retain their influence as key institutional investors in the corporate governance of their investee companies. There has also been a notable increase in the overseas level of ownership—this is particularly noteworthy because it has increased from 7 per cent in 1963 to 41.2 per cent in

Table 6.1 Summary of main categories of share ownership in the UK 1963–2010

Type of investor	1963	2010
	%	%
Individuals	54	11.5
Insurance companies	10	8.6
Pension funds	6	5.1
Unit trusts	1	6.7
Other financial institutions	11.3	16.0
Overseas	7	41.2

Source: *Ownership of UK Quoted Shares 2010* (Office for National Statistics (ONS), 2012)

(Other categories owning shares include banks, investment trusts, public sector, private non-financial companies, and charities)

2010. Many of the overseas holdings are US investors (56 per cent), with the other large hold-ings being European (28 per cent), and Asian (11 per cent). The US institutional investors tend to be much more proactive in corporate governance and this stance has started to influence the behaviour of both UK institutional investors and UK companies. The extent of institu-tional share ownership can be seen quite clearly in Figure 6.1, which shows the beneficial ownership of UK shares at the end of 2010. Similarly, the influence of overseas investors on corporate UK is shown by their level of equity ownership.

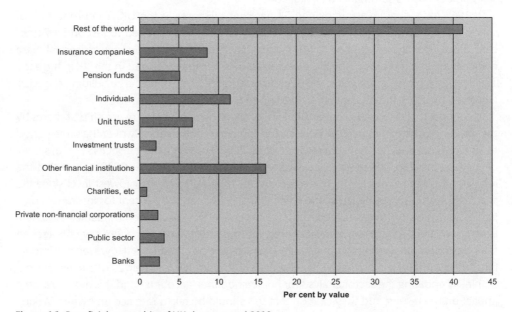

Figure 6.1 Beneficial ownership of UK shares at end 2010

Influence of institutional investors

Given the size of their shareholdings, the power of the institutional investors cannot be doubted. In his seminal work, Hirschman (1970) identified the exercise of institutional power within an 'exit and voice' framework, arguing that 'dissatisfaction [may be expressed] directly to management' (the *voice* option) or by selling the shareholding (the *exit* option). The latter choice is not viable for many institutional investors given the size of their holdings or a policy of holding a balanced portfolio.

The Cadbury Committee (1992) viewed institutional investors as having a special respon-sibility to try to ensure that its recommendations were adopted by companies, stating that 'we look to the institutions in particular . . . to use their influence as owners to ensure that the companies in which they have invested comply with the Code'. A similar view was expressed in the Greenbury Report (1995), as one of the main action points is 'the investor institutions should use their power and influence to ensure the implementation of best practice as set out in the Code'. Similarly, in the Hampel Report (1998), it states 'it is clear . . . that a discus-sion of the role of shareholders in corporate governance will mainly concern the institutions'.

Therefore, three influential committees, which have reported on corporate governance in the UK, have clearly emphasized the role of institutional investors. The institutional investors' potential to exert significant influence on companies has clear implications for corporate governance, especially in terms of the standards of corporate governance and issues concerned with enforcement. Until the revision of the Combined Code in 2010, the Combined Code included principles of good governance relating to institutional shareholders. However, when the Combined Code was revised and renamed the UK Corporate Governance Code in 2010, the section on institutional shareholders was removed and a new UK Stewardship Code was introduced (discussed later).

In 2002 Hermes, a large and influential institutional investor based in the UK, issued *The Hermes Principles*. The first principle was that 'companies should seek an honest, open and ongoing dialogue with shareholders'. This clearly reflects Hermes' intention to have a dialogue with its investee companies. Similarly, in *The Hermes Corporate Governance Principles* (2006), global principle 3 relating to the board of directors, states that 'the board is responsible for facilitating a satisfactory dialogue with the shareholders'. In 2010 Hermes published *The Hermes Responsible Ownership Principles* detailing what they expect of listed companies and what listed companies can expect from them. Hermes' expectations of listed companies encompass 12 principles relating to transparency and communication; corporate culture; strategy; financial disciplines and structure, and risk management; stakeholders, environmental and social issues; and governance. In turn, listed companies can expect five core principles of stewardship and engagement that Hermes feels responsible shareholders ought to observe. These are a clearly communicated set of expectations on investor communications, corporate culture, operations, strategy, financial disciplines and structure, sustainability and governance; a consistent approach; a thorough understanding of markets and companies around the world; a long-term perspective when exercising ownership rights; and a constructive, confidential dialogue with boards and senior management.

The perception of the key role to be played by institutional investors is not purely a UK phenomenon. Useem (1996) detailed the rise of 'investor capitalism' in the USA and described how the concentration of shares, and hence power, into a relatively small number of hands, has enabled institutional investors to challenge management directly on issues of concern. Monks (2001) identified 'global investors' as being

> the public and private pension funds of the US, UK, Netherlands, Canada, Australia and Japan. Through extrapolating the specific holding of a number of the largest pension schemes, we conclude that the level of ownership in virtually all publicly quoted companies in the world is large enough to permit the effective involvement of owners in the governance of those corporations.

Similarly, in the context of the Australian market, Bosch (1993) stated that 'institutional shareholders because of their increasing influence, by virtue of their size, should take an active interest in the governance of the Company and develop their own principles of good practice'.

This emphasis is to be expected from countries such as the USA, UK, and Australia, which all have a significant concentration of share ownership in the hands of institutional investors. However, the Centre for European Policy Studies (CEPS) 1995 report stated that 'in any attempt to understand the control of corporations, the role of insurance companies, pension funds, and other institutional investors, and other actors, such as employees or banks, has to be taken into account to different extents in European countries'. The report goes on to state:

> International diversification and increasing cross-border activity of institutional investors will accelerate this process. American and British pension funds, in particular, which represent about 72 per cent of total pension fund assets in the western world, can be instrumental in changing corporate governance standards as a result of the active stance towards investment that is required by local laws and codes.

The aspect of foreign share ownership should not be underestimated, as these 'new' investors in Europe will tend to be institutional investors from the USA, the UK, and other countries. The large proportion of institutional share ownership in both the USA (where around 55 per cent of US equities are owned by institutional investors and 80 per cent of all share trades are made by institutional investors) and the UK (where institutional ownership is around 65–80 per cent) mean that the voice of the institutional investor cannot go unheard. The Federation of European Securities Exchanges (FESE) (2008) highlights the trend towards higher ownership by foreign investors in the listed shares of European exchanges.

Mallin and Melis (2010) highlight that shareholders are the providers of risk capital and therefore they need to be able to protect their investment by ensuring that a competent board is in place to manage the company and to ensure that effective strategies are in place for the company's overall corporate performance and long-term sustainability. Well governed companies which consider all the business' risks, both financial and non-financial, are perceived as less likely to operate in a way that reduces the value of shareholders' investments and hence impacts negatively on other stakeholders. McCahery *et al.* (2010) find that corporate governance is of importance to institutional shareholders in their investment decisions and a number of them are willing to engage in shareholder activism. Over the last five years or so there has been increasing pressure from government, ultimate beneficiaries, and various stakeholders on institutional investors to engage with their investee companies.

Stewardship

The concept of 'stewardship' has also come to the fore, as we shall see in the discussion of the ISC recommendations on the responsibilities of institutional investors, and the subsequent development of the Stewardship Code in 2010, which is discussed in detail below. However, it is useful at this point to consider what is meant by 'stewardship'. Tomorrow's Company (2009) has contributed significantly to the stewardship debate and declares that 'Stewards are people who look after the resources entrusted to them . . . stewardship is the process through which shareholders, directors, and others seek to influence companies in the direction of long-term, sustainable performance that derives from contributing to human progress and the well-being of the environment and society'. Moreover 'The main resources with which institutional shareholders are entrusted are their client's funds . . . once the institution uses a client's fund to buy shares in a company this reinforces the shareholder's interest in the stewardship of that company' (Tomorrow's Owners, 2009).

Talbot (2010) states that 'shareholder stewardship requires institutional shareholders to take an active role in corporate governance and empowers them, both legally and morally, to do so. Previous conceptions of stewardship viewed directors and not shareholders as worthy stewards of the company's best interests.' Whilst FairPensions (2011), in a detailed discussion encompassing various dimensions of fiduciary responsibility, conclude that 'there is a need to align the legal framework governing investors with the "enlightened shareholder value" ethos underpinning the duties of company directors, encouraging a responsible, long-term approach to serving beneficiaries' interests'.

Development of guidance on institutional investors' responsibilities

The power of institutional investors such as those cited above clearly cannot be under-estimated, and the influence that they can wield is enormous. The institutional investors may be influenced in their views by the various institutional investor representative groups in the UK. Large institutional investors, mainly insurance companies and pension funds, usually belong to one of two representative bodies that act as a professional group 'voice' for their views. These two bodies are the Association of British Insurers (ABI) and the National Association of Pension Funds (NAPF). Both the ABI and the NAPF have best practice corporate governance guidelines, which encompass the recommendations of the Combined Code. They monitor the corporate governance activities of companies and will provide advice to members. Institutional investors will generally consult ABI and/or NAPF reports on whether particular companies are complying with 'good' corporate governance practice, as well as undertaking their own research and analysis. Most large institutional investors have terms of reference that incorporate corporate governance aspects, or have issued separate corporate governance guidelines. These guidelines are generally based around the Combined Code recommendations, and further guidance that may have been issued by the NAPF or ABI. Companies will try to ensure that they meet these guidelines.

The Myners Report on institutional investment, issued in 2001 by HM Treasury, concentrated more on the trusteeship aspects of institutional investors and the legal requirements for trustees, with the aim of raising the standards and promoting greater shareholder activism. For example, the Myners Report expects that institutional investors should be more proactive especially in the stance they take with underperforming companies. In 2007 the NAPF published the results of its review of the extent to which pension fund trustees were complying with the principles. The report stated 'the recommendations set out in this report provide a framework for developing further the Principles so that they remain relevant for the world in which pension fund trustees operate today'. Subsequently HM Treasury published *Updating the Myners Principles: A Response to Consultation* in 2008. There are six principles identified: effective decision-making; clear objectives; risk and liabilities; performance assessment; responsible ownership; transparency and reporting. The report emphasized greater industry ownership of the principles and places the onus on trustees to report on their own practices.

The Institutional Shareholders' Committee (ISC), whose members comprise the ABI, the NAPF, the Association of Investment Trust Companies (AITC), and the Investment Management Association (IMA), issued a statement on the responsibilities of institutional investors in late 2002 (the ISC was renamed in the summer of 2011, as the Institutional Investor Committee (IIC) whose members are the NAPF, the ABI and the IMA).

The ISC (2002) states that the policies on activism that it describes 'do not constitute an obligation to micro-manage the affairs of investee companies, but rather relate to procedures designed to ensure that shareholders derive value from their investments by dealing effectively with concerns over underperformance. Nor do they preclude a decision to sell a holding, where this is the most effective response to such concerns'. In other words, the exercise of 'voice' is recommended but 'exit' is not precluded.

The ISC recommends that institutional investors should have a clear statement of their policy on activism and on how they will discharge their responsibilities. The policy would be a public document and would address the following areas:

- how investee companies will be monitored;
- the policy for requiring investee companies' compliance with the Combined Code;
- the policy for meeting with an investee company's board and senior management;
- how any conflicts of interest will be dealt with;
- the strategy on intervention;
- an indication of when and how further action may be taken;
- the policy on voting.

It also recommends that institutional investors should monitor performance. Monitoring performance should be a regular process, clearly communicable and checked periodically for its effectiveness. It should include reviewing annual reports and accounts, circulars and resolutions, and attending company meetings. In particular, institutional shareholders should try to satisfy themselves that the investee company's board and subcommittee structures are effective, and that independent directors provide adequate oversight, and maintain a clear audit trail of their meetings and of votes cast on company resolutions, in particular contentious issues. The ISC states that these actions should help institutional investors 'to identify problems at an early stage and minimize any loss of shareholder value'.

The ISC advocates that institutional investors intervene when necessary and such intervention may occur when they have concerns about a range of issues, including: the company's strategy; its operational performance; its acquisition/disposal strategy; independent directors failing to hold executive management properly to account; internal controls failing; inadequate succession planning; an unjustifiable failure to comply with the Combined Code; inappropriate remuneration packages; the company's approach to corporate social responsibility. Boards should be given the chance to respond constructively but if they do not, then the institutional investors may choose to escalate their action through a range of ways, including intervening jointly with other institutions on particular issues, making a public statement in advance of the company's general meeting, or requisitioning an extraordinary general meeting possibly to change the boards. Finally, institutional investors should evaluate and report on the outcomes of their shareholder activism.

As might be inferred from its content, the ISC statement is aimed at significantly enhancing 'how effectively institutional shareholders discharge their responsibilities in relation to the companies in which they invest'. It is a milestone in the encouragement of institutional shareholder activism in the UK.

The ISC published a review of its 2002 *Statement of Principles* on the responsibilities of institutional shareholders and their agents in September 2005. The review monitored the progress of the statement for the two years since its launch in 2002 and concluded that there had been a general increase in the level of engagement of institutional investors with their investee companies. The *Statement of Principles* issued in 2002 has stayed the same but with two modifications to the wording: the word 'activism' has been replaced with 'engagement', in order 'to emphasise the importance now attached by institutional investors to developing a high-quality all-round relationship with the companies in which they invest'; given that it is a listing requirement that companies must comply with the Combined Code (2003) or explain why they do not, there is no need for institutional investors to state in their policy that they require investee companies to do this. In addition, it is recommended that pension funds should incorporate the principles into their Statement of Investment Principles, and that corporate governance aspects could be more integrated with the investment process. The ISC further reviewed and updated the *Statement of Principles* in 2007, resulting in a recommendation for institutional investors to publish a policy on voting disclosure. The revised statement sets out how disclosure can be achieved in a flexible and cost-effective manner, using a 'comply or explain' approach. Voluntary public disclosure is desirable but may not be appropriate in all cases, in which case 'a reasoned explanation' should be provided of the non-disclosure. The most cost-effective method of disclosure is usually via a website. Institutions may disclose by exception, i.e. where they have departed from their published voting policy, or they may choose to disclose their voting on each and every vote. Voting disclosure should not jeopardize the creation of value through engagement with investee companies, therefore disclosure should take place only after the relevant general meeting. Institutional investors should review their policy on voting disclosure on a regular basis, usually as part of the wider review of the policy on engagement.

The International Corporate Governance Network (ICGN) produced a *Statement of Shareholder Responsibilities* (2007) which set out the ICGN's view of the responsibilities of institutional shareholders both in relation to their external role as owners of company equity, and also in relation to their internal governance. Both these areas are of interest to beneficiaries and other stakeholders. Ownership of equity carries important responsibilities, and the rights attached to share ownership must be exercised responsibly. Responsible ownership requires high standards of transparency, probity, and care on the part of institutions. Furthermore, the ICGN (2009) stated: 'It will help establish a role for governance and shareholders, as well as preserve shareholder rights if institutions formally commit to the principles laid out in the "ICGN Statement of Principles on Institutional Shareholder Responsibilities (2007)"'.

In June 2009 the ISC published a paper on *Improving Institutional Investors' Role in Governance* aimed at enhancing the quality of dialogue between institutional investors and all companies 'to help improve long term returns and the alignment of interests, reduce the risk of catastrophic outcomes due to bad strategic decisions or poor standards of governance, and help with the efficient exercise of governance responsibilities'. The suggested improvements include clearer mandates for fund managers, the development of collective dialogue, chairs of board committees to stand for re-election each year, raised standards at institutional investors, and enhancements to the Combined Code.

In November 2009 the ISC issued the *Code on the Responsibilities of Institutional Investors*. The Code built on the statements on institutional investors' responsibilities issued previously by the ISC. The ISC stated that 'the Code aims to enhance the quality of the dialogue of institutional investors with companies to help improve long-term returns to shareholders, reduce the risk of catastrophic outcomes due to bad strategic decisions, and help with the efficient exercise of governance responsibilities'.

Following on from the financial crisis, an independent review of the governance of banks and other financial institutions was carried out by Sir David Walker. The Walker Review published its final recommendations in November 2009, and nine of its thirty-nine recommendations related to the role of institutional shareholders' communication and engagement (emphasizing the development and regulatory sponsorship of a Stewardship Code). When the UK Corporate Governance Code was issued in 2010, a Stewardship Code was produced alongside, largely based on the ISC Code discussed earlier, and the first of its kind in the world.

UK Stewardship Code 2010

The Financial Reporting Council (FRC) issued the UK Stewardship Code in June 2010, which set out the good practice on engagement with investee companies that it believes institutional shareholders should aspire to. As mentioned earlier, the UK Stewardship Code is largely based on the ISC 'Code on the Responsibilities of Institutional Investors', in fact only a few minor amendments were made to the latter before it was adopted as the UK Stewardship Code, with the FRC assuming responsibility for its oversight.

The seven principles of the UK Stewardship Code are that institutional investors should:

- Principle 1—publicly disclose their policy on how they will discharge their stewardship responsibilities.
- Principle 2—have a robust policy on managing conflicts of interest in relation to stewardship and this policy should be publicly disclosed.
- Principle 3—monitor their investee companies.
- Principle 4—establish clear guidelines on when and how they will escalate their activities as a method of protecting and enhancing shareholder value.
- Principle 5—be willing to act collectively with other investors where appropriate.
- Principle 6—have a clear policy on voting and disclosure of voting activity.
- Principle 7—report periodically on their stewardship and voting activities.

The Stewardship Code is applied on a 'comply or explain' basis. The UK Stewardship Code applies to firms who manage assets on behalf of institutional shareholders such as pension funds, insurance companies, investment trusts, and other collective vehicles. However, pension fund trustees and other owners may also monitor company performance and so the FRC encourages all institutional investors to report whether, and how, they have complied with the Stewardship Code. The FRC expects such firms to disclose on their websites how they have applied the Stewardship Code or to explain why it has not been complied with.

There has generally been a good take-up of the Stewardship Code, with over 180 asset managers, over 50 asset owners, and 14 service providers signing up to it. Whilst most of those signing up are supportive of the Stewardship Code's principles, Mallin (2012) reports that statements that organizations will not be complying with the Stewardship Code fall into two groups: (i) those not signing based on their specific investment strategy (for example, they do not invest in UK equities), and (ii) those who do not commit to codes in individual jurisdictions.

The Stewardship Code has generally been well received and may be emulated by other countries where appropriate. Its effectiveness will be measured by the extent to which there is full engagement with investee companies, with appropriate monitoring and the use of the various tools of corporate governance.

Interestingly, the European Fund and Asset Management Association (EFAMA) published the *EFAMA Code for External Governance: Principles for the exercise of ownership rights in investee companies* in April 2011. There are six principles for investment management companies (IMCs) detailing how they should:

- have a documented policy available to the public on whether, and if so how, they exercise their ownership responsibilities;
- monitor their investee companies;
- establish clear guidelines on when and how they will intervene with investee companies to protect and enhance value;
- consider cooperating with other investors, where appropriate, having due regard to applicable rules on acting in concert;
- exercise their voting rights in a considered way;
- report on their exercise of ownership rights and voting activities and have a policy on external governance disclosure.

Private equity and sovereign wealth funds (SWFs)

Two types of investor that have gained increasing influence and prominence during the last decade are private equity firms and SWFs. In each case there has been some unease about the lack of transparency associated with these types of investor. As a result, pressure has been brought to bear to encourage more disclosure and transparency by these funds. We will look first at private equity funds.

Private equity

A private equity fund is broadly defined as one that invests in equity which is not traded publicly on a stock exchange. Sometimes private equity firms acquire companies, which may be large well-known companies, and the funds for such deals often come from institutional investors. Private equity investments can be broadly divided into categories including venture capital, buy-out, acquisition of a significant portion or a majority control in a more mature company, investment in a distressed company, or investment in a company where value can be unlocked.

The Walker Working Group (Private Equity Working Group on Transparency and Disclosure) published, in November 2007, *Guidelines for Disclosure and Transparency in Private*

Equity. These guidelines are aimed at private equity firms authorized by the Financial Services Authority and by UK portfolio companies owned by private equity funds.

Walker Guidelines for Disclosure and Transparency in Private Equity

The voluntary guidelines were drawn up for the British Private Equity and Venture Capital Association (BVCA). The guidelines place much greater onus on private equity funds to provide more details of the financial performance of companies they take over. The new rules require private equity companies to publish accounts for the larger companies they own no later than six months after financial year-ends.

Since the publication of the guidelines, about a dozen private equity firms—including Apax Partners, Terra Firma, Permira and Cinven—have published annual reviews, giving details of their senior managers, investors, strategies, and portfolio companies. Sir Michael Rake, Chairman of the Walker Guidelines Monitoring Group, in an interview with the *Financial Times* in August 2008 stated that thirty-two private equity firms and fifty-five portfolio companies have committed to comply with the Walker Recommendations.

The Organisation for Economic Co-operation and Development (OECD) (2008a and 2008b) also published two useful documents in relation to private equity firms. These were the *Codes and Industry Standards Covering the Behaviour of Alternative Investors*, which is a list of private sector initiatives aimed at addressing policy issues, and *The Role of Private Equity and Activist Hedge Funds in Corporate Governance—Related Policy Issues*. The latter document concludes that private equity firms and activist hedge funds often act as informed owners and are more active in monitoring the performance of companies and their management than other institutional investors. The report also concluded that any corporate governance concerns that relate to governance practices by private equity firms and activist hedge funds are best addressed within the framework of the existing OECD Principles.

Sovereign Wealth Funds (SWFs)

An SWF is a fund owned by a government and these funds are often very large and influential. TheCityUK Research (2012) published a useful summary of the size of the SWF market. Table 6.2 highlights the largest of the SWFs and shows how China accounts for 29 per cent, followed by the United Arab Emirates 16 per cent, Norway 12 per cent, and Saudi Arabia 10 per cent. Norway's SWF, which accounts for 12 per cent, has stakes in some 3,500+ companies but is seen as being fairly transparent and relatively unthreatening, whereas the sovereign funds of some of the Middle and Far Eastern sovereign funds are seen as being much more opaque. This can become a problem when these funds start to buy into strategic businesses, and their motivation and long-term investment strategy is unknown.

The Santiago Principles

The International Working Group of Sovereign Wealth Funds (IWG), with a membership of 26 countries with SWFs, was established in May 2008. The IWG met three times to identify and draft a set of generally accepted principles and practices (GAPP) that properly reflects their investment practices and objectives: the Santiago Principles.

Table 6.2 SWFs market share by country

End 2011	US$bn	% share
China	1,411	29
United Arab Emirates	783	16
Norway	560	12
Saudi Arabia	478	10
Singapore	405	8
Kuwait	296	6
Russia	114	2
Others	753	16
Total	**4,800**	**100***

*Rounded
Source: SWF Institute, TheCityUK estimates.

The GAPP are underpinned by the following guiding objectives for SWFs:

- to help maintain a stable global financial system and free flow of capital and investment;
- to comply with all applicable regulatory and disclosure requirements in the countries in which they invest;
- to invest on the basis of economic and financial risk and return-related considerations; and
- to have in place a transparent and sound governance structure that provides for adequate operational controls, risk management, and accountability.

Members of the IWG 'either have implemented or intend to implement the following principles and practices, on a voluntary basis, *each of which is subject to* home country laws, regulations, requirements and obligations' [emphasis in original].

There are 24 GAPP which cover areas such as:

- the legal framework of the SWF;
- its policy and purpose;
- the requirement for clear and public disclosure of policies and of statistical data;
- a sound governance framework which establishes a clear and effective division of roles and responsibilities in order to facilitate accountability and operational independence in the management of the SWF to pursue its objectives;
- a defined accountability framework;
- the publication of an audited set of financial statements in a timely manner;
- professional and ethical standards in SWFs;
- an investment policy that is clear and consistent with the SWF's defined objectives, risk tolerance, and investment strategy;
- shareholder ownership rights that are viewed as a fundamental element of the SWF's equity investments' value;

- a framework that identifies, assesses, and manages the risks of its operations;
- a regular review of the extent to which the GAPP have been followed.

These GAPP should help ensure that there is more confidence in the activities of SWFs, which will help maintain stability in international financial markets and ensure that there is more trust in them.

Institutional investors' relationship with investee companies

Corporate governance may be used as a tool for extracting value for shareholders from underperforming, undervalued companies. This approach has been very successful for Lens Inc., CalPERS, Hermes, and Active Value Advisors, to name but a few. By targeting companies that are underperforming in one of the main market indices, and analyzing those companies' corporate governance practices, improvements can be made that unlock the hidden value. These improvements often include replacing poorly performing directors and ensuring that the companies comply with perceived best practice in corporate governance.

Corporate governance may also be used to help restore investor confidence in markets that have experienced financial crises. We have seen this happening in the last few years in Malaysia, Japan, and India, for example. In these countries, as in a number of other countries that have similarly been affected by a lack of investor confidence, particularly overseas investor confidence, new or improved corporate governance practices have been introduced. Key features of these changes include measures to try to improve investor confidence by improving transparency and accountability in these markets.

We have seen earlier that there is increasing pressure on institutional investors to engage with their investee companies from a number of sources, including government. The EU also identified, in the Commission Green Paper on Corporate Governance in Financial Institutions and Remuneration Policies 2010, that 'a lack of appropriate shareholder interest in holding financial institutions' management accountable contributed to poor management accountability and may have facilitated excessive risk taking in financial institutions'. Some of the reasons cited include the cost of engagement, the difficulty of valuing the return on engagement, and the uncertainty of the outcome of engagement, including 'free rider' behaviour.

In the UK the Department of Business, Innovation & Skills commissioned Professor John Kay to assess the effect of UK equity markets on the competitiveness of UK business. The *Kay Review of UK Equity Markets and Long-Term Decision Making, Interim Report* was published in February 2012. It highlighted a number of areas based on the submissions received and on discussions with market participants. An area of concern is the issuance of quarterly or interim earnings statements by companies, as this can lead to a short-term focus by investors (and companies) rather a longer term perspective.

The OECD (2011) in its publication *The Role of Institutional Investors in Promoting Good Corporate Governance* reviewed the role of institutional investors, including their engagement with investee companies, the incentives they have to promote engagement, and the barriers to engagement. It covers twenty-six jurisdictions with an in-depth review of Australia, Chile, and Germany. The review demonstrates that institutional investors can play an important role in jurisdictions characterized by both dispersed and concentrated ownership. However, the report points out that 'the nature of institutional investors has evidently evolved over the years into a complex system of financial institutions and fund management companies with their own corporate governance issues and incentive structures'.

The ICGN issued the *ICGN Model Mandate Initiative* in 2012, which discusses model contract terms between asset owners and their managers. It identifies areas that are most significant in this regard: standards and high-level commitment; risk management; integration of long-term factors; stewardship activities; long-termism and alignment; and commission and counterparties. In another section on accountability and reporting it points out 'as important as setting standards within fund management contracts is how clients can effectively call their fund managers to account in respect of these mandates'.

From the discussion earlier, it is clear that with institutional investors under the spotlight and an emphasis on their stewardship role, we can expect to see more use being made of the tools of corporate governance.

Tools of corporate governance

(i) One-to-one meetings

The meetings between institutional investors and companies are extremely important as a means of communication between the two parties. This is one clear example of the way in which individual investors are at a disadvantage to institutional investors: corporate management will usually only arrange such meetings with large investors who are overwhelmingly institutional investors.

A company will usually arrange to meet with its largest institutional investors on a one-to-one basis during the course of the year. The meetings tend to be at the highest level and usually involve individual key members of the board in a meeting once, or maybe twice, a week. Their 'target' institutional investor audience will include large shareholders (perhaps the top thirty) and brokers' analysts (perhaps the top ten), and any large investors who are underweight or selling their shares. In addition, they will tend to phone an institutional investor if they have not seen them in the last twelve to eighteen months. Meetings are often followed up with phone calls by the firm to the institutional investor to ensure that everything has been discussed.

The issues that are most discussed at these meetings between firms and their large institutional investors include areas of the firm's strategy and how the firm is planning to achieve its objectives, whether objectives are being met, and the quality of the management. Institutional investors are seen as 'important for the way the business is managed', and their views may be fed back to the board in the planning process, and incorporated, as appropriate, in an annual strategy paper. They are seen as having a collective influence, with management paying most attention to the commonality of institutional investors' views in meetings over time. The firms want to ensure that institutional investors understand the business and its strategy so that the value of the business is fully recognized.

As a way of saying 'well done', Hermes has sent letters to various companies stating when they found their annual report particularly informative and useful in terms of various areas, for example, directors' remuneration and risk management. In 2008 the Institute of Chartered Secretaries and Administrators (ICSA) and Hermes joined forces to launch the ICSA Hermes Awards for UK companies whose annual reports and accounts achieved best practice in governance disclosure.

(ii) Voting

The right to vote that is attached to voting shares (as opposed to non-voting shares) is a basic prerogative of share ownership, and is particularly important given the division of ownership (shareholders) and control (directors) in the modern corporation. The right to vote can be seen as fundamental for some element of control by shareholders.

The institutional investors can register their views by postal voting, or, in many companies, the facility to vote electronically is now available. Most of the large institutional investors now have a policy of trying to vote on all issues that may be raised at their investee company's annual general meeting (AGM). Some may vote directly on all resolutions, others may appoint a proxy (which may be a board member). Generally, an institutional investor will try to sort out any contentious issues with management 'behind the scenes'; however, if this fails, then they may abstain from voting on a particular issue (rather than voting with incumbent management as they generally would) or they may actually vote against a resolution. In this case, they would generally inform the firm of their intention to vote against. It tends to be corporate governance issues that are the most contentious, particularly directors' remuneration and lengths of contract.

The high level of institutional share ownership in the UK has been discussed earlier. Looking back at the Cadbury Report (1992), this states: 'Given the weight of their votes, the way in which institutional investors use their power . . . is of fundamental importance'. It encourages institutional investors to 'make positive use of their voting rights and disclose their policies on voting'.

A number of similar statements can be found in the guidelines issued by various institutional investor representative groups. For example, the two main groups representing institutional investors in the UK, the NAPF and the ABI, both advocate voting by institutional investors. NAPF (1995) refers to 'the powerful vote' and 'encourage—as a matter of best practice—the regular exercise of proxy votes by pension funds'; ABI recommends that 'large shareholders should vote wherever possible and support boards of directors unless they have good reason for doing otherwise'. In 1999 the ABI and NAPF issued some joint guidance on responsible voting in which they emphasized the importance of voting and advocated that voting should be done in a considered fashion rather than 'box ticking', that it could contribute to effective corporate governance, and that it could be seen as an integral part of the investment management function.

So, it would seem that the main institutional investor representative groups in the UK are in agreement that votes should be exercised on a regular basis in an informed manner.

There have been a number of efforts to try to ensure that voting levels do improve. These include the NAPF *Report of the Committee of Inquiry into UK Vote Execution* (1999). The report identified various impediments to voting, a major one being the cumbersome and outdated paper-based system. As a result of this, a number of projects were established to try to find a suitable electronic voting system to make voting easier and the process more efficient. The

NAPF report additionally identified a number of other areas of concern, including a 'lack of auditability or adequate confirmatory procedure in the voting system' and communication problems between the pension funds, fund managers, custodians, registrars, and companies. It recommended that:

- regular considered voting should be regarded as a fiduciary responsibility;
- voting policy ought to be specifically covered by agreement;
- the UK's voting system should be modernized;
- companies themselves should actively encourage voting;
- member associations should offer help and guidance;
- registrars should support electronic voting arrangements;
- voting in the context of stock lending should be re-examined;
- custodians should actively assist in the voting process.

The Shareholder Voting Working Group (SVWG) was established in 1999, under the chairmanship of Terry Pearson, as an industry-wide body to address the issue of improving the voting process in the UK. The SVWG has subsequently been chaired by Paul Myners and has issued several reports on the impediments to voting UK shares.

The SVWG issued its fourth report in July 2007. The report states that voting levels have risen to over 60 per cent up from 50 per cent some three years ago. The report details the various impediments to voting, highlighting the complexity of the voting system, and making recommendations on a number of areas to help improve the situation and remedy the problem of 'lost' votes. The report recommends that the voting system should be more efficient and transparent, and specifically highlights that institutional shareholders could be doing more to try to ensure that their votes were appropriately recorded. The report cited The Combined Code on Corporate Governance (2006), which stated: 'institutional shareholders should take steps to ensure their voting instructions are translated into practice' (supporting principle to Principle E3). The sentiment remained the same in the Combined Code (2008) although the phrase 'voting instructions' was replaced with 'voting intentions'.

Voting levels by institutional investors in the UK have gradually begun to increase in recent years, with voting levels in the FTSE 100 companies rising to just over 70 per cent according to Manifest (2011). Institutional investors recognize though that unless voting levels increase across their investee companies in the next couple of years, the government may make voting mandatory. Whilst the question of mandatory voting has been fairly widely discussed in the UK, there is no real consensus on this issue. However, there is undoubtedly a sense that institutional investors should have a more active involvement, especially in areas of corporate governance such as voting, and, in the course of time, if voting levels do not improve, then voting may well become mandatory. There is also a concern to try to ensure that individual shareholders who hold shares through nominees and not directly do not lose their right to vote; this is another dimension of institutional investor power and influence.

The situation in continental Europe is rather different because the shareholder structure in many European countries differs quite significantly from that in the UK: for example, large banks and corporations tend to dominate German and French companies, whilst Italian companies tend to be dominated by non-financial holding companies and families. However, the report of the CEPS working party set up to give policy directions on the future of corporate governance in Europe stated: 'Shareholders should be given the responsibility to exercise their voting rights in an informed and independent manner. This activity should also be adapted to the growing internationalization of shareholding and not be limited to national borders'. This seems to indicate that whatever the shareholding structure in a particular country, the vote is seen as being of importance, and once again informed voting is emphasized. It is also interesting to note the reference to the internationalization of shareholdings and the implication that cross-border holdings should be voted.

In 2002 the EU High-Level Group of Company Law Experts, chaired by Jaap Winter, emphasized the importance of facilitating voting by electronic and other means, and also of enabling cross-border voting. The recommendations of this group fed into the EU Communication, 'Modernizing Company Law and Enhancing Corporate Governance in the European Union—A Plan to Move Forward'. Approximately one-third of the share capital of EU listed companies in any given country is held by non-residents. Non-residents may face a number of obstacles when trying to exercise their shareholder rights, such as lack of sufficient information being received in a timely manner, share blocking, and difficulties in voting cross-border shares. In the context of shareholder rights, two main objectives were identified: (i) 'to strengthen shareholder rights and third party protection, with a proper distinction between categories of companies'; and (ii) 'to foster efficiency and competitiveness of business, with special attention to some specific cross-border issues'. In practice, this led to the issue in January 2006 of a Directive on Shareholders' Rights, which made the following proposals to enhance shareholders' rights:

- General meetings should be convened with at least one month's notice. All relevant information should be available on that date at the latest, and posted on the issuer's website. The meeting notice should contain all necessary information.
- Share blocking should be abolished and replaced by a record date, which should be set no earlier than 30 days before the meeting.
- The right to ask questions should be accessible to non-residents. The maximum shareholding thresholds to benefit from the right to table resolutions should not exceed 5 per cent, in order to open this right to a greater number of shareholders while preserving the good order of general meetings.
- Proxy voting should not be subject to excessive administrative requirements, nor should it be unduly restricted. Shareholders should have a choice of methods for distance voting.
- Voting results should be available to all shareholders and posted on the issuer's website.

The EU Directive (2007a) was formally adopted in June 2007 and had to be incorporated into Member States' laws by summer 2009 and 'will ensure in particular that shareholders have timely access to the complete information relevant to general meetings and facilitates the exercise of voting rights by proxy. Furthermore, the directive provides for the replacement of share blocking and related practices through a record date system'.

In June 2007 the European Commission (2007b) published an external study on proportionality between capital and control in EU listed companies. Proportionality is the relationship between capital and control ('one share, one vote'). The study, carried out by Institutional

Shareholder Services Europe (ISS Europe), the European Corporate Governance Institute (ECGI) and the law firm Shearman & Sterling LLP, found that 'on the basis of the academic research available, there is no conclusive evidence of a causal link between deviations from the proportionality principle and either the economic performance of listed companies or their governance. However, there is some evidence that investors perceive these mechanisms negatively and consider more transparency would be helpful in making investment decisions'.

In December 2007, the OECD published a paper on the *Lack of Proportionality Between Ownership and Control: Overview and Issues for Discussion*. The paper states that 'proportionality between corporate ownership and control implies that any shareholder owns the same fraction of cash flow rights and voting rights'. In some countries there is a departure from this principle of proportionality and this may cause concern. The paper highlights that the cost of regulating proportionality would be significant and that a preferred approach is to strengthen corporate governance frameworks and, where necessary, target specific problems in some countries with regulation.

Like the UK, the US stock market is dominated by institutional investors. One significant difference from the UK though is that private pension funds are mandated to vote by the Department of Labor's (DOL) regulations governing proxy voting by Employee Retirement Income Security Act (ERISA) funds. ERISA was enacted in 1974 and established federal fiduciary standards for private pension funds. The fiduciary duty is deemed to encompass voting. The DOL has, especially in more recent years, been fairly proactive in monitoring compliance with ERISA, and in offering interpretive advice on it. Early in 1994 Olena Berg, Assistant Secretary for Pension and Welfare Benefits, clarified the issue of global voting by stating that 'voting foreign proxies should be treated the same way as voting domestic proxies'. However, it was recognized that voting overseas proxies can be an expensive business and it is advised that fiduciaries look at possible difficulties of voting a particular stock *before* purchasing it and also evaluate the cost of voting the shares against the potential value to the plan of voting the shares. Combined with the dramatic growth in the level of US institutional investors' holdings of overseas equities, this pronouncement can also be expected to have a significant effect on the attitude towards voting in the overseas countries in which US institutional investors hold equities.

ERISA does not apply to public pension funds but the major public pension funds tend to vote their own shares or instruct their managers how to vote. Funds such as the California Public Employees' Retirement System (CalPERS), the New York City Employees' Retirement System (NYCERS), and the State of Wisconsin Investment Board (SWIB) all have a policy of voting all their shares. CalPERS, the USA's largest pension fund and the third largest in the world, makes available its voting actions on its website.

In the Australian context, the Bosch Committee (1993) stated that institutional investors should 'take an active interest in the governance of their company' and commented that shareholders in general should make 'a sufficient analysis to vote in an informed manner on all issues raised at general meetings'. Stephen Smith, Chairman of the Parliamentary Joint Committee on Corporations and Securities, argued that 'institutional investors have a clear moral, if not legal, obligation to examine each proposal and decide how they will best exercise their voting rights'. In its 1995 guidelines, the Australian Investment Managers' Association recommended that 'voting rights are a valuable asset of the investor and should be managed with the same care and diligence as any other asset', and urges that 'institutions should support boards by positive use of their voting power unless they have good reasons for doing otherwise'.

A survey of institutional investors carried out by the ICGN in 2001 found that most institutional investors state that they try to exercise their overseas proxies but that there may be problems in trying to do so. Problems that may be encountered when trying to vote cross-border include the following:

- timing problems whereby just a couple of weeks' notice of the agenda items to be voted on at the companies' AGM may be given, making for a very tight deadline;
- information relating to agenda items being insufficient and/or in a foreign language, making detailed analysis of items very difficult in the available timescale;
- the blocking or depositing of shares, which means that shares have to be deposited with a central depository, public notary, or depositary named by the company, and so cannot be traded for a period of time before the company's AGM (usually between five and eight days);
- voting procedures or methods may be problematic in cross-border voting, for example, having physically to attend the AGM to vote rather than being able to send in votes by post or other appropriate means.

Recent developments in a number of countries, including various EU countries, have gone some way towards addressing a number of these issues.

However, the OECD (2011) identified that a key problem is that 'domestic investors in many jurisdictions do not vote their foreign equity. This is important because foreign shareholders make up around 30 per cent of ownership in many jurisdictions. Barriers to cross-border voting that raise the costs of exercising voting rights remain, but evidence shows that there is also a lack of knowledge by institutional investors about foreign companies in their portfolios.'

Whilst there remain a number of barriers to the effective exercise of voice by means of voting, it is, though, a powerful and public means of exercising voice. We are likely to see increased voting levels over time as there is both increasing pressure from institutional investors on companies to try to ensure a more efficient and effective voting system, and pressure from governments on institutional investors for more institutional investors to vote regularly. Over the last decade there has been a slow increase in voting levels and maybe the threat of mandatory voting is receding. However, if institutional investor voting levels are not sustained, and increased over time, then the UK government may legislate so that voting becomes mandatory; but this is something that both the government and institutional investors would prefer not to happen, as it is felt that this might lead to mere 'box ticking' rather than to considered voting.

(iii) Shareholder proposals/resolutions

Shareholder proposals or shareholder resolutions are quite widespread in the USA, with 800–900 per annum. In the USA shareholder proposals have often been in relation to social, environmental, or ethical issues. However, it is expected that in future increasing numbers will relate to dissatisfaction with executive remuneration packages.

In contrast, in the UK a company has a duty to circulate resolutions proposed by share-holders and intended to be moved at an AGM if a certain number of members request it. The number of members necessary is: (i) members having 5 per cent of the voting power of the company, or (ii) 100 or more shareholders whose paid-up capital averages at least £100 each. The resolution may be circulated at the expense of the members making the request, unless the company resolves otherwise. Given the practical difficulties of meeting either of these two conditions, the number of shareholder proposals in the UK has tended to be low, usually fewer than ten per annum. However, it is expected that the number will increase given the dissatisfaction with executive remuneration, which seems to have already triggered an increased number of shareholder proposals.

(iv) Focus lists

A number of institutional investors have established 'focus lists', whereby they target underperforming companies and include them on a list of companies that have underperformed a main index, such as Standard and Poor's. Underperforming the index would be a first point of identification; other factors would include not responding appropriately to the institutional investor's enquiries regarding underperformance, and not taking account of the institutional investor's views. After being put on the focus list, the companies receive the often unwanted attention of the institutional investors who may seek to change various directors on the board.

(v) Corporate governance rating systems

With the increasing emphasis on corporate governance across the globe, it is perhaps not surprising that a number of corporate governance rating systems have been developed. Examples of firms that have developed corporate governance rating systems are Deminor, Standard and Poor's, and Governance Metrics International (GMI). The rating systems cover several markets: for example, Deminor has tended to concentrate on European companies, whilst Standard and Poor's has used its corporate governance rating system in quite different markets, such as Russia. GMI ratings cover a range of countries, including the USA, various countries in the Asia-Pacific region and Europe. These corporate governance rating systems should be of benefit to investors, both potential and those presently invested, and to the companies themselves.

In turn, the ratings will also be useful to governments in identifying perceived levels of corporate governance in their country compared to other countries in their region, or out-side it, whose companies may be competing for limited foreign investment. In emerging market countries in particular, those companies with a corporate governance infrastructure will, *ceteris paribus*, be less subject to cronyism and its attendant effects on corporate wealth. These companies will tend to be more transparent and accountable, and hence more attrac-tive to foreign investors.

A corporate governance rating can be a powerful indicator of the extent to which a company currently is adding, or has the potential to add in the future, shareholder value. This is because a company with good corporate governance is generally perceived as more attractive to investors than one without. Good corporate governance should, for example, indicate a board that is prepared to participate actively in dialogue with its shareholders, ensuring the effective exercise of voice (Hirschman 1970) thus enabling investors to articulate their interests.

An appropriate approach for a corporate governance rating system is first to have a rating of the corporate governance in a given country, for example:

- How transparent are accounting and reporting practices generally in the country?
- Are there existing corporate governance practices in place?
- Is there a code of best practice?
- To what extent is that code complied with?
- What sanctions are there against companies which do not comply?

Having set the scene in any given country, the individual company can then be given a corporate governance rating. With regard to the individual company, the ratings will generally be based on the company's approach to the rights of shareholders, the presence of independent non-executive (outside) directors, the effectiveness of the board, and the accountability and transparency of the company. Corporate governance rankings of companies in, for example, the banking sector can be assessed both within a country and also across countries, providing a valuable additional indicator/comparator benchmark for investors.

Overall, corporate governance rating systems should provide a useful indication of the corporate governance environment in specific countries, and in individual companies within those countries. Such systems will provide a useful benchmark for the majority of investors who identify good corporate governance with a well-run and well-managed company, and investors will increasingly take into account companies' governance profiles in investment decisions.

Corporate governance and corporate performance

Is there a link between corporate governance and corporate performance? Whilst there have been many studies carried out on this area, the evidence appears to be fairly mixed.

One of the earlier and much-quoted studies is that of Nesbitt (1994). Nesbitt reported positive long-term stock price returns to firms targeted by CalPERS. Nesbitt's later studies show similar findings. Subsequently, Millstein and MacAvoy (1998) studied 154 large publicly traded US corporations over a five-year period and found that corporations with active and independent boards appear to have performed much better in the 1990s than those with passive, non-independent boards. However, the work of Dalton et al. (1998) showed that board composition had virtually no effect on firm performance, and that there was no relationship between leadership structure (chief executive officer (CEO)/chairman) and firm performance. Patterson (2000), of the Conference Board, produced a comprehensive review of the literature relating to the link between corporate governance and performance, and stated that the survey did not present conclusive evidence of such a link.

Whilst the evidence seems to be quite mixed, there does appear to be a widely held perception that corporate governance can make a difference to the bottom line. The findings of a survey by McKinsey (2002) found that the majority of investors would be prepared to pay a premium to invest in a company with good corporate governance. The survey states that 'good' governance in relation to board practices includes a majority of outside directors who are truly independent, significant director stock ownership and stock-based compensation, formal director evaluations, and good responsiveness to shareholder requests for governance information. The findings indicate that investors would pay 11 per cent more for the shares of a well-governed Canadian company, 12 per cent more for the shares of a well-governed UK company, and 14 per cent more for the shares of a well-governed US company, compared to shares of a company with similar financial performance but poorer governance practices. The premiums rise to 16 per cent for a well-governed Italian company, 21 per cent for a Japanese company, 24 per cent for a Brazilian company, 38 per cent for a Russian company and, at the top of the scale with the highest premium for good governance, 41 per cent for a well-governed Moroccan company. It is therefore the investor's perception and belief that corporate governance is important and that belief leads to the willingness to pay a premium for good corporate governance.

Some of the significant papers that that have found evidence of a positive link include Gompers *et al.* (2003) and Deutsche Bank (2004a and 2004b). Gompers *et al.* (2003) examined the ways in which shareholder rights vary across firms. They constructed a 'Governance Index' to proxy for the level of shareholder rights in approximately 1,500 large firms during the 1990s. An investment strategy that bought firms in the lowest decile of the index (strongest rights) and sold firms in the highest decile of the index (weakest rights) would have earned abnormal returns of 8.5 per cent per year during the sample period. They found that firms with stronger shareholder rights had higher firm value, higher profits, higher sales growth, lower capital expenditures, and made fewer corporate acquisitions. Deutsche Bank (2004a and 2004b) explored the implications of corporate governance for portfolio management and concluded that corporate governance standards are an important component of equity risk. Its analysis also showed that for South Africa, Eastern Europe, and the Middle East, the performance differential favours those companies with stronger corporate governance.

Hermes (2005) provided a succinct summary of academic and practitioner research in this area, splitting it into three categories: opinion-based research (such as McKinsey (2002); focus list research and performance of shareholder engagement funds (such as 'the CalPERS effect', on which there were various studies such as Nesbitt (1994)); and finally, governance ranking research (such as Deutsche Bank, 2004). Hermes concludes its 2005 review of the literature by stating that it recognizes that a number of the authors of the various studies cited in the review have mentioned that there is further empirical work needed on the issue of causation but that, 'nevertheless, we consider there to be sufficient evidence in support of our view that good corporate governance improves the long-term performance of companies'.

In 2007 Hermes published another summary of the research in this area, identifying the missing links. The effectiveness of engagement is highlighted by the study carried out by Becht *et al.* (2009) whereby the researchers were given unlimited access to Hermes' resources, including letters, memos, minutes, presentations, transcripts/recordings of telephone conversations, and client reports, documenting its work with the companies in which Hermes' UK Focus Fund invested in a period over five years (1998–2004). They reviewed all forms of public and private engagement with 41 companies. They found that when the engagement objectives led to actual outcomes, there were economically large and statistically significant positive abnormal returns around the announcement date. On the basis of their findings, they concluded that shareholder activism can produce corporate governance changes that generate significant returns for shareholders.

Lantz *et al.* (2010), in a study of French companies, found that institutional investors are becoming more active in their portfolio management. They point out that since 1999, So-ciété des Bourses Françaises (SBF) 120 companies in France that do not respect the 'Code of Best Practices on Corporate Governance as set out by the AFG' are added to a widely circu-lated 'target list'. They examine the AFG alerts on financial performance, using a short-term event study methodology and their findings indicate a negative effect on the wealth of shareholders on the day of the alert. They conclude, therefore, that the impact depends on past performance measured by book ratios or expressed in relation to the future premium opportunity for shareholders.

Renders *et al.* (2010) report that, in a cross-European sample, their results 'imply that corporate-governance ratings are relevant and that in adhering to good corporate-governance practices, companies can significantly improve their performance'. Aggarwal *et al.* (2011) found that institutional investors influence the development of corporate governance in other coun-tries, and especially in terms of improving investor protection in countries where it is weaker than their own. They provide evidence that 'institutional ownership has a direct effect on cor-porate governance outcomes, functioning as a disciplinary mechanism in terminating poorly performing CEOs. Furthermore, increases in institutional ownership lead to increases in firm valuation, suggesting that institutional investment not only affects governance mechanisms, but also has real effects on firm value and board decisions . . . we conclude that monitoring and activism by institutions travel beyond country borders and lead to better firm performance'.

In sum, the evidence, both academic and practitioner, points on balance towards the view that good corporate governance helps realize value and create competitive advantage; this is more of an intuitive feeling because the studies are trying to single out corporate governance variables that may affect performance and this is very difficult to do. However, shareholder activism is the key to ensuring good corporate governance and, without this, there is less accountability and transparency, and hence more opportunity for management to engage in activities that may have a negative effect on the bottom line.

The global financial crisis has highlighted the importance of corporate governance in res-toring trust in global capital markets. The ICGN issued two statements on the global financial crisis, one in late 2008 and one in March 2009. The latter statement pointed out that 'institu-tional shareholders must recognize their responsibility to generate long term value on behalf of their beneficiaries, the savers and pensioners for whom they are ultimately working', and 'shareholders should take governance factors into account and consider the riskiness of a company's business model as part of their investment decision-making. Governance should not be a parallel activity. It needs to be integrated into investment'. Furthermore in its con-clusions, the ICGN (2009) statement emphasizes 'securing and maintaining the rights of shareholders and developing the transparency needed for them to exercise these rights in a responsible, informed, and considered way'.

Conclusions

In this chapter, the extent of institutional share ownership, and hence the growth of institutions' power and influence, has been examined. The chapter highlights the emphasis that is increasingly placed on the role of institutional investors in corporate governance in a global context. The tools of governance for institutional investors, including one-to-one meetings, voting, shareholder proposals/resolutions, the use of focus lists and rating systems are discussed.

We have seen how, in the UK and the USA, institutional investors have become very important over the last forty years as their share ownership has increased and they have become more active in their ownership role. Institutional investors tend to have a fiduciary responsibility, i.e. the responsibility to act in the best interests of a third party (generally the beneficial or ultimate owners of the shares). Until recently, this responsibility has tended to concentrate on ensuring that they invest in companies that are not only profitable but that will continue to have a growing trend of profits. Whilst this remains the case, governments and pressure groups have raised the question of how these profits are achieved. We now see institutional investors being much more concerned about the internal governance of the company and also the company's relationship with other stakeholder groups. The growth of institutional investor interest in socially responsible investment is the subject of Chapter 7.

Summary

- Institutional investors, such as large pension funds, insurance companies, and mutual funds, have become the largest shareholders in many countries, having significant shareholdings in the companies in which they invest.

- Sovereign wealth fund, private equity firms, and hedge funds have all come under the spotlight in relation to corporate governance issues.

- The relationship between institutional investors and their investee companies is very important. Institutional investors can have a powerful 'voice' in their investee companies.

- There is an increased emphasis on the stewardship role that should be played by institutional investors.

- The 'tools' of governance include one-to-one meetings, voting, shareholder proposals/ resolutions, focus lists, and rating systems.

- The evidence as to whether 'good' corporate governance impacts on corporate performance is rather mixed but, looking at it another way, good governance can help ensure that companies do not fail. Also, a company with good corporate governance is more likely to attract external capital flows than one without.

Example: Bellway Plc, UK

This is an example of a company that did not engage fully with its major shareholders in relation to its executive remuneration policy; as a result there was a shareholder rebellion over its remuneration report.

Bellway Plc is the fourth largest house builder in the UK. In January 2009 it held its AGM at which the majority of shareholders voted against its remuneration report. This was the first defeat of its kind in the UK since the GlaxoSmithKline remuneration report was rejected in 2003. The ABI had issued a 'red top' alert (indicating a breach of corporate governance best practice) as it felt that management had abandoned their original bonus targets when it became apparent that they were not going to meet these targets, but awarded themselves bonuses anyway. This meant that the directors had bonuses of

(continued)

55 per cent of their salaries in a year when shares in Bellway lost 28 per cent of their value and sales fell by 50 per cent. It should be remembered that the vote on the remuneration report is an advisory one, and the directors are under no obligation to pay back their bonuses. However, Bellway has stated: 'The board has noted shareholders' views . . . and believes it was wrong in not consulting with major shareholders earlier. It therefore proposes to review future policy on this matter, in consultation with them, in the coming months'. This example clearly highlights the need for boards to have an informed dialogue with their major shareholders, and to take their views into account.

In 2012 all resolutions, including the vote on the report on directors' remuneration were passed, although a minority of 2.69 per cent of shareholders voted against the report.

Example: Eli Lilly & Company, USA

This is an example from the USA of the use of a focus list by an institutional investor to highlight perceived poor corporate governance in Eli Lilly & Company.

Eli Lilly & Company is a global pharmaceutical company and one of the world's largest corporations headquartered in the USA. CalPERS is one of the largest and most influential pension funds in the USA and is active in pursuing good corporate governance in its investee companies. It included Eli Lilly on its 2009 corporate governance focus list of poorly performing companies (the company had also been included on its 2007 list). This was because its stock (shares) had underperformed relative to the Russell 1000 index and its industry peer index over the three- and five-year time periods ending 27 February 2009. In addition, CalPERS was concerned that the board had adopted a default provision under Indiana law which prohibits shareowners from amending the bylaws. Only 4 per cent of companies in the Russell 1000 employ such restrictions on shareowner rights and the board of Eli Lilly was unwilling to remove this restriction. CalPERS stated that

> In light of a majority approved shareowner proposal at the 2008 Annual Meeting, the Board of Directors has opted not to take necessary action to seek shareowner approval to amend the articles of incorporation for the purpose of removing the supermajority voting requirements . . . The company would not agree to allow shareowners the right to call a special meeting and/or act by written consent . . . The company would not agree to adopt an annual non-binding advisory vote on executive compensation practices.

Eli Lilly responded by saying that it would seek shareowner approval at the 2009 annual meeting to eliminate its classified board structure (a classified board structure is one where directors may serve for different periods of time, often longer periods of time than shareholders would usually like to see, and so the directors may become entrenched or non-responsive). The company did try to remove its classified board structure at both the 2007 and 2008 annual meetings, but did not succeed due to its 80 per cent supermajority voting requirements (supermajority voting requirements are where a high level of shareholder approval, in this case 80 per cent, is needed to approve certain changes, so where less than 80 per cent is achieved, an amendment cannot be passed). CalPERS is seeking to allow a simple majority of shareowners (51 per cent) the right to amend the bylaws.

A review of the proxy statement for 2011 shows that the board did ask for a 'vote for' for two resolutions (i) to approve amendments to the articles of incorporation to provide for annual election of all directors, and (ii) to approve amendments to the articles of incorporation to eliminate all supermajority voting requirements. However, both of these resolutions each required an 80 per cent supermajority vote and they again appeared on the 2012 proxy statement so it seems that the supermajority vote in favour has proved difficult to achieve.

(Note: From November 2010 CalPERS adopted a new approach for engaging with underperforming companies through private contacts and proxy actions rather than by posting to a public 'name and shame' focus list).

Mini case study   Rio Tinto Plc, UK

This is an interesting example of institutional investors trying to protect their interests when they feel that the company's proposed strategy is not in the best interests of the current shareholders. After institutional investors expressed their concerns, the board engaged in dialogue with them to discuss these concerns and explain their strategy more fully.

Rio Tinto is a leading international mining group headquartered in the UK, combining Rio Tinto Plc, a London and New York Stock Exchange (NYSE) listed company, and Rio Tinto Limited, which is listed on the Australian Securities Exchange. The group's activities are the finding, mining, and processing of mineral resources. Its major products include aluminium, copper, diamonds, energy (coal and uranium), gold, industrial minerals (borax, titanium dioxide, salt, talc), and iron ore.

In February 2009 Rio Tinto announced a deal with Aluminium Corporation of China (Chinalco) which would create a strategic partnership through joint ventures whilst also giving Rio Tinto a cash injection from Chinalco. The cash injection would help solve some of the financial problems arising from Rio Tinto's large US$39 billion debt burden. However, the cash injection would involve the sale of stakes in prized mines and also the issue of US$7.2 billion of convertible bonds to Chinalco, together raising some US$19.5 billion.

However, investors, including Legal General Investment Management (the second largest share-holder in Rio Tinto), Scottish Widows Investment Partnership, and Aviva Investors were concerned that this proposed deal would result in a dilution of their shareholdings as they had not been offered the opportunity to participate in a rights issue. Rights issues have been a traditional way to raise funds from existing shareholders in the UK, Europe, and Australasia. Existing shareholders are offered the chance to acquire new shares, at a discount, in proportion to their existing holding. Shareholders taking up the rights will retain the same proportion of the share capital overall as they had prior to the rights issue. However, shareholders not taking up the rights issue shares will have a lower proportion of the company's share capital than they did prior to the rights issue, i.e. their stake will be diluted. To avoid any dilution that would occur when companies do not offer shares to their existing shareholders first, in some jurisdictions the concept of pre-emption rights (that is, new shares have to be offered to existing shareholders first) has long been enshrined in company law. In addition to the concern over the lack of opportunity to existing shareholders to partake in any new issues of shares, the institutional investors pointed out that potential conflicts of interest could arise if Chinalco had seats on the Rio Tinto board, and also held stakes in some of Rio Tinto's best assets.

Interestingly, Jim Leng, who was the Chairman Designate for Rio Tinto, resigned over the matter as he had reservations about the Chinalco deal and favoured a rights issue. However, Tom Albanese, the Chief Executive, and Paul Skinner, who was due to retire from the Chairman's post and make way for Jim Leng, both argued in favour of the Chinalco deal.

Institutional investors threatened to vote against the deal, and the board engaged in dialogue with the investors to try to convince them to approve the deal. However, many of the institutional investors still favoured a rights issue over the proposed deal. In May 2009 Chinalco walked away from the proposed deal with Rio Tinto amid the intense investor pressure, and Rio Tinto announced a rights issue. Chinalco participated in the rights issues along with other shareholders, taking up the rights offered.

In December 2010 Rio Tinto and Chinalco signed a non-binding Memorandum of Understanding (MoU) to establish a landmark exploration joint venture in China, with Chinalco holding a 51 per cent interest in the joint venture and Rio Tinto holding a 49 per cent interest.

In 2012 Rio Tinto completed an agreement with the Aluminum Corporation of China Limited (Chalco), a listed arm of Chinalco, to set up a joint venture for the development of the Simandou iron ore mine in Guinea, West Africa. According to the agreement, Rio Tinto and Chinalco will hold 53 per cent and 47 per cent stakes, respectively, in the joint venture, which translates into a 50.35 per cent and 44.65per cent interest in the Simandou project; the remaining 5per cent will go to the International Finance Corporation, a member of the World Bank Group.

Questions

The discussion questions to follow cover the key learning points of this chapter. Reading of some of the additional reference material will enhance the depth of the students' knowledge and understanding of these areas.

1. Why has the influence of institutional investors grown so much in recent years, and what role do you think institutional investors should play in corporate governance?
2. How do SWFs differ from 'traditional' institutional investors?
3. To what extent is the internationalization of investment portfolios responsible for institutional investors' increased interest in corporate governance?
4. What 'tools of governance' do institutional investors have at their disposal?
5. What evidence is there to show that 'good' corporate governance can improve corporate performance?
6. 'Institutional investors have a responsibility to vote the shares in their investee companies.' Critically discuss this statement.

References

ABI/NAPF (1999), *Responsible Voting—A Joint ABI-NAPF Statement*, ABI/NAPF, London.

Aggarwal, R., Erel, I., Ferreira, M., and Matos, P. (2011), 'Does Governance Travel Around the World? Evidence from Institutional Investors', *Journal of Financial Economics*, Vol. 100 (1), pp. 154–81.

Becht, M., Franks, J., Mayer, C., and Rossi, S. (2009), 'Returns to Shareholder Activism—Evidence from a Clinical Study of the Hermes UK Focus Fund', *The Review of Financial Studies*, Vol. 22, Issue 8.

Berle, A.A. and Means, G.C. (1932), *The Modern Corporation and Private Property*, Macmillan, New York.

Bosch, H. (1993), *Corporate Practices and Conduct*, Business Council of Australia, Melbourne.

Cadbury, Sir Adrian (1992), *Report of the Committee on the Financial Aspects of Corporate Governance*, Gee & Co. Ltd, London.

Combined Code (2003), *The Combined Code on Corporate Governance*, FRC, London.

CEPS (1995), *Corporate Governance in Europe*, Brussels.

——(2006), *The Combined Code on Corporate Governance*, FRC, London.

——(2008), *The Combined Code on Corporate Governance*, FRC, London.

Dalton, D.R., Daily, C.M., Ellstrand, A.E., and Johnson, J.L. (1998), 'Meta-analytic Reviews of Board Composition, Leadership Structure, and Financial Performance', *Strategic Management Journal*, Vol. 19, No. 24.

Deutsche Bank (2004a), *Global Corporate Governance Research*, 'Beyond the Numbers—Corporate Governance in the UK', February.

——(2004b), *Global Corporate Governance Research*, 'Beyond the Numbers—Corporate Governance in South Africa', October.

European Commission (2007a), *Directive 2007/36/EC Shareholders' Rights*, EU, Brussels.

——(2007b), *Report on the Proportionality Principle in the EU*, external study by ISS Europe, the ECGI, and Shearman & Sterling LLP, EU, Brussels.

——(2010), *Green Paper on Corporate Governance in Financial Institutions and Remuneration Policies*, European Commission, Brussels.

——(2011), Green Paper, *The EU Corporate Governance Framework*, European Commission, Brussels.

EFAMA (2011), *EFAMA Code for External Governance: Principles for the exercise of ownership rights in investee companies*, EFAMA, Brussels.

FairPensions (2011), *Protecting Our Best Interests, Rediscovering Fiduciary Obligation*, FairPensions, London.

FESE (2008), *Share Ownership Structure in Europe*, FESE Economics and Statistics Committee, Brussels.

FRC (2010), *UK Corporate Governance Code*, FRC, London.

FRC (2010), *UK Stewardship Code*, FRC, London.

Gompers, P.A., Ishii, J.L., and Metrick, A. (2003), 'Corporate Governance and Equity Prices', *Quarterly Journal of Economics*, Vol. 118, No. 1 (February).

Greenbury, Sir Richard (1995), *Directors' Remuneration*, Gee & Co. Ltd, London.

Hampel, Sir Ronnie (1998), *Committee on Corporate Governance: Preliminary Report*, Gee & Co. Ltd, London.

Hermes (2002), *The Hermes Principles*, Hermes Pensions Management Ltd, London.

—— (2005), *Corporate Governance and Corporate Performance*, Hermes Investment Management Ltd, London.

—— (2006), *The Hermes Corporate Governance Principles*, Hermes Investment Management Ltd, London.

—— (2007), *Corporate Governance and Performance– The Missing Links*, Hermes Investment Management Ltd, London.

—— (2010), *The Hermes Responsible Ownership Principles*, Hermes Pensions Management Ltd, London.

Hirschman, A.O. (1970), *Exit, Voice, and Loyalty*, Harvard University Press, Cambridge, MA.

HM Treasury (2008), *Updating the Myners Principles: A Response to Consultation*, HM Treasury, London.

ISC (2002), *The Responsibilities of Institutional Shareholders and Agents—Statement of Principles*, ISC, London.

—— (2005), *Review of the Institutional Shareholders' Committee Statement of Principles on the Responsibilities of Institutional Shareholders and Agents*, ISC, London.

—— (2007), *The Responsibilities of Institutional Shareholders and Agents—Statement of Principles*, ISC, London.

—— (2009), *Improving Institutional Investors' Role in Governance*, ISC, London.

—— (2009), *Code on the Responsibilities of Institutional Investors*, ISC, London.

ICGN (2007), *Statement of Shareholder Responsibilities*, ICGN, London.

—— (2008), *Statement on the Global Financial Crisis*, ICGN, London.

—— (2009), *Second Statement on the Global Financial Crisis*, ICGN, London.

—— (2012), *ICGN Model Mandate Initiative*, ICGN, London.

International Financial Services London (2009), *Sovereign Wealth Funds 2009*, March, IFSL Research, London.

IWG (2007), *Sovereign Wealth Funds, Generally Accepted Principles and Practices—Santiago Principles*, IWG, London.

Kay, J. (2012), *The Kay Review of UK Equity Markets and Long-Term Decision Making, Interim Report February 2012*, Department for Business, Innovation & Skills, London.

Lantz, J.-B., Montandrau, S., and Sahut, J.-M. (2010), 'Activism of Institutional Investors, Corporate Governance Alerts and Financial Performance', *International Journal of Business*, Vol. 15, No. 2, pp. 221–40.

Mallin C.A. (2012), 'The Stewardship Code', Working Paper, Birmingham Business School.

—— and Melis, A. (2010), 'Shareholder Rights, Shareholder Voting and Corporate Performance', forthcoming Journal of Management and Governance, available on Online First 11/5/10, **http://www.springerlink.com/content/ x6751r152n771546/fulltext.pdf**

Manifest (2011), *Proxy Voting 2010*, Manifest Information Services Ltd, Essex.

McCahery J. A., Starks, L.T., and Sautner, Z. (2010), 'Behind the Scenes: The Corporate Governance Preferences of Institutional Investors', *Tilburg Law School Research Paper No. 010/2010*. Available at SSRN: **http://ssrn.com/abstract=1571046**

McKinsey & Co. (2002), *Global Investor Opinion Survey: Key Findings*, McKinsey & Co., London.

Millstein, I.M. and MacAvoy, P.W. (1998), 'The Active Board of Directors and Performance of the Large Publicly Traded Corporation', *Columbia Law Review*, Vol. 98, No. 21.

Monks, R. (2001), *The New Global Investors*, Capstone Publishers, London.

Myners, P. (2001), *Myners Report on Institutional Investment*, HM Treasury, London.

—— (2007), *Review of the Impediments to Voting UK Shares*, IMA, London.

National Association of Pension Funds (1995), *Voting guidelines*, NAPF, London.

—— (1999), *Report of the Committee of Inquiry into UK Vote Execution*, NAPF, London.

—— (2007), *Institutional Investment in the UK—Six Years On*, NAPF, London.

Nesbitt, S.L. (1994), 'Long-term Rewards from Shareholder Activism: A Study of the "CalPERS Effect"', *Journal of Applied Corporate Finance*, No. 5.

OECD (2007), *Lack of Proportionality Between Ownership and Control: Overview and Issues for Discussion*, OECD, Paris.

—— (2008a), *Codes and Industry Standards Covering the Behaviour of Alternative Investors*, OECD, Paris.

—— (2008b), *The Role of Private Equity and Activist Hedge Funds in Corporate Governance—Related Policy Issues*, OECD, Paris.

—— (2011), *The Role of Institutional Investors in Promoting Good Corporate Governance*, OECD, Paris.

ONS (2012), *Ownership of UK Quoted Shares 2010*, ONS, Newport.

Patterson, D.J. (2000), *The Link Between Corporate Governance and Performance, Year 2000 Update*, Conference Board, New York.

Renders A., Gaeremynck A., and Sercu P. (2010), 'Corporate-Governance Ratings and Company Performance: A Cross-European Study', *Corporate Governance: An International Review*, Vol. 18(2), pp. 87–106.

SVWG (2005), *Review of the Impediments to Voting UK Shares*, SVWG, London.

Talbot, L. E. (2010), 'The Coming of Shareholder Stewardship: A Contextual Analysis of Current Anglo-American Perspectives on Corporate Governance', *Warwick School of Law Research Paper No. 2010/22*. Available at SSRN: **http://ssrn.com/abstract=1676869**

The CityUK Research (2012), *Sovereign Wealth Funds 2012*, The CityUK Research, London.

Tomorrow's Owners (2009), *Tomorrow's Owners Stewardship of Tomorrow's Company*, Tomorrow's Owners, London.

Useem, M. (1996), *Investor Capitalism—How Money Managers Are Changing the Face of Corporate America*, BasicBooks, Harper Collins, New York.

Walker, D. (2009), *A Review of Corporate Governance in UK Banks and Other Financial Industry Entities, Final Recommendations*, HM Treasury, London.

Walker Working Group (Private Equity Working Group on Transparency and Disclosure) (2007), *Guidelines for Disclosure and Transparency in Private Equity*, Walker Working Group, London.

Useful websites

www.abi.org.uk The website of the Association of British Insurers offers topical articles on a range of corporate governance issues of particular relevance to the UK's insurance industry.

http://blog.thecorporatelibrary.com/ The website of the Corporate Library, which has comprehensive information about various aspects of corporate governance including shareholders and stakeholders (renamed the GMI blog).

www.calpers.ca.gov The website of the California Public Employees' Retirement System, a large pension fund active in corporate governance matters.

www.bis.gov.uk The Department for Business, Innovation & Skills website offers a range of information including ministerial speeches and regulatory guidance.

http://ec.europa.eu/internal_market/company/index_en.htm The website of the European Union covering company law and corporate governance aspects.

www.fese.be The website of the Federation of European Securities Exchanges which covers its activities in promoting relations between global stock exchanges.

www.manifest.co.uk The website of Manifest, providing information about global proxy governance matters.

www.napf.co.uk The website of the National Association of Pension Funds offers topical articles on a range of corporate governance issues of particular relevance to UK pension funds.

www.swfinstitute.org The website of the Sovereign Wealth Fund Institute covering various aspects of SWFs.

www.thecityuk.com The website of The CityUK, which has information about UK financial services at home and overseas.

 For further links to useful sources of information visit the Online Resource Centre **www.oxfordtextbooks.co.uk/orc/mallin4e/**

 **FT Clippings**

FT: Institutions wary of full disclosure on how they vote

By Ruth Sullivan

April 29, 2012

Shareholders are increasingly flexing their muscles on both sides of the Atlantic, particularly over the size of executive remuneration, most notably for bankers.

In the US in the past few weeks shareholders have used their advisory say on pay to reject the pay award of Citigroup's chief executive, while in the UK investors have forced Barclays to accept tougher bonus conditions for its boss Bob Diamond. Nearly a third of the bank's shareholders failed to support its remuneration report at the annual general meeting on Friday.

Yet in spite of the flurry of activism, institutional investors are still reluctant to disclose publicly how they vote on pay in the UK.

Recent research from Pirc, the corporate governance group, shows slow growth in publishing voting information in spite of a "comply or explain" requirement to do so under the UK Stewardship Code.

The study shows only 27 asset managers—out of the 175 that have signed up to the code—have disclosed a full voting record, with just 50 providing some level of voting data.

Tom Powdrill, a spokesman for Pirc, says: "A long tail of asset managers do not do it [full disclosure]. Some only give headline statistics without any breakdown, not providing anything of value and others just report votes against [a resolution] or abstentions." The data suggest "the remaining two-thirds do not comply with the code, which states institutional investors should publicly disclose voting records or explain why not," he adds.

Many of the smaller asset managers choose to explain rather than to comply.

The most common reason for non-disclosure is that such information is confidential or should be shared only with the client.

Smaller asset managers may have fewer resources to tackle the work involved in disclosing information but Mr Powdrill dismisses this argument. "It is not an onerous task for any asset manager, regardless of size, as it just takes a few hours. Investors are free to choose how frequently they wish to disclose voting information, with some reporting quarterly and others monthly or annually," he says.

Greater disclosure on voting information is also useful for the companies in which asset managers invest, particularly if there is a lack of engagement. "Companies want to know how their investors are voting as it gives them guidance," says one US proxy agency.

If there is not enough support for a voluntary approach, perhaps the UK should follow the US where it is mandatory for mutual funds to publicly disclose how they vote. All asset managers with more than $100m under management will have to follow suit if draft legislation is adopted.

Such an approach recently gained support from Chuka Umunna, the UK's shadow business secretary. Keen to increase transparency, Mr Umunna brought forward a proposed change to the financial services bill that would force institutional investors such as asset managers to say how they voted on executive pay packages.

Asset managers are not enthusiastic about the proposal. Colin Melvin, chief executive of Hermes Equity Ownership Services, an advisory service funded by

25 institutional investors, believes it is good practice to disclose (and does so) but maintains a mandatory approach would not help.

"It would not do the end client any good but might [just] lead to boosting the revenues of proxy agencies," he says. A better approach is to "attack the root cause of the problem, which is to clarify what is the fiduciary duty of asset managers".

Guy Jubb, head of corporate governance at Standard Life Investments, says taking the mandatory route to disclosure would "give rise to people dumping information that would not be useful".

While Standard Life is a signatory to the Stewardship Code, Mr Jubb says if asset managers put all their voting information on their websites "people would not see the wood for the trees". The number of people gaining access to the voting data on Standard Life's website is already disappointing, he says, and more information would not improve traffic volume.

Looking at the growth of disclosure in the UK over the past five years, Pirc estimates it would take almost 10 years before half of the Stewardship Code signatories disclose a full record. "Progress in disclosure could [even] slow in the next few years as some asset managers may believe their

explanations for non-compliance are sufficient. The Stewardship Code is unlikely to result in standardised disclosure of full voting records across the industry any time soon," says Mr Powdrill. The group supports a mandatory approach.

In the UK greater transparency on executive pay packets is likely to come from plans proposed by Vince Cable, business secretary, to make shareholder votes binding on future pay policies. This would approve salary increases and the level of performance-related pay and would also require boards to gain a majority of between 50 to 75 per cent of shareholder votes for a pay policy to be approved.

Such moves come as politicians worry that the current advisory vote on remuneration is not tackling the issue of high pay.

Many asset managers are not in favour of a binding vote on pay and worry about the detail of such legislation. The government "needs to find the right balance between accountability and practicality", says Mr Jubb.

In the US, where shareholders are into their second year of say on pay activity, there is also little appetite for a binding vote. "Investors are happy with a non-binding say on pay. If it were binding people would be more reluctant to use it," says the proxy agency.

FT: Boards wake up to a shareholder spring

By Kate Burgess and Dan McCrum

May 4, 2012

A new mood of militancy is bowling through this year's season of public get-togethers between companies and their shareholders. And it is extraordinary for several reasons.

For decades annual meetings have been polite affairs. The big institutional

insurance and pension fund managers, who own the bulk of shares, usually back management having thrashed out concerns privately long before they reach the ballot box.

Not this year. There has been a breakdown in discussions with several boards after institutions accused them of persistently rewarding executives with multimillion-pound bonuses despite anaemic performances. This comes against a backdrop of deepening anxieties about jobs, wages, and returns on savings. Shareholders have simply lost patience with persistently poor returns over five years.

This week investors in Aviva refused to back the UK insurer's pay plans for top executives. It is only the fourth FTSE 100 company to lose the vote in Britain's decade-long history of having a say on pay.

The backlash started against banks paying large chunks of profits to staff. Just over half of Citigroup's shareholders refused to back its remuneration scheme last month. Then swaths of UBS' shareholders this week voted against the management's performance and its pay plans.

In the UK, nearly a third of Barclays' investors refused to back its pay report, despite a last-minute dash to deflect shareholder anger by publicly promising to boost dividends and cut the bonus of its chief executive Bob Diamond.

One seasoned adviser to Barclays remarked: "After that, Barclays remuneration committee meetings will never be the same again".

And it is not hedge funds, activist arbitrageurs or corporate governance nuts that are leading the protests. "This is the City turning on the City. That is what is so remarkable about this so-called shareholder spring," says one UK-based proxy adviser.

Those rebelling are long-term corporate backers such as BlackRock, Invesco, Aviva's investment arm and Standard Life. Now they are taking the battle beyond the banks to other companies and other countries.

In Europe, the backlash over executive pay is still largely confined to the banks. But Susannah Haan, secretary-general of the Federation of European Issuers, says: "European companies understand it is coming".

So far the uprising has cost two UK chief executives their jobs. Two weeks ago David Brennan, chief executive of AstraZeneca, bowed to pressure from the pharmaceutical group's top shareholders and stepped down at the annual meeting. This week Sly Bailey quit as chief executive of media group Trinity Mirror days before the annual meeting and after the company failed to find a compromise over her £1.7m pay package.

Investors are not going into battle lightheartedly. "Bringing these things to a head is very destabilising—for companies, employees and our investment," says the chief investment officer of one group.

But the head of another leading shareholder group says: "We are fed up with companies coming back with poorly structured pay plans year after year." Another says: "We have reached a point where we are saying we have to change the mindset and if that requires sacrificing a head, so be it." The no-votes do not simply reflect poor communication between boards and owners, says Robert Talbut, chief investment officer of Royal London Asset Management. Nor, he adds, should the no-votes be seen as a sudden knee jerk. Instead, they reflect calls for "fundamental reform" aligning pay to performance.

Keith Skeoch, chief executive of Standard Life Investments, says: "Boards have to get away from the idea of delivering large lumps of annual income [to executives]".

Pay is also the flashpoint for wider shareholder dissatisfaction. The no-votes signal concerns about a wider board malfunction, explains Sarah Wilson, chief executive at Manifest, a voting agency. "Remuneration is the window to the soul of the company. It objectively measures the links between incentives, behaviour, strategy and outcomes," she says.

The sudden burst of protest has in part been driven by the US where investors have had an advisory vote on pay for two years.

Last year 41 companies' pay plans were turned down within the Russell 3000 index. So far this year, eight have suffered the same fate, with the Citi vote setting a new high water mark.

"The Citi vote was electrifying. It shook us all up big time," says an EU-based investor. It shows that—contrary to the beliefs of some chief executives—US shareholders do care about pay if not aligned to performance.

Bank boards in the US, UK and Europe redoubled attempts to allay investor concerns over bonuses, says ISS, a proxy voting adviser. The say on pay in the US "has stiffened the sinews of shareholders and regulators and the contagion is spreading to other territories, such as Australia, South Africa and Europe," says Tom Gosling, pay consultant at PwC.

Even without the US impetus, many shareholders in Europe who have long had a vote on remuneration reports have been spoiling for a fight. Politics has been driving pay up the agenda amid criticism that investors failed to act like owners and did not curb the outsize executive incentives blamed for fuelling the financial crisis.

In 2010 the European Commission issued a green paper on the governance and pay at banks querying "the effectiveness of corporate governance rules based on the presumption of effective control by shareholders". Confidence in the model "has been severely shaken, to say the least," it said. That year the UK came up with the Stewardship Code setting out a blueprint for enhancing shareholders' engagement with companies.

Mr Skeoch of Standard Life says the code has galvanised shareholders. "Investors are a lot more joined up about issues. They are much more prepared to vote to signal intentions—and they will do so internationally." The code has not, however, staved off government intervention. UK politicians are proposing to make the vote on pay binding. Shareholders do not much like the idea but recognise the political will behind it, given the widening gap between ordinary workers' pay and bosses' bonuses.

As one investor comments: "Boards can't sack lots of people and then immediately come back with a pay rise for executives. Consciously or unconsciously it is distasteful." But some shareholders resent being squeezed between what one described as "unembarrassable" boards and policy makers who expect investors to act as board consciences.

Ms Wilson from Manifest adds: "Shareholders don't want to micromanage or set pay. That is not their job. This is about stiffening the resolve of remuneration committees." So will companies continue to suffer public beatings? We've seen these shareholder springs before. In 2009, 59 per cent of shareholders voted Shell's pay plans down. But the threatened wider revolt never materialised as corporate returns recovered.

"Is the trend here to stay?" asks Amra Balic, head of corporate governance for Europe Middle East and Africa at BlackRock. "It depends on whether companies learn anything from this year's experience."

7 Socially Responsible Investment

Learning Objectives

- To be aware of the origins of socially responsible investment
- To understand the different approaches that may be used for socially responsible (ethical) investment
- To appreciate the role of institutional investors in socially responsible investment
- To be aware of the different ethical indices that may be used to assess the performance of socially responsible funds
- To be aware of the evidence analyzing the performance of socially responsible investment funds

Introduction

We have seen that corporate governance is concerned with many facets of a business and how that business is managed. The previous chapter highlighted how, over the last 40 years, institutional investor share ownership has increased substantially and the majority of UK equity is now owned by institutional investors. In recent years, there has been an increasing awareness of socially responsible investment (SRI) issues in the UK, and these have, in many cases, become an integral part of corporate governance policies, both of individual companies and of institutional investors.

SRI involves considering the ethical, social, and environmental performance of companies selected for investment as well as their financial performance. The phrase 'ethical investment' is often used interchangeably with the phrase 'socially responsible investment'.

The origins of SRI lie in various religious movements such as the Quakers and the Methodists. From the nineteenth century onwards, religious groups such as these have sought to invest their funds without compromising their principles. So, for example, the churches would avoid investing in companies involved in alcohol and gambling. This type of policy is common across many religions, including Christianity and Islam. During the course of the twentieth century there were various incidences with which religious groups sought to avoid investment contact, latterly one such incidence has been the avoidance of involvement with tobacco companies. It is worth mentioning that US church groups tend to be one of the most active in putting forward socially based shareholder proposals at companies' annual general meetings. Such shareholder proposals include areas such as trying to ensure that advertising does not encourage young people to smoke.

SRI covers a wide range of areas, including genetic engineering, the environment, employment conditions, and human rights. Recent cases of companies highlighted for not being socially responsible include those that have used child labour in the manufacture of their clothes overseas and retailers selling carpets that have been made by small children who are exploited by working long hours for little, if any, pay.

SRI and corporate governance

Increasingly, institutional investors have become aware of the importance of SRI on a number of fronts: client demand, corporate citizenship, and potential economic benefits. The Organisation for Economic Co-operation and Development (OECD) (1998) corporate governance report stated:

> In the global economy, sensitivity to the many societies in which an individual corporation may operate can pose a challenge. Increasingly, however, investors in international capital markets expect corporations to forego certain activities—such as use of child or prison labour, bribery, support of oppressive regimes, and environmental disruption—even when those activities may not be expressly prohibited in a particular jurisdiction in which the corporation operates.

It is key to the development of SRI that the large institutional investors in both the UK and the USA have become more involved and willing to screen potential investments as appropriate. Increasingly, this approach is fuelled by client demand for SRI. A number of pension schemes in the UK, including British Coal and the Universities Superannuation Scheme, have asked their fund managers to take ethical and social issues into account in their investment strategy. A further motivation for SRI is highlighted by the OECD (1998): 'In accommodating the expectations of society, corporations must not lose sight of the primary corporate objective, which is to generate long-term economic profit to enhance shareholder (or investor) value. The Advisory Group recognises that, over the long term, acting as a responsible corporate citizen is consistent with this economic objective'.

The growing awareness of SRI and the involvement of the government via legislation means that institutional investors are becoming increasingly active in this field, for example, by setting up special funds or screening existing and potential investments. The value of UK ethical funds increased substantially in the last decade, rising from £1.465 billion in 1997 to £11.3 billion at the end of June 2011 (Ethical Investment Research Services (EIRIS) 2012). It is expected that this trend will continue given the clear indication of the growing interest in this area.

An important development in the UK was that, from 3 July 2000, pension fund trustees have had to take account of SRI in their Statement of Investment Principles. This change means that pension fund trustees must state 'the extent (if at all) to which social, environmental or ethical considerations are taken into account in the selection, retention, and realisation of investments' (amendment to Pensions Act 1995). Therefore pension fund trustees are required to state their policy on social, environmental, and ethical issues, and if they do not have a policy in place, then this provision will also highlight that fact. A survey of pension fund trustees carried out by Gribben and Gitsham (2006), found that 'only one in ten trustees believe that companies are providing sufficient information to enable social and environmental impacts and risks to be assessed effectively'.

More recently Boersch (2010) reported the results of a survey conducted by Allianz Global Investors and the Centre for European Economic Research (ZEW) amongst pension experts in France, Germany, Italy, the Netherlands, Switzerland and the UK on the future of SRI in pension fund portfolios. He stated that, 'on average, most of the pension experts surveyed believe that, in the future, SRI criteria will play an increasingly important role in how pension funds make investment decisions. Environmental criteria are considered to be the most important element of the SRI concept. Respondents agreed that the growing SRI trend is being driven much less by the expectation of higher returns or lower risk as it is by public pressure.'

Strategies for SRI

EIRIS is a leading provider of independent research into corporate social, environmental, and ethical performance, and was established in 1983 to help investors make responsible investment decisions. EIRIS has identified three basic strategies for SRI:

- **Engagement**—identify areas for improvement in the ethical, social, and environmental policies of the companies invested in, and encourage them to make improvements.
- **Preference**—fund managers work to a list of guidelines that trustees prefer companies invested in to meet.
- **Screening**—trustees ask for investments to be limited to companies selected (screened) for their ethical behaviour. May be 'positive' or 'negative' screening.

EIRIS provides more detailed definitions for each of these strategies as follows.

Engagement

Engagement involves identifying areas for improvement in the ethical, social, and environmental policies of the companies invested in, and encouraging them to make those improvements. This can be done by:

- the investor telling the companies their policy and letting them know how it affects their decisions to invest in a company or respond to takeovers and share issues;
- the investor trying to persuade the company, via regular meetings, to improve their practices on issues such as employment practices, recycling, and pollution reduction;
- offering to help them formulate their own policy; this might be done through existing corporate governance voting policies by extending them to include ethical issues.

Preference

Fund managers work to a list of guidelines that the trustees prefer the companies they invest in to meet. They then select investments or portfolio weightings in these companies, taking into account how closely a company meets, or sets about meeting, these parameters. This approach also enables the investor to integrate ethical with financial decision-making; in cases where two companies get a similar rating against traditional financial indicators, they can be compared against the investor's ethical indicators, and the company with the better all-round performance is selected.

Screening

Trustees ask the fund manager to limit their investments to a list of companies selected (screened) for their ethical behaviour. They may be companies whose conduct is viewed positively, such as those with good employment practices or those taking active steps to reduce levels of pollution. Or they may be selected for not indulging in certain 'negative' practices or proscribed industries, for example, the armaments industry.

Institutional investors' policies

In 1996 the National Association of Pension Funds (NAPF), in its guidance on good corporate governance, stated that:

> NAPF believes it is inconceivable that, in the long run, a company can enhance shareholder value unless it takes good care to retain and develop its customer relationships; unless it provides encouragement to its employees; unless it develops effective relationships with its suppliers so that they can see the common interest in working to lower costs; unless it pays proper attention to preserving its 'licence to operate' from the community.

The sentiments embodied in this statement have become broadly accepted, and in the context of SRI, the last point is particularly pertinent: one has to have regard to the impact of a business's activities on the community at large and all that that implies, including the impact on the environment, and ethical aspects.

In 2009 the NAPF issued its *Responsible Investment Guidance*. The guidance states that the NAPF approach is based on two key principles: 'Corporate responsibility, which encompasses the environmental, social and governance issues managed by the companies and other assets in which pension funds invest, is an integral part of good corporate governance. The development and oversight of an appropriate Corporate Responsibility Policy thus falls to their boards' and 'Funds should give careful consideration to the extent to which they wish their managers to take responsible investment issues into account when implementing their investment policies and reporting on them'. Furthermore, the report states that 'pension schemes and their advisers, have an important role to play in encouraging higher standards of corporate responsibility'.

A number of institutional investors have policies in place regarding SRI. The policies may be separate or incorporated as part of the institutional investors' wider corporate governance policies. Several of the largest UK institutional investors have made statements on SRI. Friends Provident stated: 'We will be using our influence as an investor to encourage companies to improve the way they (investee companies) manage environmental and ethical issues'. Friends Provident's approach is called the 'Responsible Engagement Overlay (REO)' and it is aimed at improving the behaviour of the companies in which it already invests.

SOCIALLY RESPONSIBLE INVESTMENT

Hermes Pensions Management Ltd is a leading UK institutional investor. In late January 2001 Hermes revised its corporate governance policies and called on UK companies to 'manage effectively relationships with its employees, suppliers, and customers, to behave ethically and to have regard for the environment and society as a whole'. Whilst asking companies to disclose their policies on an annual basis, Hermes asked that the remuneration committee in each company, when setting incentive pay, consider the effect on the company's performance of social, environmental, and ethical matters. There should be a credible system for verifying the accuracy of social disclosures, and directors should take social issues into account when assessing risk. The statement issued by Hermes had the backing of eight investor institutions who expected to incorporate it into their policies.

In 2002 Hermes introduced *The Hermes Principles*. Hermes advocates that companies should be able to demonstrate that their investment decisions are sound and also demonstrate ethical behaviour. In the section on social, ethical, and environmental aspects, Hermes has two principles: principles 9 and 10. Principle 9 states: 'Companies should manage effectively relationships with their employees, suppliers and customers and with others who have a legitimate interest in the company's activities. Companies should behave ethically and have regard for the environment and society as a whole'. This principle identifies the importance of considering both stakeholder views and having regard to social responsibility aspects. Principle 10 states: 'Companies should support voluntary and statutory measures which minimise the externalisation of costs to the detriment of society at large'. This principle discourages companies from making business successful at the expense of society at large. *The Hermes Corporate Governance Principles* (2006) reiterate the aforesaid principle 9, but also states in principle 5 that 'we consider socially, ethically and environmentally responsible behaviour as part of the management process that companies should undertake in order to maximize shareholder value in the long term rather than as an end in itself'. Companies are encouraged to comply with internationally recognized guidelines and principles on social, ethical, and environmental matters. In 2010 Hermes published *The Hermes Responsible Ownership Principles* detailing what they expect of listed companies and what listed companies can expect from them. Hermes' expectations of listed companies encompass twelve principles, which include two relating to stakeholders, environmental, and social issues. In turn, listed companies can expect five core principles of stewardship and engagement that Hermes feels responsible shareholders ought to observe; these include sustainability and governance, a long-term perspective when exercising ownership rights, and a constructive, confidential dialogue with boards and senior management.

Recognition of the growing importance of SRI was also evidenced by the Association of British Insurers (ABI) (2001) with the publication of its disclosure guidelines on SRI. The main focus of the guidelines is the identification and management of risks arising from social, environmental, and ethical issues that may affect either short-term or long-term business value. The flip side of this is that appropriate management of these risks may mean opportunities to enhance value. To this end, the guidelines recommend that the board should receive adequate information to make an assessment of the significance of social, environmental, and ethical matters that are relevant to the business and that there are appropriate systems in place for managing this type of risk, including 'performance measurement systems and appropriate remuneration incentives'. Furthermore, the guidelines state that the company's policies and procedures for managing this type of risk should be disclosed in the annual report, and not in any separate summary accounts nor on a dedicated social responsibility website. The ABI (2003) reviewed the level of compliance with its guidelines on SRI and found that 'two thirds of the FTSE 100 companies made either adequate or full disclosure . . . in their annual report that their boards have assessed the business and reputational risks arising from the way they manage social, environmental and ethical issues, and that these risks are being properly managed'.

The ABI issued its *Guidelines on Responsible Investment Disclosure* in February 2007, which updated and replaced its *Socially Responsible Investment Guidelines* (2001). The updated guidelines highlight aspects of responsibility reporting on which shareholders place particular value. This is narrative reporting, which 'sets environmental, social, and governance (ESG) risks in the context of the whole range of risks and opportunities facing the company; contains a forward looking perspective; and describes the actions of the Board in mitigating these risks'. They also state that 'investors continue to believe that, by focusing on the need to identify and manage ESG risks to the long and short-term value of the business, the guidelines highlight an opportunity to enhance value' and 'Reporting in connection with these risks should be set firmly in the context of the full range of strategic, financial and operational risks facing the business'.

There is also an emphasis that for institutional investors' consideration of these risks and opportunities should be in the context of their overarching objective of enhancing shareholder value; it should be an integral part of the investment process, rather than a separate 'add-on' consideration.

The guidelines give guidance to companies as to what disclosures an institutional investor might expect to see in a company's annual report. These disclosures include whether, as part of its regular risk assessment procedures, it takes account of the significance of ESG matters to the business of the company; whether ESG (as well as other) risks have been identified and systems are in place to manage such risks; and whether account is taken of ESG matters in the training of directors. With regard to the remuneration report, the remuneration committee should state whether it is able to consider corporate performance on ESG issues when setting remuneration of executive directors, and if not, why not; and also whether the remuneration committee has ensured that the incentive structure for senior management does not raise ESG risks by inadvertently motivating irresponsible behaviour.

The UK Sustainable Investment and Finance Association (UKSIF) is an active force in promoting the adoption, and propounding the virtues, of SRI in the UK. Its members encompass a wide range of interested parties, including fund managers, organizations, companies, and individuals. In 2010 UKSIF published *Focused on the Future: Celebrating ten years of responsible investment disclosure by UK occupational pension funds*. The report highlights ten key actions to ensure the protection and enhancement of pension fund assets through responsible ownership and investment. These are:

- **Sustainability governance**—Pension fund trustees and insurance company boards will increase their skills in sustainability governance; it will become good practice to have at least one member with sustainability expertise.
- **Transparency**—Major pension funds will implement web-based disclosure of how their responsible investment strategies are implemented.

- **Leadership**—Major new pension providers, such as the UK's NEST Corporation, will sign and implement the UN-backed *Principles for Responsible Investment*, and seek to be beacons for responsible ownership and investment.
- **Public procurement**—Public sector asset owners, such as UK local government pension schemes, will be required by governments to sign and implement the UN-backed *Principles for Responsible Investment*.
- **Responsible procurement**—Pension funds will demand responsible investment as part of risk transfer negotiations (e.g. pension fund buy-outs) and for both established investment services and emerging asset classes.
- **Empowering shareholders as owners**—A forward-looking resilience and sustainability strategy will be published annually addressing opportunities, risks and economic and social impact; companies will put this to a shareholder vote; executive pay will be linked to key sustainability achievements.
- **Responsible pension plan sponsorship**—Companies will encourage responsible investment by the occupational or personal pension funds they sponsor or provide access to; sustainability expertise will be made available as part of the employer's pension fund support.
- **Scrutiny from non-governmental organizations (NGOs)**—NGOs will build capacity and consumer support for understanding, scrutinising and challenging pension and insurance investment decisions.
- **Support from the professions**—Professional associations will promote responsible investment skills development and encourage debate on the social and environmental impact of investment regulation, policies and decisions.
- **Integration into investment management**—Asset managers will build responsible ownership and investment into marketing and promotion, service development strategies and staff development. This will play a key role in rebuilding trust in financial services.

FairPensions campaigns for major institutional investors to adopt responsible investment using shareholder power to hold companies to account. FairPensions report (2009) highlights that major UK pension funds are now acknowledging the potential that 'non-financial' issues have to affect the value of investments, however, many still lack key strategies to manage these risks. Catherine Howarth, the Chief Executive of FairPensions, said: 'Pension funds are now recognising that "non-financial" issues can become financial issues, but many still need to match words with deeds if they are to be ready for major challenges associated with issues like climate change'. The report highlights that the importance of ESG issues is 'a truth universally acknowledged' but not universally acted upon, that is, that the institutional investors' *Statement of Investment Principles* acknowledges the potential importance of ESG factors in the investment process, but then this may not be fully reflected in the detailed policy, implementation, and performance monitoring; they also highlight that 'there are a number of pension funds which, given their sponsoring companies' public profile on corporate social responsibility, could be expected to have pension schemes that are responsible investment leaders, but in practice appear to fall short of expectations'. In relation to transparency, the report finds evidence of 'a discernable correlation between pension schemes that are more transparent and those with well-defined policy and practice for managing ESG-related risks and opportunities'.

FairPensions (2010), in a review of the approach of insurance companies to ESG issues, states that 'Responsible investment focuses on the integration into investment decisions of those environmental, social and governance ("ESG") issues that can be material to long term shareholder value. The corporate fall-out from the Gulf of Mexico oil spill and the hacking scandal at News International should have removed all doubt about the financial relevance of ESG issues. Indeed governance failures within banks are widely regarded as one of the critical elements of the financial crisis. Yet our findings suggest that many insurance companies still view ESG issues as being relevant only to specialist "SRI" funds.' Therefore, insurance companies appear to lag behind other pension providers on responsible investment.

In the USA there has long been an active movement for SRI. The main thrust has tended to come from church groups and ethical/environmental groups with investment interests. They have been particularly active in putting forward shareholder proposals at investee companies; it is not unusual for literally hundreds of shareholder proposals to relate to SRI. Whilst the large institutional investors have not tended to be so active in putting forward shareholder proposals (they tend to have other ways of making their 'voice' heard), they have often supported shareholder proposals put forward by these interest groups.

However, for the last few years, the Teachers' Insurance and Annuity Association–College Retirement Equities Fund (TIAA–CREF) has taken an active stand in trying to promote and ensure good workplace practice, for example. CalPERS, the USA's largest institutional investor, issued its *Global Principles of Accountable Corporate Governance* in February 2009, revised in November 2011, which state

> CalPERS expects companies whose equity securities are held in the Fund's portfolio to conduct themselves with propriety and with a view toward responsible corporate conduct. If any improper practices come into being, companies should move decisively to eliminate such practices and effect adequate controls to prevent recurrence. A level of performance above minimum adherence to the law is generally expected. To further these goals, in September 1999 the CalPERS board adopted the Global Sullivan Principles of Corporate Social Responsibility.

In Europe too, in a number of countries including France, Germany, Belgium, the Netherlands, and Denmark, there is a growing awareness of SRI. For example, in Germany, from January 2002, every pension fund provider had to inform members in writing about whether, and in what form, social, ethical, and ecological aspects are taken into consideration. Whilst in Denmark large businesses are covered by a statutory requirement which means that from 2009 they had to report on the business's social responsibility policies, including any standards, guidelines or principles for social responsibility the business employs; how the business translates its social responsibility policies into action, including any systems or procedures used; and the business's evaluation of what has been achieved through social responsibility initiatives during the financial year, and any expectations it has regarding future initiatives. Similarly, there is a growing interest in SRI across the globe, for example, in Japan and also in Australia where a description of the extent to which investment products take account of social, ethical, and environmental issues is required. The European Commission

(2008) identifies the strong growth of the SRI market in European countries in recent years and states, 'there is some evidence that mainstream analysts and investors are attaching more importance to social and environmental issues'.

The UN *Principles for Responsible Investment* (PRI), launched in 2006, now have over 1050 signatories managing US$ 30 trillion. Eurosif (2010) state that total SRI assets under management in Europe had reached €5 trillion, as at December 31, 2009. This represents a spectacular growth compared to two years ago when it was €2.665 trillion.

International guidance

There have been a large number of international guidelines and statements that are relevant to the area of SRI. These include:

- *Global Sullivan Principles* (1977, 1999)—principles that are directed towards increasing corporate social responsibility (CSR) throughout the world, based on self-help.

- The *MacBride Principles* (1984)—consist of nine fair employment, affirmative action principles.

- Coalition for Environmentally Responsible Economies (Ceres) (1989)—a coalition of environmental, investor, and advocacy groups working together for sustainability in areas such as environmental restoration and management commitment. In 2010 Ceres published 'The 21st Century Corporation: The Ceres Roadmap for Sustainability'. It analyses the drivers, risks, and opportunities involved in making the shift to sustainability, and details strategies and results from companies that are taking on these challenges.

- *UN Global Compact* (1999)—nine principles relating to the areas of human rights, labour standards, and environmental practices. In 2004 a tenth principle against corruption was added.

- OECD *Guidelines for Multinational Enterprises* (2000, updated most recently in 2011)—cover areas such as disclosure, environment, employment, industrial relations, bribery, and consumer interests.

- *Global Reporting Initiative (GRI) Sustainability Guidelines* (2002, updated most recently in 2011)—the United Nations Environment Programme (UNEP) and Ceres formed a partnership in 1999 to encourage NGOs, business associations, corporations, and stakeholders to undertake sustainability reporting.

- EC CSR—a *Business Contribution to Sustainable Development* (2002) encourages an EU framework for the development of SRI, especially promoting transparency and convergence of CSR practices and instruments. Revised in 2011 with the EU *A Renewed Strategy 2011–14 for Corporate Social Responsibility*.

- The UN *Principles for Responsible Investment* (PRI) were issued in 2006. The PRI were developed by an international group of institutional investors reflecting the increasing relevance of environmental, social and corporate governance issues to investment practices. The process was convened by the UN Secretary-General. The PRI state:

As institutional investors, we have a duty to act in the best long-term interests of our beneficiaries. In this fiduciary role, we believe that environmental, social, and corporate governance (ESG) issues can affect the performance of investment portfolios (to varying degrees across companies, sectors, regions, asset classes and through time). We also recognize that applying these Principles may better align investors with broader objectives of society.

Signatories to the PRI commit to:

- incorporating ESG issues into investment analysis and decision-making processes;
- being active owners and incorporating ESG issues into ownership policies and practice;
- seeking appropriate disclosure on ESG issues by the entities in which they invest;
- promoting acceptance and implementation of the Principles within the investment industry;
- working together to enhance their effectiveness in implementing the Principles, and reporting on their activities and progress towards implementing the Principles.

In 2011 a document entitled *PRI Report on Progress 2011* was published. The report highlights progress made to date, special initiatives that have been undertaken, and areas for improvement. In April 2012, a new reporting framework was piloted. The new reporting framework has been designed through an extensive consultation process to achieve three main sets of objectives for signatories: to ensure transparency and accountability of the PRI initiative and its signatories, to encourage signatory transparency on responsible investment activities, and to provide tools to allow signatories to measure their performance with objective indicators.

Given that SRI and CSR are very much developing areas, further guidelines/revisions to existing guidelines are to be expected. However, it is becoming increasingly clear that companies will have to consider these as mainstream issues rather than as peripheral optional extras.

CSR indices

A number of stock market indices of companies with good CSR have been launched in recent years. These include the Ethibel Sustainability Index and the Domini Social Index, although perhaps the two most well-known are the FTSE4Good Indices and the Dow Jones Sustainability Indices (DJSI).

The FTSE4Good was launched in 2001 and is designed to reflect the performance of socially responsible equities. It covers four markets: the UK, USA, Europe, and global. It uses criteria for judging CSR based on three areas: human rights, stakeholder relations, and the environmental impact of a company's activities. When developing these criteria, the FTSE-4Good drew on various international guidelines and statements, including the *UN Global Compact*, the OECD *Principles for Multinational Enterprises*, the *Global Sullivan Principles*, the *Ceres Principles*, the *Caux Roundtable Principles*, and the *Amnesty International Human Rights Principles for Companies*. There are four tradable and five benchmark indices that make up the FTSE4Good index series. In 2004 the FTSE4Good Japan index (benchmark only) was launched, enabling investors to identify Japanese companies, within the FTSE Global Equity Index Series, which meet a set of internationally supported standards of CSR. A committee of independent practitioners in SRI and CSR review the indices to ensure that they are an accurate reflection of best practice.

The DJSI are aimed at providing indices to benchmark the performance of investments in sustainability companies and funds. DJSI describes corporate sustainability as 'a business approach that creates long-term shareholder value by embracing opportunities and managing risks deriving from economic, environmental and social developments'. Components are selected by a systematic corporate sustainability assessment and include only the leading sustainability companies worldwide, thereby providing a link between companies that implement sustainability principles and investors who wish to invest in that type of company. Areas that receive higher weighting in arriving at the corporate sustainability assessment criteria include corporate governance, scorecards and measurement systems, environmental performance, and external stakeholders.

In March 2003 Business in the Community (BITC) reported on the launch of its first Corporate Responsibility Index. Companies who wished to be rated completed a substantial online survey of areas such as their corporate strategy, the integration of CSR into the company's operations, management practice, performance and impact (social and environmental), and assurance. The answers enabled BITC to score the companies. In general, the results revealed that companies seem better at creating CSR strategy than at implementing it effectively in their companies. The Corporate Responsibility Index follows a systematic approach to managing, measuring, and reporting on responsible business practices, companies are assessed using a framework that incorporates: corporate strategy, including looking at the main risks in the company and how these are dealt with at senior levels; integration, which includes looking at how companies embed CSR in the organization; management, which builds on the integration aspect looking at how companies are managing their risks and opportunities in the areas of community, environment, marketplace and workplace; and performance and impact, which asks companies to report performance in a range of social and environmental impact areas.

Corporate social responsibility (CSR)

CSR was conceptualized by Carroll (1979) as follows: 'the social responsibility of business encompasses the economic, legal, ethical, and discretionary expectations that society has of organizations at a given point in time'. This can be explained further as the business having a responsibility to produce goods that it sells at a profit, to abide by legal requirements, to do what is right and fair, and to do what might be desired of companies in terms of supporting the local community and making charitable donations. Carroll (2006) states: 'It appears that the corporate social responsibility concept has a bright future because, at its core, it addresses and captures the most important concerns of the public regarding business and society relationships'.

Gray et al. (1987) identified many of the accounting and accountability issues associated with corporate social reporting. Given the emphasis now being placed on SRI, it is not surprising that CSR has gained more prominence in recent years along with an emphasis on the company's board for its responsibility for relations with its stakeholders. Cadbury (2002) states that 'the broadest way of defining social responsibility is to say that the continued existence of companies is based on an implied agreement between business and society' and that 'the essence of the contract between society and business is that companies shall not pursue their immediate profit objectives at the expense of the longer term interests of the community'.

With the recognition that companies should not pursue profit without regard to the impact on wider societal interests, we can see a link with both agency theory and stakeholder theory discussed in Chapter 2. Whilst the directors manage the company on behalf of the shareholders (an agency relationship), the interests of stakeholders should also be taken into account (stakeholder theory). A Friedmanite view of the firm, whereby there is an emphasis on the purely financial aspects of the business, is no longer appropriate in a society that is increasingly taking an inclusive view of business.

Many companies have responded to this more inclusive approach by starting to report not just the traditional financial performance of the company (the bottom line) but also the 'triple bottom line', which essentially encompasses economic profit, social, and environmental performance. The triple bottom line conveys a wider information set than financial information, and helps to present the wider picture of the company's performance in relation to social and environmental matters. These aspects should now be incorporated in the business review as part of the company's annual report to provide a deeper understanding of the impact of the company's activities on society. The Companies Act (2006) expects directors to disclose more information relating to the risks affecting the company, an analysis of the performance of the company over the year, and consideration of shareholder and stakeholder interests. These requirements will therefore also add to the wider information on environmental, social, and ethical issues disclosed in the annual report and accounts.

In Chapter 4 recent developments in EU and UK company law were highlighted. These will impact on companies' reporting in relation to CSR as companies need to disclose analysis of their performance, where appropriate, based on non-financial key performance indicators (KPIs) as well as financial KPIs.

Aguilera et al. (2006) argue that key differences between the UK and the USA in the importance ascribed to a company's social responsibilities reflect differences in the corporate governance arrangements in these two countries. They explore differences between institutional investors in the UK and in the USA concerning CSR, and identify that UK institutional investors are focused on the long term, whereas the US institutional sector is dominated by mutual funds that may have a shorter term outlook. However, they feel that 'US companies may well gravitate toward British CSR disclosure norms as a positive side effect of globalization'.

Liebman (2008) notes that:

> At present the notion of Corporate Social Responsibility has narrowed down to a mere issue of corporate governance. What is at risk is the crucial relation between politics and the economy—or, between 'the market' and 'regulations'—and what is at stake is the principle of the 'primacy of politics', which has long since been recognized as the cornerstone of modern democracy. Considering the limited effects of State regulations, this principle may only be preserved by a careful balance between legal rules—flowing from different sources or from accords but, in any event, subject to enforcement by the appropriate authority vested to

that effect—and commitments unilaterally undertaken by enterprises on a strictly voluntary basis and typically expressed in codes of ethics of various contents and inspirations.

Clearly both regulation and voluntary actions together may seem to be the most effective approach.

Waddock (2008) identifies 'an emerging institutional infrastructure around corporate responsibility that has resulted in the evolution of initiatives such as the Global Reporting Initiative, the social investment movement, and related efforts that place more emphasis on corporate responsibility, accountability, transparency, and sustainability'. Many multinational companies are now responding to this corporate responsibility infrastructure as corporate responsibility has become an area that companies cannot ignore.

Carroll and Shabana (2010) discuss how

the broad view of the business case justifies CSR initiatives when they produce direct *and* indirect links to firm performance. The advantage of the broad view over the narrow view is that it allows the firm to benefit from CSR *opportunities*. The broad view of the business case for CSR enables the firm to enhance its competitive advantage and create win-win relationships with its stakeholders, in addition to realizing gains from cost and risk reduction and legitimacy and reputation benefits, which are realized through the narrow view.

In terms of links between aspects of market and corporate governance structures, and CSR, Gamerschlag *et al.* (2011), in a paper examining the determinants of voluntary CSR disclosure in a sample of 130 listed German companies, find that

CSR disclosure is positively associated with higher company visibility, a more dispersed shareholder ownership structure, and US cross-listing (a proxy for US stakeholders' interest in the company). Profitability only affects CSR disclosure's environmental dimension. Furthermore, our results show that CSR disclosure is affected by industry membership and firm size: companies from 'polluting industries' tend to have a higher level of environmental disclosures. Finally, big companies disclose more than small companies.

Kock *et al.* (2012) build on a stakeholder–agency theoretical perspective to explore the impact of particular corporate governance mechanisms on firm environmental performance. They find that 'several important corporate governance mechanisms such as the board of directors, managerial incentives, the market for corporate control, and the legal and regulatory system determine firms' environmental performance levels. These results suggest that these different governance mechanisms resolve, to some extent, the existing divergence of interests between stakeholders and managers with respect to environmental activities'.

The impact on shareholder value

An important facet of SRI is whether there is a beneficial effect on shareholder value (the value of the investment). Clearly, the OECD (1998) believes this to be so as it states that 'acting as a responsible citizen is consistent with this economic objective [of generating long-term economic profit to enhance shareholder (or investor) value]'.

There have been a number of studies that have looked at the performance of SRI funds but there has been no definitive outcome one way or another as to whether SRI funds outperform non-SRI funds. In the UK studies have included those by Luther *et al.* (1992), who found weak evidence of some overperformance, on a risk-adjusted basis, by 'ethical' unit trusts, although they pointed out that ethical investment seemed to be skewed towards smaller market capitalized companies. In an extension of the paper, Luther and Matatko (1994) found that ethical funds had returns that were highly correlated with a small company index, hence abnormal returns may have been attributable more to a small company bias than to an ethical one. Mallin *et al.* (1995) analysed the performance of ethical funds and found that, on the mean excess returns, ethical funds appeared to underperform both non-ethical funds and the market in general, whereas on a risk-adjusted basis, ethical funds outperformed non-ethical funds. Research by Lewis and Mackenzie (2000), which utilized a questionnaire survey, highlighted the fact that institutional investors show general support for engaging in lobbying activity and the development of dialogue in order to improve corporate practice and influence companies to improve their ethical and environmental performance. Kreander *et al.* (2002) investigated the financial performance of forty 'ethical' funds from seven European countries. The results suggested that very few ethical funds significantly outperform a global benchmark after adjusting for risk; conversely, none of them significantly underperformed either. Kreander *et al.* (2005) studied the performance of sixty European funds from four countries and used a matched-pair approach for fund evaluation. They found no difference between ethical and non-ethical funds according to the performance measures employed. Schröder (2007) analysed whether stock indices that represent SRI exhibit a different performance compared to conventional benchmark indices. He found that SRI stock indices do not exhibit a different level of risk-adjusted return from conventional benchmarks. However, many SRI indices have a higher risk relative to the benchmarks.

Capelle-Blancard and Monjon (2011) examine the popularity of SRI in newspapers and academic journals; it seems that most of the papers on SRI focus on financial performance. They state 'the question of the financial performance of the SRI funds is certainly relevant, but maybe too much attention has been paid to this issue, whereas more research is needed on a conceptual and theoretical ground, in particular the aspirations of SRI investors, the relationship between regulation and SRI, as well as the assessment of extra-financial performances'.

In the context of corporate performance and sustainability, Ameer and Othman (2012) point out that 'sustainability is concerned with the impact of present actions on the ecosystems, societies, and environments of the future. Such concerns should be reflected in the strategic planning of sustainable corporations. Strategic intentions of this nature are operationalized through the adoption of a long-term focus and a more inclusive set of responsibilities focusing on ethical practices, employees, environment, and customers.' They posit that companies that have regard to these responsibilities 'under the term superior sustainable practices' will have better financial performance than those that do not. They examine the top 100 sustainable global companies in 2008 selected from a universe of 3,000 firms from the developed countries and emerging markets. They find 'significant higher mean sales growth, return on assets, profit before taxation, and cash flows from operations in some activity sectors of the sample companies compared to the control companies over the period of 2006–2010. Furthermore, our findings show that the higher financial performance of sustainable companies has increased and been sustained over the sample'.

Given that SRI is now increasingly perceived as a mainstream element of good corporate governance, the importance of SRI will continue to gain momentum. Certainly in Europe, the European Commission (2008) in its *European Competitiveness Report* had a section entitled 'Overview of the links between Corporate Social Responsibility and Competitiveness' and this section clearly identified that the European Commission believes that CSR can have a positive impact at every level on the countries in the EU. In October 2011 the EU issued *A Renewed EU strategy 2011–14 for Corporate Social Responsibility*. The report states that

> the economic crisis and its social consequences have to some extent damaged consumer confidence and levels of trust in business. They have focused public attention on the social and ethical performance of enterprises. By renewing efforts to promote CSR now, the Commission aims to create conditions favourable to sustainable growth, responsible business behaviour and durable employment generation in the medium and long term.

It states that to fully meet their social responsibility, enterprises 'should have in place a process to integrate social, environmental, ethical and human rights concerns into their business operations and core strategy in close collaboration with their stakeholders'. The new policy puts forward an action agenda for the period 2011–14 covering eight areas, including:

- enhancing the visibility of CSR and disseminating good practices;
- improving company disclosure of social and environmental information (the new policy confirms the Commission's intention to bring forward a new legislative proposal on this issue);
- better aligning European and global approaches to CSR, highlighting:
  - the OECD *Guidelines for Multinational Enterprises*;
  - the ten principles of the *UN Global Compact*;
  - the *UN Guiding Principles on Business and Human Rights*;
  - the International Labour Organization (ILO) *Tripartite Declaration of Principles Concerning Multinational Enterprises and Social Policy*;
  - the ISO 26000 *Guidance Standard on Social Responsibility*.

Conclusions

SRI and CSR are of growing importance in many countries. Across the world there has been an increasing recognition that companies cannot operate in isolation from the ecosystem in which they operate, they must take into consideration the impact of their activities on various stakeholder groups, and the impact of their operations on both the local environment and the global environment. Therefore in many countries there has been a significant upward trend in SRI and governments have made it very much an agenda item. In the UK legislation means that it is an important item for consideration for pension fund trustees. In the USA it is an area that has a high profile and in which there is continuing interest. There are ongoing developments in continental Europe, Australia, and Japan, to name but a few countries, to encourage more SRI.

Institutional investors have developed policy statements on SRI either as separate statements or as an integrated part of their corporate governance policies. A number of institutional investors have developed their SRI analytical capability with new appointments or additional resources. Increasingly, SRI is seen as a mainstream corporate governance issue and, as well as the social and environmental benefits to be gained from SRI, there is the increasing perception that it can help to maintain or increase shareholder value. Together, these are two advantages that should mean that SRI will continue to grow apace.

Summary

- SRI involves considering the ethical, social, and environmental performance of companies as well as their financial performance. The origins of SRI lie in various religious movements that, from the nineteenth century onwards, sought to invest their funds without compromising their principles.
- There are three basic strategies for SRI: engagement, preference, and screening.
  - **Engagement**—identify areas for improvement in the ethical, social, and environmental policies of the companies invested in, and encourage them to make improvements.
  - **Preference**—fund managers work to a list of guidelines that trustees prefer companies invested in to meet.
  - **Screening**—trustees ask for investments to be limited to companies selected (screened) for their ethical behaviour.
- Many institutional investors have developed SRI policies/guidelines; others have incorporated their views on SRI into their mainstream corporate governance policies.
- SRI indices measure the level of CSR in equities. Companies are included in the indices, or score well in them, if they have a good record on CSR.
- The evidence regarding financial performance of SRI (ethical) funds is rather inconclusive but they do not underperform the market generally.

Example: Novo Nordisk, Denmark

This is an example of a Scandinavian company that is committed to CSR and has comprehensive disclosure of its policies. It utilizes the triple bottom line in its reporting. It is included in both the FTSE4Good and the Dow Jones Sustainability Indices.

Novo Nordisk is a focused healthcare company, being a world leader in diabetes care. It is the twelfth largest company in Denmark, measured by turnover, and second largest in terms of its profitability. Its sustainability report states: 'In our vision of sustainability, corporate commitment is aligned with personal values'. It believes that it is possible to balance business concerns with those of stakeholders, and use the triple bottom line to frame this belief. The triple bottom line encompasses social and environmental responsibility, and economic viability. Social responsibility includes employees, people whose healthcare it serves, and local/global communities; environmental responsibility includes the environment itself, animal welfare and bioethics; financial and economic viability includes corporate growth, national growth, and investors' expectations.

The overall strategy is based on a three-tier approach: the corporate governance structure defines its commitments; a stakeholder engagement approach means it can stay attuned to stakeholder issues and concerns; and target-setting with systematic follow-up procedures aids ongoing improvement and better organizational practices.

Novo Nordisk has received a number of awards in the past and at the 2009 World Economic Forum held in Davos, Novo Nordisk was once again rated amongst the 100 most sustainable companies in the world in the Global 100 list. The Global 100 was first launched in 2005 and Novo Nordisk has been on the list since then. The Global 100 companies are sustainable in the sense that they have displayed a better ability than most of their industry peers to identify and effectively manage material environmental, social, and governance factors impacting the opportunity and risk sides of their business.

In 2010 Novo Nordisk won the UK's Learning and Leadership for Sustainable Excellence Award by the Great Place to Work® Institute. The award recognizes organizations that help employees and leaders understand and respond to socio-environmental challenges. Novo Nordisk demonstrates a company-wide commitment to corporate social responsibility, supported by evidence of strong employee engagement in volunteer programmes and a genuine commitment to climate change.

Example: PUMA AG, Germany

PUMA is an example of a leading manufacturer of sports goods which in 2011 produced an Environmental Profit and Loss Account, the first company to do so.

PUMA is one of the world's leading sport lifestyle companies that designs and develops footwear, apparel and accessories. PUMA has been a member of the DJSI since 2006 and the FTSE4Good since 2005, and has won numerous awards for its CSR.

PUMA produces a GRI Index Report and gives a detailed breakdown of its performance against various GRI framework criteria. They have combined their financial and sustainability report into one document but nonetheless, despite the integrative approach, they still aim for a GRI 'A+' grade. The financial and non-financial information were externally verified by their auditors, Pricewaterhouse-Coopers (PwC).

In 2011 PUMA produced its Environmental Profit and Loss Account (E P&L) which was ground breaking, being the first one of its kind. PUMA state:

> The E P&L seeks to answer the seemingly simple question: How much would our planet ask to be paid for the services it provides to PUMA if it was a business? And how much would it charge to clean up the 'footprint' through pollution and damage that PUMA leaves behind? Our operations and supply chain depend on nature for services such as fresh water, clean air, healthy biodiversity and productive land. The PUMA E P&L is the first attempt to measure the immense value of these services to a business, and the true costs of a business's impacts on nature. The PUMA E P&L is simply a means of placing a monetary value on the environmental impacts along our entire value chain.

PUMA consulted with various experts in the community and also referred to academic publications, and then concluded that their most significant environmental impacts are greenhouse gas emissions, water use, land use, air pollution, and waste. Therefore, these are the impacts that are included in the E P&L.

The E P&L acts as a strategic tool to identify the area to which PUMA should direct its sustainability initiatives (for example, identifying more sustainable materials); as a risk management tool (for

(continued)

example, to help manage underlying risks from rising raw material costs, and the impact of the changing climate on resources and the changing water availability); and as a transparency tool (for example, to show to stakeholders the extent of PUMA's environmental impacts).

PUMA makes the point that: 'Luckily even those concerned only about bottom-lines and not the fate of nature are beginning to realize that the sustainability of business itself depends on the long-term viability of ecosystems'.

PUMA has a number of programmes through which they provide concrete examples of their vision and help to build a more sustainable future for the company and its stakeholders. These programs are: PUMA.Safe (focusing on environmental and social issues), PUMA.Peace (supporting global peace), and PUMA.Creative (supporting artists and creative organizations).

Looking at one of these programmes, PUMA.Safe, it engages in capacity building activities in various countries. Its activities include health check-ups for staff in Cambodia; training in the management systems and grievance/complaint/suggestion system for workers' representatives and middle management for their factory in Georgia; freedom of association protocol training for issues related to collective bargaining, the formation of unions etc. in their factory in Indonesia; training in Turkey for supporting human rights, enhancement of communication, and combating abuse in the workplace; and the Better Work Vietnam (BWV) initiative, managed by the ILO and the International Finance Corporation, in which factories that sign up are assessed regularly and supported by the BWV team.

In relation to the PUMA.Peace programme, in December 2010, the prestigious Peace and Sports Awards organizing committee awarded PUMA the 'Best Corporate Social Responsibility Award' in recognition of the PUMA.Peace project's contribution to world peace.

 ## Mini case study   Vodafone, UK

This is an example of a company, the shares of which are included in many ethical investment funds because of its good record on social, environmental, and ethical issues. It is listed in the FTSE4Good and Dow Jones Sustainability Indices.

Vodafone is one of the largest companies in Europe. It made history with the first UK mobile call on 1 January 1985, and since then has gone on to become one of the largest communications companies in the world. By December 2008 Vodafone had over 289 million customers. In 2008 it was rated first in the Accountability Ratings, which evaluate companies drawing on information that companies put into their public reporting, as well as data on their actual social and environmental performance. It rates companies on four 'domains': strategic intent, governance and management, engagement, and operational performance. Out of a maximum available of 100, Vodafone scored 77.7 (the second placed company, General Electric, scored 70.2). Clearly then, Vodafone is high profile in terms of its CSR as well as its financial and sectoral performance.

In Vodafone, the executive committee—which focuses on the group's strategy, financial structure and planning, succession planning, organizational development, and group-wide policies—is the reporting line for corporate responsibility (CR) issues, indicative of the importance that it places on these issues.

Vodafone's CR Report for the year ending March 2008 highlights that Vodafone's 'business strategy and our CR strategy are inseparable. Meeting society's needs creates enormous opportunities to grow our business'. In his Chief Executive's letter, Arun Sarin states: 'At Vodafone, corporate responsibility plays a significant role in helping us achieve our global strategic objectives. We believe that if you want to achieve commercial success on a sustainable basis, you need to conduct business in a responsible way. That's why our commercial strategies are designed with good CR practice in mind'.

In the CR Report, it is emphasized that CR is one of the company's top priorities and that this is substantiated with key objectives in the company's five-year plan.

The CR Report is comprehensive and provides a good picture of the depth of Vodafone's CR activities. A useful summary of various objectives and commitments that Vodafone set itself in order to help improve its CR performance is shown at the end of the report, detailing key issues, what Vodafone said that it would do in relation to each issue, and the deadline for the action to occur. An example is the reuse and recycling of mobile phones in relation to which Vodafone committed to collect a further 1.5 million handsets by March 2009; send for reuse and recycling 95 per cent of network equipment waste during 2008/9; and assess mobile phone collection, reuse, recycling, and disposal in a major Indian city by March 2009. In addition, Vodafone conducted environmental audits of local recycling suppliers in ten of their operating companies in 2007/8. These audits focused specifically on the suppliers' environmental credentials in addition to site evaluations as part of their general supply-chain management.

Vodafone meets regularly with large institutional investors to discuss a variety of topics, including CR issues. Vodafone's commitment to CR has made it a popular choice for inclusion in ethical investment funds.

The Corporate Register Reporting Awards recognized Vodafone's contribution with the award of 'Best Carbon Disclosure' in 2010, and then the award of First Runner-up with its Sustainability Report for the year ending 31 March 2011.

Questions

The discussion questions to follow cover the key learning points of this chapter. Reading of some of the additional reference material will enhance the depth of the students' knowledge and understanding of these areas.

1. Why might institutional investors be interested in SRI?
2. Why are more companies becoming interested in their social and environmental policies?
3. In what ways might institutional investors decide on which companies to invest in when considering their social responsibility policies?
4. Do you think that investors should be willing to sacrifice financial return, if necessary, in order to have a portfolio that is comprised of SRIs?
5. 'Companies are about making money, not about social responsibility.' Critically discuss this statement.
6. 'CSR is the first casualty in an economic downturn as companies will choose to cut back on this area.' Critically discuss this statement in the light of the global financial crisis and the potential implications for the SRI of institutional investors.

References

ABI (2001), *Socially Responsible Investment Guidelines*, ABI, London.

—— (2003), *FTSE 100 Companies Respond Positively to the ABI SRI Guidelines*, ABI Media Centre News Release 13/02, 3 February.

—— (2007), *Guidelines on Responsible Investment Disclosure*, ABI, London.

Aguilera, R.V., Williams, C.A., Conley, J.M., and Rupp, D. (2006), 'Corporate Governance and Social Responsibility: A Comparative Analysis of the UK and the US', *Corporate Governance: An International Review*, Vol. 14, No. 3, pp. 147–58, May.

Ameer, R. and Othman, R. (2012), 'Sustainability Practices and Corporate Financial Performance: A Study Based on the Top Global Corporations', *Journal of Business Ethics*, Vol. 108, No. 1, pp. 61–79.

Boersch, A. (2010), 'Doing Good by Investing Well—Pension Funds and Socially Responsible Investment: Results of an Expert Survey', *Allianz Global Investors International Pension Paper No. 1/2010*. Available at SSRN: **http://ssrn.com/abstract=1607730 or http://dx.doi.org/10.2139/ssrn.1607730**

Cadbury, Sir Adrian (2002), *Corporate Governance and Chairmanship: A Personal View*, Oxford University Press, Oxford.

CalPERS (2011), *Global Principles of Accountable Corporate Governance*, CalPERS, California.

Capelle-Blancard, G. and Monjon, S. (2011), 'Trends in the Literature on Socially Responsible Investment: Looking for the Keys Under the Lamppost' *Business Ethics: A European Review*. Forthcoming, available at SSRN: **http://ssrn.com/abstract=1978815**

Carroll, A.B. (1979), 'A Three-dimensional Conceptual Model of Corporate Social Performance', *Academy of Management Review*, No. 4.

——(2006), 'Corporate Social Responsibility: A Historical Perspective', in M.J. Epstein and K.O. Hanson (eds), *The Accountable Corporation*, Praeger Publishers, Westport, CA.

——and Shabana K.M. (2010), 'The Business Case for Corporate Social Responsibility: A Review of Concepts, Research and Practice', *International Journal of Management Reviews*, Vol. 12, Issue 1, March 2010, pp. 85–105.

EIRIS (2012), *The Ethical Investor*, EIRIS, London.

European Commission (2002), *Corporate Social Responsibility: A business contribution to Sustainable Development*, EC, Brussels.

——(2008), *European Competitiveness Report 2008*, EC, Brussels.

——(2011), *A Renewed EU strategy 2011–14 for Corporate Social Responsibility*, EC, Brussels.

Eurosif (2010), *European SRI Study 2010*, Eurosif, Paris.

FairPensions (2009), *Responsible Pensions? UK Occupational Pension Schemes' Responsible Investment Performance 2009*, FairPensions, London.

——(2010), *The Stewardship Lottery*, FairPensions, London.

Gamerschlag R., Moëller K. and Verbeeten F. (2011), 'Determinants of voluntary CSR disclosure: empirical evidence from Germany', *Review of Managerial Science*, 5, 233–62.

Gray, R.H., Owen, D., and Maunders, K. (1987), *Corporate Social Reporting: Accounting and Accountability*, Prentice Hall International, London.

Gribben, C. and Gitsham, M. (2006), *Will UK Pension Funds Become More Responsible? A Survey of Trustees*, 2006 edn, Ashridge Centre for Business and Society & Just Pensions/UKSIF, London.

Hermes (2002), *The Hermes Principles*, Hermes Pensions Management Ltd, London.

——(2006), *The Hermes Corporate Governance Principles*, Hermes Pensions Management Ltd, London.

——(2010), *The Hermes Responsible Ownership Principles*, Hermes Pensions Management Ltd, London.

Kock, C. J., Santaló, J., and Diestre, L. (2012), 'Corporate Governance and the Environment: What Type of Governance Creates Greener Companies?', *Journal of Management Studies*, Vol. 49, Issue 3, pp. 492–514.

Kreander, N., Gray, R.H., Power, D.M., and Sinclair, C.D. (2002), 'The Financial Performance of European Ethical Funds 1996–1998', *Journal of Accounting and Finance*, Vol. 1.

——————————(2005), 'Evaluating the Performance of Ethical and Non-Ethical Funds: A Matched Pair Analysis', *Journal of Business Finance and Accounting*, Vol. 32, Nos 7, 8, September/October.

Lewis, A. and Mackenzie, C. (2000), 'Support for Investor Activism Among UK Ethical Investors', *Journal of Business Ethics*, April.

Liebman, S. (2008), *Multi-Stakeholders Approach to Corporate Governance and Labor Law: A Note on Corporate Social Responsibility*, 31 March, available at SSRN: **http://ssrn.com/abstract=1114969**

Luther, R.G. and Matatko, J. (1994), 'The Performance of Ethical Unit Trusts: Choosing an Appropriate Benchmark', *British Accounting Review*, Vol. 26.

——————and Corner, C. (1992), 'The Investment Performance of UK "Ethical" Unit Trusts', *Accounting, Auditing and Accountability*, Vol. 5, No. 4.

Mallin, C.A., Saadouni, B., and Briston, R.J. (1995), 'The Financial Performance of Ethical Investment Funds', *Journal of Business Finance and Accounting*, Vol. 22, No. 4.

NAPF (2009), *Responsible Investment Guidance—March 2009* NAPF, London.

OECD (1998), *Corporate Governance: Improving Competitiveness and Access to Capital in Global Markets*, Report to the OECD by the Business Sector Advisory Group on Corporate Governance, OECD, Paris.

——(2011) *Guidelines for Multinational Enterprises*, OECD, Paris.

Schröder, M. (2007), 'Is there a Difference? The Performance Characteristics of SRI Equity Indices', *Journal of Business Finance & Accounting*, Vol. 34, Nos 1–2.

UK Sustainable Investment and Finance Association (UKSIF) (2010), *Focused on the Future: Celebrating ten years of responsible investment disclosure by UK occupational pension funds*, UK Sustainable Investment and Finance Association (UKSIF), London.

UN (2006), *Principles for Responsible Investment*, New York.

——(2011), *Principles for Responsible Investment, Report on Progress*, New York.

Waddock, S. (2008), 'Building a New Institutional Infrastructure for Corporate Responsibility', *Academy of Management Perspectives*, Vol. 22, No. 3.

Useful websites

www.ceres.org The website of Ceres, the national network of investors, environmental organizations, and other public interest groups working with companies and investors to address sustainability challenges such as global climate change.

www.eiris.org The website of the Ethical Investment Research Services has information on various aspects of ethical investment.

www.forumethibel.org The website of ETHIBEL, an independent consultancy agency for SRI.

www.eurosif.org The website of Eurosif, which contains information about SRI.

www.fairpensions.org.uk The website of FairPensions, which campaigns for major institutional investors to adopt responsible investment.

www.ftse.com/Indices/FTSE4Good_Index_Series/index.jsp The website of the FTSE4Good index provides information about the composition of the index and related material.

www.hermes.co.uk The Hermes website contains information related to various corporate governance issues.

www.globalreporting.org The website of the Global Reporting Initiative, which has details of the GRI Guidelines and Reporting Framework.

www.ilo.org The website of the International Labor Organization has details of international labor standards.

www.oecd.org The website of the Organisation for Economic Co-operation and Development, which has details of the Guidelines for Multinational Enterprises and other developments.

www.sustainability-index.com/ The website of the Dow Jones Sustainability Indexes provides information about the indexes, which track the financial performance of the leading sustainability-driven companies worldwide.

www.thesullivanfoundation.org/about/global-sullivan-principles The website of the Global Sullivan Principles of Corporate Social Responsibility.

www.unglobalcompact.org/ The website of the UN Global Compact, a strategic policy initiative for businesses that are committed to aligning their operations and strategies with ten universally accepted principles in the areas of human rights, labour, environment, and anti-corruption.

www.unpri.org The website for the UN Principles of Responsible Investment.

 For further links to useful sources of information visit the Online Resource Centre **www.oxfordtextbooks.co.uk/orc/mallin4e/**

Part Two case study   Institutional investors and SRI

This case study illustrates how, when an influential group of institutional investors work together, they can influence the operations of their investee companies which are in a country where there are human rights abuses, political instability, and unacceptable risks. This action was part of the SRI remit of the institutional investors.

The political instability and human rights abuses make Myanmar a very difficult country in which to undertake business. As well as the physical dangers of such operations, companies might be subject to negative press campaigns by 'pressure' groups and corruption attempts locally. A number of the largest UK and European institutional investors—including Aviva, Co-operative Insurance Services, Ethos Investment Foundation, Friends Ivory & Sime, Henderson Global Investors, PGGM and the Universities Superannuation Scheme—joined forces to launch 'Business Involvement in Myanmar (Myanmar)—A statement from institutional investors'. The statement called on companies to justify their involvement in Myanmar, given the risks that such activity may pose to shareholders, and sought assurance that company boards had considered fully these risks, and had effective policies and procedures in place to manage them. Having such risk assessment and management procedures in place is in accordance with the ABI's guidelines on SRI.

One of the institutional investors involved in launching the statement, Aviva, met with one of their investee companies, British American Tobacco (BAT) to discuss BAT's joint venture with the military government to manufacture cigarettes in Myanmar. Subsequently, in July 2003, the British government requested BAT reconsider its investment in Myanmar. BAT stated: 'We have reached what we believe is a balanced solution to meet the British government's requirement while maintaining local employment prospects and the continued orderly and responsible local marketing of our brands'. On 18 June 2004 it sold its 60 per cent shareholding in Rothmans of Pall Mall Myanmar Pte Limited (RPMM) to Distinction Investment Holdings, a Singapore-based investment company. The remaining 40 per cent of RPMM is owned by the Myanmar government. BAT stated: 'We have licensed brands to the new owner to manufacture and market them locally through RPMM, enabling its continued operation as a going concern and good local employer'. BAT would not necessarily have chosen to leave Myanmar, maybe feeling that it could influence the local situation more by maintaining a presence there, but given the British government's request, it decided to withdraw.

Another company that has come under considerable pressure to withdraw from Myanmar is Total Oil, which operates the Yadana natural gas pipeline from Myanmar to Thailand. Various governments disapprove of this operation and Total Oil has come under considerable pressure to end its arrangement with the Burmese government. At the time of writing this matter was still unresolved. However, human rights abuses continue to be a problem in Myanmar with the military government cracking down on personal and political freedom. Institutional investors, with the increasing emphasis on SRI and the management of all risks, continue to exert influence on those companies that still operate in Myanmar.

Recently there have been significant changes in Myanmar with wide-ranging reforms being introduced in 2011 and 2012. These have led to much greater freedom of information, freedom of speech, and political reforms. These democratic reforms have led to international sanctions against the country being dropped by the EU. Furthermore, there have been economic reforms and in May 2012, Myanmar finalized a foreign investment law that includes details of tax exemptions, legal structures, and incentives for foreign companies. Also in May 2012, UN Secretary-General Ban Ki-moon launched the Local Network of the *UN Global Compact* in Myanmar; 15 Burmese companies signed up to the ten principles of the *UN Global Compact*.

These changes will likely mean that institutional investors will reconsider their position regarding Myanmar, however the legal structures need strengthening in the country and there is evidence of widespread corruption, so it may take some time before this happens.

 **FT Clippings**

FT: Managers 'talk more than walk' on SRI

By Ruth Sullivan

April 1, 2012

Expectations that socially responsible investing (SRI) would move from niche to mainstream have not been fulfilled. However, although asset managers' commitment remains patchy, a growing focus on good governance is likely to trigger more progress.

"There is lots of activity but mainstreaming into the core [investment] process is still not happening enough," says Raj Thamotheram, president of the Network for Sustainable Financial Markets. "There is a gap between the walk and the talk," he adds.

One of the telling signs is the lack of sell-side research that incorporates environmental, social and governance factors. "Banks like Deutsche and JPMorgan used to provide ESG reports but they no longer do it, having stopped in 2007 and 2009 respectively. This is a major step back," says Mr Thamotheram.

He points to the Enhanced Analytics Initiative which, between 2004 and 2008, encouraged the growth of ESG research. Its aim was to stimulate sell-side analysts to produce research incorporating ESG issues in such a way that fund managers could integrate them into their investment decisions.

The initiative later became part of the UN Principles for Responsible Investment Enhanced Research Portal where it has been "more or less forgotten because it is just too hard to do", according to Mr Thamotheram.

Will Oulton, European head of responsible investment at Mercer, the consultant, agrees. The EAI "has lost momentum on the sell side in the past few years since it was taken over by the PRI", he says.

A recent global survey by Mercer shows portfolio managers are failing to make headway on integrating ESG in the investment process and to follow good stewardship practice, with only 9 per cent of more than 5,000 ESG strategies gaining top ratings between 2008 and 2011.

In spite of such findings Mr Oulton says he expects to see more progress in the next few years as public awareness and industry debate on governance heats up and guidance on how to improve the relationship between asset owners and their agents is put into practice.

Mr Oulton believes one of the main challenges facing asset managers is getting consistent high quality ESG data on companies or sectors that is useful for investment decisions.

This view is echoed by Gerrit Heyns, partner in Osmosis Investment Management. It is difficult to get hard numbers in some ESG areas, particularly the social one, he says. Osmosis looks at factors it can measure in constructing its Climate Solutions Index and Model of Resource Efficiency Index, using information on companies' water and fossil-fuel-based energy consumption and their waste production.

Information that companies disclose to investors is material and "has to be measured, audited, monitored and reported, so it ends up being a proxy for good governance", says Mr Heyns. Companies identified by Osmosis' research tend to have a higher return on equity and better growth, he says.

He believes there is too much pressure on fund managers to take action on the ESG front. Investors are playing the role they should simply by being in the market and contributing to price discovery. The market is generally right, he maintains, and information on a company is all in the price.

At Allianz Global Investors, chief investment officer Andreas Utermann points to the added value investment managers in the group gain from research carried out by an in-house team of analysts dedicated to socially responsible investment strategies.

Research from RCM, part of the AGI group, shows investors could have added 1.6 percentage points a year to their investment returns between 2006 and 2010 by allocating to portfolios investing in companies with above average ESG ratings.

AGI decided a few years ago to integrate SRI strategies across all its assets. "We believe demand for SRI strategies is going to grow, although it may be slow, and we want to be ahead of the curve," says Bozena Jankowska, global head of sustainability research at RCM.

Others have taken a similar route to integration. First State Investments, part of the asset management division of the Commonwealth Bank of Australia, uses ESG factors to inform its views on growth, risk and quality of management.

"ESG analysis is particularly useful for [analysing] quality of management,"

says Amanda McCluskey, head of responsible investment at First State. "A company with poor safety performance has poor management quality." An increasing awareness of the risks involved in investing in companies with poor governance is triggering demand from asset managers and asset owners for ways to assess this, according to Eiris, the independent ESG research group. Last week the organisation launched a global sustainability ratings service providing investors with an assessment of the sustainability performance of more than 3,000 global public companies.

There are also other positive indicators. "UNPRI signatories [with a total of $30tn assets under management] make up about 15 per cent of the global institutional investor market, with big US players such as Goldman Sachs Asset Management, BlackRock, AllianceBernstein and Pimco adding their names recently," says Mr Thamotheram.

While this is a step in the right direction Mr Oulton says asset managers need to work out how to take the next step. "Asset managers tend to sign up and then work out how to do it. The numbers are rising but there is lag time in what they actually do," he says.

FT: Stock exchanges urged to make ESG demands

By Mike Scott

April 22, 2012

There are increasing calls for stock exchanges to become more involved in efforts to encourage the companies that list on them to consider more seriously environmental, social and governance issues.

"It is part of their job and they do not do enough," says Jon Williams, a partner

in the Sustainability and Climate Change practice at PwC.

Partly, this is due to their structures: many of the biggest bourses are now listed companies themselves, under pressure to generate returns for their shareholders. "Exchanges make money through volume. The best thing for their business is volatility," Mr Williams says. "It is all part of the short termism that pervades the financial markets." However, exchanges also have a utility function that goes far wider than their own shareholders—and that is to help provide sustainable capital markets that are more resilient than they proved to be during the financial crisis. Steve Waygood, head of sustainability research and investment at Aviva, says: "If we do not have capital markets structured in a sustainable fashion, we cannot ensure that the cost of capital is higher for unsustainable behaviour. It is the responsibility of exchanges to promote responsible investment and corporate behaviour via disclosure." An increasing number of exchanges seem to agree. A recent report* from the Sustainable Stock Exchanges Initiative surveyed 27 of the world's biggest exchanges and found 76 per cent thought they had a responsibility to encourage greater corporate responsibility. However, they were also quick to point out there was no money in this for them and that, "in an increasingly global and competitive market and with a reduced regulatory function, there are limits to the actions they can take on sustainability".

"The most obvious tool they can use is their listing requirements." There is nothing to stop exchanges from requiring certain disclosures of ESG practices, or saying that companies must put their sustainability report to the AGM alongside the financial report," PwC's Mr Williams says.

"Aviva does this and it forces them to treat it with the same rigour as the annual report." A growing number of exchanges are introducing sustainability-related requirements on a comply-or-explain basis, but it is notable that the prime movers are in emerging markets. "Emerging markets see sustainability as helping to bring the overall standard of performance up for them and the companies that list on them," says Thomas Kuh, executive director for ESG indices at MSCI. "Developed markets are at best passive in this area." At NYSE Euronext, for example, Michelle Greene, head of corporate responsibility talks about "celebrating the good work of companies

leading on sustainability, highlighting what they are doing and allowing others to learn from best practice. Our approach is more carrot than stick." Meanwhile, the LSE directs inquiries about sustainability and ESG matters to subsidiary FTSE, which runs the FTSE4Good indices. While these are valuable for investors looking to invest in a best-in-class sustainability strategy, "large investors buy the whole market, not a subset", says Mr Williams, meaning there is a need for measures that improve the performance of all companies.

Emerging market bourses are taking a more proactive approach, with exchanges in South Africa, Brazil and Malaysia among those that require companies to publish sustainability reports or explain why not.

In South Africa, where the JSE has incorporated the King Code of Corporate Governance into its listing requirements, Michelle Joubert, head of investor relations, says: "As an exchange in a developing country, it is incumbent on us to ensure the development of communities and consumers." "That encourages the growth of the economy and the companies listed on the JSE. If we don't play a role in encouraging our companies to think about sustainability issues, we're not doing our job." This is particularly important for South Africa, not just because of its apartheid past and the social issues that has created but also because of the predominance of mining and extractive companies on the JSE and in the country's economy.

BM&F Bovespa also stresses the importance of Brazil's natural resources as a reason for its focus on sustainability.

"Emerging markets do not have the burden of the old economy that Europe and North America have," says Mr Williams.

"They want to create exchanges for the new economy while the make-up of the LSE, for example, is very carbon- and resource-heavy. It would be a real shame if, at a time when the world is moving to a lower-carbon, lower-energy model, London were to find itself excluded from that new economy." The Sustainable Stock Exchange Initiative is calling on policymakers and regulators to support the introduction of guiding principles to enhance ESG disclosure by companies in their markets, something supported by 80 per cent of respondents to the survey.

The initiative wants to see all nations at Rio+20 commit "to develop a convention requiring on a report or explain basis the integration of material sustainability issues within the report and accounts of all listed and large private companies".

Sustainable Stock Exchanges: Real Obstacles, Real Opportunities
© 2012 *The Financial Times Ltd.*

Part 3

Directors and Board Structure

8

Directors and Board Structure

⦿ Learning Objectives

- To be aware of the distinction between unitary and dual boards
- To have a detailed understanding of the roles, duties, and responsibilities of directors
- To understand the rationale for key board committees and their functions
- To be able to critically assess the criteria for independence of non-executive (outside) directors
- To comprehend the role and contribution of non-executive (outside) directors
- To be aware of the importance of board evaluation, succession planning, and board diversity

Introduction

This chapter covers the board structure of a company. The discussion encompasses the function of a board and its subcommittees (the most common ones being the audit, remuneration, nomination, and risk committees); the roles, duties, and responsibilities of directors; and the attributes and contribution of a non-executive (outside) director. Whilst the context is that of a UK company, much of the material is appropriate to other countries that also have a unitary (one-tier) board structure and may also be generalized to a dual (two-tier) board structure.

Unitary board versus dual board

A major corporate governance difference between countries is the board structure, which may be unitary or dual depending on the country. As in the UK, in the majority of EU Member States, the unitary board structure is predominant (in five states, the dual structure is also available). However, in Austria, Germany, the Netherlands, and Denmark, the dual structure is predominant. In the dual structure, employees may have representation on the supervisory board (as in Germany, covered in detail in Chapter 10) but this may vary from country to country.

Unitary board

A unitary board of directors is the form of board structure in the UK and the USA, and is characterized by one single board comprising both executive and non-executive directors. The unitary board is responsible for all aspects of the company's activities, and all the directors are working to achieve the same ends. The shareholders elect the directors to the board at the company's annual general meeting (AGM).

Dual board

A dual board system consists of a supervisory board and an executive board of management. However, in a dual board system, there is a clear separation between the functions of supervision (monitoring) and that of management. The supervisory board oversees the *direction* of the business, whilst the management board is responsible for the *running* of the business. Members of one board cannot be members of another, so there is a clear distinction between management and control. Shareholders appoint the members of the supervisory board (other than the employee members), whilst the supervisory board appoints the members of the management board.

Commonalities between unitary and dual board structures

There are many similarities in board practice between a unitary and a dual board system. The unitary board and the supervisory board usually appoint the members of the managerial body: the group of managers to whom the unitary board delegates authority in the unitary system and the management board in a dual system. Both bodies usually have responsibility for ensuring that financial reporting and control systems are operating properly and for ensuring compliance with the law.

Usually, both the unitary board of directors and the supervisory board (in a dual system) are elected by shareholders (in some countries, such as Germany, employees may elect some supervisory board members).

Advocates of each type of board structure identify their main advantages as: in a one-tier system, there is a closer relationship and better information flow as all directors, both executive and non-executive, are on the same single board; in a dual system, there is a more distinct and formal separation between the supervisory body and those being 'supervised', because of the separate management board and supervisory board structures. These aspects are discussed further in Chapter 10. However, whether the structure is unitary or dual, many codes seem to have a common approach to areas relating to the function of boards and key board committees, to independence, and to the consideration of shareholder and shareholder rights.

The UK Corporate Governance Code

In Chapter 3, the *Cadbury Code of Best Practice* was cited as having influenced the development of corporate governance codes in many countries. The Cadbury Code clearly emphasizes, inter alia, the central role of the board, the importance of a division of responsibilities at the

Box 8.1 The UK Corporate Governance Code

Section A: Leadership

A.1 **The Role of the Board** Every company should be headed by an effective board that is collectively responsible for the long-term success of the company.

A.2 **Division of Responsibilities** There should be a clear division of responsibilities at the head of the company between the running of the board and the executive responsibility for the running of the company's business. No one individual should have unfettered powers of decision.

A.3 **The Chairman** The chairman is responsible for leadership of the board and ensuring its effectiveness on all aspects of its role.

A.4 **Non-executive Directors** As part of their role as members of a unitary board, non-executive directors should constructively challenge and help develop proposals on strategy.

Section B: Effectiveness

B.1 **The Composition of the Board** The board and its committees should have the appropriate balance of skills, experience, independence, and knowledge of the company to enable them to discharge their respective duties and responsibilities effectively.

B.2 **Appointments to the Board** There should be a formal, rigorous, and transparent procedure for the appointment of new directors to the board.

B.3 **Commitment** All directors should be able to allocate sufficient time to the company to discharge their responsibilities effectively.

B.4 **Development** All directors should receive induction on joining the board, and should regularly update and refresh their skills and knowledge.

B.5 **Information and Support** The board should be supplied in a timely manner with information in a form and of a quality appropriate to enable it to discharge its duties.

B.6 **Evaluation** The board should undertake a formal and rigorous annual evaluation of its own performance and that of its committees and individual directors.

B.7 **Re-election** All directors should be submitted for re-election at regular intervals, subject to continued satisfactory performance.

Section C: Accountability

C.1 **Financial and Business Reporting** The board should present a balanced and understandable assessment of the company's position and prospects.

C.2 **Risk Management and Internal Control** The board is responsible for determining the nature and extent of the significant risks it is willing to take in achieving its strategic objectives. The board should maintain sound risk management and internal control systems.

C.3 **Audit Committee and Auditors** The board should establish formal and transparent arrangements for considering how they should apply the corporate reporting, and risk management and internal control principles, and for maintaining an appropriate relationship with the company's auditor.

Section D: Remuneration

D.1 **The Level and Components of Remuneration** Levels of remuneration should be sufficient to attract, retain, and motivate directors of the quality required to run the company successfully, but a company should avoid paying more than is necessary for this purpose. A significant proportion of executive directors' remuneration should be structured so as to link rewards to corporate and individual performance.

D.2 **Procedure** There should be a formal and transparent procedure for developing policy on executive remuneration and for fixing the remuneration packages of individual directors. No director should be involved in deciding his/her own remuneration.

Section E: **Relations with Shareholders**

E.1 **Dialogue with Shareholders** There should be a dialogue with shareholders based on the mutual understanding of objectives. The board as a whole has responsibility for ensuring that a satisfactory dialogue with shareholders takes place.

E.2 **Constructive Use of the AGM** The board should use the AGM to communicate with investors and to encourage their participation.

Source: *The UK Corporate Governance Code*, (Financial Reporting Council (FRC), 2010). © Financial Reporting Council Limited (FRC). Adapted and reproduced with the kind permission of the Financial Reporting Council, Aldwych House, 71–91 Aldwych, London WC2B 4HN. All rights reserved. For further information please visit www.frc.org.uk or call +44 (0)202 7492 2300.

head of the company, and the role of non-executive directors. There have been a number of revisions to UK corporate governance codes, as detailed in Chapter 3, culminating in the issuance of the *UK Corporate Governance Code* (2010) which has its main principles listed under five headings: Leadership, Effectiveness, Accountability, Remuneration, and Relations with Shareholders. These are detailed in Box 8.1.

The *UK Corporate Governance Code* (hereafter 'the Code') is appended to the Listing Rules by which companies listed on the London Stock Exchange must abide. However, companies can conform to the Code's provisions on a 'comply or explain' basis. 'Comply or explain' means that the company will generally be expected to comply with the provisions of the Code, but if it is unable to comply with a particular provision, then it can explain why it is unable to do so. Institutional investors and their representative groups monitor carefully all matters related to the Code, and will contact companies if they have not complied with a provision of the Code and protest if the company does not have an appropriate reason for non-compliance.

The board of directors

The board of directors leads and controls a company and hence an effective board is fundamental to the success of the company. The board is the link between managers and investors, and is essential to good corporate governance and investor relations.

Given the UK's unitary board system, it is desirable that the roles of chairman and chief executive officer (CEO) are split because otherwise there could be too much power vested in one individual. The chairman is responsible for the running of the board whilst the CEO is responsible for the running of the business. The Code (2010) states that 'the roles of chairman and chief executive should not be exercised by the same individual' (para A.2.1). When a CEO retires from his/her post, he/she should not then become chairman of the same company (exceptionally, a board may agree to a CEO becoming chairman, but in this case, the board should discuss the matter with major shareholders setting out the reasons, and also declare these in the next annual report). The Higgs Review (2003) reported that only five FTSE 100 companies had a joint chairman/CEO, whilst this figure rose to 11 per cent of companies outside the FTSE 350.

Role of the board

The board is responsible for: determining the company's aims and the strategies, plans, and policies to achieve those aims; monitoring progress in the achievement of those aims (both from an overview company aspect and also in terms of analysis and evaluation of its own performance as a board and as individual directors); and appointing a CEO with appropriate leadership qualities. Sir Adrian Cadbury (2002) gives an excellent exposition of corporate governance and chairmanship, and the role and effectiveness of the board in corporate governance.

In a study of the changing role of boards, Taylor et al. (2001) identified three major challenges facing company boards over the forthcoming five-year period. These challenges were to build more diverse boards of directors, to pay more attention to making their boards more effective, and to be able to react appropriately to any changes in the corporate governance culture. By building better boards, innovation and entrepreneurship should be encouraged and the business driven to perform better. The board will focus on the value drivers of the business to give the firm competitive advantage. Clearly, the composition of the board will play a key role in whether a company can successfully meet these challenges. The presence of the most suitable non-executive directors will help the board in this task. The role and appointment of non-executive directors is discussed in more detail later.

Epstein and Roy (2006) state that,

high-performance boards must achieve three core objectives:

1. provide superior strategic guidance to ensure the company's growth and prosperity;
2. ensure accountability of the company to its stakeholders, including shareholders, employees, customers, suppliers, regulators and the community;
3. ensure that a highly qualified executive team is managing the company.

Decisions relating to board composition and structure will be of fundamental importance in determining whether, and to what extent, the board is successful in achieving these objectives.

Role, duties, and responsibilities

It is essential that the role, duties, and responsibilities of directors are clearly defined. The Code (2010) states that, 'the board's role is to provide entrepreneurial leadership of the company within a framework of prudent and effective controls which enables risk to be assessed and managed' (para A.1). Directors should make decisions in an objective way and in the company's best interests.

The board should have regular meetings, with an agenda, and there should be a formal schedule of matters over which the board has the right to make decisions. There should be appropriate reporting procedures defined for the board and its subcommittees. As mentioned earlier, the roles of chair and CEO should preferably be split to help ensure that no one individual is too powerful. The board should have a balance between executive and non-executive directors. All directors should have access to the company secretary and also be able to take independent professional advice. The Code (2010) recommends that directors should receive appropriate training when they are first appointed to the board of a listed company.

According to UK law, the directors should act in good faith in the interests of the company, and exercise care and skill in carrying out their duties.

In November 2006 the Companies Act (2006) finally received Royal Assent after a prolonged period in the making. The Act updates previous Companies Acts legislation, but does not completely replace them, and it contains some significant new provisions that will impact on various constituents, including directors, shareholders, auditors, and company secretaries. The Act draws on the findings of the Company Law Review proposals.

The main features of the Act are as follows:

- directors' duties are codified;
- companies can make greater use of electronic communications for communicating with shareholders;
- directors can file service addresses on public record rather than their private home addresses;
- shareholders will be able to agree limitations on directors' liability;
- there will be simpler model Articles of Association for private companies, to reflect the way in which small companies operate;
- private companies will not be required to have a company secretary;
- private companies will not need to hold an AGM unless they agree to do so;
- the requirement for an Operating and Financial Review (OFR) has not been reinstated, rather companies are encouraged to produce a high-quality Business Review;
- nominee shareholders can elect to receive information in hard copy form or electronically if they wish to do so;
- shareholders will receive more timely information;
- enhanced proxy rights will make it easier for shareholders to appoint others to attend and vote at general meetings;
- shareholders of quoted companies may have a shareholder proposal (resolution) circulated at the company's expense if received by the financial year end;
- whilst there has been significant encouragement over a number of years to encourage institutional investors to disclose how they use their votes, the Act provides a power that could be used to require institutional investors to disclose how they have voted.

All parts of the Act were in force by October 2008 with certain provisions taking effect much earlier, for example, company communications to shareholders, including electronic communications, took effect from January 2007.

Overall there seems to be an increasing burden for quoted companies whilst the burden seems to have been reduced for private companies. In terms of the rights of shareholders these are enhanced in a number of ways, including greater use of electronic communications, more information, enhanced proxy rights, and provision regarding the circulation of shareholder proposals at the company's expense. Equally, there is a corresponding emphasis on shareholders' responsibilities with encouragement for institutional shareholders to be more active and to disclose how they have voted.

Given that the company is comprised of different shareholders, it may not be possible for the directors, whilst acting in the interest of the company as a whole, to please all shareholders at all times. In order to perform their role to best effect, it is vital that directors have access to reliable information on a timely basis. It is an essential feature of good corporate governance that the board will, in its turn, be accountable to shareholders and provide them with relevant information so that, for example, decision-making processes are transparent.

The roles of the CEO, chairman, senior independent director, and company secretary are now discussed.

Chief executive officer (CEO)

The CEO has the executive responsibility for the running of the company's business, whereas the chairman has responsibility for the running of the board. The two roles should not therefore be combined and carried out by one person, as this would give an individual too much power.

One particular problem that arises from time to time is whether a retiring CEO should become chairman of the same company. This is generally discouraged because a chairman should be independent. The Code (2010) states:

> A chief executive should not go on to be chairman of the same company. If exceptionally a board decides that a chief executive should become chairman, the board should consult major shareholders in advance and should set out its reasons to shareholders at the time of the appointment and in the next annual report. (para. A.3.1)

As well as a lack of independence, there is a feeling that it might cause problems for any incoming CEO if the retired CEO is still present at a senior level in the company (in the role of chairman) because he/she may try to become more involved in the running of the company rather than the running of the board (in his/her new role as chairman).

Various institutional bodies have made their views known on this issue: for example, Research Recommendations Electronic Voting (RREV), a joint venture between the National Association of Pension Funds (NAPF) and Institutional Shareholder Services (ISS), states that 'the normal application of the NAPF policy is to vote against the re-election of a director with the roles of both chief executive and chairman'. Hermes, in *The Hermes Corporate*

Governance Principles, states that it is generally opposed to a CEO becoming chairman of the board at the same company.

Chairman

The chairman is responsible for the running of the board and for ensuring that the board meets frequently, that directors have access to all the information they need to make an informed contribution at board meetings, and that all directors are given the opportunity to speak at board meetings.

As Sir Adrian Cadbury (2002) observed: 'the primary task of chairmen is to chair their boards. This is what they have been appointed to do and, however the duties at the top of a company may be divided, chairing the board is their responsibility alone' (p. 78). He also succinctly highlights an important difference between CEOs and chairmen:

> the difference between the authority of chairmen and that of chief executives is that chairmen carry the authority of the board, while chief executives carry the authority delegated to them by the board. Chairmen exercise their authority on behalf of the board; chief executives have personal authority in line with the terms of their appointment. (p. 99.)

The chairman should hold meetings with the non-executive directors without the executives present. The *Combined Code* (2006) stated that no individual should hold more than one chairmanship of a FTSE 100 company, however, the *Combined Code* (2008) removed this restriction. One rationale for this change is that limiting an individual to chairing just one FTSE 100 company took no account of what other activities he/she might be engaged in; these other activities might not be onerous in which case it would be feasible to chair more than one FTSE 100 company. The Code (2010) states that the board should not agree to a full-time executive director taking on more than one non-executive directorship in a FTSE 100 company or the chairmanship of such a company, (B.3.3).

McNulty *et al.* (2011), in a study of 160 chairs of 500 FTSE listed companies, find that 'by linking board structure, board process and the exercise of influence, the study reveals both differences amongst chairs in how they run the board, but also that chairs' differ in the influence they exert on board-related tasks. Full-time executive chairs exert their greatest influence in strategy and resource dependence tasks whereas part-time, non-executive chairs seem to exert more influence over monitoring and control tasks'.

Senior independent director

The Code (2010) provides for the appointment of a senior independent director (SID) who should be one of the independent non-executive directors. The Code (2010) states: 'the senior independent director should be available to shareholders if they have concerns which contact through the normal channels of chairman, chief executive or finance director has failed to resolve or for which such contact is inappropriate' (para. A.4.1).

The Hermes Corporate Governance Principles also see the SID as providing an additional communication channel to shareholders and states: 'if the chairman of the board is not independent, then the board should appoint a senior independent director whose role would include reviewing the performance of the chairman' (para. 3.4). The non-executive directors should meet without the chairman present at least annually in order to appraise the chairman's performance, and on other occasions as necessary. At these times, the SID would lead the meeting.

Company secretary

The company secretary, like the directors, must act in good faith and avoid conflicts of interest. The company secretary has a range of responsibilities, including facilitating the work of the board by ensuring that the directors have all the information they need for the main board and also for the board subcommittees (commonly audit, remuneration, and nomination), and that such information flows well between the various constituents. The company secretary advises the board, via the chairman, on all governance matters and will assist with the professional development needs of directors and induction requirements for new directors.

The dismissal of the company secretary is a decision for the board as a whole and not just the CEO or chairman.

Board subcommittees

The board may appoint various subcommittees, which should report regularly to the board, and although the board may delegate various activities to these subcommittees, it is the board as a whole that remains responsible for the areas covered by the subcommittees. Charkham (2005) states:

> committees of the board are used for various purposes, the main one being to assist the dispatch of business by considering it in more detail than would be convenient for the whole board . . . the second purpose is to increase objectivity either because of inherent conflicts of interest such as executive remuneration, or else to discipline personal preferences as in the exercise of patronage.

The Cadbury Report recommended that an audit committee and a remuneration committee should be formed, and also stated that a nomination committee would be one possible way to make the board appointments process more transparent.

The Higgs Review (2003) reported that most listed companies have an audit committee and a remuneration committee. Only one FTSE 100 company did not have an audit committee or remuneration committee, whilst 15 per cent of companies outside the FTSE 350 did not have an audit committee. Adoption of nomination committees has tended to be less prevalent with the majority (71 per cent) of companies outside the FTSE 350 not having a nomination committee. FTSE 100 companies have tended to adopt nomination committees with the exception of six companies. The Code (2010) states that there should be a nomination committee to lead the board appointments process.

Audit committee

The audit committee is arguably the most important of the board subcommittees.

The Smith Review of audit committees, a group appointed by the FRC, reported in January 2003. The review made clear the important role of the audit committee: 'while all directors have a duty to act in the interests of the company, the audit committee has a particular role, acting independently from the executive, to ensure that the interests of shareholders are properly protected in relation to financial reporting and internal control' (para. 1.5). The review defined the audit committee's role in terms of 'oversight', 'assessment', and 'review', indicating the high-level overview that audit committees should take; they need to satisfy themselves that there is an appropriate system of controls in place but they do not undertake the monitoring themselves.

It is the role of the audit committee to review the scope and outcome of the audit, and to try to ensure that the objectivity of the auditors is maintained. This would usually involve a review of the audit fee and fees paid for any non-audit work, and the general independence of the auditors. The audit committee provides a useful 'bridge' between both internal and external auditors and the board, helping to ensure that the board is fully aware of all relevant issues related to the audit. The audit committee's role may also involve reviewing arrangements for whistle-blowers (staff who wish confidentially to raise concerns about possible improper practices in the company). In addition, where there is no risk management committee (discussed later), the audit committee should assess the systems in place to identify and manage financial and non-financial risks in the company.

The guidance was updated in 2005 and subsequently a new edition of the guidance was issued in October 2008. A limited number of changes were made to implement some of the recommendations of the Market Participants Group (MPG), established to provide advice to the FRC on market-led actions to mitigate the risk that could arise in the event of one or more of the Big Four audit firms leaving the market. The main changes to the guidance are that audit committees are encouraged to consider the need to include the risk of the withdrawal of their auditor from the market in their risk evaluation and planning; and that companies are encouraged to include in the audit committee's report information on the appointment, reappointment or removal of the auditor, including supporting information on tendering frequency, the tenure of the incumbent auditor, and any contractual obligations that acted to restrict the committee's choice of auditor. In addition, there have been a small number of detailed changes to the section dealing with the independence of the auditor, to bring the guidance in line with the Auditing Practices Board's Ethical Standards for auditors. An appendix has also been added containing guidance on the factors to be considered if a group is contemplating employing firms from more than one network to undertake the audit.

The Code (2010) states that,

the board should establish an audit committee of at least three, or in the case of smaller companies, two, independent non-executive directors. In smaller companies the company chairman may be a member of, but not chair, the committee in addition to the independent non-executive directors, provided he or she was considered independent on appointment as chairman. The board should satisfy itself that at least one member of the audit committee has recent and relevant financial experience. (para. C.3.1.)

In September 2011 the FRC announced that it intended to consult on proposed changes to the Code in relation to audit committees and audit retendering. It is possible that further changes may be proposed as a consequence of the Sharman Panel of Inquiry into 'going concern' and the Department for Business, Innovation & Skills consultation on narrative reporting, the outcomes of both of these being available in 2012. Any changes agreed as a result will be incorporated into the revised Code that will apply from 1 October 2012.

Spira (2002) provides a useful insight into the processes and interactions of audit committees, and highlights the importance of the composition of audit committees. The audit committee should comprise independent non-executive directors who are in a position to ask appropriate questions, so helping to give assurance that the committee is functioning properly. Turley (2008) highlights how 'the role and significance of the audit committee as a governance structure have developed substantially during the last decade'.

Zaman et al. (2011) examine the influence of audit committee effectiveness, a proxy for governance quality, on audit fees and non-audit services fees. They find that after controlling for board of director characteristics, there is a significant positive association between audit committee effectiveness and audit fees, only for larger clients. Their results indicate that

> effective audit committees undertake more monitoring which results in wider audit scope and higher audit fees. Contrary to our expectations, we find the association between audit committee effectiveness and non-audit service fees to be positive and significant, especially for larger clients. This suggests that larger clients are more likely to purchase non-audit services even in the presence of effective audit committees probably due to the complexity of their activities. Overall, our findings support regulatory initiatives aimed at improving corporate governance quality.

Remuneration committee

The area of executive remuneration is always a 'hot issue' and one that attracts a lot of attention from investors and so, perhaps inevitably, the press. Indeed, since the financial crisis there seems to be an insatiable appetite for stories about excessive executive remuneration. Executive remuneration itself is covered in some detail in Chapter 9, whilst the structure of the remuneration committee is detailed now.

The Code (2010) states that 'the board should establish a remuneration committee of at least three, or in the case of smaller companies, two independent non-executive directors' (para. D.2.1). The remuneration committee should make recommendations to the board, within agreed terms of reference, on the company's framework of executive remuneration and its cost; it should determine on their behalf specific remuneration packages for each of the executive directors, including pension rights and any compensation payments.

The establishment of a remuneration committee (in the form recommended by the Code) prevents executive directors from setting their own remuneration levels. The remuneration committee mechanism should also provide a formal, transparent procedure for the setting of executive remuneration levels, including the determination of appropriate targets for any performance-related pay schemes. The members of the remuneration committee should be identified in the annual report. The remuneration of non-executive directors is decided by the chairman and the executive members of the board. The company chairman may serve on—but should not chair—the remuneration committee where he/she is considered independent on appointment as the chairman.

However, Bender (2011) states:

> The market they [remuneration committees] use to derive comparative data is not a market as such, it is a collection of self-selected elite peers. The much-vaunted independence of the non-executives on the remuneration committee in itself means that they have incomplete knowledge of the company and the individuals being compensated, and asymmetry of information leaves them at the wrong end of a power imbalance. In all, the realities of how committees actually operate differ considerably from the rhetorics with which they describe their compliance with the unattainable Ideal.

Nomination committee

In the past directors were often appointed on the basis of personal connections. This process often did not provide the company with directors with appropriate business experience relevant to the particular board to which they were appointed. The board would also not have a balance in as much as there would be a lack of independent non-executive directors.

The Code (2010) advocates a formal, rigorous, and transparent procedure for the appointment of new directors and states that 'there should be a nomination committee which should lead the process for board appointments and make recommendations to the board. A majority of members of the nomination committee should be independent non-executive directors' (para. B.2.1). The chair of the committee may be the chairman of the company or an independent non-executive director but the chairman should not chair the nomination committee when it is dealing with the appointment of a successor to the chairmanship.

The nomination committee should evaluate the existing balance of skills, knowledge, and experience on the board, and utilize this when preparing a candidate profile for new appointments. The nomination committee should throw its net as wide as possible in the search for suitable candidates to ensure that it identifies the best candidates. In an often rapidly changing business environment, the nomination committee should also be involved with succession planning in the company, noting challenges that may arise and identifying possible gaps in skills and knowledge that would need to be filled with new appointments. As with the other key board committees, the members of the nomination committee should be identified in the annual report.

It is important that the board has a balanced composition, both in terms of executive and non-executive directors, and in terms of the experience, qualities, and skills that individuals bring to the board.

The Institute of Directors (IoD) published some useful guidance in this area. Box 8.2 shows an extract from *Standards for the Board* (2006) in relation to an action list for deciding board composition.

Guo and Masulis (2012), in a sample of 1,280 firms listed on the New York Stock Exchange (NYSE) or Nasdaq, use the mandatory changes in board composition brought about

> ## Box 8.2 Action list for deciding board composition
>
> - Consider the ratio and number of executive and non-executive directors.
> - Consider the energy, experience, knowledge, skill and personal attributes of current and prospective directors in relation to the future needs of the board as a whole, and develop specifications and processes for new appointments, as necessary.
> - Consider the cohesion, dynamic tension and diversity of the board and its leadership by the chairman.
> - Make and review succession plans for directors and the company secretary.
> - Where necessary, remove incompetent or unsuitable directors or the company secretary, taking relevant legal, contractual, ethical, and commercial matters into account.
> - Agree proper procedures for electing a chairman and appointing the managing director and other directors.
> - Identify potential candidates for the board, make selection and agree terms of appointment and remuneration. New appointments should be agreed by every board member.
> - Provide new board members with a comprehensive induction to board processes and policies, inclusion to the company and to their new role.
> - Monitor and appraise each individual's performance, behaviour, knowledge, effectiveness and values rigorously and regularly.
> - Identify development needs and training opportunities for existing and potential directors and the company secretary.
>
> *Source: Standards for the Board* (IoD, 2006)

by the new exchange listing rules following the passage of the Sarbanes-Oxley Act (SOX) to estimate the effect of overall board independence and nominating committee independence on forced CEO turnover. Their evidence suggests that 'greater representation of independent directors on board and/or nominating committee leads to more effective monitoring. Our finding that nominating committee independence significantly affects the quality of board monitoring has important policy implications given the intense debate on the costs and benefits of mandatory board regulations since the passage of SOX'.

Risk committee

Risk of various types features significantly in the operation of many businesses. Although not a recommendation of the Code, many companies either set up a separate risk committee or establish the audit committee as an audit and risk committee. Of course, it is essential that directors realize that they are responsible for the company's system of internal controls and have mechanisms in place to ensure that the internal controls of the company and risk management systems are operating efficiently.

Equally, many companies, particularly larger companies or those with significant transactions overseas, may find that they have interest or currency exposures that need to be covered. The misuse of derivatives through poor internal controls and lack of monitoring led to the downfall of Barings Bank (as detailed in Chapter 1) and other companies may be equally at risk. A risk committee should therefore comprehend the risks involved by, inter alia, using derivatives, and this would necessitate quite a high level of financial expertise and the ability to seek external professional advice where necessary.

Pathan (2009), using a sample of 212 large US bank holding companies over the period 1997–2004, examines the relevance of bank board structure on bank risk-taking. He finds that 'strong bank boards (boards reflecting more of bank shareholders interest) particularly small and less restrictive boards positively affect bank risk-taking. In contrast, CEO power (CEO's ability to control board decision) negatively affects bank risk-taking'.

Meanwhile Yatim (2010), in a study of 690 firms listed on the Bursa Malaysia for the financial year ending in 2003, finds

> a strong support for an association between the establishment of a risk management committee and strong board structures. Specifically, the result shows that firms with higher proportions of non-executive directors on boards and firms that separate the positions of chief executive officers and board chairs are likely to set up a stand-alone risk management committee. Firms with greater board expertise and board diligence are also likely to establish a risk management committee. These findings suggest that stronger boards demonstrate their commitment to and awareness of improved internal control environment.

Ethics committee

Following the collapse of Enron more companies introduced ethics committees as a board subcommittee. Companies may try to ensure that there is a strong organizational ethic by cascading an ethics code throughout the company, from director level to the worker on the shop floor. Many corporate governance codes are silent on any explicit mention of ethics committees, although the spirit of corporate governance recommendations is to act in an ethical way. This lack of an explicit mention is perhaps rather surprising given the frequent 'breaches' of perceived good corporate governance: infringement of shareholder rights, fraud, and excessive executive remuneration. As we have seen in Chapter 6, institutional shareholders are being exhorted to engage more fully with their investee companies, to act more as shareowners, and hopefully to encourage companies to behave more ethically. In Chapter 7 we saw that the management of, inter alia, ethical issues can be seen as a form of risk management.

Stevens et al. (2005) state that

> the extent to which ethics codes are actually used by executives when making strategic choices as opposed to being merely symbolic is unknown ... We find that financial executives are more likely to integrate their company's ethics code into their strategic decision processes if (a) they perceive pressure from market stakeholders to do so (suppliers, customers, shareholders, etc.); (b) they believe the use of ethics codes creates an internal ethical culture and promotes a positive external image for their firms; and (c) the code is integrated into daily activities through ethics code training programs. The effect of market stakeholder pressure is further enhanced when executives also believe that the code will promote a

positive external image. Of particular note, we do not find that pressure from non-market stakeholders (e.g., regulatory agencies, government bodies, court systems) has a unique impact on ethics code use.

Crane *et al.* (2008) highlight that ethics programmes may involve a smaller cost now and result in significant savings in the future: 'In the United States, for example, corporations can significantly reduce their fine once they have been found guilty in criminal procedures by showing that an effective ethics program was in place'.

Non-executive directors

Non-executive directors are a mainstay of good governance. The non-executive director's role essentially has two dimensions. One dimension—which has been given much emphasis in the last decade—is as a control or counterweight to executive directors, so that the presence of non-executive directors helps to ensure that an individual person or group cannot unduly influence the board's decisions. The second dimension is the contribution that non-executive directors can make to the overall leadership and development of the company. Some argue that there may be a conflict in these two roles because non-executive directors are expected both to monitor executive directors' actions and to work with executive directors as part of the board. This idea of a potential conflict in the roles is an area discussed by Ezzamel and Watson (1997).

The Cadbury Report (1992) stated that 'given the importance of their distinctive contribution, non-executive directors should be selected with the same impartiality and care as senior executives' (para. 4.15). Non-executives should ideally be selected through a formal process and their appointment should be considered by the board as a whole.

The Cadbury Report also emphasized the contribution that independent non-executive directors could make, stating 'the Committee believes that the calibre of the non-executive members of the board is of special importance in setting and maintaining standards of corporate governance' (para. 4.10). The importance of non-executive directors was echoed in the Organisation for Economic Co-operation and Development (OECD) Principles: 'Boards should consider assigning a sufficient number of non-executive board members capable of exercising independent judgement to tasks where there is a potential for conflict of interest. Examples of such key responsibilities are financial reporting, nomination and executive and board remuneration.'

The Code (2010) also recognizes the important role to be played by independent non-executive directors:

> as part of their role as members of a unitary board, non-executive directors should constructively challenge and help develop proposals on strategy . . . [they] should scrutinise the performance of management in meeting agreed goals and objectives and monitor the reporting of performance. They should satisfy themselves on the integrity of financial information and that financial controls and systems of risk management are robust and defensible. They are responsible for determining appropriate levels of remuneration of executive directors and have a prime role in appointing, and where necessary removing, executive directors, and in succession planning. (para. A.4.)

Independence of non-executive directors

Although there is a legal duty on all directors to act in the best interests of the company, this does not of itself guarantee that directors will act objectively. To try to ensure objectivity in board decisions, it is important that there is a balance of independent non-executive directors. This idea of independence is emphasized again and again in various codes and reports: for example, Cadbury (1992) stated that 'apart from their directors' fees and shareholdings, they [non-executive directors] . . . should be independent of management and free from any business or other relationship which could materially interfere with the exercise of their independent judgement' (para. 4.12). The OECD (1999) also considered this issue: 'Board independence usually requires that a sufficient number of board members not be employed by the company and not be closely related to the company or its management through significant economic, family or other ties. This does not prevent shareholders from being board members'. Subsequently, the OECD (2004) stated that 'board independence . . . usually requires that a sufficient number of board members will need to be independent of management'. The Higgs Review (2003) stated that 'a board is strengthened significantly by having a strong group of non-executive directors with no other connection with the company. These individuals bring a dispassionate objectivity that directors with a closer relationship to the company cannot provide' (para. 9.5).

The Code (2010) states that 'the board should identify in the annual report each non-executive director it considers to be independent. The board should determine whether the director is independent in character and judgement and whether there are relationships or circumstances which are likely to affect, or could appear to affect, the director's judgement' (para. B.1.1).

'Independence' is generally taken as meaning that there are no relationships or circumstances that might affect the director's judgement. Situations where a non-executive director's independence would be called into question include:

- where the director was a former employee of the company or group within the last five years;
- where additional remuneration (apart from the director's fee) was received from the company;
- where the director had close family ties with the company's other directors and advisors;
- where he/she had a material business relationship with the company in the last three years;
- where he/she had served on the board for more than ten years; where he/she represented a significant shareholder.

There is some discussion as to whether the number of non-executive directorships that any one individual can hold should be defined. Of course, if an individual were to hold many non-executive directorships, for example, ten or more, then it is arguable whether that individual could devote enough time and consideration to each of the directorships. On the other hand, it may be perfectly feasible for an individual to hold, for example, five non-executive directorships. It really depends on the time that an individual has available, on the level of commitment, and whether any of the multiple non-executive directorships might lead to the problem of interlocking directorships whereby the independence of their role is compromised. An interlocking relationship might occur through any of a number of circumstances, including family relationship, business relationship, or a previous advisory role (such as auditor), which would endanger the fundamental aspect of independence. However, the independence of non-executive directors is an area of corporate governance that institutional investors and their representative groups monitor very carefully and disclosure of biographical information about directors and increasing use of databases of director information should help to identify potential problems in this area. The Code (2010) states that 'non-executive directors should undertake that they will have sufficient time to meet what is expected of them' and 'their other significant commitments should be disclosed to the board before appointment, with a broad indication of the time involved and the board should be informed of subsequent changes' (para. B.3.2). It is recommended that a full-time executive director should not take on 'more than one non-executive directorship in a FTSE 100 company nor the chairmanship of such a company' (para. B.3.3).

Morck (2008) discussed the fact that behavioural issues are important in corporate governance, citing Milgram's (1974) findings that human nature includes 'a reflexive subservience' to people perceived to be legitimate authorities, like corporate CEOs. Morck states that 'effective corporate governance reforms must weaken this reflexive subservience. Corporate governance reforms that envision independent directors (dissenting peers), non-executive chairs (alternative authority figures), and fully independent audit committees (absent authority figures) aspire to a similar effect on corporate boards—the initiation of real debate to expose poor strategies before they become fatal'.

Yeh et al. (2011), using the data of the twenty largest financial institutions from G8 countries (Australia, Canada, France, Germany, Italy, Japan, UK, and USA), of which four are common law countries and four civil law countries, find that the 'performance during the crisis period is higher for financial institutions with more independent directors on auditing and risk committees. The influence of committee independence on the performance is particularly stronger for civil law countries. In addition, the independence-performance relationships are more significant in financial institutions with excessive risk-taking behaviors'.

Contribution of non-executive directors

The necessity for the independence of the majority of non-executive directors has been established above, and the 'right' non-executive directors can make a significant contribution to the company. When non-executive directors are being sought, the company will be looking for the added value that a new appointment can make to the board. The added value may come from a number of facets: their experience in industry, the City, public life, or other appropriate background; their knowledge of a particular functional specialism (for example, finance or marketing); their knowledge of a particular technical process/system; their reputation; their ability to have an insight into issues discussed at the board and to ask searching questions. Of course, these attributes should be matched by the non-executive director's independence and integrity. The *Cadbury Code of Best Practice* (1992) stated that 'non-executive directors should bring an independent judgement to bear on issues of strategy, performance, resources, including key appointments, and standards of conduct' (para. 2.1).

As well as their contribution to the board, non-executive directors will serve on the key board committees (audit, remuneration, and nomination) as described earlier. However, it is not recommended that any one non-executive director sits on all three of these board committees. The Code (2010) refers to the benefits of 'ensuring that committee membership is refreshed and that undue reliance is not placed on particular individuals' (para. B.1).

Higgs Review

The Higgs Review, chaired by Derek Higgs, was established by the Department of Trade and Industry (DTI) in 2002 to review the role and effectiveness of non-executive directors. The Higgs Review was discussed in more detail in Chapter 3. Its recommendations caused much discussion but most of them were incorporated into the Combined Code (2003, 2006, 2008) and the subsequent UK Corporate Governance Code (2010), although some in a modified form.

In 2006 the FRC published *Good Practice Suggestions from the Higgs Report*. These include guidance on the role of the chairman and the non-executive director, and a summary of the principal duties of the remuneration and nomination committees. In 2010 the FRC published the *Guidance on Board Effectiveness*, which relates primarily to Sections A and B of the Code on the leadership and effectiveness of the board. The guidance was developed by the Institute of Chartered Secretaries and Administrators (ICSA) on the FRC's behalf, and replaces 'Suggestions for Good Practice from the Higgs Report' (known as the Higgs Guidance), which has been withdrawn.

The Association of British Insurers (ABI) issued its first Report on Board Effectiveness in 2011. The report focuses on three areas that the ABI believes helps ensure that the board is effective and contributes to the company's success. These areas are board diversity, succession planning, and board evaluation. The ABI states: 'These issues do not stand alone. Selecting the best individuals from a diverse talent pool, planning for succession and replacement, and regularly evaluating the board to determine its effectiveness, cover the lifecycle of a board. That is why they are important'.

Director evaluation

In the Hampel Committee Final Report (1998), it was suggested that boards consider the introduction of formal procedures to 'assess both their own collective performance and that of individual directors' (para 3.13). In a widely cited report of institutional investor opinion, McKinsey (2002) defined 'good' board governance practices as encompassing a majority of outside (non-executive) directors, outside directors who are truly independent with no management ties, and under which *formal director evaluation is in place*.

The evaluation of directors has two dimensions, which are the evaluation of the board as a whole and the evaluation of individual directors serving on the board. Most annual reports are not forthcoming on how these evaluations may be carried out in their business, and indeed KPMG (2002) found, in a survey of corporate governance in Europe, that only 39 per cent of UK respondents had a regular process for the evaluation of the board. However, this was considerably better than the figure for the European countries as a whole, which was only 17 per cent.

In terms of the evaluation of the board as a whole, there are several approaches that might be utilized. These approaches include, first, a structured questionnaire to evaluate how the board is performing in key areas (such as achieving key goals that have been set), and informal discussion between the chairman of the board and the directors, which would cover a wide range of strategic and operational issues (such as how well do the board dynamics work, and how well do the board subcommittees work).

The evaluation of individual directors provides individual directors with the opportunity to discuss key areas with the chairman on a one-to-one basis. It is an important process for finding out just how comfortable an individual director is, what areas he/she might be able to contribute to more effectively, and whether there are any barriers to full participation in the board's activities (for example, lack of information to enable an informed discussion).

These evaluations will contribute to the establishment of the performance criteria that will help to achieve the corporate objectives and which are used in helping to align the performance of directors with the interest of shareholders.

It does seem clear that, in order to determine whether boards of directors as a whole, and directors as individuals, are performing to the best of their ability, there should be evaluation of the board as a whole, the board leadership, and the individual directors. Many boards are silent on this issue, indicating either that they do not have evaluation procedures in place or that they do not wish to disclose them if they have. If the latter is the case, then one has to ask whether the reluctance to disclose is because the evaluation process is not robust enough to stand up to scrutiny. If the former is the case, that is, that there are no evaluation or assessment procedures in place, then equally one has to ask why not. This information will be very helpful in setting performance-related pay for directors and helping to eliminate the unease that many investors feel about executive remuneration levels.

The area of board evaluation has been taken up by the Code (2010), which includes the principle that 'the board should undertake a formal and rigorous annual evaluation of its own performance and that of its committees and individual directors' (para. B.6). The board should disclose in the annual report the way in which the performance evaluations have been carried out. The Code recommends that, at least every three years, evaluation of FTSE 350 companies should be externally facilitated. Furthermore, 'non-executive directors, led by the senior independent director, should be responsible for performance evaluation of the chairman, taking into account the views of executive directors', (para. B.6.3).

Van den Berghe and Levrau (2004), in a study of the boards of directors of thirty companies listed on Euronext Brussels and Nasdaq Europe, found that there were a number of areas where better understanding was needed of elements that determined board effectiveness. They also found that board evaluation was not as widespread as might be hoped. Epstein and Roy (2006) state that it is important to evaluate both the board as a whole and individual directors, as this may help highlight deficiencies. Metrics for evaluation should be relevant and linked to the inputs, such as attendance at board meetings, and outputs, such as stock price. A balanced scorecard approach, derived from the work of Kaplan and Norton (1992, 2000) is an appropriate tool for director evaluation.

Wong (2011) highlights that the global financial crisis has prompted more debate on how the effectiveness of the board might be improved. He points out that

> despite considerable reforms over the past two decades, boards—particularly at financial institutions—have been criticized recently for failing to properly guide strategy, oversee risk management, structure executive pay, manage succession planning, and carry out other essential tasks. This article argues that the lack of attention to behavioral and functional considerations—such as director mindset, board operating context, and evolving human dynamics—has hampered the board's effectiveness.

He makes various recommendations alongside 'establishing core building blocks such as appropriate board size, well-functioning committees, proficient company secretarial support, and professionally-administered board evaluation'.

The ABI (2011) find that in 2010/11, 95.9 per cent of FTSE 100 and 96.2 per cent of FTSE 250 companies stated that they conducted a board evaluation. For companies listed in both 2009/10 and 2010/11, 16.2 per cent of FTSE 100 companies and 5.1 per cent of FTSE 250 companies conducted external evaluations in both years.

Succession planning

The Code (2010) describes non-executive directors as having a key role to play in the succession planning of the company, and states: 'The board should satisfy itself that plans are in place for orderly succession for appointments to the board and to senior management, so as to maintain an appropriate balance of skills and experience within the company and on the board and to ensure progressive refreshing of the board', (para. B.2).

Naveen (2006) found that 'a firm's propensity to groom an internal candidate for the CEO position is related to firm size, degree of diversification, and industry structure. My results also suggest that succession planning is associated with a higher probability of inside succession and voluntary succession and a lower probability of forced succession'.

Larcker and Tayan (2010) state that whilst one of the most important decisions for a board of directors is the selection of the CEO, 'survey data indicates that many boards are not prepared for this process. In recent years, shareholder groups have pressured boards to increase transparency about their succession plans'.

The Spencer Stuart 2011 UK Board Index, reporting on the current board trends and practices at major UK companies, finds that 'chairman succession planning is not widely discussed in most boardrooms because there are few formal mechanisms for addressing the issue beyond the chairman's annual review with the senior independent director. For such a critical appointment it is surprising how little has been written and how seldom the chairman succession planning process is openly discussed, (Will Dawkins)'.

Board diversity

An area that is attracting increasing interest is that of board diversity whereby diversity is defined broadly in terms of gender or nationality. It may be argued that board diversity enables different perspectives to be taken on various issues given that men and women may approach issues from different viewpoints and may have different behavioural patterns as well; similarly individuals from different ethnic backgrounds may bring additional cultural insights to the boardroom.

Concerned by the lack of progress with the representation of women on UK boards, the UK's Coalition Government invited Lord Davies to review the situation, to identify the barriers that were preventing more women from reaching the boardroom, and to make recommendations as to how this situation might be redressed. Lord Davies' report, *Women on Boards*, was published in February 2011 and reviewed the current situation on UK boards (FTSE 350) and considered the business case for having gender-diverse boards.

A number of recommendations were made, including that the chairmen of FTSE 350 companies should state the percentage of women that they aim to have on their boards in 2013 and 2015, and that FTSE 100 companies should aim for a minimum 25 per cent women in the boardroom by 2015 although many might achieve a higher figure. Quoted companies should annually disclose the proportion of women on the board, women in senior executive positions, and female employees in the organizations as a whole. Furthermore, Lord Davies recommended that the FRC amend the Code to require listed companies to establish a policy on boardroom diversity, including measurable objectives for implementing the policy, and disclose a summary of the policy and the progress made towards achieving the objectives each year. It was also recommended that executive search firms should draw up a voluntary code of conduct addressing gender diversity and best practice, covering the relevant search criteria and processes in relation to FTSE 350 board appointments. Early in 2012 there was a follow-up report published which indicated that, over the year since the original report was published, the biggest ever reported increase in the percentage of women on boards was evidenced.

In May 2011 the FRC began consulting on possible amendments to the Code that would require companies to publish their policy on boardroom diversity and report against it annually, as recommended by the Davies Report (2011) and to consider the board's diversity amongst other factors, when assessing its effectiveness. In October 2011 the FRC announced that these changes would be implemented in a revised version of the Code, which will be issued in 2012 and will apply to financial years beginning on or after 1 October 2012.

The changes affect two sections of the Code. First, in relation to Section B.2.4, where it is proposed that the work of the nomination committee should be described in a separate section of the annual report, including the process used in relation to board appointments. This section should include a description of 'the board's policy on diversity, including gender, any measurable objectives that it has set for implementing the policy, and progress on achieving the objectives. An explanation should be given if neither an external search consultancy nor open advertising has been used in the appointment of a chairman or a non-executive director.' Secondly, in relation to Section B6 where 'the evaluation of the board should consider the balance of skills, experience, independence and knowledge of the company on the board, its diversity, including gender, how the board works together as a unit, and other factors relevant to its effectiveness.'

Following on from the publication of *Women in economic decision-making in the EU: Progress Report* in March 2012, the European Commission is considering legislation to improve the gender balance on the boards of listed companies. The Progress Report showed that a number of countries in the EU—France, the Netherlands, Italy and Belgium—enacted legislative measures in 2011 aimed at improving gender balance in company boards, and that other countries (for example, Spain since 2007 and Norway since 2003) already had quota systems in place at 40 per cent. However, in January 2012 the average number of female board members in the largest companies listed in the EU was only 13.7 per cent compared to 11.8 per cent in 2010. Moreover, only 3.2 per cent of chairpersons were women in January 2012 compared to 3.4 per cent in 2010.

What does the academic evidence have to say about board diversity? Carter *et al.* (2003) examine the relationship between board diversity and firm value for Fortune 1000 firms. Board diversity is defined as the percentage of women, African-Americans, Asians, and Hispanics on the board of directors. After controlling for size, industry, and other corporate governance measures, they find significant positive relationships between the fraction of women or minorities on the board and firm value. They also find that the proportion of women and minorities on boards increases with firm size and board size but decreases as the number of insiders increases. For women, there is an inverse relationship between the percentage of women on boards and the average age of the board.

Carter *et al.* (2007) analysed both the diversity of the board and of important board committees, in all firms listed on the Fortune 500 over the period 1998–2002, to gain greater insight into the way diversity affects board functions and, ultimately, shareholder value. Their findings support the view that board diversity has a positive effect on financial performance. The evidence on board committees indicates that gender diversity has a positive effect on financial performance primarily through the audit function of the board whilst ethnic diversity impacts financial performance through all three functions of the board: audit, executive compensation, and director nomination.

Erkut *et al.* (2008) show that, based on interviews with 50 women directors, twelve CEOs, and seven corporate secretaries from Fortune 1000 companies, a critical mass of three or more women directors can cause a fundamental change in the boardroom and enhance corporate governance. The content of boardroom discussion is more likely to include the perspectives of multiple stakeholders; difficult issues and problems are less likely to be ignored or brushed aside; and boardroom dynamics are more open and collaborative.

Grosvold and Brammer (2011) find that 'as much as half the variation in the presence of women on corporate boards across countries is attributable to national institutional systems and that culturally and legally-oriented institutional systems appear to play the most significant role in shaping board diversity'.

Ferreira (2011) discusses the potential costs and benefits of board diversity arising from the academic literature. The costs include conflict, lack of co-operation, and insufficient communication; choosing directors with little experience, inadequate qualifications, or who are overused; and conflicts of interests and agenda pushing. The benefits include creativity and different perspectives; access to resources and connections; career incentives through signaling and mentoring; and public relations, investor relations, and legitimacy. From his discussion of board diversity literature, he concludes that 'making a business case for women in the boardroom on the basis of statistical evidence linking women to profits obviously creates the possibility of a business case against women if the evidence turns out to suggest that women reduce profits . . . the research on board diversity is best used as a means to understand the costs and benefits of diversity in the workplace and to study corporate governance issues'.

Conclusions

In this chapter the different types of board structure, unitary or dual, have been discussed. We have seen that the UK has a unitary board structure and that the predominant form of board structure in Europe is also the unitary board structure. The roles and responsibilities of the board, including those of the chair, CEO, senior independent director, and company secretary, have been reviewed.

The role and contribution to be made by key board subcommittees, including audit, remuneration, nomination, risk, and ethics committees are discussed. The increasing emphasis on the importance of the role of non-executive (outside) directors is shown, and the definition of the important criterion of the 'independence' of non-executive directors is analysed, together with the role that non-executive directors play on a company's key board subcommittees. In future, it is likely that non-executive directors will be called upon to play an ever more important role as investors look to the audit committees, in particular, to restore and enhance confidence in companies.

The key areas of board evaluation, succession planning, and board diversity are covered. The impact of board diversity, in terms of gender and ethnicity, is discussed, and the low proportion of female directors and directors from different ethnic groups is highlighted.

Summary

- Board structure may be unitary (single tier) or dual (two tier). In a dual structure there is a supervisory board as well as an executive board of management. Usually, both the unitary board of directors and the supervisory board (in a dual system) are elected by shareholders.
- The board of directors leads and controls the company, and is the link between managers and investors.
- It is desirable to split the roles of chair and CEO so that there is not too much power invested in one individual. The chair is responsible for the running of the board, whilst the CEO is responsible for running the business.
- The board may delegate various activities to board subcommittees, the most common being the audit, remuneration, nomination, risk, and ethics committees.
- The board should include an appropriate number of independent non-executive (outside) directors. The non-executive directors bring a balance to the board, and their experience and knowledge can add value to the board. The non-executive directors make a key contribution through their membership of the board subcommittees.
- Boards should include due consideration of key areas including board evaluation, succession planning, and board diversity.
- Boards should have appropriate diversity in their composition; this should strengthen boards as they will be more capable of reflecting the views of the various stakeholder groups.

Example: Statoil Hydro, Norway

Statoil Hydro is one of Norway's largest companies. There are a number of legal requirements in Norway relating to members of the board which Statoil Hydro is subject to. There is a Norwegian legal requirement for at least 40 per cent of the board members to be female, which means that its board is more diverse than is common in most other countries. Also the companies' employees can be represented by three board members.

Statoil Hydro was established in October 2007 following the merger between Statoil and Hydro's oil and gas activities. It is an international energy company primarily focused on upstream oil and gas operations, and operates in thirty-nine oil and gas fields, whilst also being the world's largest operator in waters more than 100 metres deep.

In the case of Statoil Hydro, its Articles of Association provide for a board of ten members. Management is not represented on the board, which appoints the president and CEO. The board is subject to Norway's rules which state that all public companies in Norway are obliged to ensure that at least 40 per cent of their board directors are women. Of the ten members, four are female and six male, which meets the legal requirement of at least 40 per cent of the board being female.

The board has two subcommittees: an audit committee and a compensation (remuneration) committee. Three of the four female directors are members of either the audit committee or the compensation committee, and a female Director, Grace Reksten Skaugen, chairs the compensation committee. This is interesting as even where females are directors in other countries, such as the UK, it is rare for them to be members of the key board committees, or indeed to chair such a committee. The fourth female Director, Lill-Heidi Bakkerud, represents the employees on the board. As well as Lill-Heidi Bakkerud, two male directors also represent the employees on the board.

Furthermore, there are another two members (both male in this case) who are in addition to the ten board members, and they are employee-elected observers and may attend board meetings but have no voting rights.

Statoil changed its organizational structure to reflect the ongoing globalization of Statoil, leverage the position on the Norwegian Continental Shelf, and simplify internal interfaces to support safe and efficient operations from 1 January 2011.

In terms of corporate governance features, the board still has 40 per cent female composition and Marit Arnstad is now the Deputy Chair of the Board.

Example: Deutsche Bank, Germany

This is an example of a well-established German bank which has good corporate governance but which suffered a drop in share price when its CEO was taken ill.

Deutsche Bank is a leading investment bank and, as a German company, it has a dual board. Its system of corporate governance has four key elements: 'good relations with shareholders, effective cooperation between the Management Board and the Supervisory Board, a system of performance-related compensation for managers and employees, as well as transparent and early reporting'.

Deutsche Bank's Supervisory Board has established five standing committees: audit, nomination, risk, mediation, and the chairman's committee. It is the latter's responsibility to

prepare the decisions for the Supervisory Board on the appointment and dismissal of members of the Management Board, including long-term succession planning. It also submits a proposal to the Supervisory Board on the compensation for the Management Board including the main contract elements and is responsible for entering into, amending and terminating the service contracts and other agreements with the Management Board members.

Dr Josef Ackermann is Chairman of the Management Board and the Group Executive Committee of Deutsche Bank. He joined the Management Board of Deutsche Bank in 1996 and was responsible for the investment banking division. In 2002 he became Spokesman of the Management Board and Chairman of the Group Executive Committee. He was appointed Chairman of the Management Board in February 2006.

In January 2009 he went to hospital feeling unwell. There was some uncertainty about the nature of his illness, and combined with poor financial results that had been released just a few hours earlier, the bank's shares fell nearly 3 per cent, although they subsequently recovered when news was given that the illness was attributable to a meal of sausages and sauerkraut, hastily eaten at the end of a busy day!

This episode highlights the nervousness that the market feels when it believes that a potential successor might not have been identified for a key role. The fear of a power vacuum or a rudderless ship sends shivers through the market. Ironically, Deutsche Bank is better prepared than many firms in terms of succession planning. In addition, Dr Ackermann's contract has now been extended from ending in 2010 to 2013, which will allow additional time to identify the most appropriate successor.

In May 2012 there is still considerable unrest at Deutsche Bank's lack of succession planning. So much so that Hermes, the UK fund manager, together with VIP, a German association of institutional shareholders, has filed 'counter resolutions' at the AGM, arguing that shareholders should withhold a usually routine confidence vote in the bank's board. This was after the bank's supervisory board failed to agree on a successor and the resulting public discussion was felt to be harmful to potential candidates and to the company itself.

 ## Mini case study   Marks and Spencer Plc, UK

This is a good example of a well-known 'blue chip' company that had good financial performance over a number of years but then hit a downturn. There were several aspects of its corporate governance that were not ideal, but the market turned a blind eye to these whilst the company was doing well. However, once the company's sales and profitability fell, there was more of a spotlight on Marks and Spencer's corporate governance. Several issues were highlighted as being less than satisfactory and, under pressure from the City, action was taken to improve these. Subsequently, however, there was more controversy as the roles of chair and CEO were combined in one individual.

Marks and Spencer Plc enjoyed an enviable reputation for many years, performing well and giving its shareholders a good return on their investment. However, there was some criticism of its corporate governance, in particular that there was a lack of sufficient independent non-executive directors. This meant that the board lacked a real balance between executive and non-executive directors, and appropriate questions might not be asked of the executive directors by the non-executive directors: for example, questions relating to the strategic direction that the company was taking, and the market it was aiming for.

In the late 1990s Marks and Spencer found that its plummeting sales and declining profits resulted in a lot of pressure to reform its corporate governance. As well as the criticism regarding non-executive directors, there was also much criticism of the pay-offs made to departing directors in the late 1990s and early 2000/01. The annual report for 2005 showed how Marks and Spencer's corporate governance had improved. The board now comprised half non-executive directors with a wide range of experience who could exercise their independent judgement on key issues. The main board committees (audit, remuneration, and nomination) were comprised of non-executive directors. There was also a Corporate Social Responsibility Committee to provide an overview of the social, environmental, and ethical impacts

(continued)

of the group's activities. Given the greater emphasis on corporate governance and the appointment in 2002 of non-executive directors, such as Paul Myners (Chair of the government-sponsored Myner's review of institutional investment), investors felt more confident in Marks and Spencer. Improved corporate governance would help the company to re-establish itself and give investors the confidence that various viewpoints would be heard on issues of strategy, performance, and resources at board meetings.

In addition to Paul Myners, a key appointment to Marks and Spencer was that of Sir Stuart Rose who was appointed to the position of CEO in May 2004. He subsequently fought off several takeover bids by Philip Green for the Marks and Spencer Group. Sir Stuart Rose had a rejuvenating effect on Marks and Spencer, and in January 2007 he was named the '2006 Business Leader of the Year' by the World Leadership Forum for his efforts in restoring the performance of the company. However, whilst Marks and Spencer's performance improved under the well-known Plan A ('there is no Plan B'), the company incurred the displeasure of investors when, in 2008, Sir Stuart Rose became both Chairman and CEO until July 2011. This combination of roles goes against the UK Combined Code's recommendations of best practice. As a result, in 2008 some 22 per cent of the shareholders did not support the appointment of Sir Stuart Rose as Chairman. By the time that Marks and Spencer's annual report 2011 was published, the situation of combining the roles of CEO and chairman was over, and the changes in the board reflect this with Marc Bolland as the CEO, and Robert Swannell as the Chairman. In addition there are twelve other directors, of whom five are female.

Questions

The discussion questions to follow cover the key learning points of this chapter. Reading of some of the additional reference material will enhance the depth of the students' knowledge and understanding of these areas.

1. What function does a board perform and how does this contribute to the corporate governance of the company?
2. What are the main subcommittees of the board and what role does each of these subcommittees play?
3. What are the main differences between a unitary board system and a dual board system?
4. How might the 'independence' of non-executive (outside) directors be defined?
5. Critically discuss the importance of board evaluations, succession planning, and board diversity for the effectiveness of the board.
6. 'Non-executive directors are a waste of time. They often have little involvement with a company and are not aware of what is really going on.' Critically discuss this statement.

References

ABI (2011), *Reporting on Board Effectiveness*, ABI, London.

Bender, R. (2011), 'The Platonic Remuneration Committee', 10 March 2011. Available at SSRN: http://ssrn.com/abstract=1782642 or http://dx.doi.org/10.2139/ssrn.1782642

Cadbury, Sir Adrian (1992), *Report of the Committee on the Financial Aspects of Corporate Governance*, Gee & Co. Ltd, London.

—— (2002), *Corporate Governance and Chairmanship*: A Personal View, Oxford University Press, Oxford.

Carter, D.A., Simkins, B.J., and Simpson, W.G. (2003), 'Corporate Governance, Board Diversity, and Firm Value', *The Financial Review*, Vol. 38.

—— D'Souza, F., Simkins, B.J., and Simpson, W.G. (2007), 'The Diversity of Corporate Board Committees and Financial Performance', available at SSRN: http://ssrn.com/abstract=972763

Charkham, J. (2005), *Keeping Better Company: Corporate Governance Ten Years On*, Oxford University Press, Oxford.

Combined Code (2003), *The Combined Code on Corporate Governance*, FRC, London.

—— (2006), *The Combined Code on Corporate Governance*, FRC, London.

—— (2008),*The Combined Code on Corporate Governance*, FRC, London.

Company Law Reform Bill (2005), Company Law Reform Bill (HL), The Stationery Office, London.

Crane, A., McWilliams, A., Matten, D., Moon, J., and Siegel, D.S. (2008), *The Oxford Handbook of Corporate Social Responsibility*, Oxford University Press, Oxford.

Davies E.M. (2011), *Women on Boards*, Department for Business, Innovation & Skills, London.

—— (2012), *Women on Boards, One Year On*, Department for Business, Innovation & Skills, London.

Epstein, M.J. and Roy, M.J. (2006), 'Measuring the Effectiveness of Corporate Boards and Directors' in M.J. Epstein and K.O. Hanson (eds), *The Accountable Corporation*, Praeger Publishers, Westport, USA.

Erkut, S., Kramer, V.W., and Konrad, A. (2008), 'Critical Mass: Does the Number of Women on a Corporate Board Make a Difference?' in S. Vinnicombe, V. Singh, R. J. Burke, D. Bilimoria, and M. Huse (eds), *Women on Corporate Boards of Directors: International Research and Practice*, Edward Elgar, Northampton, MA.

European Commission (2012), *Women in Economic Decision-Making in the EU: Progress Report*, European Commission, Brussels.

Ezzamel, M. and Watson, R. (1997), 'Wearing Two Hats: The Conflicting Control and Management Roles of Non-Executive Directors', in K. Keasey, S. Thompson, and M. Wright (eds), *Corporate Governance: Economic, Management and Financial Issues*, Oxford University Press, Oxford.

Ferreira, D. (2011), 'Board Diversity', in H. Kent Baker and R. Anderson (eds), *Corporate Governance, A Synthesis of Theory, Research and Practice*, The Robert W. Kolb Series in Finance, John Wiley & Sons Inc., New Jersey.

FRC (2006), *Good Practice Suggestions from the Higgs Report*, FRC, London.

—— (2008), *Guidance on Audit Committees*, FRC, London.

—— (2010), *The UK Corporate Governance Code*, FRC, London.

—— (2010), *Guidance on Board Effectiveness*, FRC, London.

—— (2011), *Developments in Corporate Governance 2011: The impact and implementation of the UK Corporate Governance and Stewardship Codes*, FRC, London.

Grosvold, J. and Brammer, S. (2011), 'National Institutional Systems as Antecedents of Female Board Representation: An Empirical Study, *Corporate Governance: An International Review*, Vol. 19 (2), pp. 116–35.

Guo, L. and Masulis, R.W. (2012), 'Board Structure and Monitoring: New Evidence from CEO Turnover', March 12, 2012. Available at SSRN: http://ssrn.com/abstract=2021468 or http://dx.doi.org/10.2139/ssrn.2021468

Hampel, Sir Ronnie (1998), *Committee on Corporate Governance: Final Report*, Gee & Co. Ltd, London.

Hermes (2006), *The Hermes Corporate Governance Principles*, Hermes Investment Management Ltd, London.

—— (2010), *The Hermes Responsible Ownership Principles*, Hermes Pensions Management Ltd, London.

Higgs, D. (2003), *Review of the Role and Effectiveness of Non-Executive Directors*, DTI, London.

IoD (2006), *Standards for the Board*, IoD and Kogan Page, London.

Kaplan, R.S. and Norton, D.P. (1992), 'The Balanced Scorecard—Measures that Drive Performance', *Harvard Business Review*, January–February, pp. 71–9.

—— (2000), 'Having Trouble With Your Strategy? Then Map It', *Harvard Business Review*, September–October, pp. 167–76.

KPMG (2002), *Corporate Governance in Europe KPMG Survey 2001/02*, KPMG, London.

Larcker, D. F. and Tayan, B. (2010), 'CEO Succession Planning: Who's Behind Door Number One?' (June 24, 2010), *Rock Center for Corporate Governance at Stanford University Closer Look Series: Topics, Issues and Controversies in Corporate Governance* No. CGRP-05. Available at SSRN: http://ssrn.com/abstract=1678062

McKinsey & Co. (2002), *Investor Opinion Survey on Corporate Governance*, McKinsey & Co., London.

Mc Nulty T., Pettigrew A., Jobome G., and Morris C. (2011), 'The Role, Power and Influence of Company Chairs', *Journal of Management and Governance*, Vol. 15, No. 1, pp. 91–121.

Milgram S. (1974), *Obedience to Authority*, Harper and Row, New York.

Morck R. (2008), 'Behavioral Finance in Corporate Governance: Economics and Ethics of the Devil's Advocate', *Journal of Management and Governance*, Vol. 12, No. 2, pp. 179–200.

Naveen, L., (2006), 'Organizational Complexity and Succession Planning', *Journal of Financial and Quantitative Analysis*, Vol. 41, Issue 3, pp. 661–83.

OECD (1999), *Principles of Corporate Governance*, OECD, Paris.

—— (2004), *Principles of Corporate Governance*, OECD, Paris.

Pathan, S. (2009), 'Strong boards, CEO power and bank risk-taking', *Journal of Banking and Finance*, 33(7), pp. 1340–50.

Smith, Sir Robert (2003), *Audit Committees Combined Code Guidance*, FRC, London.

Spencer Stuart (2011), *2011 UK Board Index*, Spencer Stuart, London.

Spira, L. (2002), *The Audit Committee: Performing Corporate Governance*, Kluwer Academic Publishers, Dordrecht.

Stevens, J., Steensma, K., Harrison, D., and Cochran, P. (2005), 'Symbolic or Substantive Document? The Influence of Ethics Codes on Financial Executives' Decisions', *Strategic Management Journal*, Vol. 26, No. 2.

Taylor, B., Stiles, P., and Tampoe, M. (2001), *The Future for the Board*, Director and Board Research, IoD, London.

Turley, S. (2008), 'Developments in the Framework of Auditing Regulation in the United Kingdom', in R. Quick, S. Turley and M. Willekens (eds), *Auditing, Trust and Governance, Regulation in Europe*, Routledge, London.

Van Den Berghe, L.A.A. and Levrau, A.P.D. (2004), 'Evaluating Boards of Directors: What Constitutes a Good Corporate Board?', *Corporate Governance: An International Review*, Vol. 12, No. 4, October.

Wong, S. C. Y. (2011), 'Elevating Board Performance: The Significance of Director Mindset, Operating Context, and Other Behavioral and Functional Considerations', Northwestern Law & Econ Research Paper No. 11-12. Available at SSRN: http://ssrn.com/abstract=1832234 or http://dx.doi.org/10.2139/ssrn.1832234

Yatim, P. (2010), 'Board structures and the establishment of a risk management committee by Malaysian listed firms', *Journal of Management and Governance*, 14(1), pp. 17–36.

Yeh Y-H., Chung H., and Liu C-L. (2011), 'Committee Independence and Financial Institution Performance during the 2007–08 Credit Crunch: Evidence from a Multi-Country Study', *Corporate Governance: An International Review*, Vol. 19, No. 5, pp. 437–58.

Zaman M., Hudaib M., and Haniffa R. (2011), 'Corporate Governance Quality, Audit Fees and Non-Audit Services Fees', *Journal of Business Finance & Accounting*, Vol. 38, Issue 1–2, pp. 165–97, January/March 2011.

Useful websites

http://blog.thecorporatelibrary.com/ The website of the Corporate Library, which has comprehensive information about various aspects of corporate governance including shareholders and stakeholders (renamed the GMI blog).

www.bis.gov.uk The website of the UK Department for Business, Innovation & Skills has a number of references to interesting material relating to directors.

www.businesslink.gov.uk The website of Business Link, the government's online resource for businesses, including detail of directors' duties.

www.conference-board.org The Conference Board is a global, independent business membership and research association working in the public interest.

www.icsa.org.uk The website of the Institute of Chartered Secretaries and Administrators has useful references to matters relating to boards and directors including board effectiveness.

www.iod.com The website of the Institute of Directors has information relating to a wide range of topics relating to directors.

www.nacdonline.org The website of the US National Association of Corporate Directors.

 For further links to useful sources of information visit the Online Resource Centre **www.oxfordtextbooks.co.uk/orc/mallin4e/**

 **FT Clippings**

FT: Increase in overseas directors in UK

By Alison Smith, Chief Corporate Correspondent

November 27, 2011

The proportion of overseas board members at the UK's biggest companies has risen by one-third in the past year, according to new research.

A study by Spencer Stuart, the headhunter, shows that foreign directors now make up 32 per cent of boards in Britain's 150 largest quoted groups, compared with 24 per cent in 2010.

The percentage of foreign directors in British companies puts the UK among the most internationally diverse countries when it comes to the boardroom.

"There are three trends behind these figures," says Edward Speed of Spencer Stuart. "Mid-cap companies are now getting a higher percentage of foreign directors; there is the influx of overseas companies with London listings; and very big traditional UK companies are taking on more directors with experience of emerging markets." Recent examples of overseas directors becoming part of UK companies include Fabio Barbosa's appointment as finance director of BG Group; and Phuthuma Nhleko's joining the boards of oil major BP and miner Anglo American.

The attraction of growth in emerging markets is contributing to the rise in the proportion of directors from beyond national boundaries at large quoted companies—to reach almost two in five in Switzerland, for example, and more than one in four for companies in France, Sweden and the UK.

"When boards are looking for non-local members to diversify their understanding of international markets, there is a very strong interest in Asia," says Bertrand Richard, partner at Spencer Stuart.

Even in the US, where companies face less pressure to internationalise,

the proportion of non-national board members in the top 200 S&P groups has risen from 6 per cent in 2006 to 8 per cent now.

At the same time, the proportion of large companies where the boards remain resolutely domestic is falling: fewer than one in five in the UK, and below half in the US.

Yet the underlying picture is less straightforward—and suggests less corporate enthusiasm for broadly diverse boards than may first appear.

First, some directors from emerging markets are appointed solely because they represent investors. Annabel Parsons, partner at international search firm Heidrick & Struggles, cites increasing levels of Chinese investment in Europe. "A high percentage of Chinese non-executives are on the board because they are shareholders," she says.

Second, while companies are keen to harness emerging markets experience, they worry about how bringing in directors from very different backgrounds will affect board balance and behaviour.

Two obvious issues are language and geography. Victor Prozesky, of Heidrick & Struggles, puts it like this: "You have to think, what strain does it put on the functioning of a board, if people cannot attend in person or attend with an interpreter?" The desire for a different perspective and yet a common language appears reflected in companies' choice of foreign board members. Among French companies, for example, many non-national directors come from Belgium, while in the US, Canada and the UK are the most popular sources of foreign directors.

Yet companies are getting used to dealing with linguistic differences in the boardroom. Some groups, such as Nokia and Skandia, run the boards in English. Even companies in countries such as France and Germany, where there is some expectation that non-nationals will understand the language, are adapting.

"In France, what we are more and more used to is a company that runs the board in French, but if non-French board members want to speak in English they can, and French board members will all understand it," Mr Richard says. As for German companies, "An interpreter in the boardroom is not as good as everyone speaking the same language, but if a board is not used to doing so, it very, very definitely limits its ability to get non-Germans." Beyond language lie cultural differences. Non-executive directors in many developed western economies are increasingly expected to play a vigorous role in the life of the company, ready to ask searching questions of executives and keep a close eye on the management of the group.

"In emerging markets, quite often the culture is consensus driven," says Ms Parsons. "That can pose quite a lot of challenges if you are putting someone with that sort of background into a board where the expectation is that non-executive directors will challenge the management." While many companies work successfully with very internationally diverse boards, some groups question whether this approach is necessarily the best way to make the most of their prospects in emerging markets.

"Having a token person from an emerging market will probably not make that much of an impact," says Ms Parsons, pointing to the research on gender diversity that suggests a shift in attitude probably requires a minimum of three women on a board.

Mr Prozesky warns that people appointed partly for emerging market credentials may find that their local expertise and network of contacts can become out of date while they have been gaining the experience in developed markets which multinational companies also value. "In some countries, when it comes to having a good network of government contacts," he says, "that can change every six weeks." But while the survey indicates that companies have embraced diversity in term of nationality, it suggests that companies will struggle to meet the recommendation by Lord Davies that FTSE100 companies should aim for a minimum 25 per cent female representation by 2015. The proportion of women on executive committees among the 50 largest quoted companies is just 11.5 per cent.

"This is not a large pool to help boards meet the 25 per cent target," says Mr Speed. "Boards will have to trawl more widely to reach it." Finance officers limit their directorships Spencer Stuart's annual board composition survey shows that the proportion of chief financial officers who are also non-executive directors at other companies has dropped from 41 per cent in 2010 to 27 per cent this year, writes Alison Smith.

Edward Speed of Spencer Stuart says that this fall is partly attributable to some finance directors being new in their posts. But, he says, some who would be comfortable with taking up an external role are facing other pressures not to spread themselves too thinly.

"Anecdotally, I think chief executives are saying to finance directors seeking to become non-executive directors 'Is this the right thing to do? And if you do take the role, don't even think about being chairman of the audit committee'".

Prominent UK finance directors that hold non-executive roles include René Médori, Anglo American's CFO who sits on the board of Scottish and Southern Energy and chairs its audit committee.

Mr Speed believes the approach of discouraging CFOs from becoming non-executives is short-sighted. "It is always a positive for boards if someone has broader experience," he says.

FT: Board make-up becomes a governance issue

By Ruth Sullivan

March 4, 2012

Regulators, politicians and shareholders are stepping up pressure on companies for greater board diversity as part of a drive to boost good governance and efficiency, forcing boards to rethink their composition.

Among shareholders calling for change in the companies in which it invests is Legal & General Investment Management, one of the UK's largest investors.

"LGIM is challenging the composition of boards and bringing diversity into the broader discussion on board nominations and succession planning. We intend to increase that pressure in the future," says Sacha Sadan, head of corporate governance.

"We want dynamic people and care about skills, nationalities and gender," he adds.

On the other side of the Atlantic, pressure from Calpers, the California Public Employees' Retirement System, the largest US public pension fund, recently forced Apple to give shareholders more influence over the election of directors, a move that other companies may have to follow.

In Japan last year, bringing in Michael Woodford, a Briton, to head Olympus, the camera maker, triggered more than just a departure from the culture of an all-Japanese executive, uncovering one of the country's biggest accounting scandals and shaking up the company.

Olympus still has a long way to go on reforms. Foreign shareholders such as F&C are voicing unhappiness over a new 11-member board, which it says consists of the company's bankers, major investors and related parties. Shareholders will vote on the board at an emergency general meeting next month.

There is increasing agreement among stakeholders that diversity at board and top executive level in terms of nationality, skills and gender leads to more transparency and improved governance practice, however painful the path.

In the US, advisory council members of the National Association of Corporate Directors maintain "lack of apparent diversity can be a sign that the board is not engaging in a rigorous search for the most qualified people, since qualified directors are not concentrated in only one race or gender but can be found in every demographic group".

The council also suggests that a low level of demographic diversity could be the result of a high proportion of board members being chief executives rather than senior managers or professionals, as the former tend to reflect a less diverse population.

A 2011 joint report by the New-York based Conference Board, NYSE Euronext and Nasdaq on diversity shows little change over the past few years on diversity of directors' professional backgrounds, with half of the board members of public companies coming from other for-profit companies. In the financial sector this rises to nearly three quarters.

Little progress has been made on increasing the number of female chief executives in large quoted companies with only 16 women CEOs in the entire S&P 500, according to S&P data for 2010.

Matteo Tonello, head of corporate leadership at the Conference Board, says the board of directors of US public companies over the past decade "has continued to draw its talent from the same old pool of individuals with top-level experience as business strategists—individuals who often know little about the new set of oversight responsibilities and, by the open admission of many of them, loathe having to deal with what they perceive as a distraction from business leadership matters".

Some stakeholders believe best practice in diversity brings more benefit to a company than improving governance in that more diversified boards lead to better performance.

"Getting the best people on boards is important to getting the best returns," according to L&G's Mr Sadan.

Helena Morrissey, chief executive of Newton Investment Management and founder of the 30 per cent Club that aims to bring more women on to UK boards, takes it further. "Board diversity is aimed at improving business decisions, reducing risk, sustaining profits growth and therefore higher long-term returns for shareholders," she maintains.

Research on the extent to which board diversity contributes to performance is growing but findings differ and it it is hard to determine cause and effect.

In terms of gender diversity, a recent Thomson Reuters report, *Women in the Workplace*, indicates share prices at companies that open job opportunities to women may fare better in volatile or falling markets.

In contrast, a study published in the North Carolina Law Review by Frank Dobbin, a Harvard sociologist, *Corporate Board Gender Diversity and Stock Performance 2011*, says studies suggest that over the long term board gender diversity does not help companies and may hurt them.

However, it concludes this is due to institutional investor bias against female appointments, as it finds that "female directors have negative effects on stock value and no effects on profits".

It adds that this is no surprise, given that other favoured corporate governance practices, such as splitting the chairman and chief executive role, do not lead to "increases in profits, stock value, or institutional holdings".

Regardless of differing opinions, regulation and guidance on diversity is clear. The US financial regulator introduced rules in 2009 requiring public companies to define and disclose their diversity policy, while in the UK the Financial Reporting Council and the revised UK Corporate Governance Code followed suit last year.

So what else is needed? Seamus Gillen, policy director at the Institute for Chartered Secretaries and Administrators, says an awareness of the issue at board level is not enough. "Boards need to have a real understanding of what diversity in a company means, the challenges it brings, and act on it," he says.

To do this boards have to work out where the gaps in skills and mindsets are within their own companies, and recruit from a wider range of people, including academics, entrepreneurs and people from other social class backgrounds, as well as women, he adds.

9 Directors' Performance and Remuneration

⊙ **Learning Objectives**

- To be aware of the main features of the directors' remuneration debate
- To know the key elements of directors' remuneration
- To assess the role of the remuneration committee in setting directors' remuneration
- To understand the different measures used to link directors' remuneration with performance
- To know the disclosure requirements for directors' remuneration
- To be aware of possible ways of evaluating directors

The directors' remuneration debate

The last decade has seen considerable shareholder, media, and policy attention given to the issue of directors' remuneration. The debate has tended to focus on four areas: (i) the overall level of directors' remuneration and the role of share options; (ii) the suitability of performance measures linking directors' remuneration with performance; (iii) the role played by the remuneration committee in the setting of directors' remuneration; (iv) the influence that shareholders are able to exercise on directors' remuneration.

The debate about directors' remuneration spans continents and is a topic that is as hotly debated in the USA as it is in the UK. Indeed, the UK's use of share options as long-term incentive devices has been heavily influenced by US practice. Countries that are developing their corporate governance codes are aware of the ongoing issues relating to directors' remuneration and try to address these issues in their own codes. In the UK the debate was driven in the early years by the remuneration packages of the directors of the newly privatized utilities. The perception that directors were receiving huge remuneration packages—and often, it seemed, with little reward to the shareholders in terms of company performance—further fuelled the interest in this area on both sides of the Atlantic. The level of directors' remuneration continues to be a worrying trend and as Lee (2002) commented 'the evidence in the US is of many companies having given away 10 per cent, and in some cases as much as 30 per cent, of their equity to executive directors and other staff in just the last five years or so. That is clearly not sustainable into the future: there wouldn't be any companies left in public hands if it were'.

It is interesting to note that a comparison of remuneration pay and incentives of directors in the USA and the UK gives a useful insight. Conyon and Murphy (2000) documented the differences in chief executive officer (CEO) pay and incentives in both countries for 1997. They found that CEOs in the USA earned 45 per cent higher cash compensation and 190 per cent higher total compensation than their counterparts in the UK. The implication is that, in the USA, the median CEO received 1.48 per cent of any increase in shareholder wealth compared to 0.25 per cent in the UK. The difference being largely attributable to the extent of the share option schemes in the USA.

The directors' remuneration debate clearly highlights one important aspect of the principal–agent problem discussed at length in Chapter 2. In this context, Conyon and Mallin (1997) highlight that shareholders are viewed as the 'principal' and managers as their 'agents', and that the economics literature, in particular, demonstrates that the compensation received by senior management should be linked to company performance for incentive reasons. Well-designed compensation contracts will help to ensure that the objectives of directors and shareholders are aligned, and so share options and other long-term incentives are a key mechanism by which shareholders try to ensure congruence between directors' and shareholders' objectives.

However, Bebchuk and Fried (2004) highlight that there are significant flaws in pay arrangements, which 'have hurt shareholders both by increasing pay levels and, even more important, by leading to practices that dilute and distort managers' incentives'. More recently the global financial crisis has served to highlight the inequities that exist between executive directors' generous remuneration and the underperformance of the companies that they direct, and the concomitant impact on shareholders who may lose vast sums of money, sometimes their life savings, and employees who may find themselves on shorter working weeks, lower incomes, or being made redundant. The International Labour Organization (ILO) 2008 reported that,

> the gap in income inequality is also widening—at an increasing pace—between top executives and the average employee. For example, in the United States in 2007, the chief executive officers (CEOs) of the 15 largest companies earned 520 times more than the average worker. This is up from 360 times more in 2003. Similar patterns, though from lower levels of executive pay, have been registered in Australia, Germany, Hong Kong (China), the Netherlands and South Africa.

Furthermore the ILO state that,

> developments in global corporate governance have also contributed to perceptions of excessive income inequality. A key development has been the use of so-called 'performance pay systems' for chief executive managers and directors . . . Importantly, empirical studies show only very moderate, if any, effects of these systems on company performance. Moreover, large country variations exist, with some countries displaying virtually no relation between performance-pay and company profits. . . . Altogether, evidence suggests that developments in executive pay may have been both inequality-enhancing and economically inefficient.

In the context of the global banking crisis, the UK's Turner Review reported in March 2009, and highlighted that executive compensation incentives encouraged 'some executives and traders to take excessive risks'. The Review emphasizes the distinction between 'short-term remuneration for banks which have received taxpayer support which is a legitimate issue of public concern, and one where governments as significant shareholders have crucial roles to play' and 'long-term concerns about the way in which the structure of remuneration can create incentives for inappropriate risk taking'. The Review therefore recommends that risk management considerations are embedded in remuneration policy, which of course has implications for the remit of remuneration committees and for the amount of time that non-executive directors may need to give.

The House of Commons Treasury Committee reporting in May 2009 on the *Banking Crisis: Reforming Corporate Governance and Pay in the City* stated:

> Whilst the causes of the present financial crisis are numerous and diverse, it is clear that bonus-driven remuneration structures prevalent in the City of London as well as in other financial centres, especially in investment banking, led to reckless and excessive risk-taking. In too many cases the design of bonus schemes in the banking sector were flawed and not aligned with the interests of shareholders and the long-term sustainability of the banks.

The Committee also refers to the complacency of the Financial Services Authority (FSA) and states 'The Turner Review downplays the role that remuneration structures played in causing the banking crisis, and does not appear to us to accord a sufficiently high priority to a fundamental reform of the bonus culture'. The Committee urges the FSA not to shy away from using its powers to sanction firms whose activities fall short of good practice. The Committee also encourages the use of deferral or clawback mechanisms to help ensure that bonus payments align the interests of senior staff more closely with those of shareholders. Moreover, the Committee believes that links should be strengthened between the remuneration, risk, and audit committees, 'given the cross-cutting nature of many issues, including remuneration' and also advocates

> that remuneration committees would also benefit from having a wider range of inputs from interested stakeholders—such as employees or their representatives and shareholders. This would open up the decision-making process at an early stage to scrutiny from outside the board, as well as provide greater transparency. It would, additionally, reduce the dependence of committees on remuneration consultants.

Sir David Walker headed a review of corporate governance in the banking sector which reported in 2009. Of its thirty-nine recommendations, twelve related to remuneration (including the role of the board remuneration committee, disclosure of executive remuneration, and the Code of Conduct for executive remuneration consultants written by the Remuneration Consultants Group). Some of the recommendations were to be taken forward by the FRC through amendments to the Combined Code, whilst others were to be taken forward by the FSA. When the UK Corporate Governance Code 2010 ('the Code') was introduced, it incorporated some of the Walker Report recommendations, including that performance-related pay should be aligned to the long-term interests of the company and to its risk policy and systems.

The Department for Business, Innovation & Skills (BIS) issued a discussion paper on executive remuneration in September 2011. The paper highlights the increasing disparity between the pay of CEOs and employees in the largest companies, and cites evidence to suggest that executive pay, particularly at CEO level in FTSE 100 companies, bears very little relationship to company performance or shareholder returns.

The High Pay Commission is an independent inquiry into high pay and boardroom pay across the public and private sectors in the UK. In 2010 they started their year-long inquiry into pay at the top of UK companies and found 'evidence that excessive high pay damages companies, is bad for our economy and has negative impacts on society as a whole. At its worst, excessive high pay bears little relation to company success and is rewarding failure.' Their report *More for Less: what has happened to pay at the top and does it matter?* issued in May 2011, stated: 'Pay is about just rewards, social cohesion and a functioning labour market, and it is the view of the High Pay Commission that the exponential pay increases at the top of the labour market are ultimately a form of market failure'. The report identifies four causes of the dramatic growth in top pay: attempts to link pay to performance, company structures fail to exert proper control over top earnings, the labour market contributes to increasing pay at the top, and the rise in individualism.

Their report *What are we paying for? Exploring executive pay and performance* (2011) finds that, in addition to an average rise in FTSE 350 salaries of 63.9 per cent between 2002 and 2010, average bonuses increased from 48 per cent to 90 per cent of salary in the same period. Comparing company performance to stock and balance sheet performance, the report suggests that 'salary growth bears no relation to either market capitalisation, earnings per share (EPS) or pre-tax profit' and that 'there is no or little relation between the total earnings trends and market capitalisation'.

The High Pay Commission's final report *Cheques with Balances: why tackling high pay is in the national interest* was issued in November 2011. The report recommends a twelve-point plan based on the principles of accountability, transparency, and fairness aimed at redressing the out-of-control executive pay spiral. The report highlights some of the excesses, for example: 'In BP, in 2011 the lead executive earned 63 times the amount of the average employee. In 1979 the multiple was 16.5. In Barclays, top pay is now 75 times that of the average worker. In 1979 it was 14.5. Over that period, the lead executive's pay in Barclays has risen by 4,899.4%—from £87,323 to a staggering £4,365,636'.

The High Pay Commission's twelve recommendations, under three headings, are as follows:

Transparency

1. Pay basic salaries to company executives (remuneration committees may elect to award one additional performance-related element only where it is absolutely necessary).
2. Publish the top ten executive pay packages outside the boardroom.
3. Standardise remuneration reports.
4. Require fund managers and investors to disclose how they vote on remuneration.

Accountability

5. Include employee representation on remuneration committees.
6. All publicly listed companies should publish a distribution statement (to show the distribution of income over a period of three years, importantly showing percentage changes in: total staff costs; company reinvestment; shareholder dividends; executive team total package; and tax paid.

7. Shareholders should cast forward-looking advisory votes on remuneration reports (votes should be cast on remuneration arrangements for three years following the date of the vote and these arrangements should include future salary increases, bonus packages and all hidden benefits, giving shareholders a genuine say in the remuneration of executives).

8. Improve investment in the talent pipeline.

9. Advertise non-executive positions publicly—(helping to make remuneration committees open to a wider group, encouraging diversity and ending the closed shop culture of appointments.

10. Reduce conflicts of interest of remuneration consultants.

Fairness

11. All publicly listed companies should produce fair pay reports.

12. Establish a permanent body to monitor high pay (on a social partnership basis, much like the Low Pay Commission by government to: monitor pay trends at the top of the income distribution; police pay codes in UK companies; ensure company legislation is effective in ensuring transparency, accountability and fairness in pay at the top of British companies; and report annually to government and the public on high pay.

Vince Cable, the Business Secretary, has taken forward ten of the twelve recommendations from the High Pay Commission. Furthermore, in January 2012 he announced the government's next steps to address failings in the corporate governance framework for executive remuneration. These included:

- greater transparency in directors' remuneration reports;
- empowering shareholders and promoting shareholder engagement through enhanced voting rights;
- increasing the diversity of boards and remuneration committees;
- encouraging employees to be more engaged by exercising their right to Information and Consultation Arrangements;
- working with investors and business to promote best practice on pay-setting.

Following this, a consultation on Executive Pay and Enhanced Shareholder Rights was launched, which provides more details on a new model for shareholder voting. The BIS website lists the main components of this as:

- an annual binding vote on future remuneration policy;
- increasing the level of support required on votes on future remuneration policy;
- an annual advisory vote on how remuneration policy has been implemented in the previous year;
- a binding vote on exit payments over one year's salary.

The outcome of the consultation, which closed in April 2012, is awaited.

As part of government reforms in this area, Deborah Hargreaves, who chaired the High Pay Commission, will run a new High Pay Centre to monitor pay at the top of the income distribution and set out a road map towards better business and economic success. In May 2012 the High Pay Centre issued *It's How You Pay It*, a report that looked at the current situation with regard to executive pay packages, the elements included in them, and how they can be calculated. The report states that: 'Levels of pay matter, and how we pay people matters too. While the corporate world has embraced wholeheartedly the idea that you can incentivise those at the top to act in the interests of shareholders, at best we can argue that evidence is unclear. At worst it is fair to say that the case against large variable awards is increasingly compelling'. The report also points out that 'providing a single figure for the pay awarded in any one year is an essential step forward for businesses' although it recognizes that this may, in itself, be a complex exercise.

As can be seen, there has been much heated debate about flawed remuneration packages which enable large bonuses to be paid even when the company has not met the performance criteria associated with those bonuses; which also allow departing directors to have golden goodbyes in the form of generous (some would say obscene) payments into their pension pots, or other means of easing their departure from the company; and bring about much distaste regarding the growing multipliers of executive remuneration compared to that of the average employee. The debate is far from over, although one thing is certain, which is that the remuneration committees and the shareholders will be looking ever more carefully at the remuneration packages being proposed for executive directors in the future, given the expectations of government and the public about what remuneration packages should look like.

Finally, the issuance in December 2010 by the FSA of 'PS10/20 Revising the Remuneration Code' should be mentioned. The revised framework for regulating financial services firms' remuneration structures and extension of the scope of the FSA Remuneration Code, arose primarily as a result of amendments to the Capital Requirements Directive (CRD3) which aimed to align remuneration principles across the EU, but also took into account provisions relating to remuneration within the Financial Services Act 2010, Sir David Walker's review of corporate governance, and also lessons learned from the FSA's implementation of its Remuneration Code. The FSA states: 'Our Remuneration Code sets out the standards that banks, building societies and some investment firms have to meet when setting pay and bonus awards for their staff. It aims to ensure that firms' remuneration practices are consistent with effective risk management'. The twelve Principles cover the three main areas of regulatory scope: governance; performance measurement; and remuneration structures. The headings encompass:

- risk management and risk tolerance;
- supporting business strategy, objectives, values and long-term interests of the firm;
- avoiding conflicts of interest;
- governance;
- control functions;
- remuneration and capital;
- exceptional government intervention;

- profit-based measurement and risk adjustment;
- pension policy;
- personal investment strategies;
- avoidance of the FSA Remuneration Code;
- remuneration structures;
- the effect of breach of the FSA Remuneration Principles.

It also introduced some new rules, for example on discretionary severance pay, linking remuneration to a firm's capital base, and discretionary pension payments.

Key elements of directors' remuneration

Directors' remuneration can encompass six elements:

- base salary;
- bonus;
- stock options;
- restricted share plans (stock grants);
- pension;
- benefits (car, healthcare, etc.).

However, most discussions of directors' remuneration will tend to concentrate on the first four elements listed earlier and this text will also take that approach.

Base salary

Base salary is received by a director in accordance with the terms of his/her contract. This element is not related either to the performance of the company nor to the performance of the individual director. The amount will be set with due regard to the size of the company, the industry sector, the experience of the individual director, and the level of base salary in similar companies.

Bonus

An annual bonus may be paid, which is linked to the accounting performance of the firm.

Stock options

Stock options give directors the right to purchase shares (stock) at a specified exercise price over a specified time period. Directors may also participate in long-term incentive plans (LTIPs). UK share options generally have performance criteria attached, and much discussion is centred around these performance criteria, especially as to whether they are appropriate and demanding enough.

Restricted share plans (stock grants)

Shares may be awarded with limits on their transferability for a set time (usually a few years), and various performance conditions should be met.

Role of the remuneration committee

The Code (2010) recommends that 'there should be a formal and transparent procedure for developing policy on executive remuneration and for fixing the remuneration packages of individual directors' (principle D.2). In practice, this normally results in the appointment of a remuneration committee.

The remuneration committee's role and composition was discussed in Chapter 8. However, in this chapter we consider the effect of remuneration committees on directors' remuneration levels in recent years. Sykes (2002) points out that, although remuneration committees predominantly consist of a majority, or more usually entirely, of non-executive directors, these non-executive directors 'are effectively chosen by, or only with the full agreement of, senior management'. Given that the non-executive directors of one company may be executive directors of another (unrelated) company, they may not be willing to stipulate demanding performance criteria because they may have a self-interest in ensuring that they themselves can go on earning a high salary without unduly demanding performance criteria being set by their own companies' remuneration committees. There is also another aspect, which is that remuneration committees will generally not wish the executive directors to be earning less than their counterparts in other companies, so they will be more inclined to make recommendations that will put the directors into the top or second quartile of executive remuneration levels. It is certainly the case that executive remuneration levels have increased fairly substantially since remuneration committees were introduced which, of course, was not the intended effect. Sykes (2002) makes the pertinent point that all the remuneration packages now so widely criticized as flawed and inappropriate were once approved by an 'independent' remuneration committee.

The performance measures that the remuneration committee decides should be used are therefore central to aligning directors' performance and remuneration in the most appropriate way. Remuneration committees are offered some general guidance by the Code (2010) recommendation that 'levels of remuneration should be sufficient to attract, retain and motivate directors of the quality required to run the company successfully, but a company should avoid paying more than is necessary for this purpose' (principle D.1).

In the UK both the National Association of Pension Funds (NAPF) and the Association of British Insurers (ABI) have been involved in the debate about executive remuneration and have issued guidance in this area. The ABI (2002) *Guidelines on Executive Remuneration* included the recommendations that:

- remuneration packages should have a balance between fixed and variable pay, and between long- and short-term incentives;
- performance-based remuneration arrangements should be demonstrably clearly aligned with business strategy and objectives;

- the remuneration committee should have regard to pay and conditions generally in the company, taking into account business size, complexity, and geographical location and should also consider market forces generally;
- share option schemes should link remuneration to performance and align the long-term interests of management with those of shareholders;
- performance targets should be disclosed in the remuneration report within the bounds of commercial confidentially considerations.

In December 2005 the ABI issued its *Principles and Guidelines on Remuneration*, which have a two-fold aim of providing 'a practical framework and reference point for both shareholders in reaching voting decisions and for companies in deciding upon remuneration policy'. The Principles and Guidelines emphasize that remuneration (committee) reports should provide a clear and full explanation of remuneration policy, showing a clear link between reward and performance and that 'shareholders believe that the key determinant for assessing remuneration is performance in the creation of shareholder value'.

In December 2007 the ABI made some minor amendments to its *Executive Remuneration—ABI Guidelines on Policies and Practices*. In September 2008 the ABI wrote a letter to the chairmen of the remuneration committees explaining that it did not plan to make any changes at that time to the ABI (2007) guidelines. However, the letter highlighted a number of areas to which the ABI wished to draw attention in the current economic climate. The points raised were:

(i) the remuneration policy should be fully explained and justified, particularly when changes are proposed. Members will carefully scrutinise remuneration uplifts, particularly increases in salaries or annual bonus levels; (ii) where a company has underperformed and seen a significant fall in its share price, this should be taken into account when determining the level of awards under share incentive schemes. In such circumstances, it is not appropriate for executives to receive awards of such a size that they are perceived as rewards for failure; (iii) shareholders are generally not in favour of additional remuneration being paid in relation to succession or retention, particularly where no performance conditions are attached; (iv) in the context of the consultation process for share incentive schemes, Remuneration Committees should ensure that shareholders have adequate time to consider the proposal and that their views are carefully considered. Relevant information related to the consultation should be clearly and fully disclosed.

In September 2011 the ABI issued the *ABI Principles of Executive Remuneration*, which are predominantly for companies with a main market listing but useful for companies on other public markets and also for other entities. The Principles relate to (in a remuneration context), the role of shareholders, the role of the board and directors, the remuneration committee, remuneration policies, and remuneration structures. There is detailed guidance for remuneration committees.

Role of remuneration consultants

Remuneration committees may draw on the advice of specialist remuneration consultants when constructing executive remuneration packages. The role of remuneration (compensation) consultants has started to receive more attention in the last few years in the academic literature. Voulgaris *et al.* (2010) in a study of 500 UK firms from the FTSE 100, FTSE 250, and the Small Cap indices, find that compensation consultants may have a positive effect on the structure of CEO pay since they encourage incentive-based compensation, and they also show that economic determinants, rather than CEO power, explain the decision to hire compensation consultants.

Murphy and Sandino (2010) examine the potential conflicts of interest that remuneration consultants face, which may lead to higher recommended levels of CEO pay. They find 'evidence in both the US and Canada that CEO pay is higher in companies where the consultant provides other services, and that pay is higher in Canadian firms when the fees paid to consultants for other services are large relative to the fees for executive-compensation services. Contrary to expectations, we find that pay is higher in US firms where the consultant works for the board rather than for management.

Similarly, Conyon *et al.* (2011), in a study of compensation consultants used in 232 large UK companies, find that 'consultant use is associated with firm size and the equity pay mix. We also show that CEO pay is positively associated with peer firms that share consultants, with higher board and consultant interlocks, and some evidence that where firms supply other business services to the firm, CEO pay is greater'.

Bender (2011), drawing on interview data with a selection of FTSE 350 companies, finds remuneration committees employ consultants for a number of reasons. First,

> the consultant is to act as an expert, providing proprietary data against which companies can benchmark pay, and giving insight and advice into the possibilities open for plan design and implementation. In this role, consultants have a direct and immediate influence on executive pay. That is, by influencing the choice of comparators, consultants both identify and drive the market for executive pay. They also bring to bear their knowledge of pay plans, and their views on what is currently acceptable to the market, thus spreading current practice more widely and institutionalizing it as—best practice.

Secondly, they act as liaisons and serve an important role in the communication with certain institutional investors. Thirdly Bender finds that they legitimize the decisions of the remuneration committee by providing an element of perceived independence but she points out that 'this route to legitimacy is under threat as various constituencies question consultants' independence'.

Also questioning the independence of remuneration consultants, Kostiander and Ikäheimo (2012), examine the remuneration consultant–client relationship in the non-Anglo-American context of Finland, focusing on what consultants do under heavy political remuneration guidance. Their findings show that 'restrictive remuneration guidelines can be ineffective and lead to standardized pay designs without providing competitive advantage. Shareholders should request greater transparency concerning remuneration design. The role of consultants should be considered proactively in the guidelines, even by limiting the length of the consultant–client relationship or increasing their transparency'.

There does therefore seem to be a growing body of evidence highlighting the role of remuneration consultants in the setting of executive remuneration, and raising issues relating to their independence and the impact on CEO pay when the remuneration consultants offer other services to the firm.

Performance measures

Performance criteria will clearly be a key aspect of ensuring that directors' remuneration is perceived as fair and appropriate for the job and in keeping with the results achieved by the directors. Performance criteria may differentiate between three broadly conceived types of measures: (i) market-based measures; (ii) accounts based measures; and (iii) individual based measures. Some potential performance criteria are:

- shareholder return;
- share price (and other market based measures);
- profit-based measures;
- return on capital employed;
- earnings per share;
- individual director performance (in contrast to corporate performance measures).

Sykes (2002) highlights a number of problems with the way in which executive remuneration is determined: (i) management is expected to perform over a short period of time and this is a clear mismatch with the underlying investor time horizons; (ii) management remuneration is not correlated to corporate performance; (iii) earnings before interest, tax, and amortisation (EBITA) is widely used as a measure of earnings and yet this can encourage companies to gear up (or have high leverage) because the measure will reflect the flow of earnings from high leverage but not the service (interest) charge for that debt. He suggests that the situation would be improved if there were: longer term tenures for corporate management; more truly independent non-executive directors; the cessation of stock options and, in their place, a generous basic salary and five-year restricted shares (shares that could not be cashed for five years).

The ABI (2002, 2005) guidelines state that total shareholder return relative to an appropriate index or peer group is a generally acceptable performance criterion. The guidelines also favour performance being measured over a period of at least three years to try to ensure sustained improvements in financial performance rather than the emphasis being placed on short-term performance. Share incentive schemes should be available to employees and executive directors but not to non-executive directors (although non-executive directors are encouraged to have shareholdings in the company, possibly by receiving shares in the company, at full market price, as payment of their non-executive director fees).

The ABI published its *Disclosure Guidelines on Socially Responsible Investment* in 2007. Interestingly, the guidelines said that the company should state in its remuneration report 'whether the remuneration committee is able to consider corporate performance on ESG [environmental, social, and governance] issues when setting remuneration of executive directors. If the report states that the committee has no such discretion, then a reason should be provided for its absence'. Also 'whether the remuneration committee has ensured that the incentive structure for senior management does not raise ESG risks by inadvertently motivating irresponsible behaviour'. These are significant recommendations in the bid to have ESG issues recognized and more widely taken into consideration.

Another area that has attracted attention, and which is addressed in joint ABI/NAPF guidance, is the area of 'golden goodbyes'. This is another dimension to the directors' remuneration debate because it is not only ongoing remuneration packages that have attracted adverse comment, but also the often seemingly excessive amounts paid to directors who leave a company after failing to meet their targets. Large pay-offs or 'rewards for failure' are seen as inappropriate because such failure may reduce the value of the business and threaten the jobs of employees. Often the departure of underperforming directors triggers a clause in their contract that leads to a large undeserved pay-off, but now some companies are cutting the notice period from one year to, for example, six months where directors fail to meet performance targets over a period of time, so that a non-performing director whose contract is terminated receives six months' salary rather than one year's salary.

The ABI/NAPF guidance emphasizes the importance of ensuring that the design of contracts should not commit companies to payment for failure; the guidance also suggests that phased payments are a useful innovation to include in directors' contracts. A phased payment involves continuing payment to a departing director for the remaining term of the contract but payments cease when the director finds fresh employment. An alternative suggested by the Myners Report (2001) is that compensation for loss of office should be fixed as a number of shares in the company (and hence the value of the compensation would be linked to the share price performance of the company).

It does seem that the days of lucrative payments for underperforming directors are drawing to a close. Furthermore, the UK's Department of Trade and Industry (DTI) issued a consultation document in summer 2003, 'Rewards for Failure: Directors' Remuneration—Contracts, Performance and Severance', which invites comment on ways in which severance pay might be limited by restricting notice periods to less than one year, capping the level of liquidated damages, using phased payments, and limiting severance pay where a company has performed poorly.

In February 2008 the ABI and the NAPF issued joint guidance entitled *Best Practice on Executive Contracts and Severance—A Joint Statement by the Association of British Insurers and the National Association of Pension Funds*. The guidance aims to assist boards and their remuneration committees 'with the design and application of contractual obligations for senior executives so that they are appropriately rewarded but are not rewarded for under-performance'. The concluding statement to the guidance succinctly sums up the views of many: 'It is unacceptable that poor performance by senior executives, which detracts from the value of an enterprise and threatens the livelihood of employees, can result in excessive payments to departing directors. Boards have a responsibility to ensure that this does not occur'.

In relation to bonuses, Fattorusso *et al.* (2007) point out that

> the focus of most criticism has been on salary, severance payments and various long-term incentives (particularly share options). However, executive bonuses have attracted little attention and have been only lightly regulated. This raises important questions. Has lighter regulation been associated with significant levels of rent extraction through bonuses, that is, a weak relation between bonus pay and shareholder returns?

In March 2012 Hermes Equity Ownership Services (Hermes EOS) and the NAPF, for the first time brought together remuneration committee members from forty-four of the FTSE 100 companies and forty-two occupational pension funds from across the globe. The dialogue focused on executive pay structures and how long-term investors can best challenge, and support companies in improving remuneration practices through engagement and the considered use of their voting powers. The intention is to shift the current political and societal debate with the view of creating greater alignment between companies and their shareholders, and to promote a culture within companies that rewards long-term success and alignment across the organization.

Remuneration of non-executive directors

The remuneration of non-executive directors is decided by the board, or where required by the articles of association, or the shareholders in general meeting. Non-executive directors should be paid a fee commensurate with the size of the company, and the amount of time that they are expected to devote to their role. Large UK companies would tend to pay in excess of £50,000 (often considerably more) to each non-executive director. The remuneration is generally paid in cash although some advocate remunerating non-executive directors with the company's shares to align their interests with those of the shareholders. However, it has generally been viewed as not being a good idea to remunerate non-executive directors with share options (as opposed to shares) because this may give them a rather unhealthy focus on the short-term share price of the company.

Nonetheless, in 2010 the International Corporate Governance Network (ICGN) published its *Non-executive Director Remuneration Guidelines and Policies*. The recommendations include that the retainer/annual fee should be the only form of cash compensation paid to non-executive directors, and that there should not be a separate fee for attendance at board meetings or at committee meetings. However, it is recognized that companies may want to differentiate the fee amount to reflect the differing workloads of individual non-executive directors, for example, where a non-executive director is also a committee chair. Interestingly, the guidelines state that, in order to align non-executive director–shareowner interests, non-executive directors may receive stock awards or similar. However, any such 'equity-based compensation to non-executive directors should be fully vested on the grant date . . . a marked difference to the ICGN's policy on executive compensation which calls for performance-based vesting on equity-based awards'.

Importantly, the ICGN also states: 'Separate from ownership requirements, the ICGN believes companies should adopt holding requirements for a significant majority of equity-based grants. These policies should require that non-executive directors retain a significant portion of equity grants until at least two years after they are retired from the board'. Such policies would help ensure that interests remain aligned.

There has been relatively little academic research into non-executive directors' remuneration. Hahn and Lasfer (2011) referred to non-executive directors' remuneration as 'an enigma'. A recent study by Gaia *et al*. (2012) compares the remuneration of independent non-executive directors in Italy and the UK. The authors find that 'independent non-executive directors do not receive performance-based remuneration except in very limited instances. In line with equity and human capital theories, we find that independent non-executive directors do receive higher remuneration when they exert more effort, have more responsibilities, and have a higher human capital'.

Disclosure of directors' remuneration

There has been much discussion about how much disclosure there should be of directors' remuneration and how useful detailed disclosures might be. The Greenbury Report, issued in the UK in 1995, was established on the initiative of the Confederation of British Industry (CBI) because of public concern about directors' remuneration. Whilst the work of the Greenbury Report focused on the directors of public limited companies, it hoped that both smaller listed companies and unlisted companies would find its recommendations useful.

Central to the Greenbury Report recommendations were the strengthening of accountability and enhancing the performance of directors. These two aims were to be achieved by (i) the establishment of remuneration committees comprised of independent non-executive directors who would report fully to the shareholders each year about the company's executive remuneration policy, including full disclosure of the elements in the remuneration of individual directors; and (ii) the adoption of performance measures linking rewards to the performance of both the company and individual directors, so that the interests of directors and shareholders were more closely aligned.

One of the Turnbull Committee recommendations (1999, revised 2005) was that boards should consider whether business objectives and the risk management/control systems of a business are supported by the performance-related reward system in operation in a company.

As part of the accountability/transparency process, the remuneration committee membership should be disclosed in the company's annual report, and the chairman of the remuneration committee should attend the company's annual general meeting to answer any questions that shareholders may have about the directors' remuneration.

The DTI published its Directors' Remuneration Report Regulations 2002. These regulations require, inter alia, that:

- quoted companies must publish a detailed report on directors' pay as part of their annual reporting cycle, and this report must be approved by the board of directors;
- a graph of the company's total shareholder returns over five years, against a comparator group, must be published in the remuneration committee report;
- names of any consultants to the remuneration committee must be disclosed, including whether they were appointed independently, along with the cost of any other services provided to the company;
- companies must hold a shareholder vote on the directors' remuneration report at each general meeting.

The stipulation that companies must hold a shareholder vote on the directors' remuneration report is an interesting one, and something that various shareholder representative groups have campaigned for over a long period of time. However, the vote is an advisory shareholder vote, but it will serve a useful purpose of ensuring that the shareholders can vote specifically on directors' remuneration, which has caused so much heated debate for so long. The other provisions will help to strengthen the role of the remuneration committee and enhance both the accountability and transparency of the directors' remuneration-setting process. The disclosures relating to the consultants used by the remuneration committee may also lead to interesting questions relating to any other services they may provide to a company to try to determine their independence.

The ILO (2008) reports:

> Disclosure practices differ widely across countries. While some countries, including France, the Netherlands, the United Kingdom and the United States require companies to report detailed compensation data in a remuneration report, others like Greece have no specific requirements . . . companies in such countries as Brazil, Germany, Japan and Mexico frequently report only aggregate data on executive compensation . . . In some countries, executives seem to consider the disclosure of the precise amount of remuneration to be a risk to their personal safety. (Leal and Carvalhal da Silva, 2005)

International guidance on executive remuneration

International Corporate Governance Network (ICGN)

The ICGN issued its recommendations on best practice for executive remuneration in 2003. It was hoped that the recommendations would create a consensus amongst both companies and investors around the world about the structure of remuneration packages.

The ICGN recommendations stated that the 'fundamental requirement for executive remuneration reporting is transparency'. This was the starting point: that there should be disclosure of the base salary, short-term and long-term incentives, and any other payments or benefits to each main board director. The remuneration committee should publish statements on the expected outcomes of the remuneration structures, in terms of ratios between base salaries, short-term bonuses, and long-term rewards, making both 'high' and 'low' assumptions as well as the 'central' case. Whilst recognizing that share options are probably here to stay, the ICGN recommendations supported the International Accounting Standards Board (IASB) proposal to expense share options through the profit and loss account.

The remuneration committee report should be presented as a separate voting item at every annual meeting (this would depend on local practice). The ICGN also urged institutional investors to devote more resources to the analysis of remuneration resolutions.

In 2004 the ICGN published statements about the compliance of each of the UK, USA, and Australia with the ICGN's Executive Remuneration Principles. Each of these countries generally complied with the principles, although each had strengths and weaknesses on particular issues.

In 2006 the ICGN approved the updated ICGN *Remuneration Guidelines*. Three principles underpin the new guidelines: transparency, accountability, and the performance basis. The guidelines state that there should also be thought given to the reputational aspects of remuneration.

At present the ICGN have circulated recommendations on non-executive director remuneration (discussed earlier) but no further guidelines on executive remuneration.

Organisation for Economic Co-operation and Development (OECD)

The OECD Corporate Governance Committee (2010) in *Corporate Governance and the Financial Crisis: Conclusions and Emerging Good Practices to Enhance Implementation of the Principles* (hereafter 'the Conclusions') noted that the ability of the board to effectively oversee executive remuneration appears to be a key challenge in practice and remains one of the central elements of the corporate governance debate in a number of jurisdictions. The nature of that challenge goes beyond looking merely at the quantum of executive and director remuneration (which is often the focus of the public and political debate), and instead more toward how remuneration and incentive arrangements are aligned with the longer term interests of the company.

Furthermore, they highlight that policymakers have 'focused more on measures that seek to improve the capacity of firm governance structures to produce appropriate remuneration and incentive outcomes. These can roughly be characterized in terms of internal firm governance (and, in particular, fostering arms-length negotiation through mandating certain levels of independence), and providing a mechanism to allow shareholders to have a means of expressing their views on director and executive remuneration'. The OECD (2011) conclude that 'aligning incentives seems to be far more problematic in companies and jurisdictions with a dispersed shareholding structure since, where dominant or controlling shareholders exist, they seem to act as a moderating force on remuneration outcomes'.

The European Commission

In April 2009 the European Commission announced new guidelines for directors' remuneration which include, inter alia, performance criteria that 'should promote the long-term sustainability of the company and include non-financial criteria that are relevant to the company's long-term value creation'; clawback provisions where variable elements of remuneration were rewarded on misleading data; and termination payments not to be paid where performance had been poor. However, these guidelines are not intended to be binding on member states. In June 2010 the EU issued a Green Paper on 'Corporate governance in financial institutions and remuneration policies'; one of the issues it consulted on was the recommendation of a binding or advisory shareholder vote on remuneration policy and greater independence for non-executive directors involved in determining remuneration policy. The Commission also consulted on this issue in the 2010 Green Paper on 'Corporate Governance in Financial Institutions'. In April 2011 another Green Paper, 'The EU corporate governance framework', was issued, with responses invited to various consultation questions. These included whether disclosure of remuneration policy, the annual remuneration report (a report on how the remuneration policy was implemented in the past year), and individual remuneration of executive and non-executive directors should be mandatory; and also whether it should be mandatory to put the remuneration policy and the remuneration report to a vote by shareholders. The final outcome of the consultation is awaited.

The Conference Board

In the USA the Conference Board Commission on Public Trust and Private Enterprise was established to address widespread abuses that led to corporate governance scandals and a resulting lack of confidence in the markets.

One area that the Commission looked at was executive compensation. The Commission reported in 2002 with principles, recommendations, and specific best practice suggestions. The seven principles relate to: the compensation (remuneration) committee and its responsibilities; the importance of performance-based compensation; the role of equity-based incentives; creating a long-term focus; accounting neutrality; shareholders' rights; and transparency and disclosure. The principles serve to clarify several areas and identify that the compensation committee—which should be comprised of directors who are free of any relationships with the company and its management—should be primarily responsible for ensuring that there is a fair and appropriate compensation scheme in place. In order to aid them in this role, the compensation committee may appoint outside consultants who should report solely to the committee. Performance-based remuneration incentives should 'support and reinforce the corporation's long-term strategic goals set by the board (for example, cost of capital, return on equity, economic value added, market share, quality goals, compliance goals, environment goals, revenue and profit growth, cost containment, cash management, etc.)'. In relation to the role of equity incentives, such as share options, the compensation committee should ensure that disclosure is made of any costs to shareholders associated with equity-based compensation such as dilution (the earnings per share after dilution should be shown). Key executives and directors should be encouraged to build up a reasonable shareholding in the corporation and hold that shareholding for the longer term.

The Commission's report is likely to influence policy in many countries, especially those countries that have already followed the US-style remuneration package and adopted share option schemes.

In spring 2009 the Conference Board announced the establishment of an Executive Compensation Task Force. They state that:

> The Task Force brings together corporations and investors, and governance, legal, compensation and ethics experts to address one of the most important issues in today's business world. The Conference Board's new Task Force is part of its broader reexamination of the foundations of the current crisis and its impact on global growth and stability as well as institutions, business organizations and markets.

In autumn 2009 the Conference Board Task Force on Executive Compensation reported and provided guiding principles for setting executive compensation, which, if appropriately implemented, are designed to restore credibility with shareholders and other stakeholders. The five principles are as follows: payment for the right things and payment for performance; the 'right' total compensation; avoidance of controversial pay practices; credible board oversight of executive compensation; and transparent communications and increased dialogue with shareholders.

Dodd-Frank Wall Street Reform and Consumer Protection Act (2010)

In July 2010 the USA passed the Dodd-Frank Wall Street Reform and Consumer Protection Act that amends US requirements relating to executive compensation practices in a number of respects. From mid-2011 the Securities and Exchange Commission (SEC) required listed companies compensation committee members to be independent directors. There are new 'say on pay' provisions such that the Act requires that, at least once every three years, there is a shareholder advisory vote to approve the company's executive compensation, as well as to approve 'golden parachute' compensation arrangements. Whilst the 'say on pay' is at least once every three years, it may occur every year.

'Say on pay'

The 'say on pay' was introduced in the UK in 2002 by the Directors' Remuneration Report Regulations. It has come very much to the fore since the financial crisis as a tool of governance activism in the context of expressing dissent on executive remuneration awards. Many countries including the USA, Australia, and various countries in Europe have introduced the 'say on pay' as a mechanism for voting against executive remuneration. In some countries, such as the UK, the 'say on pay' vote is an advisory one (at least for the time being), whilst in other countries it is a binding vote on which the board must take action.

As mentioned earlier, in the USA, the Dodd-Frank Wall Street Reform and Consumer Protection Act (2010), under new 'say on pay' provisions, requires that at least once every three years there is a shareholder advisory vote to approve the company's executive compensation as disclosed pursuant to SEC rules. The 'say on frequency' provision requires companies to put to a shareholder advisory vote every six years whether the 'say on pay' resolution should occur every one, two, or three years.

Conyon and Sadler (2010), in a study of shareholder voting behaviour in the UK from 2002-7, find that there is

> little evidence of widespread and deep shareholder voting against CEO pay. Critics of CEO pay may be surprised, as one frequently proposed remedy for excess pay has been to give shareholders a voice. The UK experience suggests that owners have not seized this opportunity to reign in high levels of executive pay . . . this noted, we do find that high CEO pay is likely to trigger greater shareholder dissent. This suggests that boards and compensation committees might try to communicate the intentions of CEO pay policies better to the firm's multiple stakeholders. Moreover, at present there is little evidence that shareholder voting dissent leads to drastic cuts in subsequent CEO pay.

Conyon and Sadler do, however, recognize that their study was carried out on pre-financial crisis data and that there may be a higher incidence of dissent post-financial crisis, especially in companies that have received financial support from governments or where executive pay is perceived to be excessively high. Recent evidence does indeed show that institutional investors are voting with much higher levels of dissent, and more frequently, against executive remuneration packages in the UK, the USA, and other countries.

Ferri and Maber (2011) examine the effect of 'say on pay' regulation in the UK. They report that

> consistent with the view that shareholders regard say on pay as a value-creating mechanism, the regulation's announcement triggered a positive stock price reaction at firms with weak penalties for poor performance. UK firms responded to negative say on pay voting outcomes by removing controversial CEO pay practices criticized as rewards for failure (e.g., generous severance contracts) and increasing the sensitivity of pay to poor realizations of performance.

Conclusions

The debate on executive directors' remuneration has rumbled on through the last decade, but with the increase in institutional investor activism, and the scandals and subsequent collapses associated with a number of large corporations in the UK, USA, and elsewhere, the focus is well and truly on curtailing excessive and undeserved remuneration packages. The global financial crisis and the collapse of various high profile banks and financial institutions has left the market reeling. There is a lack of public confidence in the boards of banks, and disbelief at some of the executive remuneration packages and ad hoc payments that have been made to executive directors. There is now an emphasis on payment for performance in a way that theoretically was present before the global financial crisis but, in practice, all too often was not. The remuneration committees, comprised of independent non-executive directors, will come under increased scrutiny as they try to ensure that executive directors' remuneration packages are fairly and appropriately constructed, taking into account long-term objectives. Central to this aim is the use of performance indicators that will incentivize directors but at the same time align their interests with those of shareholders, to the long-term benefit of the company. Shareholders in many countries now have a 'say on pay', either in the form of an advisory or a binding vote, and seem increasingly active in expressing their dissent on executive remuneration.

Summary

- The debate on executive directors' remuneration has been driven by the view that some directors, and especially those directors in the banking sector, are being overpaid to the detriment of the shareholders, the employees, and the company as a whole. The perception that high rewards have been given without corresponding performance has caused concern, and this area has increasingly become the focus of investor activism and widespread media coverage.

- The components of executive directors' remuneration are base salary, bonuses, stock options, stock grants, pension, and other benefits.

- The remuneration committee, which should be comprised of independent non-executive directors, has a key role to play in ensuring that a fair and appropriate executive remuneration system is in place.

- The role of the remuneration consultant is a complex one and there may be potential conflicts of interest.

- There are a number of potential performance criteria that may be used to incentivize executive directors. These are market-based measures (such as share price), accounts-based measures (such as earnings per share), and individual director performance measures.

- It is important that there is full disclosure of directors' remuneration and the basis on which it is calculated.

- There seems to be a trend towards convergence internationally in terms of the recommendations for the composition, calculation, and disclosure of executive directors' remuneration.

- The 'say on pay' is a mechanism for investors to express their approval or dissent in relation to executive remuneration packages and has become widely adopted.

Example: AstraZeneca Plc, UK

This is an example of a company that came under shareholder pressure over its executive remuneration package, and its financial performance and strategy.

AstraZeneca is a global biopharmaceutical company operating in over one hundred countries. Their primary focus is the discovery, development, and commercialization of prescription medicines for six important areas of healthcare: cardiovascular, gastrointestinal, infection, neuroscience, oncology, and respiratory/inflammation.

At 31 December 2011 AstraZeneca's board comprised two executive directors (the CEO and chief financial officer) and nine non-executive directors, of whom three are female, one of these being the senior independent non-executive director. There are no female executive directors on the board. In terms of international directors, two directors are French, three are from the USA, five from the UK, and one from Sweden.

There are four principal board committees: audit; remuneration; nomination and governance; and science committees. The remuneration committee is comprised of four independent non-executive directors, one of whom, John Varley, is the Chair of the remuneration committee.

In the spring of 2012 AstraZeneca announced that it would be making around 12 per cent of its staff redundant; yet just a few weeks later, it announced a substantial increase in the pay of its CEO, David Brennan, to £9.27 million. A substantial part of this came from a long-term incentive scheme but AstraZeneca nonetheless increased David Brennan's basic pay and bonus by some 11 per cent. This was at a time when AstraZeneca's shares had fallen 13 per cent over the past year, whereas its peer group had seen increases of more than 4 per cent during the same time. However, John Varley pointed out that AstraZeneca's core earnings per share had risen during 2011. There was investor pressure over David Brennan's remuneration package at a time when AstraZeneca's performance has, in their eyes, been disappointing, and there has also been concern over the company's strategy going forwards. In April 2012 David Brennan stepped down as CEO of AstraZeneca after shareholder pressure to do so.

Example: American International Group (AIG), USA

This is an example of one of the largest American insurers that has received federal government bail-out money but has continued to pay retention bonuses to its senior employees.

AIG has been kept afloat by more than US$170 billion in public money since September 2008. A furore broke out after it was revealed that large bonuses were being paid to executives only a few months after AIG received federal support. The American Federation of Labor and Congress of Industrial Organizations (AFL-CIO), a voluntary federation of fifty-six national and international labour unions and representing 11 million members, was one of the groups astounded at the payouts at a time when thousands are losing their jobs. AFL-CIO were particularly incensed about these payments, which 'were in the form of "retention" bonuses to employees of its financial products division, which sold the complex derivatives at the heart of the company's financial troubles . . . AIG's poor pay practices expose the fallacy of "pay for performance." The potential windfalls for executives were so massive they had nothing to lose by taking on huge risks to create the illusion of profits.'

The CEO, Edward Liddy, asked the senior employees to pay back the bonuses, totalling US$165 million, urging them to 'do the right thing'. Many of them have now done so.

In recent years, the US government has been looking into how the oversight of executive compensation might be changed. One area where a significant change has occurred is the introduction of the 'say-on-pay' legislation whereby shareholders have the right to vote on directors' remuneration. In July 2010 new 'say on pay' provisions were introduced by the Dodd-Frank Wall Street Reform and Consumer Protection Act 2010, whereby at least once every three years, there is a shareholder advisory vote to approve the company's executive compensation.

In 2011 using the 'say on pay', shareholders voted overwhelmingly in favour of AIG's executive remuneration. Subsequently, in February 2012 AIG reported a US$19.8 billion profit for its fourth quarter but US$17.7 billion of that profit was a tax benefit from the US government. The company made relatively little during the quarter from its actual operations. Ironically, the tax benefit will also benefit employees who are paid based on the company's performance. However, the US Treasury Department has ordered that nearly seventy top executives in AIG to take a 10 per cent pay-cut, and the pay for the CEO was frozen at 2011 levels. Nonetheless, AIG's CEO is still expected to receive US$10.5 million.

 ## Mini case study   Aviva Plc, UK

This is an example of a company that is itself renowned for its corporate governance activism in its investee companies but which suffered a defeat of its executive remuneration proposals via the 'say on pay' and also saw the departure of its CEO soon afterwards.

Aviva is the UK's largest insurer and one of Europe's leading providers of life and general insurance with over 36,000 employees and some 43 million customers worldwide.

Its board of directors consists of twelve directors of whom eight are independent non-executive directors (three of these independent non-executive directors are female, there being no female executive directors on the board), plus the chairman, the executive deputy chairman, the chief financial officer, and the executive director for developed markets. There are five key board committees: audit, remuneration, nomination, corporate responsibility, and risk. The remuneration committee comprises three independent non-executive directors, one of whom chairs it. The remuneration committee, like many, seeks the advice of remuneration consultants when setting the pay packages for its executive directors, and the activities of the remuneration committee note that during 2011 the remuneration committee approved the appointment of FIT Remuneration Consultants in place of AON Hewitt New Bridge Street.

During the first part of 2012 Andrew Moss, the CEO of Aviva, announced restructuring plans which included Aviva Investors shedding more than one-tenth of its workforce; subsequently, in April 2012 he announced a simplification of the management structure, which saw some of its most respected executives leaving the company. At around this time, ABI issued an 'amber alert' over Aviva's remuneration report. With investor concern about Aviva's executive pay proposals mounting, Aviva announced that it would review the executive pay proposals. Andrew Moss declined a pay rise of £46,000 but, nonetheless, looking back at 2011, his pay (excluding a long-term share incentive plan) rose by around 8.5 per cent, whilst Aviva's shares lost around one-quarter of their value, which raised shareholders' concerns of reward for poor performance. However, the unease from institutional investors was not just about the executive pay proposals but also about the performance of Aviva in recent years, with share prices falling and Aviva underperforming compared to its peers. In early May 2012 Aviva became one of the few companies in the UK to suffer a shareholder defeat of its executive remuneration proposals since the 'say on pay' was introduced in the UK some ten years ago. Just over a week later, Andrew Moss resigned from his post as CEO of Aviva.

(continued)

Questions

The discussion questions to follow cover the key learning points of this chapter. Reading of some of the additional reference material will enhance the depth of the students' knowledge and understanding of these areas.

1. What factors have influenced the executive directors' remuneration debate?

2. Why is the area of executive directors' remuneration of such interest to investors, and particularly to institutional investors?

3. What are the main components of executive directors' remuneration packages?

4. Critically discuss the roles of the remuneration committee and remuneration consultants in setting executive directors' remuneration.

5. Critically discuss the performance criteria that may be used in determining executive directors' remuneration.

6. Critically discuss the importance of executive director remuneration disclosure.

References

ABI (2002), *Guidelines on Executive Remuneration*, ABI, London.

—— (2005), *Principles and Guidelines on Remuneration*, ABI, London.

—— (2007), *Disclosure Guidelines on Socially Responsible Investment*, ABI, London

—— (2007), *Executive Remuneration—ABI Guidelines on Policies and Practices*, ABI, London.

—— (2008), *Best Practice on Executive Contracts and Severance—A Joint Statement by the Association of British Insurers and National Association of Pension Funds*, ABI/NAPF, London.

—— (2011), *ABI Principles of Executive Remuneration*, ABI, London.

Bebchuk, L. and Fried, J. (2004), *Pay Without Performance: The Unfulfilled Promise of Executive Compensation*, Harvard University Press, Boston, MA.

Bender, R. (2011), 'Paying for advice: The role of the remuneration consultant in U.K. listed companies', *Vanderbilt Law Review*, Vol. 64(2), pp. 361–96.

BIS (2011), *Executive Remuneration Discussion Paper*, September 2011, BIS, London.

Combined Code (2008), *The Combined Code on Corporate Governance*, Financial Reporting Council, London.

Conference Board (2002), *Commission on Public Trust and Private Enterprise Findings and Recommendations Part 1: Executive Compensation*, Conference Board, New York.

—— (2009), *The Conference Board Task Force on Executive Compensation*, Conference Board, New York.

Conyon, M.J. and Mallin, C.A. (1997), *Directors' Share Options, Performance Criteria and Disclosure: Compliance with the Greenbury Report*, ICAEW Research Monograph, London.

—— and Murphy, K.J. (2000), 'The Prince and the Pauper? CEO Pay in the United States and United Kingdom', *The Economic Journal*, Vol. 110.

—— and Sadler, G.V. (2010), 'Shareholder Voting and Directors' Remuneration Report Legislation: Say on Pay in the UK', *Corporate Governance: An International Review*, Vol. 18(4), pp. 296–312.

—— Peck S.I. and Sadler G.V. (2011), 'New Perspectives on the Governance of Executive Compensation: an Examination of the Role and Effect of Compensation Consultants', *Journal of Management and Governance*, Vol. 15, No.1, pp. 29–58.

Dodd-Frank Wall Street Reform and Consumer Protection Act (2010), USA Congress, Washington DC.

DTI (2002), The Directors' Remuneration Report Regulations 2002 (SI No. 2002/1986), DTI, London.

—— (2003), 'Rewards for Failure: Directors' Remuneration—Contracts, Performance and Severance', DTI, London.

European Commission (2009), *Commission Recommendation on Directors' Remuneration*, April 2009, Brussels.

—— (2010), Green Paper on Corporate Governance in Financial Institutions and Remuneration Policies, European Commission, June 2010, Brussels.

—— (2011), Green Paper on the EU Corporate Governance Framework, European Commission, April 2011, Brussels.

Fattorusso, J., Skovoroda, R., and Bruce, A. (2007), 'UK Executive Bonuses and Transparency—A Research Note', British Journal of Industrial Relations, Vol. 45, No. 3.

Ferri, F. and Maber, D. A. (2011), 'Say on Pay Votes and CEO Compensation: Evidence from the UK', Review of Finance, forthcoming. Available at SSRN: http://ssrn.com/abstract =1420394

FRC (2010), UK Corporate Governance Code, Financial Reporting Council, London.

FSA (2010), PS10/20 Revising the Remuneration Code, FSA, London.

Gaia S., Mallin C.A., and Melis A. (2012), 'Independent Non-Executive Directors' Remuneration: A Comparison of the UK and Italy', Working Paper, Birmingham Business School.

Greenbury, Sir R. (1995), Directors' Remuneration: Report of a Study Group Chaired by Sir Richard Greenbury, Gee Publishing Ltd, London.

Hahn, P. and Lasfer, M. (2011), 'The compensation of non-executive directors: rationale, form, and findings', Journal of Management and Governance, 15(4), pp. 589–601.

High Pay Centre (2012), It's How You Pay It, High pay Centre, London.

High Pay Commission (2011), More for Less: what has happened to pay at the top and does it matter? Interim Report, May 2011, High Pay Commission, London.

—— (2011), What are we paying for? Exploring executive pay and performance, September 2011, High Pay Commission, London.

—— (2011), Cheques with Balances: Why tackling high pay is in the national interest, Final Report, November 2011, High Pay Commission, London.

House of Commons Treasury Committee (2009), Banking Crisis: Reforming Corporate Governance and Pay in the City, Ninth Report of Session 2008-09, House of Commons, The Stationery Office, London.

ICGN (2003), Best Practices for Executive and Director Remuneration, ICGN, London.

—— (2004a), Australian Compliance 2004 with ICGN's Executive Remuneration Principles, ICGN, London.

—— (2004b), UK Compliance 2004 with ICGN's Executive Remuneration Principles, ICGN, London.

—— (2004c), US Compliance 2004 with ICGN's Executive Remuneration Principles, ICGN, London.

—— (2006), Remuneration Guidelines, ICGN, London.

—— (2010), Non-executive Director Remuneration Guidelines and Policies, ICGN, London.

ILO (2008), World of Work Report 2008: Income Inequalities in the Age of Financial Globalization, International Institute for Labour Studies, Geneva, Switzerland.

Kostiander, L. and Ikäheimo, S., (2012), '"Independent" Consultants' Role in the Executive Remuneration Design Process under Restrictive Guidelines', Corporate Governance: An International Review, 20(1) pp. 64–83.

Leal, R.P.C. and Carvalhal da Silva, A. (2005), Corporate Governance and Value in Brazil (and in Chile), available at SSRN: http://ssrn.com/abstract=726261 or DOI: 10.2139/ssrn.726261

Lee, P. (2002), 'Not Badly Paid But Paid Badly', Corporate Governance. An International Review, Vol. 10, No. 2.

Murphy, K.J. and Sandino, T. (2010), 'Executive pay and "independent" compensation consultants' Journal of Accounting and Economics, Vol. 49, Issue 3, pp. 247–62.

Myners, P. (2001), Institutional Investment in the UK: A Review, HM Treasury, London.

OECD (2010), Corporate Governance and the Financial Crisis: Conclusions and Emerging Good Practices to Enhance Implementation of the Principles, OECD, Paris.

—— (2011), Board Practices: Incentives and Governing Risks, OECD, Paris.

Sykes, A. (2002), 'Overcoming Poor Value Executive Remuneration: Resolving the Manifest Conflicts of Interest', Corporate Governance: An International Review, Vol. 10, No. 4.

Turnbull Committee (1999), Internal Control: Guidance for Directors on the Combined Code, ICAEW, London.

Turner Review (2009), A Regulatory Response to the Global Banking Crisis, March 2009, FSA, London.

Voulgaris G., Stathopoulos K., and Walker M. (2010), 'Compensation Consultants and CEO Pay: UK Evidence', Corporate Governance: An International Review, Vol. 18(6), pp. 511–26.

Walker, D. (2009), A Review of Corporate Governance in UK Banks and Other Financial Industry Entities, Final Recommendations, HM Treasury, London.

Useful websites

www.abi.org.uk The website of the Association of British Insurers has guidelines on executive remuneration issues.

http://blog.thecorporatelibrary.com/ The website of the Corporate Library, which has comprehensive information about various aspects of corporate governance including shareholders and stakeholders; and executive remuneration. (Renamed the GMI blog.)

www.conference-board.org/ The Conference Board website gives details of its corporate governance activities and publications including those relating to executive remuneration (compensation).

www.bis.gov.uk The Department for Business, Innovation & Skills website offers a range of information including ministerial speeches and regulatory guidance.

www.highpaycentre.org The website of the High Pay Centre which contains a range of documents and reports relating to executive remuneration.

www.highpaycommission.co.uk/facts-and-figures/ The website of the High Pay Commission, which contains a range of documents and reports relating to executive remuneration.

www.icgn.org The website of the International Corporate Governance Network contains various reports it has issued in relation to directors' remuneration.

www.ivis.co.uk The website of Institutional Voting Information Service, providers of corporate governance voting research. The service has developed from the low key, proactive, but non-confrontational approach to corporate governance adopted by the ABI. Includes ABI Guidelines such as those on executive remuneration.

www.napf.co.uk The website of the National Association of Pension Funds has guidelines on various corporate governance issues.

www.parliament.uk/treascom This website has the publications of the Treasury Committee.

For further links to useful sources of information visit the Online Resource Centre
www.oxfordtextbooks.co.uk/orc/mallin4e/

 Part Three case study   Royal Bank of Scotland Plc, UK

This case study draws together a number of the issues covered in this section of the book relating to a dominant CEO, the lack of appropriate questioning of strategy by the board, and perceived overly generous executive remuneration packages.

The Royal Bank of Scotland (RBS) Plc hit the headlines when it had to be bailed out by the UK government in 2008 to the tune of £20 billion with the government becoming a 70 per cent shareholder. The government has also underwritten £325 billion of RBS assets in an effort to stabilize the bank. In common with various other well-known financial institutions in the UK, USA, and elsewhere, RBS had been badly affected by the global financial crisis which, ironically, the financial institutions themselves had helped to cause. Following the initial shock that such a well-known name needed to be rescued by public funding, came the angry outcry at the remuneration packages being paid out to top executives, even after the bank had been bailed out.

In 2007 Sir Fred Goodwin, CEO of RBS at that time, received a salary of £1.29 million and a bonus of £2.86 million, a total of £4.15 million. This package was more than the CEO of any of Lloyds TSB, HBOS, or Barclays received. Under Sir Fred's time as CEO, RBS followed two strategic decisions that ultimately contributed to it incurring massive losses of £24 billion in 2008. The first was that goodwill on past acquisitions had to be written down, and the second was losses arising from its expansion into investment banking and toxic assets. The board has been criticized for not standing up to Sir Fred who has been accused of not only going on a seven-year acquisition spree but also paying generous prices for the acquisitions. Sir Fred subsequently left RBS after being given early retirement at the age of fifty but with a pension of over £700,000 per annum, which caused even more anger. Despite requests from the government asking him not to take this huge amount, Sir Fred initially remained unmoved and legal enquiries indicated that the terms of the arrangement meant that he could not be forced to pay it back. However, the annual pension has now been reduced substantially although anger at Sir Fred remains high.

Needless to say, at RBS's annual general meeting the remuneration report received an 80 per cent vote against it, clearly displaying the institutional shareholders' disapproval.

RBS' corporate governance was criticized as it was perceived as having a dominant CEO combined with a board comprised of directors who had either been on the board for some years and hence might be seen as being rather too 'cosy' with the CEO, or directors who had limited banking experience. Lord Paul Myners has viewed bank boards generally as inadequate: 'The typical bank board resembles a retirement home for the great and the good: there are retired titans of industry, ousted politicians and the occasional member of the voluntary sector. If such a selection, more likely to be found in *Debrett's Peerage* than the City pages, was ever good enough, it is not now'.

Following on from the disastrous financial performance in 2008, and the criticism across the board from angry investors, an angry government, and an angry public, RBS reduced its board size from sixteen to twelve, the latter including three new non-executive directors who had received UK government approval. Sir Sandy Crombie, CEO of Standard Life, the insurer, became the bank's senior independent director in June 2009, which should greatly have strengthened the RBS board.

The FSA Report (2011) into the failure of the RBS highlighted a number of factors that contributed to the bank's downfall and also stated that 'the multiple poor decisions that RBS made suggest, moreover, that there are likely to have been underlying deficiencies in RBS management, governance and culture which made it prone to make poor decisions'. Sentiment against Sir Fred Goodwin continued to run high and in early 2012 Sir Fred Goodwin was stripped of his knighthood, awarded in 2004 for his services to banking, as he was the dominant decision-maker in RBS in 2008 when decisions were made that contributed significantly to RBS's problems and to the financial crisis.

During 2012 RBS was once again caught up in the executive pay furore, and the wave of shareholder activism and public sentiment were directed at RBS's CEO, Stephen Hester, who decided to waive £2.8 million in salary and long-term incentives.

 FT Clippings

FT: Trinity Mirror investors rebel over pay

By Salamander Davoudi, Media Correspondent

May 10, 2012

Investors underlined their dissatisfaction with the pay culture at Trinity Mirror on Thursday as 45 per cent voted against its 2012 executive pay plan in the latest example of shareholders taking action against perceived corporate excess.

Sly Bailey, the chief executive who resigned last week, saw 14.5 per cent of votes cast against her re-election for the time she remains and 17 per cent voted against Jane Lighting, the chair of the remuneration committee.

Investors in Trinity have repeatedly demanded a substantial cut in Ms Bailey's pay in the light of the group's share price performance. Trinity's market capitalisation has dwindled from £1.1bn when she joined in 2003 to about £84m today. Trinity has paid no dividend since 2008.

Fewer than half of all shareholders voted for the remuneration report as 15 per cent of votes were withheld. Twenty-two per cent voted against executives' long-term incentive plan.

With the exception of the outgoing chairman, Sir Ian Gibson, all other directors were re-elected with a majority of 98 per cent or more.

Ms Bailey is expected to leave Trinity, the publisher of the Mirror and the People, at the end of the year. She resigned amid investor anger over her £1.7m pay package.

At the company's annual meeting shareholders were critical of how Trinity had been run and expressed anger over Ms Bailey's remuneration.

Steve Bennett, shareholder, said: "What is going on? When you read the Mirror it talks about fat cats and bonuses. Why don't you look in your own back yard? I have no confidence in the board. All I can say is that you are fired." His comments were met with a round of applause.

Sir Ian defended her package: "We have not been rewarding our people irresponsibly. Our payment structure is not out of line," adding that Ms Bailey would not be getting a pay-off. He said that the board had delivered on the strategy required.

Chris Morley, shareholder and member of the National Union of Journalists, said: "It has been a strategy of despair rather than success and achievement." The company announced that in the 17 weeks to April net debt was reduced by £24m to £197m. The pension deficit fell by £54m to £176m.

Trinity Mirror has forecast that in May, revenues would fall 5 per cent year-on-year, with advertising income down 10 per cent and circulation revenue down 4 per cent.

Sir Ian said: "This is a secure business, it is in tough times but it is not in crisis. Many of our competitors, if they were not privately owned, would be in crisis." "It is false to say that the business in 2003/4 or 1989 or even now is as efficient as it ought to be. It can be more efficient and should be more efficient even now." The shares rose 3.5p to 33.75p.

FT: Shareholders lose patience on bankers' pay

By Dan McCrum in New York and Kate Burgess in London

April 20, 2012

Vikram Pandit, Citigroup's chief executive, turned around this week to find that the crowd of supporters he thought he had at his back had melted away. Without an overt campaign or agitation from a leading activist, shareholders simply refused to approve his $15m pay package.

He was not the only one to be shocked when over half of the votes cast on pay at the bank's annual meeting were against or withheld. The vote made Citi the first big, financial company in the US to have suffered such a defeat. Patrick McGurn, general counsel at shareholder voting agency ISS, says the rebellion came out of the blue. "We hadn't heard any drum beat about pay." Many companies thought they had filed the rough edges off controversial pay schemes, he says, and pay had fallen down the agenda. But days later, on the other side of the Atlantic, Barclays bowed to investor protest at a package for chief executive Bob Diamond that included a "tax equalisation" payout of £5.75m.

Boards looking at their own pay scales are now faced with the question of whether such shareholder unrest is an aberration, confined to the banks, or if it signifies a more assertive stance from investors that is here to stay.

Investors' tempers have been fraying for some time. Poor returns are testing their patience, while politicians are increasing the pressure on shareholders to exercise their powers and hold directors to account after the failings of the financial crisis.

At Citi, investors have suffered 90 per cent decline in their shares over the past decade. A cash bonus of $5.3m and $8m in deferred stock and cash for Mr Pandit rubbed salt into their wounds. Mr Diamond's take home pay last year rose 25 per cent to about £25m, all in, when shares in Barclays fell by about 3 per cent.

"What Citi tells us is that shareholders don't have short memories, they aren't looking at what happened in the last 18 months, they are looking at what happened since 2007," said Anne Simpson, head of corporate governance for Calpers, the largest US public pension fund, which voted against the pay arrangements at the bank.

The head of governance at one large, global fund manager, said the Citi vote would resonate across the corporate world, and was a sign of things to come. "This is the second year that US shareholders have had a say on pay and they have found their feet. They feel more confident in expressing their views—not just about US banks." In part it reflects a broader debate about pay. In the US attention has begun to focus on the rewards going to the richest segment of society after more than two decades where incomes for the majority have been static, after adjusting for inflation.

The focus on pay also reflects regulatory changes introduced last year as part of financial reform legislation. All US-listed companies must now hold an advisory "say on pay" vote at their annual meeting.

Congressman Barney Frank, an architect of the reforms, says the Citi vote "will encourage shareholders throughout the financial sector to take their responsibilities seriously. And the result should be a reduction in the excessive levels of compensation to financial company executives." But anger over remuneration goes beyond financial services, focusing concerns about strategy, management and performance and galvanising investors in a way that no other issue does, say voting and pay consultants.

Many companies have consulted investors and changed plans again and again in recent months to avoid public confrontation. Two companies that failed to receive shareholder support last year, Jacobs Engineering Group and Beazer Homes, took pains to recraft their pay packages and both received more than 95 per cent support this year.

Such votes, even when just advisory, are also widely credited with forcing boards of companies to talk to their owners, and it has given investors a way to shape the companies they own more directly by setting management incentives.

Michael McCauley, head of corporate governance for Florida's public pension fund, says that investors are thinking about pay in the context of three to five years. "It's not just about share price performance, it's about the change in pay relative to performance." Even so, some boards have remained impervious to calls to link payouts clearly to performance, warn shareholders. These companies will come under fire at annual meetings this year in a way they have not seen before.

Turnouts are already rising, particularly in Europe. In part this is because US shareholder groups, which are diversifying overseas, are obliged by US law to cast their votes. Meanwhile European institutions are on notice from politicians, regulators and their clients to make every vote count.

Investors say that in the UK, for instance, no-votes will rise. And abstentions and withheld votes will no longer be used as a way of subtly reprimanding boards. "People now see abstentions as a wasted action," says Robert Talbut of Royal London Asset Management and chairman of the Association of British Insurer's investment committee. Votes against the re-election of individual directors, especially those serving on remuneration committees, are also expected to rise.

Investors were already expecting a set-to at Barclays' meeting in London next Friday. The board has for months tried to justify to investors the £5.75m "tax equalisation" payment and explain why Mr Diamond's bonus was so high.

Now Mr Diamond has promised investors a higher share of profits and said he will forgo half of his bonus until performance improves. Is it enough? Standard Life Investments, previously a vocal opponent, now says it will vote for the plan. But several are still threatening to vote no.

In the US there have been only four votes against pay packages so far this year, but the annual meeting season has only just got under way. Roughly three-quarters of companies will face investor votes in the next two months. Unresponsive executives will pay a hefty price.

Part 4

International Corporate Governance

Corporate Governance in Continental Europe

Learning Objectives

- To understand the background to the development of corporate governance codes in Europe
- To be aware of the main differences in corporate governance in Continental European countries
- To have a detailed knowledge of the corporate governance codes for a range of Continental European countries
- To be able to evaluate whether corporate governance codes are converging or diverging

Background

As in other countries across the globe, the interest in corporate governance in Continental European countries has grown considerably in the last decade. Its importance for the development of capital markets and investor confidence has been widely appreciated. The realization that the barriers between different countries' capital markets are declining with the adoption of the euro, the internationalization of cross-border portfolios, and technological advances means that corporate governance practices of individual countries increasingly need to satisfy certain perceived core principles of accepted good practice. We have seen that the Cadbury Code (1992) and the Organisation for Economic Co-operation and Development (OECD) Principles (1999, 2004) have been influential in the determination of these core principles.

The increase in both privatizations of former state-owned enterprises, and mergers and acquisitions in many countries has also led to a need for better corporate governance, as wider shareholder groups are created and providers of finance need to be sure that their investment will be protected.

The work of La Porta *et al.* (1998) suggests that countries that have a civil law/code often have a limited protection of minority shareholders; in addition, these countries often have a concentrated share ownership structure rather than a more dispersed shareholder base, such as that in the UK or the USA. This aspect should be borne in mind when analyzing the corporate governance of Continental European countries.

Franks and Mayer (1995) used the terms 'insider' and 'outsider' systems to differentiate between two types of ownership and control structures. In the outsider system, there is dispersed ownership of corporate equity amongst a large number of outside investors (as in both the UK and the USA), whereby institutional investor ownership is predominant, although the institutional investors do not tend to hold large shareholdings in any given company, hence they have little direct control. In contrast, in an insider system, such as in many Continental European countries, ownership tends to be much more concentrated, with shares often being owned either by holding companies or families (although the state still plays an important role in France, for example).

Sometimes, a corporate governance system may also be termed 'bank-oriented' or 'market-oriented'. A bank-oriented system implies that banks play a key role in the funding of companies and so may well be able to exercise some control via the board structure (for example, bank representatives may have seats on the supervisory board in German companies); in contrast, a market-oriented system is one where banks' influence is not prevalent in the same way and does not infiltrate the corporate structure. Becht and Mayer (2001) make an interesting observation about this distinction: they state that the balance of evidence provided by various studies shows that 'the distinction between bank- and market-oriented financial systems is therefore fragile. In contrast, the differences in ownership and control of corporations . . . are pronounced'.

It is also likely that, over time, the remaining influence of banks in terms of direct influence in a company will reduce, and it will be the distinction between ownership and control that helps drive and shape corporate governance reform. Of course, such reform will be within the context of the legal and capital market structure of the various countries. Needless to say, as EU reforms lead to more 'common' requirements of countries and hence to more harmonization, companies and, where appropriate, their corporate governance systems will need to provide for certain of these aspects. EU directives may have an immediate or a more long-term effect on corporate governance. Two examples are the European Works Councils Directive 94/95 ([1994] OJ L254/64), which is concerned with the establishment of European Works Councils for informing and consulting employees, and the Large Holdings Directive (EEC 88/627), whereby voting blocks of 10 per cent or more in companies have to be disclosed.

Subsequently, the EU Accounts Modernization Directive was intended to produce more comparability across the financial reporting of its Member States. By its provisions, companies in various countries in the EU are subject to common standards of both the level and content of disclosures. The Directive was discussed in more detail in Chapter 4.

However, there have also been developments in relation to the Action Plan on Modernizing Company Law and Enhancing Corporate Governance in the EU, which was presented in 2003. The then European Commissioner, Charlie McCreevy, launched a consultation on the Action Plan. Following on from the consultation process, various priorities were identified: shareholders' rights and obligations, internal control, and the modernization and simplification of European Company Law. Also in 2006 amendments to the fourth and seventh Company Law Directives were issued with the aim of enhancing confidence in financial statements and annual reports. These amendments prescribe that, inter alia, listed companies must now publish a separate corporate governance statement in the annual report, and board members are to take collective responsibility for the annual report and accounts.

More recently in 2011 the EU issued the Green Paper on the EU Corporate Governance Framework, which launched a public consultation on possible ways forward to improve existing corporate governance mechanisms. The Green Paper contains three chapters: boards, shareholders, and the 'comply or explain' principle. The objective of the Green Paper is to have a broad debate on the issues raised. The consultation period ended in July 2011 with the final report expected in 2012.

As already mentioned, apart from ownership structure, the main differences in corporate governance codes amongst Continental European countries stem from companies law and securities regulation. Gregory and Simmelkjaer (2002) identify the main differences as being: employee representation; social/stakeholder issues; shareholder rights and participation mechanics; board structure, roles, and responsibilities; supervisory body independence and leadership; board committees; disclosure.

Table 10.1 Predominant board and leadership structure

Member State	Board structure	Employee role in supervisory body
Austria	Two-tier	Yes
Belgium	Unitary*	No
Denmark	**Two-tier**	Yes
Finland	Unitary*	Articles may provide
France	Unitary*	Articles may provide (and Advisory)
Germany	Two-tier	Yes
Greece	Unitary*	No
Ireland	Unitary	No
Italy	Unitary**	No
Luxembourg	Unitary	Yes
Netherlands	Two-tier	Advisory
Portugal	Unitary* **	No
Spain	Unitary	No
Sweden	Unitary	Yes
United Kingdom	Unitary	No

*Other structure also available   **Board of auditors also required
Source: Comparative Study of Corporate Governance Codes (Gregory and Simmelkjaer, 2002)
©European Communities 2002, Internal Market Directorate General

Table 10.1 highlights the predominant board and leadership structure in a number of European countries. The table shows that most European countries have a unitary board structure, although the majority also have the option of a dual structure. A number of countries provide for employee representation on, or a role in, the supervisory board; there is separate supervisory and managerial leadership in the companies in countries where the board structure is dual.

Table 10.2 indicates the key distinctions between the supervisory board and the management board. The supervisory board is elected by shareholders and employees, and it in turn appoints the management board. The supervisory board has a control function whereas the management board manages the business.

Table 10.2 Summary of key differences between supervisory and management boards

Supervisory board	Management board
Members (shareholder representatives) are elected by the shareholders in general meeting; members (employee representatives) are nominated by the employees	Members are appointed by the supervisory board
Controls the direction of the business	Manages the business
Oversees the provision of information and ensures appropriate systems have been put in place by the management board	Provides various financial information and reports; and puts appropriate systems in place, e.g. a risk management system

The next sections will look at several countries in more detail: Germany, Denmark, France, and Italy. These countries have been chosen because they represent different board structures and ownership patterns: Germany and Denmark each have a two-tier board structure but with different corporate ownership structures; France has a unitary board structure but the other structure is also available; and Italy has a unitary board structure but a board of auditors is also required.

Germany

Charkham (1994) stated that 'if there were a spectrum with "confrontation" at one end and "co-operation" at the other, we would confidently place German attitudes and behaviour far closer to the "co-operation" end than, say, those of the British or Americans'. This is an important statement in the context of understanding the philosophy of the German approach to business and to companies, whereby the shareholders are but one of a wider set of stakeholder interests with the employees and customers being given more emphasis. Charkham (1994) finds this approach evidenced in the industrial relations of German companies: 'Good industrial relations . . . would not be prominent in works on corporate governance systems in most countries, or at best would be regarded as peripheral. In Germany, however, good industrial relations are much nearer centre stage.' This is evidenced in the Works Constitution Act 1972, which sets out the rights of the works council and, broadly speaking, deals with all matters pertaining to the employees' conditions of employment. Works councils are part of the cooperative process between workers and employers, the idea being that co-determination (the right to be kept informed of the company's activities and to participate in decisions that may affect the workers) means that there is a basis for more trust and cooperation between workforce and employers. The Co-determination Act 1976 defines the proportion of employee and shareholder representatives on the supervisory board (*Aufsichtsrat*) and also stipulates that a director on the management board has special responsibility for labour-related matters.

The business structure in Germany is detailed in Wymeersch (1998), where he identifies the most used business types in various Continental European states. In Germany, as far as the larger business entities are concerned, the business types tend to be either public (*Aktiengesellschaft, AG*) or private companies limited by shares (*Gesellschaft mit beschrankter Haftung, GmbH*). However, he identifies a hybrid that is also used in Germany, specifically, a hybrid of the *GmbH & Co. KG*, combining the advantages of the unincorporated *Kommanditgesellschaft* and the limited liability of *GmbH*.

In Germany as in many Continental European countries and the UK, there is a trend away from individual share ownership. The most influential shareholders are financial and non-financial companies, and there are significant cross-holdings, which mean that when analyzing share ownership and control in Germany, one needs to look also at the links between companies. Banks, and especially a few large banks, play a central role in German corporate governance, with representation on the supervisory boards of companies and links with other companies. Charkham (1994) identifies a number of reasons as to why banks are influential in Germany. First, there is direct ownership of company shares by banks; secondly, German shareholders generally lodge their shares with banks authorized to carry out their voting instructions (deposited share voting rights, or DSVR); thirdly, banks tend to lend for the long term and hence develop a longer term relationship with the company (relationship lending); and fourthly, banks offer a wide range of services that the company may find it useful to draw upon. Given these factors, banks tend to build up a longer term, deeper relationship with companies, and their expertise is welcomed on the supervisory boards. Hence the German corporate governance system could be termed an 'insider' system. A more detailed analysis is beyond the scope of this text but a comprehensive analysis is provided in Prigge (1998).

The German corporate governance system is based around a dual board system, and, essentially, the dual board system comprises a management board (*Vorstand*) and a supervisory board (*Aufsichtsrat*). The management board is responsible for managing the enterprise. Its members are jointly accountable for the management of the enterprise and the chairman of the management board coordinates the work of the management board. The supervisory board appoints, supervises, and advises the members of the management board and is directly involved in decisions of fundamental importance to the enterprise. The chairman of the supervisory board coordinates the work of the supervisory board. The members of the supervisory board are elected by the shareholders in general meetings. The co-determination principle provides for compulsory employees representation. So, for firms or companies that have more than five hundred or two thousand employees in Germany, employees are also represented in the supervisory board, which then comprises one-third employee representative or one-half employee representative respectively. The representatives elected by the shareholders and representatives of the employees are equally obliged to act in the enterprise's best interests.

The idea of employee representation on boards is not always seen as a good thing because the employee representatives on the supervisory board may hold back decisions being made that are in the best interests of the company as a whole but not necessarily in the best interests of the employees as a group. An example would be where a company wishes to rationalize its operations and close a factory but the practicalities of trying to get such a decision approved by employee representatives on the supervisory board, and the repercussions of such a decision on labour relations, prove too great for the strategy to be made a reality.

Table 10.3 Key characteristics influencing German corporate governance

Feature	Key characteristic
Main business form	Public or private companies limited by shares
Predominant ownership structure	Financial and non-financial companies
Legal system	Civil law
Board structure	Dual
Important aspect	Compulsory employee representation on supervisory board

The committee on corporate governance in Germany was chaired by Dr Gerhard Cromme and is usually referred to as the Cromme Report or Cromme Code. The code harmonizes a wide variety of laws and regulations, and contains recommendations and also suggestions for complying with international best practice on corporate governance.

The Cromme Code was published in 2002 (amended in 2005) and has a number of sections, which are discussed below.

(i) Shareholders and the general meeting

At the general meeting, the management board submits the annual and consolidated financial statement, and the general meeting decides on the appropriation of net income and approves the decisions of the management board and the supervisory board. An important aspect of the general meeting is that it elects the shareholders' representatives to the supervisory board and also, generally, the auditors.

The shareholders' right to vote is facilitated in a number of ways, including by the personal exercise of shareholders' voting rights, and by the use of proxies.

(ii) Cooperation between the management board and the supervisory board

It is essential that the management board and the supervisory board cooperate closely for the benefit of the enterprise. The Cromme Code defines the management board's role as coordinating the enterprise's strategic approach with the supervisory board and discussing the implementation of strategy with the supervisory board at regular intervals. There are certain situations, such as those relating to the enterprise's planning, business development, risk situation, and risk management, when the management board should inform the supervisory board immediately of any issues.

The supervisory board is able to specify the management board's information and reporting duties in more detail. It is essential that there is open discussion between the management board and supervisory board as well as amongst the members within each of those two boards. The management board and the supervisory board report each year on the enterprise's corporate governance in the annual report and they should explain any deviations from the Cromme Code. The company shall keep previous declarations of conformity with the Code available for viewing on its website for five years.

(iii) Management board

The composition of the management board is determined by the supervisory board, and should be reported in the notes to the accounts. Any conflict of interest should be disclosed to the supervisory board. The Cromme Code states that 'the management board is responsible for independently managing the enterprise' with a view to acting in the enterprise's best interest, and endeavouring to increase the sustainable value of the enterprise. As mentioned earlier, the management board develops the enterprise's strategy and coordinates with the supervisory board on this issue.

The Cromme Report provides for the compensation to be comprised of a fixed salary and variable component. As in many other countries, the variable compensation element should be linked to the business performance as well as long-term incentives. Stock options are mentioned as one possible element of variable compensation components and these should be linked to certain performance criteria, such as the achievement of predetermined share prices.

(iv) Supervisory board

It is important that the composition of the supervisory board reflects a suitable level of knowledge, ability, and experience to be able properly to carry out the tasks relevant to the business. There should be an adequate number of independent members. 'Independence' will mean no business or personal relations with the company or its management board that cause a conflict of interest. To help maintain its independence, not more than two former members of the management board should be members of the supervisory board. The former management board chairman or a management board member should not generally become supervisory board chairman or chairman of a supervisory board committee. Supervisory board members should not have directorships or similar positions or indeed have advisory roles with important competitors of the enterprise.

The supervisory board carries out a number of important functions, including the regular provision of independent advice and supervision to the management board on the management of the business. The management and supervisory boards should ensure that there is a long-term succession plan in place. The supervisory board may delegate some duties to other committees, which include compensation and audit committees. The chairman of the supervisory board, who should not be the chairman of the audit committee, coordinates work within the supervisory board, chairs its meetings and attends to the affairs of the supervisory board externally.

It is worth elaborating on the committees that may be formed with a remit for various delegated areas. These may include (i) the audit committee (the chairman of the audit committee should not be a former member of the management board of the company) and the chairman of the audit committee should have specialist knowledge and experience in the application of accounting principles and internal control processes; (ii) and a compensation committee to look at the compensation of the management board and may also look at the appointment of members of the management board.

The compensation of members of the supervisory board is specified either by a resolution of the general meeting or in the articles of association. Members of the supervisory board may receive performance-related compensation as well as fixed compensation. The compensation of the supervisory board members should be disclosed in the corporate governance report.

An interesting disclosure required by the Cromme Code is that if a supervisory board member takes part in less than half of the meetings of the supervisory board in a financial year, then this will be noted in the report of the supervisory board. Any conflicts of interest should be reported to the supervisory board and the supervisory board would then inform the general meeting of any conflicts of interest together with how these conflicts have been treated.

(v) Transparency

The Code provides that the management board should disclose immediately any facts that might affect the enterprise's activities and which are not publicly known. The report emphasizes that all shareholders should be treated equally in respect of information disclosure and that the company may use appropriate media, such as the internet, to inform the shareholders and investors in an efficient and timely manner. There is disclosure required in terms of the shareholdings, including options and derivatives, which are held by individual management board and supervisory board members. These must be reported if they directly or indirectly exceed 1 per cent of the shares issued by the company. These disclosures should all be included in the corporate governance report.

(vi) Reporting and audit of the annual financial statements

The Code states that the supervisory board or the audit committee should obtain a statement from the proposed auditor clarifying whether there are any 'professional, financial or other relationships' that might call the auditor's independence into question. Interestingly, this statement should include the extent to which other services have been performed for the company in the past year, especially in the field of consultancy, or which are contracted for the following year. It is the supervisory board that concludes agreement on the auditor's fee.

From the discussion earlier, it can be seen that the defining feature of Germany's corporate governance system is the significant role played by the supervisory board. In addition, the supervisory board has compulsory representation of workers via the co-determination rules. This can have an important impact on key strategic decisions, for example, if a German company decides that it needs to close one of its subsidiaries, then it may prefer to close down a subsidiary overseas, in a country such as the UK, which has a unitary board structure and hence no supervisory board with employee representation. Employees in the UK would therefore be in a weaker position than their German counterparts, and have less influence over any closure decision.

It is interesting to note that Charkham (2005), in reviewing corporate governance developments in Germany, is of the opinion that 'internal and external developments have put pressure on it, but its main provisions remain intact. The factors for change have been the diminishing role of the banks, the international governance codes and principles, and the international capital markets'.

In November 2005 Germany abolished the requirement for shares to be blocked in advance of a shareholder meeting. Blocking had meant that shares could not be traded for a period of time before a company's general meeting if the holder of the shares wished to be able to vote on the resolutions tabled for the general meeting. Therefore, it had effectively been a deterrent to voting because institutional investors often could not afford to be in a position whereby they were unable to trade their shares.

Legal changes required companies to disclose pay details for executive directors, effective for annual reports for 2006 onwards. However, company management may propose that disclosure is limited and if the proposal is approved by 75 per cent of its shareholders, then the additional disclosure does not have to be given. An amended version of the *German Corporate Governance Code* was published in 2006 and recommended that various executive remuneration disclosures should be made in the corporate governance report. Companies would be obliged to disclose if they were to deviate from these recommendations.

There were minor amendments to the *German Corporate Governance Code* in 2007 and 2008. In the foreword to each of these codes, it is mentioned that the European Company or Societas Europaea (SE) gives German enterprises the opportunity to opt for the unitary board system, in which case the form that co-determination would take would be a matter for agreement between the company management and the employees. Also, there is now a recommendation in the section on the 'Supervisory Board' that the supervisory board should form a nomination committee composed exclusively of shareholder representatives, which should propose suitable candidates to the supervisory board for recommendation to the company's general meeting.

Further updates to the Code took place in 2009 and 2010. In 2009 the foreword to the Code included mention that the Code clarifies the obligations of the management board and the supervisory board 'to ensure the continued existence of the enterprise and its sustainable creation of value in conformity with the principles of the social market economy (interest of the enterprise)'. Therefore the interests of the shareholders, the employees, and other stakeholders will be taken into account. Other amendments in 2009 relate to remuneration and board composition, including diversity:

- the full supervisory board should determine the total compensation of individual members of the management board based on their individual performance, the performance of the business, the economic outlook and the remuneration levels in peer group companies;
- external compensation experts may be called upon for advice;
- the compensation structure should be oriented towards sustainable growth and should not encourage the taking of unnecessary risks;
- the supervisory board should have regard to diversity when appointing the members of the management board;
- the supervisory board and the management board should engage in long-term succession planning;
- management board members should not become members of the supervisory board within two years of the end of their appointment unless their appointment is based on a proposal presented by shareholders holding more than 25 per cent of the voting rights;
- members of the supervisory board should not hold more than three supervisory board memberships in non-group listed companies.

In 2010 amendments to the Code focused on shareholders' rights, remuneration, and diversity:

- the general meeting can vote on the remuneration system for members of the management board (reflecting the growing focus on executive pay);
- the forms for postal voting should be included on the company's website;
- diversity, with appropriate consideration of women, should be taken into account by the management board when filling managerial positions in the company, and by the supervisory board when making appointments to the management board;
- the supervisory board should 'specify concrete objectives regarding its composition which . . . take into account the international activities of the enterprise . . . and diversity. These concrete objectives shall, in particular, stipulate an appropriate degree of female representation';
- in relation to training, the 2010 Code adds the provision 'the members of the supervisory board shall on their own take on the necessary training and further education measures required for their tasks. They shall be supported by the company appropriately'.

Goergen *et al.* (2008) review the governance role of large shareholders, creditors, the product market and the supervisory board, and also discuss the importance of mergers and acquisitions, the market in block trades, and the lack of a hostile takeover market. They find that

> the German system is characterised by a market for partial corporate control, large shareholders and bank/creditor monitoring, a two-tier (management and supervisory) board with co-determination between shareholders and employees on the supervisory board, a disciplinary product-market, and corporate governance regulation largely based on EU directives but with deep roots in the German codes and legal doctrine. Another important feature of the German system is its corporate governance efficiency criterion which is focused on the maximisation of stakeholder value rather than shareholder value. However, the German corporate governance system has experienced many important changes over the last decade. First, the relationship between ownership or control concentration and profitability has changed over time. Second, the pay-for-performance relation is influenced by large shareholder control: in firms with controlling blockholders and when a universal bank is simultaneously an equity- and debtholder, the pay-for-performance relation is lower than in widely-held firms or blockholder-controlled firms. Third, since 1995 several major regulatory initiatives (including voluntary codes) have increased transparency and accountability.

Odenius (2008) reviews Germany's corporate governance system and the effectiveness of recent reforms. He states that since the early 1990s far-reaching reforms have complemented the traditional stakeholder system with important elements of the shareholder system. He raises the important question of whether these reforms have created sufficient flexibility for the market to optimize its corporate governance structure within well-established social and legal norms. He concludes that there is scope for enhancing flexibility in three core areas, relating to internal control mechanisms, especially the flexibility of board structures; self-dealing; and external control, particularly take-over activity.

v. Werder and Talaulicar (2011) reviewed corporate governance developments in Germany in recent years and point out that 'regulatory changes are primarily aimed at further improving the modalities of managing and supervising corporations within the corporate governance system in order to attenuate its downsides and to develop its strengths. In this regard, an accelerating pace as well as an increasing intensity of reforms is to be observed.'

Denmark

Denmark has a quite different ownership structure from that of, say, the USA, the UK, or most other European countries. The ownership is quite concentrated and there is a widespread existence of foundation ownership. This means that some of the largest Danish companies are controlled by a foundation (i.e. a legal entity without owners often created to administer a large ownership stake in a particular company). There is also significant institutional investor share ownership in Denmark, with institutional investors owning approximately 35 per cent of market value of Danish equity. Like Germany, corporate governance in Denmark is focused on a dual board structure. The Danish Companies Act provides that half the members elected by the shareholders, or by other parties entitled to appoint directors, will be elected by the employees, with a minimum of two (this provision applies to companies with at least thirty-five employees).

The Nørby Committee's report was published in 2001 and made recommendations for corporate governance in Denmark. The foreword to the report very much emphasized that this was a voluntary code and that it was really up to the individual companies as to whether they actually followed it, but that the Nørby Committee believed that it was in companies' best interests to do so. The Committee tried to make the recommendations operationally practical, although it emphasized that the recommendations be followed by companies of their own accord, so these were non-binding recommendations. However, the Committee felt that it was in the companies' own interests to follow the recommendations and did think it important that companies stated to what extent they had followed the recommendations. The report built on the OECD basic values of openness, transparency, responsibility, and equality. The Nørby Committee felt that because, internationally, there is a growing interest in corporate governance and rise in investors demanding more and better information about managements' actions and the companies' long-term goals and strategy, it was important that Denmark also had a set of corporate governance recommendations. The Committee believed that there should be more demands on listed companies than on unlisted

Table 10.4 Key characteristics influencing Danish corporate governance

Feature	Key characteristic
Main business form	Public or private companies limited by shares
Predominant ownership structure	Institutional investors and foundation ownership
Legal system	Civil law
Board structure	Dual
Important aspect	Many shares have multiple voting rights

companies; it also recommended that state companies complied with the recommendations, where relevant. The Nørby report was split into seven sections, outlined later.

The Nørby Committee's (2001) recommendations formed the basis for further corporate governance developments in Denmark. In late 2002 the Copenhagen Stock Exchange appointed an independent corporate governance committee to develop further corporate governance for Danish listed companies. Various international initiatives occurred that impacted on corporate governance thinking in Denmark. These included the US Sarbanes–Oxley Act (2002), the *UK Combined Code* (2003), and EU initiatives such as the Action Plan (2003) to modernize company law and enhance corporate governance in the EU (see earlier for more detail). In the light of these various international developments, it was decided to revisit the original Nørby recommendations to see what revisions might be needed.

In December 2003 the Copenhagen Stock Exchange Committee on Corporate Governance issued its report, often referred to as Nørby (2003). A subsequent update was made in August 2005, being Nørby (2005), and an important development was that the Copenhagen Stock Exchange incorporated the Nørby (2005) Committee's revised recommendations for corporate governance into the disclosure requirements for listed companies, 'obliging the companies, in accordance with the "comply or explain" principle, to include in their future annual reports a statement on how they address the Recommendations'. The fundamentally important aspect here is transparency. As in the UK, companies may comply by explaining how and why they do not comply with a particular recommendation. It is the disclosure and transparency aspects that enable shareholders and other stakeholders to understand better what is going on in the company.

The focus of the original Nørby (2001) recommendations plus the additional recommendation, and the revisions to these by subsequent committees, are now outlined, these being the recommendations as at August 2005.

(i) The role of the shareholders and their interaction with the management of the company

The report emphasizes the importance of communication and dialogue between management and shareholders, in order to ensure that the company's funds are appropriately utilized and that the company continues to be competitive and to create value. The report lays great importance on the role of the annual general meeting (AGM) as a medium for communication and decision. The report recommends that the shareholders should be facilitated in using their rights, both in terms of communications and also in terms of voting rights. Denmark has a dual voting system, in other words, some shares have multiple voting rights, but the report states that voting rights differentiation or restricting the number of votes that an individual shareholder can cast or restricting the number of shares that an individual shareholder may own in the company are not recommended. If any of these restrictions already apply, then the board should look at these and decide whether it is possible to revoke them. Shareholders should receive sufficient notice of the AGM.

(ii) The role of the stakeholders and their importance to the company

The report emphasizes the importance of dialogue with stakeholders, i.e. anyone who 'is directly affected by the company's decisions and business'. The interaction is emphasized as being of great importance and the company should have policies or guidelines in appropriate areas, such as environmental and social issues.

(iii) Openness and transparency

Openness and transparency are seen as essential in providing continuous and timely information to the shareholders and other stakeholders of the company. The report recommends that investor relations should be based on continuous dialogue and that investor relations might be enacted in various ways such as investor meetings, use of information technology, use of the Internet, etc. The company should prepare its company report according to the relevant Danish rules but it is also recommended to apply international accounting standards.

(iv) The tasks and responsibilities of the supervisory board

The report states that 'the supervisory board is responsible for safeguarding the interests of the shareholders, with care and due consideration of the interests of the other stakeholders'. There is an emphasis on the development and implementation of strategies for the company, and the board's essential tasks are concerned with this area, as well as with areas such as risk management, appointing a qualified management, and trying to ensure good relations with a company's stakeholders. The chairman's task is to run the board and to ensure that these meetings are run effectively and efficiently, and it is recommended that a deputy chairman is also appointed. There should be established procedures as to how management reports to the board and how the board and management communicate.

(v) Composition of the supervisory board

The board should be comprised of directors who have the relevant and necessary knowledge and professional experience to contribute positively to the board, so that the strategic and managerial tasks of the board can be effectively carried out. When nominations are made to the AGM, then certain information should be provided about the directors, including the requirements of professional qualifications, international experience, and so on. It is recommended that when directors join the board they, in collaboration with the chairman, decide on any relevant or supplementary training that may be necessary. Every year, the supervisory board should assess whether the competence and expertise of its members needs to be updated.

The board size is recommended to be such that it allows for constructive debate and effective decision-making, and ensures that the supervisory board members' experience and capabilities match the company's requirements. The independence of directors is emphasized, directors should be able to act independently of special interests and hence at least half of the supervisory board members should be independent. In this context, 'independent' means that the director should not have been an employee in the company or have been employed by the company within the past five years; nor should he/she be, or have been, a member of the executive board of the company; nor a professional consultant to the company; nor have any other strategic interest in the company other than that of a shareholder. The annual report would contain information about the directors elected by the general meeting, including the directors' occupations; their other managerial positions or directorships in Danish as well as foreign companies; and how many shares, options, and warrants each director owns in the company. It is recommended that the board meets at regular intervals. Individual directors should be able to allocate sufficient time for their duties and it is recommended that a supervisory board member who is also a member of the executive board of an active company should not fill more than three ordinary directorships, or one chairmanship and one ordinary directorship, in companies that are not part of the group. Directors should retire at an age agreed by the supervisory board.

The supervisory board should consider whether to establish board committees, such as audit, remuneration, and nomination committees. If such committees are established, terms of reference should be drawn up for each committee. Members' names should be listed in the annual report in relation to each committee. Where such committees are established, it is important to ensure that information relevant to the whole supervisory board is made available to all its members and not just to the members of an individual committee. There should be self-assessment of the board's work on an annual basis and this should take account of the strategic goals and plans, and whether these are being realized. The procedures for self-assessment should be included in the annual report.

(vi) Remuneration of the members of the supervisory board and the executive board

The report emphasizes the importance of a competitive remuneration scheme for attracting and keeping competent directors and managers. It is important that principles and guidelines are established, and that there should be incentives that reflect the interests of the shareholders and the company. Whilst stating that the remuneration of the directors may include incentive schemes (including bonus schemes and shares at market price), the report does not recommend that it consists of share option schemes. However, where share or subscription options are used, these should be set up as roll-over schemes (the options are allocated and expire over a number of years). There should be transparency in this important area and directors' remuneration should be published in the annual report. Information about severance schemes should be disclosed in the company's annual report.

(vii) Risk management

It is important that the board considers risk management and that the company has an efficient risk management system. The board should monitor this area and ensure that the systems are working efficiently. The annual report should contain information about risk management activities.

(viii) Audit

An essential part of the supervisory board's work is to ensure a competent and independent audit. The framework for the auditor's work should be decided upon by the supervisory and executive boards. Each year the supervisory board should also detail the scope of any non-audit services provided by the auditor to help ensure the auditor's independence. The supervisory board should review and assess, at least annually, the internal control systems of the company. The supervisory board should discuss with the auditor the accounting policies, together with important accounting estimates. The result of the audit should be discussed at meetings with the supervisory board.

From the discussion above, it can be seen that the Danish corporate governance system is developing rapidly, with a move to a 'comply or explain' basis. As with Germany, the dual board system may mean that Danish employees are at an advantage if the company's strategy requires that part of the company be closed down; the closure is more likely to hit part of the company located in a country with a unitary board structure, where employees have less influence.

There were minor amendments to the Danish *Corporate Governance Code* in February 2008 in relation to section (vi) earlier, relating to remuneration of the members of the supervisory and executive boards; and in December 2008 in relation to section (iii) openness and transparency, and section (v) composition of the supervisory board. In relation to section (vi) the contents of the remuneration policy should be disclosed on the company's website as well as in the annual report. In relation to section (iii) the company may publish details of a non-financial nature including diversity aspects (such as gender and age) within the supervisory board, the executive board and the company more generally. Finally, in relation to section (v), the composition of the supervisory board should be regularly reviewed, including in relation to diversity (such as gender and age).

The Companies Act 2009 introduced new generic terms for the governing bodies of Danish companies being the supreme governing body (essentially aimed at the board of directors or the supervisory board) and the central governing body (essentially aimed at the board of directors or the executive board of companies that have a supervisory board/executive board). Further amendments were made to the Danish *Corporate Governance Code* in 2010 and 2011. The revisions in 2010 were made as a response to the Danish Companies Act 2009, the Financial Statements Act, and the Act on Approved Auditors and Audit Firms, in addition to European Commission recommendations, including those on remuneration of listed companies' governing bodies. Developments in foreign recommendations on corporate governance were also taken into account. Amendments include that the company's central governing body should have a corporate social responsibility policy, and that consideration be given as to whether to establish a whistle-blowing scheme.

In 2008 the Danish Venture Capital and Private Equity Association (DVCA) introduced guidelines to help create greater openness and transparency in private equity funds in Denmark. The guidelines, using a 'comply or explain' approach, apply at both company level and fund level, i.e. both the private equity funds and the companies in which they invest are expected to be more open and transparent.

France

The corporate governance system in France is set in a civil law context and, traditionally, does not offer good protection to minority investors. The French government has been an important stakeholder, partly because of its direct shareholdings in French industry (although this has declined with the privatizations in recent years) and also because of the fact that many civil servants are appointed to corporate boards. Wymeersch (1998) states that takeovers, particularly of recently privatized firms, are prevented by the *noyaux durs* (hard core), which comprise a series

Table 10.5 Key characteristics influencing French corporate governance

Feature	Key characteristic
Main business form	Public or private companies limited by shares
Predominant ownership structure	State, institutional investors, individuals
Legal system	Civil law
Board structure	Unitary (but other structure possible)
Important aspect	Many shares have multiple voting rights

of holdings by financial institutions, banks, and insurance companies to help stabilize the French industrial sector. In addition, control may be enhanced by multiple voting rights attaching to shares, a construct that is against generally accepted corporate governance best practice.

There are various business forms available in France of which the two we are most concerned with are the *Sociétés anonymes (SAs)*, which is essentially like a public company in the UK, and the *Sociétés à responsabilité limitée (SARL)*, which is a limited liability company along the lines of a limited company in the UK. The French corporate governance system places a lot of emphasis, and power, on the *président directeur-général (PDG)* of a company. This is in line with the French tradition of centralized leadership and power.

France has a predominantly unitary board system, although the option to have a dual board exists. Similarly, there is provision for employee involvement where this is provided for by the articles of the company. French corporate governance codes therefore need to take account of this diversity of structure.

The first French corporate governance report was the Viénot Committee report in 1995 (Viénot I). The Viénot Committee was established by two employers' federations (MEDEF and AFEP-AGREF) and with the support of leading private sector companies; it was chaired by Marc Viénot, head of Société Générale. The second Viénot report (Viénot II) was issued in 1999. Subsequent to Viénot II, the corporate governance environment became further complicated by the introduction of 'new economic regulations' in 2001 that gave companies with a unitary board structure the choice of separating the functions of chairman and chief executive officer (CEO) or keeping them joint. The corporate governance report of a working group chaired by Daniel Bouton (President of Société Générale) was then issued in October 2002.

Bouton Report (2002)

The Bouton Report recommended incremental improvement rather than any radical reform. Part 1 of the report was split into six areas: the role and operation of the board of directors, the board of directors' composition, evaluation of the board of directors, the audit committee, the compensation committee, and the nominating committee. Part 2 of the report contained some recommendations on strengthening the independence of statutory auditors (with specific reference of the importance of this area in the context of the Enron affair). Part 3 covered financial information, accounting standards and practices, and discussed the importance of high quality financial information and disclosures and the means to achieve them. Let us now look at Part 1 of the Bouton Report in more detail.

(i) Role and operation of the board of directors

In line with the earlier Viénot reports, the Bouton Report emphasized that there should be specialized committees to undertake work in the areas of:

- reviewing the financial statements;
- monitoring the internal audit function;
- selection of statutory auditors;
- deciding a policy on remuneration and stock options;
- appointing of directors and corporate officers (chairman, CEO, and chief operating officer in a unitary board system; chairman and members of the management board in a dual board system).

The report highlighted the importance of strategy and stated that the directors' internal rules of operation should specify board procedures for dealing with key strategic issues, such as issues relating to the company's financial position.

The importance of directors' access to information on a timely basis was also emphasized as an 'essential requirement for the satisfactory performance of their duties'. The report stated that information of a negative nature (if such arises) should also be supplied to the directors. A crucial feature relating to the interpretation of any information by directors was that newly appointed directors should have the facility to obtain additional training concerning specific facets of the company (such as its lines of business and markets). There was also provision for the directors to meet key executives of the company without, if they so wished, the corporate officers being present.

(ii) Board of directors' composition

The report recognized that the quality of the board is dependent on its membership and that directors should be sound characters with integrity, be knowledgeable about the business, be active in their role as directors (competently discussing strategy and other issues in board meetings), and should have regard to the interest of all shareholders.

The report advocated that half of the board be comprised of independent directors in companies that have a dispersed ownership structure and no controlling shareholders. This was an increase on the Viénot II report, which had called for boards to be comprised of one-third independent directors. The report defined 'independence' as: 'A director is independent when he or she has no relationship of any kind whatsoever with the corporation, its group or the management of either that is such as to colour his or her judgement'. This is a fairly encompassing, yet at the same time succinct, definition.

(iii) Evaluation of the board of directors

The report recommended annual evaluations via a debate at board level about its operation each year. At least every three years, there should be a formal evaluation, possibly under the leadership of an independent director, with help from an appropriate consultant. Shareholders would be kept informed each year via the annual report of evaluations carried out and the steps taken as a result.

(iv) The audit committee

The report recommended that the audit committee should be comprised of two-thirds independent directors and that there should not be any corporate officers as members. As well as any financial or accounting expertise that the audit committee members may already possess, they should also be informed of 'the company's specific accounting, financial and operating procedures'.

The audit committee should draw up rules of operation detailing responsibilities and operating procedures, and these should be approved by the board, to which the audit committee should also report so that the board is fully informed. Furthermore, the annual report should describe the work carried out by the audit committee. It is expected that the audit committee should interview the external auditors (whose appointment process they should drive) and the head of internal audit, and be able to call upon outside experts as necessary. The audit committee should also monitor auditor independence, including the amount of fees paid to the audit firm and what proportion those fees represent in relation to the audit firm's total billings.

(v) Compensation committee

The report recommended that the compensation committee should be comprised of a majority of independent directors and that there should not be any corporate officers as members. The compensation committee should draw up rules of operation, detailing responsibilities, and operating procedures, and these should be approved by the board, to which the compensation committee should also report so that the board is fully informed. Furthermore, the annual report should describe the work carried out by the compensation committee.

Under French law, the annual report should include a discussion of the principles and processes applied in the setting of the corporate officers' compensation. The Bouton Report required that the compensation committee defines how the variable element of directors' compensation will be set, and ensures that this is consistent with the annual performance evaluation of the corporate officers and with the company's medium-term strategy.

The Bouton Report highlighted some significant differences relating to stock options under French law, compared to some other countries. First, 'only the general meeting of shareholders has the power to authorize the granting of options, to set their maximum number and to determine the main conditions of the granting process'; secondly, 'the exercise price of the options, which is set based on stock prices at the time of granting, cannot subsequently be revised or altered regardless of stock price trends'; thirdly, 'the holding period of options . . . is directly determined in practice by tax rules', being five years' minimum period from the date of grant for options granted prior to April 2000 (four years' minimum for options granted subsequently); and fourthly, 'directors who are neither corporate officers nor employees are barred by law from receiving stock options'.

(vi) Nominating committee

The Bouton Report emphasized the importance of the nominating committee, which should include the chairman of the board as a member, because he/she 'plays an essential role in shaping the future of the company, and is in charge of preparing the future membership of leadership bodies'. There should be a formal procedure in place to select future independent directors, and the annual report should include a description of the work of the nominating committee.

The Bouton Report recommended that its proposals be implemented as soon as possible, but at the latest, by the end of 2003 (see later). Companies should include a discussion in their annual report of the extent to which the recommendations have been implemented. The events at Enron, in particular, were clearly in the minds of the Bouton working group when they stated. 'Although procedural rules and recommendations concerning the operation of the board and its committees are essential corporate governance standards, any procedure will only be as good as the people implementing it. ENRON complied formally with all these rules and was even considered a model of corporate governance!' It is really a case of substance over form: companies may comply with the letter of a code but do they comply with the spirit of it too? That will be the ultimate decider as to whether there are more Enrons in the future.

On a separate note, France published a decree in February 2002 setting out mandatory disclosure by companies in their annual report, and accounts of the social and environmental impact of their activities. It came into force in 2003 for all annual reports.

(vii) Social and environmental issues

Areas where disclosures take place are community indicators, which are primarily qualitative, and these focus on companies' integration with local communities and engagement with stakeholder groups. Labour standards are also addressed with disclosure required on how subsidiaries respect International Labour Organization (ILO) conventions and how the company promotes them with its subcontractors. Environmental indicators cover areas such as emissions to air, water, and ground, implementation of management systems, and compliance with mainstream standards of practice or certification. Whilst these provisions are comprehensive, the question remains as to what could be done if a company did not comply and therefore the effectiveness of this legislation may, in practice, be limited.

In August 2003 France enacted new laws relating to financial security with the aim of restoring the trust of investors in French markets. The changes included that there should be improved transparency with more information provided to shareholders, including a separate report on the internal control procedures of the company, and a new procedure for the appointment of external auditors.

In October 2003 AFEP and MEDEF published *The Corporate Governance of Listed Corporations*, a document that provided a set of principles of corporate governance based on consolidation of the 1995, 1999 (Viénot I and II) and 2002 (Bouton) AFEP and MEDEF reports. The report does not add to the Viénot and Bouton reports, the substance of which is retained; rather, it collates the recommendations into a single set of principles. The principles cover various aspects of the board of directors, independent directors, board evaluation, meeting of the board and the committees, and board committees (such as audit, compensation, and nominations), and directors' compensation. The principles utilize a 'comply or explain' approach with regard to which recommendations a company has adopted. In December 2010 AFEP and MEDEF published the *Corporate Governance Code of Listed Corporations* which consolidates the earlier corporate governance publications, including the Viénot reports, the Bouton Report, recommendations made in 2007 and 2008 concerning the compensation of executive directors of listed companies, and the recommendation made in 2010 concerning strengthening women's representation within boards.

The Association Française de la Gestion Financière (AFG) is the French Asset Management Association which represents and promotes the interests of the French asset management industry. In 2011 it issued the ninth version of its recommendations on corporate governance, which constitute shareholder voting criteria for its members.

Lee and Yoo (2008) provide an interesting discussion about the competing rationales for corporate governance in France. Their analysis

> shows that both converging and diverging forces of institutional change coexist, shaping selective responses to globalization. While the adoption of the shareholder model is necessary for resource acquirement from the global capital markets, resource allocation in the cooperative innovation systems reinforces the stakeholder model. The French case confirms the sustainability of distinctive institutional complementarities, albeit with selective adaptation based on a sense-making social compromise.

Gomez (2011), when discussing corporate governance developments in France, highlights three areas that he feels will need to be tackled in coming years: the isolation of CEOs, CEO succession planning, and the effective role of shareholders. He highlights the growing importance of corporate governance in France such that 'the more a company is known to be influential in French society, the more the question of whether or not it is being well "governed" becomes publicly debated and receives media coverage'.

Italy

Bianchi et al. (2001) identify seven different company types in Italy. However, the main business forms are the *societa di persone*, or partnership, which generally has unlimited liability, and the *societa di capitali*, or limited liability companies. Furthermore, their analysis of direct ownership for both listed and unlisted companies in Italy finds that 'a major role is played by families, coalitions, the State and above all by other companies. The largest stake in listed and unlisted companies is held by other non-financial or holding companies. Contrary to other European countries, the amount held by financial institutions is limited' (p. 154). They do, however, comment that the situation is changing as pyramidal private groups are simplifying, and hence both banks and institutional investors are starting to play a more important role.

Italy has traditionally had a unitary board structure but a board of auditors is also required. However, the corporate governance situation in Italy has been subject to a number of revisions in recent years. In 1998 the then Director General of the Italian Treasury, Mario Draghi, introduced corporate governance rules, a series of legislative measures that became known as the Draghi Law. These rules enhanced transparency of listed companies, discussed the structure for decision-making within companies, and also looked at the area of internal control. Minority shareholders benefited from this legislation and it also strengthened the position of Italian companies with reference to the confidence with which they were perceived by international investors.

The Draghi Law also required the establishment of a board of auditors comprised of at least three individuals, all of whom should be independent of the company's directors and employees. Members of the board of auditors have to fulfill experience and other criteria. The role of the board of auditors includes reviewing the company's organizational structure, its internal control system, its accounting system, and its administrative system.

Table 10.6 Key characteristics influencing Italian corporate governance

Feature	Key characteristic
Main business form	Limited liability companies; partnerships
Predominant ownership structure	Non-financial/holding companies; families
Legal system	Civil law
Board structure	Unitary
Important aspect	Board of auditors required

In 1998 the Borsa Italiana introduced a corporate governance report that became known as the Preda Report, named after its chairman. The Preda Code of Conduct (1999) introduced recommendations regarding the composition of the board, the formation of key board committees, the roles of chairman and CEO, and the independence of directors. However, the code was a voluntary code and companies could disclose the extent to which they had adopted or complied with the code. It must be said that the code was not as comprehensive as, for example, the UK Combined Code. For example, it said that the majority of a company's remuneration committee members should be non-executive but it did not really talk about their independence. So, given the current climate where there is a lot of focus and emphasis on corporate governance, in 2002 a revised report, known as 'Preda 2' was issued. The Preda 2 report dealt with a number of areas relating to corporate governance, which are now looked at in more detail.

(i) Role of the board of directors

The Preda code identifies the role of the board of directors as, inter alia:

- to examine and approve the company's strategic operational and financial plans;
- to establish appropriate committees, which should report regularly to the board of directors;
- to consult with the board of auditors on the remuneration for directors recommended by the special committee (remuneration committee);
- to allocate the total amount to which the members of the board and the executive committee are entitled;
- to supervise the general performance of the company;
- to report to the shareholders at shareholders meetings.

The code defines the objective as creating value for the shareholders. The report mentions that the emphasis placed on shareholder value, apart from reflecting an internationally prevalent approach, is in conformity with Italian law, which sees the interest of the shareholders as the main point of reference for the directors.

The code emphasizes that it is important for listed companies to be governed by a board that meets at regular intervals and that has an efficient way of operating. The directors are expected to exercise independent judgement (regardless of whether they are executive or non-executive).

When directors accept a board appointment, they should do so on the basis that they have the requisite skills and knowledge, and that they can devote the appropriate amount of time to the directorship. They should also take into account how many other directorships they might actually have. Each year the annual report should publish details of other positions held by the directors on other boards of companies or as auditors of listed companies.

(ii) Composition of the board of directors

The board is made up of executive directors and non-executive directors, and the report emphasizes the role that non-executive directors can play. Normally, non-executive directors in Italy will outnumber the executive directors and the contribution that non-executive directors bring is in terms of their expertise of a general strategic or specific technical nature, which has been acquired outside the company. The other area where non-executive directors can be particularly helpful is where the interests of the executive directors and the shareholders might not coincide, and in that case, the non-executive directors can help to assess proposals with greater detachment.

(iii) Independent directors

There should be an adequate number of independent non-executive directors and the definition that is given in the code broadly encompasses the generally accepted definition of what an independent director is: for example, they should not be engaged in business relationships with the company or its subsidiaries, or with the executive directors or shareholders or group of shareholders who control the company in such a way as would influence their own judgement. They should not be immediate family members of the executive directors of the company. In terms of owning shares, they may own shares, but not such a quantity that would enable them to have control over the company or to exercise significant influence. A new provision, which is quite an interesting one, is that the directors' independence would be periodically assessed by the board on the basis of information provided. The results of that test of independence will then be communicated to the market. The presence of independent directors is recognized as one way of trying to represent the interest of all shareholders, whether majority or minority shareholders.

(iv) Chairman of the board of directors

The chairman is responsible for calling meetings of the board, ensuring the activities of the board are coordinated, and for chairing the meetings effectively and efficiently. The board may delegate power to the chairman and that should be disclosed in the annual report, i.e. which powers have actually been delegated. In Italy it is quite common that the chairman and managing director roles may be combined into one position or, alternatively, they may be separate positions with their own tasks.

(v) Information to be provided to the board of directors

The executive committee and managing directors should periodically report to the board of directors on activities performed in the exercise of their delegated powers; they are asked to provide the board of directors and the board of auditors with the same information.

(vi) Confidential information

The report emphasizes the confidentiality of information that directors receive in the performance of their work and asks them to comply with procedures for communicating such information to third parties, as appropriate. The code recommends the adoption of internal procedures so that the disclosure of transactions carried out by 'relevant persons' (insider dealings) is appropriately dealt with. Further, the code states that, if a nomination committee is established—which is one way of ensuring a transparent selection procedure— then that committee should be comprised of a majority of non-executive directors. Nomination committees will also be particularly appropriate where the shareholder base is quite diverse. Any proposals for potential directors should be accompanied by details of the personal traits and professional qualifications of the candidates, and this information should be deposited at the company's registered office at least ten days before the date fixed for the shareholders meeting or at the time the election lists, if provided for, are deposited.

(vii) Remuneration of directors

It is recommended that the board of directors form a remuneration committee that is comprised of the majority of non-executive directors. The remuneration committee would make recommendations to the board of directors regarding remuneration issues. It is also recommended that, of the total remuneration, a part should be linked to the company's profitability and maybe to the achievement of certain objectives. However, the Preda code does give companies a lot of flexibility in this area and states that it is really up to the board of directors acting on the remuneration committee's recommendations as to whether they do actually use systems of remuneration that are linked to results, which might include stock options, and setting the objectives for managing directors.

(viii) Internal control

The report recognizes the importance of internal controls and that the responsibility for an internal control system lies with the board of directors. The board of directors is therefore tasked with the duty of instituting a system of internal control and periodically checking that that system is functioning as expected. An internal control committee may be established and this would be made up of non-executive directors, the majority being independent. The head of internal audit may also head up the internal control system. It is important that the internal control system is monitored and that there are appropriate reports to enable any inadequacies to be remedied. The internal control committee would assess the proposals of audit firms (external auditors), and also report to the board of directors on its activity and the adequacy of the internal control system at least once every six months.

(ix) Transactions with related parties

Transactions with related parties should comply with criteria of substantial and procedural fairness and the board should be informed in detail of the existence, potential or actual, of the interest that has arisen. Any directors concerned with the related party transaction would have to leave the board meeting when the issue is actually being discussed.

(x) Relations with institutional investors and other shareholders

The chairman of the board of directors and the managing director should actively endeavour to develop a dialogue with shareholders and institutional investors based on recognition of their reciprocal roles. They might designate a person or create a corporate structure that would be responsible for this function, which would presumably be along the lines of an investor relations department. The report recognizes the importance of continuous communication with shareholders and that it is important to both present and prospective shareholders.

(xi) Shareholders' meetings

The report recognizes the importance of shareholders' meetings and believes that directors should encourage and facilitate as broad a participation in the meetings as possible. All directors should usually attend shareholders' meetings, which are seen as an opportunity to provide shareholders with information about the company. It is important that a procedure is set in place to ensure that the meeting is conducted in an orderly manner and effectively, and also to guarantee that each shareholder may speak on matters on the agenda, meaning that the rights of each shareholder are guaranteed.

(xii) Members of the board of auditors

Any proposals for appointment to the position of auditor should be accompanied by detailed information regarding the personal traits and professional qualifications of the candidates (a similar process to the appointment of the independent directors). The members of the board of auditors act autonomously with respect to shareholders, including those who elected them. In other words, they would represent the interest of the generality of shareholders rather than those who actually appointed them specifically. Any documents and information that come their way in the performance of their duties must be treated with confidentiality.

In 2006 Borsa Italiana issued a new corporate governance code to take account of changes in good governance practices internationally. Whilst the order of contents was similar to that of the 2002 code, the structure changed: principles were elaborated on with application criteria and comments, which helped to define the range of the principles and criteria, and also examples were given. New features included:

- the introduction of recommendations on the limit of roles held by each director and annual self-assessment by the board;
- the introduction of a lead independent director;

- recommendations on the internal control system;
- the promotion of initiatives to encourage shareholder participation in shareholders' meetings and the exercise of their rights.

In 2010 there was a revision to the article in the 2006 code relating to remuneration of directors and key management personnel, such that 'a significant part of the remuneration shall be linked to achieving specific performance objectives, possibly including non-economic objectives'. Moreover, in relation to non-executive directors, 'the remuneration of non-executive directors shall be proportionate to the commitment required from each of them, also taking into account their possible participation in one or more committees'. In December 2011 the *Corporate Governance Code* was substantially updated and now contains ten articles:

- Article 1—Role of the Board of Directors;
- Article 2—Composition of the Board of Directors;
- Article 3—Independent directors;
- Article 4—Internal committees of the Board of Directors;
- Article 5—Appointment of directors;
- Article 6—Remuneration of directors;
- Article 7—Internal control and risk management system;
- Article 8—Statutory auditors;
- Article 9—Relations with the shareholders;
- Article 10—Two tier and one-tier systems.

A significant legal change was introduced in April 2012 by Article 36 of Decree Law No. 201 of 6 December 2011, converted into Law No. 214/2011, in relation to the financial sector, which means that it is illegal for a person to hold more than one seat on a board in a financial institution operating in the same sector or market.

Melis (2006) provided an insightful discussion of the development of corporate governance in Italy, highlighting: the Draghi Law (1998) as a cornerstone with its explicit aim to strengthen minority shareholders' rights; the Preda Code of Conduct (1999, 2002), which has had a significant impact on the corporate governance structure of Italian listed companies; and the important innovation given by the 2004 company law reform, which gave companies the freedom to choose between three different board models. Portolano (2008) also cited the importance of this Italian corporate reform, which now provides for three different management models for Italian companies:

> the traditional model, which allows shareholders to appoint a board of directors with responsibility for managing the company and a panel of statutory auditors with responsibility for auditing the accounts and ensuring compliance with law; the German model, comprising a Board of Directors and a Supervisory Panel; and the Anglo-Saxon model, providing for a Board of Directors and an internal Audit Committee.

However, at that time only a very small number of companies had diverged from the traditional model.

Enriques (2009) provided an interesting discussion of corporate governance reforms in Italy. He believed that the corporate governance legal framework was much improved as a result of the reforms but felt that further changes could be made to improve the protection of investors against expropriation by corporate insiders. However, he also pointed out that changes to the legal and political cultures in Italy would help ensure the effectiveness of corporate governance reforms.

Melis and Gaia (2011) review developments in corporate governance in Italy and conclude that whilst the overall awareness of the importance of corporate governance has increased amongst senior managers, directors, and investors, Italian listed companies tend to 'whenever possible, avoid complying with "unfavourable" laws and/or recommendations and are prone to creative compliance, that is formal compliance, rather than to respect the spirit of recommendations (or law).'

Bianchi *et al.* (2011) state that nearly 86 per cent of Italian listed companies claim to be in formal compliance with the provisions of the Italian *Corporate Governance Code*. However, when they devise a governance indicator (CoRe) to try to assess the actual, or effective, levels of compliance with the Italian *Corporate Governance Code* in terms of listed companies' procedures for dealing with related party transactions (RPTs), they find that 'the companies' level of effective compliance with regard to RPTs is considerably lower than their publicly reported levels of formal compliance' and that 'higher levels of effective compliance tend to be found in companies where (1) minority shareholders have appointed one or more directors; (2) independent directors serve on important committees; and (3) there are significant holdings by institutional investors—particularly foreign investors—who participate in general shareholder meetings.'

Convergence or divergence

We have seen that the main differences in corporate governance codes amongst Continental European countries stem from companies law and securities regulation. The ownership structure varies across Continental European countries and those countries with a civil law/code tend to have poorer protection of minorities, which is not attractive for smaller shareholders or for those investing from overseas. Van den Berghe (2002) concludes that 'a serious tension is growing between capital markets, which are gradually globalising, and the economic and legal environments (like the company models involved, the governance recommendations and legal rules) that are still quite divergent. This gap creates pressure on firms that want to enter the capital market with structures and governance environments that are not up to the global standards of the capital markets' (p. 167). Gregory (2005) reviews the various developments in international corporate governance, highlighting both the commonalities and the remaining differences, which indicate that there is a move towards convergence, albeit gradual and incomplete. Solomon (2007) states that 'there is increasing evidence that corporate governance standardization at a global level is desirable, in order to increase cross-border institutional investment and to reduce cost of capital for multi-national companies'. Clarke (2007) believes that

as pressures to conform to international standards and expectations increase, the resilience of historical and cultural differences will continue. The business case for diversity is, if anything, even more compelling . . . However, an enduring lesson of the recent experience of corporate governance failure, is that it is in the interest of firms, investors and economies wherever they are based in the world, and whatever system they adopt, to commit to strive for the highest standards of governance.

More recently, Martynova and Renneboog (2010) in a study of a comprehensive comparative analysis of corporate governance regulatory systems and their evolution over the last fifteen years in thirty European countries and the US find that 'while varying degrees of creditor protection that were recently introduced in national bankruptcy laws show that the global convergence of legal systems towards a single system of corporate regulation is unlikely, there are still signs of increasing convergence by national corporate governance regulations towards a shareholder-based regime when the protection of (minority) shareholders is considered'.

Whilst recognizing that 'one size does not fit all' in terms of corporate governance, institutional investors are increasingly converging on the basic characteristics of good corporate governance, encompassing such areas as basic shareholder rights, independence of directors, and presence of key board committees. Therefore it is likely that, over time, there will be convergence on the fundamental aspects of good corporate governance, notwithstanding that ownership structures and legal systems may vary. The EU Corporate Governance Framework recommendations have implications for a more consistent approach to issues, such as boards and shareholders' rights across EU Member States and will continue to be a powerful force towards convergence on various aspects of corporate governance.

Conclusions

This chapter has shown how corporate governance has developed in a number of Continental European countries. Spurred by the development of capital markets, the influence of institutional investors, and a growing desire for more transparency and disclosure following various high-profile financial scandals across the globe, Continental Europe has responded by improving its corporate governance to provide increased disclosure and accountability. Although corporate ownership structures may differ across Europe, and some countries have a unitary board whilst others have a dual board, there does seem to be agreement on some of the fundamental aspects of corporate governance, which is leading towards a convergence of corporate governance in key areas.

Summary

- Corporate governance codes in Continental Europe have developed against a backdrop of varying legal and ownership structures. Whilst idiosyncratic features of countries influence the development of individual codes, there seems to be a consensus on certain key issues, for example, more transparency and disclosure, accountability of the board, and the independence of at least a portion of the directors.

- Most European countries have a unitary board structure, although the majority also have the option of a dual structure.

- Germany has a dual board structure and co-determination means that employees are represented on the supervisory board. Banks are quite influential in the German corporate governance system. The Cromme Code harmonized a wide variety of laws and regulations, and contained recommendations and suggestions for complying with international best practice on corporate governance. The amended Corporate Governance Code (2006) updates the earlier provisions of the Cromme Code, and subsequent amendments were made annually between 2007 and 2010.

- Denmark also has a dual board structure. Its ownership structure is unusual because there is widespread foundation ownership. The Nørby Code and subsequent updates made recommendations on corporate governance in Denmark and a 'comply or explain' approach is now followed.

- France has a predominantly unitary board system although the option to have a dual board exists. Building on the earlier Viénot reports, the Bouton Report recommended incremental improvements rather than any radical reform. AFEP and MEDEF produced a single set of corporate governance principles that drew together the earlier recommendations of Viénot and Bouton. France has some comprehensive recommendations regarding disclosure of social and environmental indicators.

- Italy has a unitary board structure but a board of auditors is also required. The Preda Codes (1 and 2) make recommendations regarding corporate governance. The Corporate Governance Code (2006) adapts the earlier principles in the light of international best practice in corporate governance. An updated Corporate Governance Code was issued in 2010 and legislation introduced in 2012 in relation to the financial sector which means that it is illegal for a person to hold more than one seat on a board in a financial institution operating in the same sector or market.

- There is much debate about whether corporate governance systems are converging or diverging. There does seem to be agreement on some of the fundamental characteristics of a sound corporate governance system, indicative of a move towards convergence. Developments such as the EU recommendations will play a key role in convergence on key aspects of corporate governance.

Example: Euro Disney, France

Many French companies have traditionally had poor disclosure of their corporate governance practices. This is changing gradually over time but good disclosure is still the exception rather than the rule. An example of good corporate governance practice and disclosure is Euro Disney.

Euro Disney is a young company. It was floated on the London, Brussels, and Paris bourses in 1989 and Disneyland Park opened in 1992. Euro Disney has attracted some 200 million visitors since opening. The Euro Disney website contains financial and other information in several languages. The corporate governance statement clarifies the governance structure of the company as being comprised of a management team and a supervisory board, the latter currently has nine members. The supervisory board has a Supervisory Board Members' Charter, which sets out the fundamental obligations that should be met. Some of the obligations in the Charter are innovative and go beyond the company's by-laws, such as requiring each board member to own at least some of the company's shares.

Euro Disney also publishes its *Corporate Responsibility (Community) Report* on the web and covers areas such as reducing waste and recycling; efforts to maintain clean air, land, and water; protecting flora and fauna; community relations; responsible development; and its employees. An example of good practice in relation to the employees, given in the 2010 Community Report, is that Euro Disney invests 4.14 per cent of annual payroll in training, equal to 300,000 hours of training. Disneyland Paris signed the Diversity Charter in 2009 in partnership with the organization IMS, Entreprendre pour la Cité and in 2010 received the Diversity Label Certificate from the AFNOR, which proves the company's commitment to the prevention of all types of discrimination, towards equal opportunity, and for the promotion of diversity.

Example: Telecom Italia, Italy

This is an example of an Italian company that has very good corporate governance practices and disclosures, and is recognized as one of the best in Italy.

Telecom Italia is heavily involved in most aspects of the telecommunications industry. The largest stake is owned by foreign institutional investors (38.37 per cent); the second largest stake (22.40 per cent) is owned by Telco S.p.A., whilst other Italian shareholders own 21.17 per cent, and Italian institutional investors own 11.47 per cent (all percentages as at 31 December 2010).

The website contains excellent information on the principles and codes that the company abides by and the *Self-Regulatory Code (2009)* is comprised of seventeen sections, including sections on the role, powers, and duties of the board of directors; composition of the board of directors; meetings of the board of directors; the chairman of the board of directors; Internal Control and Corporate Governance Committee; meetings of shareholders; and relations with shareholders. An annual corporate governance report is produced and contains a comprehensive review of Telecom Italia's corporate governance. For example, in 2010 the board of directors met nine times with the average duration of meetings being approximately 3.7 hours. The percentage of attendance was 92.43 per cent (95.55 per cent for independent directors). Telecom Italia's by-laws stipulate that the board of directors should comprise between seven and nineteen members; it is presently fifteen members with five of these being independent. Legislative Decree No. 27/2010 (implementing the so-called Shareholders' Rights Directive) led to the company's by-laws regulation governing the process of appointing the board of directors to be amended in 30 September 2010. Therefore the board of directors is appointed on the basis of slates presented by persons entitled to vote holding a total of at least 0.5 per cent of the ordinary share capital or such different proportion as required by Consob (this was set at 1 per cent for Telecom Italia). Telecom Italia's Corporate Governance Report 2010 explains that four-fifths of the directors to be elected are chosen from the slate that obtains more votes (the so-called Majority Slate) in the order they are listed on the slate; in the event of a fractional number, it shall be rounded down to the nearest whole number. The remaining directors are chosen from the other slates.

There is also detailed disclosure of directors' remuneration in the annual financial statements and in the annual corporate governance report. In addition, there is disclosure of other positions held by directors. Under Telecom Italia's *Self-Regulatory Code (2009)*, a director is not allowed to be a member of the board of directors or auditors of more than five companies other than companies that are directed or coordinated by Telecom Italia, or are Telecom Italia subsidiaries or affiliates, when the companies in question are listed and included in the S&P/MIB index and/or operate prevalently in the financial sector on a public basis and/or engage in banking or insurance. However, the limit is reduced to three for executive positions in such companies.

Mini case study: Siemens, Germany

The example of Siemens has been chosen as the company was rocked by a scandal in 2006/7. This case highlights the corporate governance structure as it is today, strengthened after the impact of the scandal a few years ago.

Siemens was founded in 1847 and is a global force in electrical engineering and electronics. The company has over 420,000 employees engaged in developing and manufacturing products, and designing and installing complex systems and projects worldwide.

In 2006 it came to light that a senior employee of Siemens had been involved in dubious payments to help secure business in several countries around the world. Siemens spent a significant amount of money dealing with the corruption scandal. Subsequently, Gerhard Cromme, who had chaired the Committee on Corporate Governance in Germany, became chairman of the supervisory board of Siemens. Compliance issues had been identified as a problem at Siemens during the time when the scandal was being perpetrated and so this area was strengthened with Gerhard Cromme stating that there should be zero tolerance of breaches of compliance procedures.

Siemens website has comprehensive information relating to its corporate governance, including the remuneration of the managing board and the supervisory board. Siemens has a two-tier governance structure with a supervisory board and a managing board. The supervisory board has twenty members—as stipulated by the German Co-determination Act, half of the members represent the company's shareholders, and half represent the company's employees—and six board committees: audit; compliance; mediation; finance and investment; nominating; and the chairman's committee. Gerhard Cromme chairs five of the committees and, although not chair of the audit committee, he is a member of it. He therefore has an excellent overview of the activities of the various committees. The managing board has ten members with the President and CEO being Peter Löscher.

The Compliance Committee comprises the chairman of the supervisory board (Gerhard Cromme), two of the supervisory board's shareholder representatives, and three of the supervisory board's employee representatives. The Compliance Committee meets at least four times a year and, where necessary, may call upon a wide range of people both within and outside the company to support its investigations.

Questions

The discussion questions to follow cover the key learning points of this chapter. Reading of some of the additional reference material will enhance the depth of the students' knowledge and understanding of these areas.

1. What factors have influenced the development of board structure in Continental European countries?

2. How might the employees' interests be represented in a company's corporate governance structure?

3. To what extent is there an emphasis on the role of non-executive directors in Continental European countries?

4. To what extent are the needs of various stakeholder groups satisfied by corporate governance structures in Continental Europe?

5. Critically discuss the case for a unitary board structure versus a dual board structure.

6. Critically discuss the extent to which you believe that corporate governance systems are converging or diverging. How might the global financial crisis have affected this?

References

AFEP and MEDEF (1999), *Report of the Committee on Corporate Governance (Viénot II)*, AFEP/MEDEF, Paris.

—— (2003), *The Corporate Governance of Listed Corporations*, AFEP/MEDEF, Paris.

—— (2008), *Corporate Governance Code of Listed Corporations*, AFEP/MEDEF, Paris.

—— (2010), *Corporate Governance Code of Listed Corporations*, AFEP/MEDEF, Paris.

AFG (2011), *Recommendations on Corporate Governance, January 2011*, AFG, Paris.

Article 36, Decree Law No. 201 (2011), *Tutela della concorrenza e partecipazioni personali incrociate nei mercati del credito e finanziari*, 6 December 2011, Italian Government, Italy.

Becht, M. and Mayer, C. (2001), 'Introduction' in F. Barca and M. Becht (eds), *The Control of Corporate Europe*, Oxford University Press, Oxford.

Bianchi, M., Bianco, M., and Enriques, L. (2001), 'Pyramidal Groups and the Separation Between Ownership and Control in Italy' in F. Barca and M. Becht (eds), *The Control of Corporate Europe*, Oxford University Press, Oxford.

—— Ciavarella A., Novembre V., and Signoretti R. (2011), 'Comply or Explain: Investor Protection Through the Italian Corporate Governance Code', *Journal of Applied Corporate Finance*, Vol. 23, Issue 1, pp. 107–21.

Bouton, D. (2002), *Promoting Better Corporate Governance in Listed Companies*, Report of the working group chaired by Daniel Bouton, AFEP/MEDEF, Paris.

Cadbury, Sir Adrian (1992), *Report of the Committee on the Financial Aspects of Corporate Governance*, Gee & Co. Ltd, London.

Charkham, J. (1994), *Keeping Good Company: A Study of Corporate Governance in Five Countries*, Oxford University Press, Oxford.

—— (2005), *Keeping Better Company: Corporate Governance Ten Years On*, Oxford University Press, Oxford.

Clarke, T. (2007), *International Corporate Governance: A Comparative Approach*, Routledge, London.

Conseil National du Patronat (CNPF) and AFEP (1995), *The Board of Directors of Listed Companies in France (Viénot I)*, CNPF/AFEP, Paris.

Corporate Governance Committee (2006), *Corporate Governance Code*, Borsa Italiana.

—— (2011), *Corporate Governance Code*, Borsa Italiana.

Cromme Code (2002), *Corporate Governance Code*, as contained in the Transparency and Disclosure Act German Government Commission.

—— (2005), *German Corporate Governance Code, as amended 2 June 2005*, Government Commission, Germany.

—— (2006), *German Corporate Governance Code, as amended 12 June 2006*, Government Commission, Germany.

—— (2007), *German Corporate Governance Code, as amended 14 June 2007*, Government Commission, Germany.

—— (2008), *German Corporate Governance Code, as amended 6 June 2008*, Government Commission, Germany.

—— (2009), *German Corporate Governance Code, as amended 18 June 2009*, Government Commission, Germany.

—— (2010), *German Corporate Governance Code, as amended 26 May 2010*, Government Commission, Germany.

DVCA (2008), *Active Ownership and Transparency in Private Equity Funds: Guidelines for Responsible Ownership and Good Corporate Governance*, DVCA, Copenhagen, Denmark.

Enriques, L. (2009), 'Modernizing Italy's Corporate Governance Institutions: Mission Accomplished?', ECGI–Law Working Paper No. 123/2009, available at SSRN: **http://ssrn.com/abstract=1400999**.

European Commission (2003), *Modernising Company Law and Enhancing Corporate Governance in the European Union*, European Commission, Brussels.

Franks, J. and Mayer, C. (1995), 'Ownership and Control', in H. Siebert (ed.), *Trends in Business Organization: Do Participation and Co-operation Increase Competitiveness?*, Mohr (Siebeck), Tubingen.

Goergen, M., Manjon, M., and Renneboog, L. (2008), 'Recent Developments in German Corporate Governance', *International Review of Law and Economics*, Vol. 28, No. 3.

Gomez, P-Y. (2011), 'From Colbert to Messier: Two Decades of Corporate Governance Reforms in France', in C.A. Mallin (ed.), *Handbook on International Corporate Governance, Country Analyses*, 2nd edition, Edward Elgar Publishing, Cheltenham.

Gregory, H. (2005), 'International Corporate Governance: A Gradual If Incomplete Convergence', in M.J. Epstein and K.O. Hanson (eds), *The Accountable Corporation*, Praeger Publishers, Westport, CA.

Gregory, H.J. and Simmelkjaer, R.T. (2002), *Comparative Study of Corporate Governance Codes Relevant to the European Union and Its Member States*, on behalf of the European Commission, Internal Market Directorate General, Weil Gotshal & Manges, New York, available at **http://europa.eu.int/comm/ internal_market/en/company/company/news/ corp-gov-codes-rpt_en.htm**

La Porta, F., Lopez de Silvanes, F., Shleifer, A., and Vishny, R. (1998), 'Law and Finance', *Journal of Political Economy*, Vol. 106, No. 6.

Lee, S.H. and Yoo, T. (2008), 'Competing Rationales for Corporate Governance in France: Institutional Complementarities between Financial Markets and Innovation Systems', *Corporate Governance: An International Review*, Vol. 16, No. 2.

Martynova, M. and Renneboog L., (2010), *A Corporate Governance Index: Convergence and Diversity of National Corporate Governance Regulations*, CentER Discussion Paper Series No. 2010-17; TILEC Discussion Paper No. 2010-012.

Melis, A. (2006), 'Corporate Governance Developments in Italy', in C.A. Mallin (ed.), *Handbook on International Corporate Governance, Country Analyses*, Edward Elgar Publishing, Cheltenham, UK.

—— and Gaia S. (2011), 'Corporate Governance in Italy: normative developments vs. actual practices', in C.A. Mallin (ed.), *Handbook on International Corporate Governance, Country Analyses*, 2nd edition, Edward Elgar Publishing, Cheltenham.

Nørby Committee (2001), *Recommendations for Good Corporate Governance in Denmark*.

—— (2003), *Report on Corporate Governance in Denmark–The Copenhagen Stock Exchange Committee on Corporate Governance*, Copenhagen Stock Exchange, Denmark.

—— (2005), *Revised Recommendations for Corporate Governance in Denmark–The Copenhagen Stock Exchange Committee on Corporate Governance*, Copenhagen Stock Exchange, Denmark.

—— (2008), *Committee on Corporate Governance's Recommendations for Corporate Governance of August 15, 2005; section VI revised by February 6, 2008; sections III and V revised by December 10, 2008*, Copenhagen Stock Exchange, Denmark.

—— (2010), *Committee on Corporate Governance's Recommendations on Corporate Governance, April 2010*, Copenhagen Stock Exchange, Denmark.

—— (2011), *Committee on Corporate Governance's Recommendations on Corporate Governance, August 2011*, Copenhagen Stock Exchange, Denmark.

Odenius, J. (2008), *Germany's Corporate Governance Reforms: Has the System Become Flexible Enough?*, IMF Working Papers, No. 8/179, available at SSRN: **http://ssrn.com/abstract=1266512**

OECD (1999), *Principles of Corporate Governance*, OECD, Paris.

—— (2004), *Principles of Corporate Governance*, OECD, Paris.

Portolano, F. (2008), 'An Imported Model of Governance', *Governance*, August 2008, Issue No. 178, Governance Publishing, Somerset.

Preda (2002), *Self Regulatory Code*, Committee for the Corporate Governance of Listed Companies, Borsa Italiana, Milan.

Prigge, S. (1998), 'A Survey of German Corporate Governance', in K.J. Hopt, H. Kanda, M.J. Roe, E. Wymeersch, and S. Prigge (eds), *Comparative Corporate Governance: The State of the Art and Emerging Research*, Oxford University Press, Oxford.

Solomon (2007), *Corporate Governance and Accountability*, John Wiley & Sons Ltd, Chichester.

v. Werder A. and Talaulicar T. (2011), 'Corporate Governance in Germany: Basic Characteristics, Recent Developments and Future Perspectives', in C.A. Mallin (ed.), *Handbook on International Corporate Governance, Country Analyses*, 2nd edition, Edward Elgar Publishing, Cheltenham.

Van den Berghe, L. (2002), *Corporate Governance in a Globalising World: Convergence or Divergence? A European Perspective*, Kluwer Academic Publishers, Amsterdam.

Wymeersch, E. (1998), 'A Status Report on Corporate Governance in Some Continental European States', in K.J. Hopt, H. Kanda, M.J. Roe, E. Wymeersch, and S. Prigge (eds), *Comparative Corporate Governance: The State of the Art and Emerging Research*, Oxford University Press, Oxford.

Useful websites

www.afg.asso.fr The website for the Association Française de la Gestion Financière (the French Asset Management Association) which represents and promotes the interests of the French asset management industry.

www.borsaitaliana.it The website of the Italian Stock Exchange, Borsa Italia, contains information about corporate governance in Italy.

www.corporategovernance.dk This website contains the Nørby Committee Report on Corporate Governance in Denmark.

www.corporate-governance-code.de The German Code of Corporate Governance can be downloaded from this website.

www.dvca.dk The website of the Danish Venture Capital and Private Equity Association, which is a member association for a broad range of high technological investors in Denmark.

www.ecgi.org The website of the European Corporate Governance Institute has comprehensive information about corporate governance, including downloadable codes/guidelines for most countries.

www.icgn.org The website of the International Corporate Governance Network contains information relating to corporate governance issues globally.

www.oecd.org The website of the Organisation for Economic Co-operation and Development has information about various corporate governance guidelines.

 For further links to useful sources of information visit the Online Resource Centre **www.oxfordtextbooks.co.uk/orc/mallin4e/**

 FT Clippings

FT: Italy groups' cross-holdings in spotlight

By Rachel Sanderson

April 26, 2012

During the annual results season in Italy, onlookers in Milan's tiny business district are treated to a spectacle.

A dozen or so black limousines drive the cobbled streets disgorging the same group of immaculately suited men at one headquarters and then another as they take their seats on the boards of the country's most powerful banks and companies.

It is a scene that has dominated Italian corporate culture since the post-war period, when a group of bankers and businessmen decided to link themselves through cross-shareholdings to defend themselves from outsiders and help each other grow. But as of this week the spectacle is about to change.

As the sovereign crisis has roiled Italian bonds, share prices and bank balance sheets, Italy's most senior leaders, from Mario Draghi, head of the European Central Bank, to Mario Monti, the technocratic prime minister, have come to question the relevance of an arcane power structure that by its very nature is all tied up in Italy.

This week a ban, imposed by Mr Monti and upheld by the Bank of Italy, comes into force that makes it illegal for the same person to hold more than one board seat in a financial institution operating in the same sector or market.

Alberto Gallo, head of European credit strategy at RBS, believes it "is a positive step in the right direction" to help bring the country back on the road to financial stability and growth.

However, Mr Gallo points out the shake-up needs to be followed by more sweeping change "to disentangle banks from their intricate web of equity and debt cross-holdings, which leave the way open to contagion risk".

Analysts estimate the reform—which some are calling one of the biggest shake-ups in corporate Italy in 60 years—will affect board seats in 1,500 companies.

However, attention is focused on some of Italy's largest financial institutions—UniCredit, the largest bank by assets; Generali, its largest insurer; and Mediobanca, a Milanese investment bank that sits at the so-called centre of Italy's "galaxy of power".

Mediobanca owns 13 per cent of Generali, while UniCredit owns 9 per cent of Mediobanca. All three groups are also linked to other companies including Telecom Italia, Pirelli and RCS Mediagroup, across an almost impenetrable web of relationships and minority stakes.

The Milanese investment bank, which sits headquartered behind the La Scala opera house in an elaborate cloistered palazzo, highlights how the cross-shareholdings business model is already starting to look outdated.

Under its chief executive Alberto Nagel, 47, and chairman Renato Pagliaro, 55, Mediobanca has undertaken some reform to diversify away from its cross-shareholdings by building a retail bank and developing an investment banking business not so reliant on Italy.

It has also introduced age limits for board members, a significant break with tradition in gerontocratic Italy.

However, the sovereign crisis and Italy's return to recession has put strain on a balance sheet weighed down by the value of its cross-shareholdings.

Mediobanca's long-envied links with Italian companies make it the country's most prolific dealmaker. But after a decade of stagnant Italian economic growth, being the banker to Italy risks being as much a liability as a boon.

Its shares have fallen 40 per cent in the past six months partly because of concern about the financial impact from its cross-shareholding. This is more than the 11 per cent fall at Intesa Sanpaolo, Italy's second largest bank by assets, which holds €60bn in Italian sovereign debt, the highest of any institution.

Academic studies have repeatedly shown the cross-shareholdings do a disservice to minority investors, instead allowing core investors who sit on one another's boards to "expropriate" funds by obtaining access to finance beyond their credit means as a result of their close relationships.

Cheuvreux analyst Atanasio Pantarrotas says while he considers Mediobanca's banking business to be more resilient than other domestic operators, "we are concerned about its holdings in Italian financial institutions".

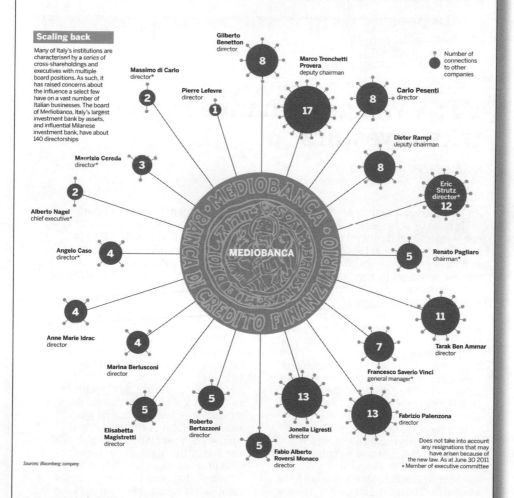

Figure 10.1 Mediobanca

Chief among them is its €2.8bn stake in Generali. But it also forecast to have to write down €120m on its exposure to Telco, a holding company linked to Telecom Italia, another strategic shareholding.

Meanwhile, analysts predict its failure to recoup its €1bn in debts from a smaller financially struggling insurance company, Fondiaria-SAI—a long-time client owned by a board member of Mediobanca—could force Mr Nagel to undertake a capital increase.

At Generali, management has ruled out a capital increase, but analysts say it remains a possibility as the insurer's balance sheet is hit by volatile equity markets and €50bn of exposure to Italian sovereign debt.

Should that come to pass, Mr Pantarrotas says it will "increase the concentration risk and put additional pressure on Mediobanca's capital ratios under Basel III framework".

Analysts and bankers predict that such financial stress—which the cross-shareholdings were initially intended to defend against—may well prove the impetus to inhabitants of Italy's "galaxy of power" to take Mr Monti's reform to its logical conclusion and start to loosen their stakes in one another.

FT: VW's governance regime irks investors

By Chris Bryant in Frankfurt

April 18, 2012

As Volkswagen's shareholders tuck into their plate of sausages at the German company's annual general meeting today some may reflect that they have an almost negligible say in how the world's biggest carmaker by revenues is run.

The influence of VW's patriarchal chairman, other Porsche family members, a local government anchor shareholder and a powerful labour force have long marked the company out as an oddity in terms of governance.

Chief among this clique is Ferdinand Piëch, supervisory chairman and the grandson of the creator of the VW Beetle, who celebrated his 75th birthday on Tuesday.

In spite of his advancing years and a recent Stuttgart court ruling (which is being appealed) that said he failed to meet his duty of care as a supervisory board member at Porsche, Mr Piëch is set to be elected on Thursday for another five-year turn as chairman. Nothing of importance happens at VW without his say-so.

For instance, VW's Audi brand announced on Wednesday that it would acquire Ducati, the luxury Italian motorcycle manufacturer. Mr Piëch adores the brand—yet analysts say it is a trophy asset that serves little strategic purpose for cash-rich VW.

Mr Piëch's wife, Ursula, whose skills are listed in a letter to shareholders as "kindergarten teacher with additional qualifications in business and law" is set to join him on the supervisory board following a shareholder vote on Thursday.

Martin Winterkorn, Mr Piëch's loyal acolyte as VW chief executive, also has grounds to celebrate after he was awarded €16.6m in annual pay and bonuses last year, all of it in cash. This was one of the highest ever payouts to a CEO of a German blue-chip company.

"What's happened in the last couple of months has been a dose of reality for investors," says Max Warbuton at Bernstein Research.

People close to VW argue that investors have few grounds for complaint. Pre-tax profits at VW more than doubled last year to €18.9bn and revenues surged to €159.3bn.

VW's share price has more than doubled since the beginning of 2010, far outperforming the blue-chip German Dax index, and shareholders are set to be rewarded this year with a healthy dividend increase.

Under Hans Dieter Pötsch, chief financial officer, VW's transparency, communication with the capital market and reputation for financial discipline is also much improved.

Yet some shareholder representatives and advisors argue that the company's alleged neglect of standard corporate governance standards could yet be its undoing.

"The concern with VW is that the corporate governance mechanisms that should be in place at a well-managed company are simply not there," says Alexander Juschus at Ivox, a German group that advises shareholders on voting at annual meetings.

Critics point to the recent history of Porsche, which reaped huge profits before almost falling into bankruptcy due to a failed attempt to acquire the much larger VW.

"The near collapse of Porsche is instructive in how weak corporate governance can cause problems," says Henning Gebhardt, head of European equities at DWS, a German institutional investor. "So long as VW continues to do well, it isn't a problem, but it could be if VW encountered difficulties again in the future." One of free-float investors' biggest concerns is that soon there may be nobody at VW to defend their interests. Mrs Piëch is set to replace Michael Frenzel, chief executive of German travel company Tui, on VW's 20-member supervisory board, bringing the total number of Porsche and Piëch-family board members to five.

Ivox has indicated to its members that they should vote against her appointment but her election is a near certainty, because of the shareholding structure. "We have issues with her qualifications. The nomination fosters diversity but the aim is to foster qualified diversity, not just diversity," says Mr Juschus.

Several prominent German corporate leaders have left VW's board in recent years, among them Gerhard Cromme, supervisory board chairman at Siemens and ThyssenKrupp. Mr Cromme was the father of Germany's corporate governance code but quit VW in 2006 after expressing his displeasure at the state of governance.

Annika Falkengren, chief executive of Swedish bank SEB, is therefore set to remain the sole independent member of the non-executive board.

"Even if you're successful . . . you need to ensure that there are still some people on the supervisory board who are willing and ready to speak up and say something critical if needs be," says Hans Hirt, head of corporate governance at Hermes Equity Ownership Services, a shareholder advisory group. Mr Hirt wrote an open letter to VW management this week upbraiding the company on its governance. "The few independent heavy hitters have left the company," he told the FT.

Mr Hirt is also critical of Mr Winterkorn's large pay: "What we would regard as appropriate is what is necessary to keep the person in the job and motivated," he says. "But I don't think it's realistic to assume that Mr Winterkorn would accept an offer from Ford any time soon. From our perspective, this amount is very questionable." VW's management and supevisory board declared in February that they were fully compliant with Germany's corporate governance code, save for certain provisions on capping severance pay and regulating the age limit of board members. "A rigid retirement age does not appear to be appropriate," VW says. As he presides over VW's AGM today, Mr Piëch will doubtless be grateful.

11

Corporate Governance in Central and Eastern Europe

 Learning Objectives

- To understand the implications of the privatization process for ownership structure in countries moving towards a market economy

- To be aware of the effect on the development of corporate governance of different privatization processes

- To have a detailed knowledge of the corporate governance systems in several Central and Eastern European countries

Introduction

More than twenty years have now passed since the Union of Soviet Socialist Republics (USSR) began to dissolve into constituent countries. The move from a command economy to a market economy is not an easy one and the countries that comprised the former USSR have achieved this transition with varying degrees of success. In general, the companies have moved from a situation where, as state-owned enterprises, they were most probably not expected to make a profit because the objective of the business was not really defined in those terms, but rather in terms of socialist goals such as full employment. This meant that, very often, the companies were highly inefficient: often using old machinery, having too large a workforce to be justified, and access to funds from the Central Bank without having to produce any repayment plans.

The success of the various countries can often be linked to the type of privatization that was followed to take businesses from state-owned enterprises to joint stock companies to public corporations. It is important to note that, in some countries, the term 'joint stock company' describes a company that has share capital which is traded on the stock exchange (essentially a public company); in other countries, the term may refer to a stage in the privatization process whereby a state-owned enterprise issues share capital to become a joint stock company, but that share capital is owned by the state with the next stage in the process being to sell the shares on to the public so that the company becomes a public corporation.

In general, there are three types of privatization process: the first is a mass privatization model, state-owned assets being distributed free of charge to the general public through vouchers that can be traded for ownership shares in state-owned firms. This model is sometimes referred to as the 'voucher privatization method' and was used in the Czech Republic and Russia. The second model allowed management and employees to buy company assets. This method was the method adopted in Poland. The third model, and arguably the one that produced the most successful results, involved selling majority control to an outside investor. The outside investor was often a foreign investor and this tended to lead first to higher expectations of the companies in which they invested and, secondly, generally better corporate governance in the companies that these outside investors bought into. This third method was followed in Hungary and Estonia.

In this chapter, we will look at four countries: the Czech Republic, Poland, Russia, and Hungary. We will look at the process of privatization that each of these countries followed and the framework for corporate governance that exists in these countries. There is clearly a link between the method of privatization used, the resultant ownership structure, and the degree or level of corporate governance that is being adopted. The method of privatization has tended to have more of an immediate impact on the development of corporate governance than the legal framework in these countries. Whilst the legal framework has been based on a command economy with state-owned enterprises, as the owners of the privatized industries find their voice, it can be expected that they will push for improved corporate governance, including better protection of minority rights. As Coffee (2002) points out:

> the more plausible explanation is that economic changes have produced regulatory changes, rather than the reverse . . . Mass privatization came overnight to the Czech Republic, and its securities market soon crashed, at least in part because of the absence of investor protections. Only then, several years later, were statutory reforms adopted to protect minority shareholders. Pistor (2000) has generalized that the same responsive reaction of law to economic change has characterized the adoption of common law reforms by transitional economies.

Privatization process and its implications

Boeri and Perasso (1998), in a study of the Czech Republic, Hungary, Poland, and Russia, highlight the effects of each of the three privatization methods on a number of outcomes. They outline the outcomes, or performance indicators, as:

> the *speed* of privatization, that is, the proportion of former state enterprises which has changed ownership within the first four years of the privatization process, the relevance of *outside ownership* (percentage of privatized enterprises with dominant outside ownership) in the resulting ownership structure of firms, and finally, the degree of *control* exerted over managerial decisions by the owners of the firm. The latter indicator is proxied by the involvement in privatization of foreign and domestic companies.

They find that the Czech Republic's speed of privatization was very rapid, resulting in significant outside ownership, but a rather weak control structure. Hungary's privatization process was less rapid but resulted in a stronger control structure and more outside ownership. Poland's process was slower but achieved a reasonable level of outside ownership and control, whilst Russia's privatization process was quite rapid but resulted in much less outside control and a poor control structure, given the initial concentration of ownership into the hands of insiders.

Table 11.1 Ownership structures of companies in selected transition countries (unweighted)

No. of companies	Czech Republic	Hungary	Poland	Romania	Russia	Ukraine
	%	%	%	%	%	%
Insiders	3	11	10	15	40	45
State	51	53	26	46	8	21
Outsiders	46	29	55	39	45	28
Individuals/families	6	8	31	20	40	22
Institutional outsiders	40	21	24	20	5	6
Others/no answer	0	7	9	0	7	6
Number of enterprises	35	38	84	41	214	87

Source: EBRD/World Bank Business Environment Survey 1999 (only medium-sized and larger companies with more than 100 employees are included here)

Looking in more detail at the ownership structure of a sample of Central and Eastern European (CEE) countries, Table 11.1 shows the dominant owners of companies in selected transition countries. The broad categories of owners are insider owners (managers and workers), outsider owners (individuals and families, and institutional outsiders such as investment funds and banks), and the state. It can be seen that the dominant owners vary across the transition countries, with the state still influential; outsiders are also influential, either in the form of individuals/families, or as institutional outsiders. It should be remembered that the privatization process will have been instrumental in determining the basic ownership structure in each of the countries, but that the data in Table 11.1 is based on a 1999 survey, several years after the initial privatization processes in each country. Nonetheless, the influence of the different privatization processes on ownership structure is still very much in evidence as, for example, in Russia, where insider ownership still retains a lot of influence.

Berglof and Pajuste (2003) highlight the fact that whilst the level of state ownership differs across countries in CEE, private ownership is becoming more dominant, with ownership being increasingly concentrated. Strong insider ownership and control, combined with poor protection of minority shareholders, makes companies less attractive to foreign investors and minority shareholders.

Aguilera *et al.* (2012) examine whether, over time, there have been significant changes in the patterns of corporate ownership amongst publicly traded firms in emerging markets, including the Czech Republic, Hungary, and Poland. Considering the period 2004–08 for CEE countries, they find that the Czech Republic has the highest remaining government ownership, that Hungary's foreign ownership is most prominent, and that Poland has relatively less concentrated ownership compared to the Czech Republic and Hungary. In their conclusions they point out that joining the EU 'triggered the impulse for the transfer of ownership from state to private hands, with the immediate consequence of large entry of foreign direct investments and its related foreign ownership of publicly traded firms'.

The Czech Republic

As discussed earlier, the Czech Republic used the voucher privatization method to privatize state-owned enterprises. Coffee (1998) details how the voucher system entitled each Czechoslovak adult to purchase a booklet of 1,000 voucher points for a cost equating to about 25 per cent of the average monthly wage at the end of 1991. For the second privatization wave in 1993/4, the price was raised by a modest amount but, by then, this accounted for less than 18 per cent of the average monthly wage. By the end of the second privatization wave, Coffee (1998) notes that 'over 80 per cent of adult Czech citizens had become shareholders in the 1849 companies that were privatized (in whole or in part)'.

The investment privatization funds (IPFs) were established shortly after the first privatization wave and bought the vouchers from individual citizens. The Czech government legislated to ensure that IPFs appointed a bank as their depository and deposited all securities and funds with it; IPFs were also required to appoint managing and supervisory boards. However, substantial holdings were still controlled by the state via the National Property Fund (NPF), which contained holdings awaiting sale, and holdings of strategic companies that may be sold at some point, such as utilities. The NPF also exercised influence via the IPFs. As Boeri and Perasso (1998) point out: 'The largest IPFs are controlled by banks, especially the big four banks, whose main shareholder, but not majority except in one case, is the state, via NPF'. Claessens et al. (1997) show that at the end of 1995, the top five IPFs owned, on average, just under 49 per cent of a firm privatized in the first wave and just under 41 per cent of a firm privatized in the second wave.

Unfortunately, the Czech voucher privatization process led to two significant shortcomings post-privatization: one was a high level of cross-ownership, resulting in a consolidation of control in the Czech banking sector; the other was the situation where, although many individuals held shares as a result of the voucher system, they formed a minority interest that had no effective legal protection. This lack of legal protection and a downturn in the Czech Republic stock market led overseas institutional investors to sell their shares and leave the market. An improved corporate governance system was seen as one way to try to ensure that foreign investment was lured back to invest in the Czech Republic.

From 1 January 2001, an extensive package of changes was introduced into the Czech Republic. These changes involved the Commercial Code, the Securities Act, and the Auditing Act. Many of the changes altered the responsibilities and rights of companies,

Table 11.2 Key characteristics influencing corporate governance in the Czech Republic

Feature	Key characteristic
Privatization method	Mass privatization via voucher
Predominant ownership structure	State; institutional outsiders (investment funds and banks)
Legal system	Civil law
Board structure	Dual
Important aspect	Influence of IPFs

board members, shareholders, and auditors, and so they were fairly wide ranging and far reaching.

The Revised Corporate Governance Code (2001), hereinafter 'the Code', set out corporate governance best practice for companies in the Czech Republic and was based on the Organisation for Economic Co-operation and Development (OECD) Principles, but reference was also made to other codes, including the Combined Code of the London Stock Exchange. The focus was on transparency and accountability because these elements are essential to encourage investor confidence. The Prague Stock Exchange recommended that companies adopted as many of the Code's provisions as they could straight away, and then explained in their annual report why they were not adopting other provisions and when they anticipated being able to do so. Additionally, it encouraged all companies listed on the second market to do the same.

The Code stated that the principles on which it was based are those of openness, integrity, and accountability, and that acceptance of these concepts would do much to remove some of the more unethical behaviour and practices prevalent in various parts of the Czech business world, and so restore an environment conducive to both strategic and portfolio investment. The Code recognized that 'good corporate governance is particularly important in the Czech Republic and other transition countries where there was no long term, continuous experience of non-state ownership of companies and the associated corporate practices'. Good corporate governance provides a framework for setting corporate objectives, and monitoring the progress towards achieving those objectives.

As in other countries around the globe, the observance and adoption of good corporate governance is an increasingly important factor for attracting investment in the Czech Republic, and much was needed to be done to rebuild the confidence of investors, because many investors had lost substantial amounts due to poor management practices, and to address the lack of investor protection, particularly of minority interests.

An important aspect of the revised Code was the emphasis on shareholder value, with the corporate governance principles contained in the Code being based on the acceptance of the improvement of shareholder value as the corporate objective.

The main provisions of the Code are now looked at in detail.

(i) 'The Company should be headed by an effective board of directors and supervisory board which should lead it and account to the shareholders. The board of directors should meet no less than once each month and the supervisory board should meet no less than ten times each year'

This part of the report covered various aspects relating to the boards. All members of the board of directors and supervisory board members are expected to bring an independent judgement to bear on issues of strategy, performance, and resources. There should be an appropriate and timely flow of information between the two boards.

There is an emphasis on independent non-executive directors. The Code stated that the supervisory board should include members of sufficient calibre and number for their views to carry significant weight. Not less than 25 per cent of the members of the supervisory board should be independent of management and free from any business or other relationship, whether with the majority shareholders or the company, which could materially interfere with the exercise of their independent judgement. Members of the supervisory board considered to be independent should be identified in the annual report. A decision to combine the role of general director and chairman of the board of directors should be explained. In either case, whether the posts are held by different people or by the same person, there should be a strong and independent non-executive element on the board, with a recognized senior member other than the chairman. These individuals should be identified in the annual report.

Companies should establish three committees, with a majority of independent members, responsible for the independent audit of the company and the remuneration (including other financial incentives) and nomination of directors and key executives.

Members of the supervisory board should be appointed by the annual general meeting (AGM) for specified terms and reappointment should not be automatic: members should be subject to re-election at intervals of no more than five years. Shareholders should be invited, specifically at the AGM, to approve all new long-term incentive schemes (including share option schemes), whether payable in cash, in kind, or shares in which members of the executive or supervisory board and senior executives will participate (as detailed in section 66, paras 2 and 3, of the Commercial Code).

This section of the Code also contains provisions that may help the members of the boards to be more competent in their job. These provisions include: members of the board of directors and the supervisory board should be able to take independent professional advice if necessary, in the context of their corporate duties, at the company's expense; they should also have access to the advice and services of the company lawyer; and they should be given appropriate training on first being appointed to the executive or supervisory board.

(ii) 'The Company should protect shareholders' rights'

Companies should make sure that there is a secure method of ownership registration, and that registered shares can be conveyed or transferred efficiently.

This part of the Code also included the recommendation that companies should inform shareholders of the date, time, and location of the AGM and provide them with appropriate information relating to agenda items. The Code emphasized that there should be early disclosure of the data on dividend and coupon payments. Companies should include a specific agenda item providing for shareholders to ask questions of the directors. Questions may be submitted in advance and there should be enough time allowed for full discussion. In the general meeting, the shareholders will elect the members of both the board of directors and the supervisory board (unlike the German model, in which the shareholders in general meeting elect the supervisory board members only).

The Code discussed the importance of voting, and stated that shareholders should be able to vote in person or in absentia (by proxy), and encouraged companies to use modern technology, such as electronic communications and electronic voting (pending the introduction of a new law sanctioning the latter), to enable as many shareholders as possible to participate. The use of electronic media would be particularly beneficial for overseas investors.

(iii) 'The Company should ensure disclosure of all capital structures and any arrangements that enable certain shareholders to obtain a degree of control disproportionate to their equity ownership. Some capital structures allow a shareholder to exercise a degree of control over the company disproportionate to the shareholders' equity ownership in the company'

The Code cited as an example cases of foreign direct investment through privatization or joint ventures, where shareholder agreements give high levels of control to the foreign shareholder. The important thing is that there is full disclosure of such arrangements.

(iv) 'The Company should ensure that all shareholders, including minorities and foreign shareholders, are treated equitably'

This principle is important to all shareholders but particularly overseas investors who are seeking assurances that they will be treated equitably. All shareholders of the same class should be treated equally: for example, within any class, all shareholders should have the same voting rights.

Members of the board and managers should be required to disclose any material interests in transactions or matters affecting the company; insider trading and abusive self-dealing should be prohibited.

Companies were encouraged to develop good relationships with their shareholders. In this context, the company's general meeting was seen as a good opportunity to develop investor relations with investors. The Code set out a 'protocol' for the general meeting, which included companies:

- arranging for the notice of the general meeting and related papers to be sent to shareholders at least 30 working days before the meeting;
- proposing a separate resolution at the general meeting on each substantially separate issue and allowing reasonable time for the discussion of each resolution;
- counting all proxy votes and announcing the proxy count on each resolution;
- arranging for the chairmen of the audit, remuneration, and nomination committees to be available to answer questions at the general meeting.

(v) 'The Company should ensure that timely and accurate disclosure is made on all material matters regarding the company, including the financial situation, performance, ownership, and governance of the company. In particular the company should observe the standards of best practice issued by the Czech Securities Commission on the contents of the annual report, half-year report and ongoing disclosure requirements'

There should be disclosure of appropriate information to enable shareholders to make decisions and assessments in relation to their investment, and to enable them to exercise their voting rights. The information should include information about: the financial and operating results of the company; the company objectives; the ownership structure of the company including:

- disclosure of major shareholders; the individual board members and key executives, and their remuneration;
- material foreseeable risk factors such as industry-specific or geographical risks and financial market risks;
- material issues regarding employees and other stakeholders.

The channels for disseminating information should provide for fair, timely, and cost-efficient access to relevant information by users, and includes the use of electronic media.

Companies were also encouraged to report on how they apply relevant corporate governance principles in practice. The board is accountable to the shareholders and should ensure that there is a proper system of internal controls and auditing procedures.

(vi) 'The board of directors should undertake all key functions in the management of the company and the supervisory board should effectively supervise such functions'

The key functions of the board include setting and reviewing corporate strategy, monitoring corporate performance, reviewing board remuneration, monitoring and managing potential conflicts of interest, ensuring the integrity of the company's accounting systems, and overseeing the process of disclosure and communications.

The Code highlighted a situation in many companies where the supervisory board and the board of directors each meet only once or twice a year, and delegate the direction of the company to a general manager who appoints his/her own management board. The Code highlighted that this is unacceptable because the general manager is an employee without official directorial responsibilities and hence not accountable to shareholders. As an interim step, the Code suggested that the general manager must be a member of the board of directors but that, within three years, companies should adopt 'a more usual structure'.

The Code stated that the corporate governance framework should ensure the strategic guidance of the company, the effective monitoring of management by the board of directors, and the board of directors' accountability to the supervisory board, company, and the shareholders. Members of both boards should act in good faith with due diligence and care, in the best interests of the company and shareholders. The Code also mentioned that both boards should consider the interests of the wider stakeholder group including employees, creditors, customers, suppliers, and local communities.

(vii) 'Institutional shareholders should act responsibly in their dealings with the company'

As with the rest of the Code, the section on institutional investors seemed to reflect what was essentially internationally recognized best practice. It is recommended that institutional investors may have a constructive dialogue with the companies in which they invest, that they should make considered use of their votes, and that they should disclose their own policies with respect to the companies in which they invest. Institutional shareholders should also, if requested, make available to their clients information on the proportion of resolutions on which votes were cast and non-discretionary proxies lodged.

(viii) 'Shareholders should have certain rights and exercise certain responsibilities in connection with the company'

This section of the Code emphasized the fact that shareholders will have more confidence in investing if there is a mechanism to ensure that they have effective redress for violation of their rights. In addition, shareholders are reminded that they have responsibilities, such as attending general meetings and voting their shares, as well as rights.

(ix) 'The role of stakeholders in corporate governance'

The role of stakeholders is recognized in this part of the Code, which stated 'the corporate governance framework should recognise the rights of stakeholders as established by law and encourage active co-operation between companies and stakeholders in creating wealth, jobs, and the sustainability of financially sound companies'. The Code cited various mechanisms that enable stakeholder participation, including employee representation on boards and employee stock ownership plans.

The Czech Code (2001) was fairly comprehensive and adoption of the recommendations by Czech companies should have helped to restore investor confidence, both that of domestic investors and also foreign investors.

However, when the revised OECD Principles were published in 2004, the Czech Securities Commission decided to update its corporate governance code as well, and in June 2004, the Czech Securities Commission issued the *Corporate Governance Code based on the OECD Principles (2004)*. The majority of the ideas contained in the 2001 Code discussed earlier were retained, however, the working group of the Securities Commission decided to follow the structure as well as the content of the OECD Principles (2004). By mapping the content and structure of the OECD Principles so closely, it was felt that this would lead to easier communication about the corporate governance of the Czech Republic with organizations such as the World Bank and with those that are familiar with the OECD Principles. Also, given various developments in corporate governance and in capital markets generally, such as the EU Action Plan discussed earlier, it was felt appropriate to update the Code. One such development relates to the European Commission's decision to leave European companies with a choice of either the unitary board or dual board structure. Where the Code (2001) tended to prefer the unitary board structure (Anglo-Saxon model), the Code (2004) leaves it up to companies as to whether they choose a dual board (German style) or unitary board (Anglo-Saxon). The Code (2004) also places more emphasis on the independence of board members.

As mentioned, the revised Czech Code (2004) mirrors both structure and content of the OECD Principles (2004) (for the detail of the OECD Principles (2004), please see Chapter 3). However, it is useful to highlight some of the additions to the revised Czech Code (2004), which include:

- the exercise of shareholders' rights should be facilitated, including participation in key corporate governance decisions, such as nomination and election of board members;
- institutional investors acting in a fiduciary capacity should disclose their corporate governance and voting policies;
- amendment to the Commercial Code to permit distance voting by electronic means;

- minority shareholders must be protected from abusive actions by, or in the interest of, controlling shareholders and should have effective means of redress;

- members of the board of directors, supervisory board, and key executives are required to disclose to the board if they have a material interest in a transaction or matter affecting the corporation;

- the rights of stakeholders, whether established in law or through mutual agreements, must be respected;

- the development of performance-enhancing mechanisms for employee participation must be allowed;

- stakeholders, including employees and their representative bodies, must be able freely to communicate their concerns about illegal or unethical practices to the supervisory board without their rights being compromised;

- the corporate governance framework must be complemented by an effective, efficient insolvency framework and by effective enforcement of creditor rights;

- the remuneration policy for members of the board of directors, the supervisory board, and key executives, and information about board members (including their qualifications, the selection process, other company directorships, and whether they are regarded as independent) must be disclosed;

- the content of any corporate governance code and the process by which it is implemented must be disclosed;

- an annual audit must be carried out by an independent, competent, and qualified auditor to provide assurance that the financial statements fairly represent the financial position and performance of the company;

- the external auditor is accountable to shareholders and owes a duty to the company to exercise due professional care in the conduct of the audit;

- the corporate governance framework must be complemented by an effective approach that addresses and promotes the provision of analysis or advice by analysts, brokers, etc. that is relevant to decisions by investors and free from material conflicts of interest that might compromise the integrity of their analysis or advice;

- appropriate and full disclosure about directors' remuneration;

- companies should publish in their annual reports a declaration of how they apply in practice the relevant principles of corporate governance contained in the Czech Code (2004);

- three separate committees responsible for the independent audit of the company, the remuneration of directors and key executives, and the nomination of directors and key executives should be established, and the mandate, composition, and working procedures of these committees must be disclosed.

The Czech Code (2004) is a comprehensive code with many explanatory notes in each section to aid the companies and investors. Adoption of the Czech Code (2004) should help to ensure that investor confidence is maintained, that shareholders' rights can be exercised more easily, and that minority shareholders are better protected.

Jandik and Rennie (2008) investigate the evolution of corporate governance and firm performance in transition economies with a focus on barriers that impeded the adoption of optimal corporate governance at Czech ammunition manufacturer Sellier and Bellot (S&B) following voucher privatization in 1993. They found that:

> Exogenously imposed diffuse ownership, combined with legal, capital market, and accounting deficiencies, contributed to poor corporate governance and weak firm performance. This study shows how legal, capital market, and accounting deficiencies hinder corporate governance evolution; it demonstrates monitoring and incentive mechanisms can create value in transition economies; it suggests effective privatisation not only involves rapid ownership transfer but careful accounting and securities regulation and legal protection.

Poland

The second model used in the privatization process was one that allowed management and employees to buy company assets. This was the method adopted in Poland from 1995, where there was a slower start to privatization than in the Czech Republic. State-owned enterprises targeted for privatization first became joint stock companies. In this instance, the joint stock company's ownership did not change, but the control structure changed to include a board of directors and the Workers' Councils, which were previously quite powerful, were disbanded, so reducing workers' power.

A defining feature of the Polish privatization process was that shares had to be included in one of 15 National Investment Funds (NIFs) established in 1995. NIFs were essentially established to manage shares that were purchased in the various privatized companies in Poland as part of the mass privatization programme. NIFs have strategic 33 per cent holdings in some firms but much smaller shares in other firms. Coffee (1998) points out that the NIFs 'remain indirectly under governmental control'. The Polish government did not allow its citizens to have vouchers that could be exchanged directly for shares in the privatized companies; rather the vouchers were exchanged for shares in the NIFs. The state also retained a significant shareholding of 25 per cent in some companies, with another 15 per cent being allotted free of charge to the workers. The investor base includes foreign investors as well as domestic, institutional, and retail investors.

Some of the firms that the NIFs are invested into required major restructuring but, sometimes, there is disagreement between the NIFs and the supervisory board as to when and how this restructuring might be undertaken. Coffee (1998) points out that 'if a proposed restructuring is politically sensitive or cuts deeply into local employment, one must suspect that labour interests and others with political clout will know how to protest effectively. Because the initial board of each NIF is governmentally appointed, there is little reason to believe that individual NIFs will feel insulated from such protests'. Therefore, the state continues to have an influential role in many companies, despite the fact that the companies are now privatized.

Poland is a country that has a civil law system. The legal framework for listed companies comprises the Commercial Code (1934) and the Code of Commercial Companies (2000). In the summer of 2002 there were two publications on corporate governance: the *Corporate Governance Code for Polish Listed Companies* and the *Best Practices in Public Companies* guidance. Both of these are now discussed in more detail.

Table 11.3 Key characteristics influencing Polish corporate governance

Feature	Key characteristic
Privatization method	Management and employees buy company assets
Predominant ownership structure	Institutional outsiders (NIFs); state; individuals/families
Legal system	Civil law
Board structure	Dual
Important aspect	Role of NIFs

Poland has a predominantly two-tier board structure comprising a supervisory board and a management board. As is usual, the supervisory board supervises the management board and oversees the company's financial statements, it also reports to the shareholders on the activities of the company. The management board conducts the day-to-day business of the company and is responsible for issues that are not within the remit of the supervisory board or the shareholders' meeting. The company's articles of association will often expand on the areas to be covered by the management board.

The final proposal of the *Corporate Governance Code for Polish Listed Companies* (hereinafter 'the Code') was published in June 2002. The Code was drawn up under the initiative of the Polish Forum for Corporate Governance established by the Gdansk Institute for Market Economics, and may also be referred to as 'the Gdansk Code'.

The Code recognizes the problems that have occurred in the past with the violation of minority rights and seeks to address these in order to help restore confidence in the Polish market. The Code largely reflects the OECD Principles (2004), the Cadbury Code (1992), and other benchmarks of international best practice. It is recommended that the Code's provisions be included in a company's articles of association. The Code expects companies to report on compliance combining annual descriptive reports and the 'comply or explain' mechanism.

The Code has seven Principles, which cover various areas of good corporate governance practice as follows.

(i) 'The main objective of the company should be to operate in the common interest of all shareholders, which is to create shareholder value'

The company's objectives should be publicized. It is important for the company to respect the rights of stakeholder groups as well. Employees are an important stakeholder group and may be offered representation on the supervisory board or the right to put forward their opinions on various matters.

(ii) 'The composition of the supervisory board should facilitate objective oversight of the company and reflect interests of minority shareholders'

The Code does not lay down the minimum number of members for the supervisory board although it envisages that there should be five or more members (except for smaller companies or where other justification exists). It is recommended that at least two of the supervisory board members should be independent (should not be linked to the company or its controlling shareholder) and should be elected without any decisive influence of the controlling shareholder. Details of candidates for supervisory board membership should be published prior to the general meeting in a timely manner to enable shareholders to vote in an informed way.

(iii) 'The powers of the supervisory board and the company by-laws should ensure an effective supervisory board process and duly secure interests of all shareholders'

The operation of the supervisory and management boards should be regulated by appropriate by-laws, and the articles of association of the company, which should be available from the company website. Members of the management board and the supervisory board should disclose any conflicts of interest; there should be regulated trading of the company shares in respect of the management and supervisory boards members (and any other person with privileged access to information) to ensure that there is no violation of the interests of shareholders and investors. Where there are transactions between the company and related parties, then these should be subject to supervisory board approval and require at least two independent board members' approval.

The supervisory board should have sufficient administrative support and also be able to hire external experts at the company's expense in pursuance of its duties. The Code also refers to the fact that many codes overseas recommend appropriate training particularly on first appointment to the board.

(iv) 'The shareholders' meeting should be convened and organized so as not to violate interests and rights of any shareholders. The controlling shareholder should not restrict the other shareholders in the effective exercise of their corporate rights'

There should be adequate notice of the meeting to enable shareholders to attend. Shareholders should be able to submit questions prior to the meeting to which the answers should be provided both in the meeting and subsequently published, where possible, on the company's website. The Code states that 'to participate in the general meeting is an inalienable right of any shareholder and should not be restricted . . . [T]his . . . gains special importance in Poland where participation in the general meeting by the way of voting by correspondence or by audio-visual means is not allowed'. Two independent supervisory board members may request that a shareholders' meeting be called, whilst company law provides for shareholders representing at least 10 per cent of the share capital to call a meeting (the company can lower this level if it thinks it appropriate). The chairman of the meeting should be impartial, and so be independent from the company and the controlling shareholder.

(v) 'The company should not apply anti-takeover defences against shareholders' interests. Changes in the company share capital should not violate interests of the existing shareholders'

The company should not use various anti-takeover devices, including acquiring its own shares for that purpose, or using voting caps, which might limit the use/number of votes by large shareholders. Management and employee stock option plan arrangements should not involve the issuance of more than 10 per cent of the total number of the company's shares over any five-year period.

(vi) 'The company should provide effective access to information, which is necessary to evaluate the company's current position, future prospects, as well as the way in which the company operates and applies the corporate governance rules'

The disclosure recommendations cover quite a comprehensive range of areas, including publishing a report, on an annual basis, providing detail of:

- the corporate governance framework, and the extent of compliance with the Code (or explain the reasons for non-compliance);
- the company's financial position and prospects, and its system of internal controls;
- the members of the management and supervisory boards, including positions held with other companies, links with shareholders, and information about remuneration.

The Code recommends that information should also be disclosed on the company's website whenever possible. The company should also disclose information about its ownership and control structure, including where there is a difference between the amount of shares owned and the amount of control, and where there are any agreements of which the company is aware that mean that shareholders might act together to vote in concert.

(vii) 'The appointment process of the company's auditor should ensure independence of the auditor's opinion'

The auditor is appointed by the supervisory board or recommended by them to the shareholders' general meeting. At least two independent board members should support the appointment resolution. The supervisory board may appoint an audit committee, comprised mainly of independent members of the supervisory board, to monitor the company's financial situation and its accounting system. There are some interesting provisions to help ensure auditor independence, which include appointing a new auditor every five years, and publishing the value of services provided by the auditor, or its subsidiaries/affiliates, in the accounting year. However, it should be noted that instead of appointing a new audit firm, the company may continue to use the same firm but with a change of personnel to a completely different audit team.

The Best Practices in Public Companies 2002 publication came out of the Best Practices Committee at Corporate Governance Forum, who stated that 'this set of best practices, established for the needs of the Polish capital market, presents the core of corporate governance standards in a public joint stock company'. There were a number of 'general rules' including: the objective of the company; the concept of majority rule and protection of the minority; the ideas of honest intentions and no abuse of rights; court control, which may apply to some issues in a company; that when expert services/opinions are sought, the experts should be independent. In addition to these general rules, there were specific guidelines relating to best practices, including: the notification and running of general meetings, and associated voting issues; the role of the supervisory board and its members; role of the management board and its members; relations with third parties, including the auditors. The Best Practices 2002 are not elaborated upon further here because the Gdansk Code, detailed earlier, also covered these areas.

The Best Practices were reviewed and amended in the light of practical experience and opinions of market participants and *Best Practices in Public Companies 2005* were issued. The amended practices included recent EU recommendations, for example, the emphasis on independence aimed at strengthening the role of non-executive or supervisory directors.

In 2007 and again in 2010 an updated *Code of Best Practice for WSE Listed Companies* was published which aims at 'enhancing transparency of listed companies, improving quality of communication between companies and investors, and strengthening protection of share-holders' rights'.

The corporate governance recommendations introduced by the Gdansk Code and the Best Practices will undoubtedly have strengthened the corporate governance of Polish companies and helped to encourage investment by restoring confidence in the market. As Rozlucki (2003) stated: 'In Poland, corporate governance has become an additional and indispensable guarantee of system stability to the financial market'. Kozarzewski (2007) carried out a cross-country comparative study of corporate governance formation in four transition countries, which differ significantly in the reform design, implementation, and outcome. His analysis showed that

> corporate governance formation in these countries is characterized by both similarities and differences. Similarities originate first of all from the common features of the historical background of these countries, the features of centrally planned economy; from the similarities of the principles of the reform programs; and from similarities of certain basic, objective regularities of the post-Communist transition. Such common features include, e.g., highly insiderized initial ownership patterns, high role of managers, high ownership concentration, dual trends of ownership structures' evolution towards concentration and outsiderization, and many others. The differences originate, among others, from the specific features of the countries' historical, cultural, and institutional heritage, the soundness of the reform design and implementation, the main characteristics of the enterprise sector, the quality of the legal base and enforcement mechanisms. Countries that had more favorable 'background' (traditions of private entrepreneurship, capacities of the elites) and during the transition period managed to create good legal background for private sector and appropriate institutions are more likely to enjoy formation of more efficient corporate governance mechanisms and patterns.

Russia

The collapse of the communist system in Russia heralded a wave of privatizations, with the privatization programme in Russia itself based on a voucher system. Pistor and Turkewitz (1996) indicate that, between January 1993 and June 1994, some 14,000–15,000 companies were sold in voucher auctions. They state that 'privatization regulations required companies with more than a thousand employees and a book value of at least 50 million rubles to set up a privatisation plan'. They highlight that there were substantial benefits available to the managers of enterprises, including subsidized equity stakes and the right to buy further shares in voucher auctions. Frydman *et al.* (1996) highlight the high participation levels of the Russian people in the voucher privatization process: 'The program did bring out a very high degree of popular participation: by July 1994, 132.7 million Russians made some use of their vouchers (even if only to sell them on the open market), and this number represents 87.8 per cent of the 151 million voucher recipients'. The privatization programme also saw the participation of privatization investment funds, which either bought shares directly or through intermediaries. After privatization, many managers bought shares from the workers. These factors contributed to a high level of ownership by insiders (managers and workers), such that managerial entrenchment became a real threat, as it meant that outside, and particularly overseas investors, would be reluctant to invest in companies where management control was high and protection of minority rights low.

Ownership in Russia is documented by Sprenger (2002), who cites some interesting surveys carried out by the Russian Economic Barometer. Table 11.4 shows the ownership change in Russian industry over the period 1995–9. What emerges is that, over time, the ownership by insiders (managers and workers) is declining whilst the ownership by outsiders is increasing, particularly ownership by individuals and financial firms, holdings, and foreign investors. Sprenger's (2005) study of 530 Russian manufacturing firms confirms the gradually decreasing ownership stakes of firms' insiders over time.

Table 11.4 Ownership change in Russia

Category of owner	1995	1997	1999
Insiders	54.8	52.1	46.2
Managers	11.2	15.1	14.7
Workers	43.6	37.0	31.5
State	9.1	7.4	7.1
Outsiders	35.2	38.9	42.4
Individuals	10.9	13.9	18.5
Non-financial firms	15.0	14.6	13.5
Financial firms, holdings, foreign investors	9.3	10.3	10.4
Others	0.9	1.6	4.3
Sample size	136	135	156

Source: Russian Economic Barometer in Kapelyushnikov (2000), cited in Sprenger (2002)

Russia, in common with other transition economies, is moving towards a market economy and has joint stock companies and limited liability companies. Minority rights have traditionally not been well looked after in Russia, so that the role and the relevance of shareholders in a company have not generally held much sway. Many foreign investors who invested in Russia post-privatization lost a lot of money as managers of the companies misused their funds and there was little effective redress. The Russian corporate governance code therefore sees it as very important to restore investor confidence in the market and to ensure that future foreign investment is encouraged by building more confidence in Russian companies.

Table 11.5 Key characteristics influencing Russian corporate governance

Feature	Key characteristic
Privatization method	Mass privatization via voucher
Predominant ownership structure	Insiders (managers and workers) although outsiders increasing
Legal system	Civil law
Board structure	Dual
Important aspect	Covers dividend payments

The *Russian Code of Corporate Governance* (hereinafter 'the Code') was issued by the Federal Securities Commission in late 2001. It had the support of both government officials and private groups, and it was hoped that compliance with the Code would be at a high level. This Code has yet to be updated and given that it has government support, it is likely that any company where the state has influence will, in theory, have to comply and also large companies that are still subject to political influence and decisions will want to comply. Also, in order to attract external direct investment, companies will want to comply with the new Code. This is particularly important given that, in the 1990s, the external investors who invested money into Russia had their fingers badly burnt when the money was pocketed by various corrupt individuals involved in companies. In order to restore confidence and to encourage more foreign investment, compliance with a corporate governance code is of prime importance.

Essentially, the Code is based on the OECD Corporate Governance Principles, but has also drawn from other international codes and guidelines. The Code has ten sections or chapters, which are now dealt with in turn.

(i) Principles of corporate governance

This chapter sets out the key principles of corporate governance and draws heavily on the OECD Principles. There should be equal treatment of shareholders, including minority and foreign investors. The key rights of shareholders are discussed, including the right to reliable registration of shares and disclosure of shares, the right to participate in profit distribution, the right to participate in managing the company by taking part in key decisions, and the right to have access to full, reliable, and timely information about the company. In terms of the protection of minority shareholders, minority shareholders have the legal right to vote on all matters of importance, including mergers and sale of substantial assets. Shareholders may vote and attend meetings both personally and by proxy.

The board of directors is responsible for the strategic management of the company and for effective control over the executive bodies of the company. The board of directors is accountable to the shareholders, with members being elected through a transparent procedure taking into account diverse shareholders' opinions. There should be 'a sufficient number' of independent directors. Various committees, including a strategic planning, audit, personnel and remuneration, corporate conflicts, risk management, and ethics committees, may be established. A managerial board should be established to manage the day-to-day activities of the company; its members should be elected by a transparent procedure.

(ii) General shareholders' meetings

The Code states: 'For a minority shareholder, the annual general shareholders' meeting is often the only chance to obtain information on the company's operations and ask the company management questions regarding the company's administration. By participating in a general shareholders' meeting, a shareholder exercises its right to be involved in the company's management.'

The Code states that shareholders should have sufficient time to prepare for an AGM and to see the resolutions to be voted on. It is recommended that notice of the meeting should be given thirty days before the AGM, which is an improvement over the twenty-day minimum notice mandated by law. The place, time, and location of the AGM should facilitate shareholders' attendance, and the Code recommends that an AGM should not start earlier than 9 a.m., nor later than 10 p.m. local time.

At the AGM, the chairman should 'act reasonably and in good faith, without using his authority to limit the rights of shareholders'. There should be a clearly formulated agenda, with all information necessary to make voting decisions. Shareholders have the right to propose agenda items and they may correspond with the company by traditional means or electronic means. During the meeting, all shareholders have an equal right to ask questions of the directors. In the past, companies have occasionally resorted to deceitful behaviour such as moving meetings at the last minute in order to stop shareholders from voting, or using technical loopholes to prevent outside shareholders from voting. In this way, they have been able to focus attention on the interest of insiders and controlling shareholders. It is hoped that the new recommendations will help to ensure that these situations do not recur.

(iii) Board of directors

The key functions of the board are defined in this section. They include strategic aspects ensuring effective control over management, resolving corporate conflict, and ensuring the effective work of the executive body. Board members should actively participate in board meetings and the board is required to meet regularly and to set up committees to discuss important issues: the Code explicitly lists a strategic planning committee, audit committee, human resources and remuneration committee, and corporate conflicts resolution committee. The compensation for board managers decided by the AGM should reflect the company's operational performance.

The Code also proposes a transparent procedure for nomination and election of board members and requires that 25 per cent of the board be independent (it is also recommended that the company's charter should provide for the board to include at least three independent directors). The 25 per cent is a lower level than one would like to see and also the definition of an independent director is often contentious in Russia. The relationship between managers, controlling shareholders, and board members in Russia has sometimes been very close, with the result that board members may be largely selected by controlling shareholders and hence under their influence, even if, in theory, they qualify as being independent.

(iv) Executive bodies

The Code refers to the executive bodies of the company, which encompass the managerial board (or management board) and the director general (akin to a chief executive officer). The executive bodies are responsible for the day-to-day operations of the company, and compliance with financial and business plans of the company. The managerial board should approve transactions involving more than 5 per cent of a company's assets, with timely notification of such transactions to the board of directors. The managerial board, like the board of directors, should work in the interests of all shareholders, and not use confidential information for personal benefit. It should take into account the interests of various stakeholder groups to try to ensure the efficient operation of the company. In particular, it should take account of the interests of employees by maintaining contact with the trade unions/professional organizations.

There is no clear recommendation regarding the size of the managerial board, rather that 'the company should proceed from the requirement that the number of members of the managerial board be optimal for productive, constructive discussion, and making prompt, informed decisions'. However, it is important that there is a transparent process for election of the director general and members of the managerial board, including making available appropriate information about the candidates.

The remuneration of the director general and managerial board members should reflect their skills and their actual contribution to the success of the company's operations.

(v) Company secretary

Perhaps one of the most radical proposals in the Code is the creation of the post of company secretary, which is a new concept for Russia. The secretary's functions would be to prepare for AGMs and board meetings, ensure the appropriate provision of information disclosure and maintenance of corporate records, consider shareholders' requests, and resolve any infringement of investors' rights. The company secretary would be appointed by the board of directors and should be granted adequate powers to perform these duties. The company secretary should inform the board chairman if anything prevents him/her from carrying out his/her duties.

(vi) Major corporate actions

The Code states that major corporate actions include reorganizations of the company and acquisition of 30 per cent or more of the outstanding shares of the company or those actions deemed to be of significant importance for the company's capital structure and financial situation. Such major corporate actions should be approved by the board of directors or extraordinary general meeting before being finalized, and also be evaluated by an independent auditor. In the case of a takeover attempt, the board of directors should inform the shareholders about its position but should not prevent the takeover if this would be against the shareholders' interests or would have a negative effect on the company.

(vii) Information disclosure

The Code states that the company information policy should make available to current and potential shareholders appropriate information. The Code lists information that should be disclosed in prospectuses, and the annual and quarterly reports; the report for the final quarter should outline the company's corporate governance policies and state whether or not it complies fully with the Code.

It is possible that there may be a potential conflict in that some information relating to 'trade or professional secrets' may be withheld if there is a need to strike a balance between transparencies and the protection of a company's interest, and this may effectively cast a shadow over disclosure.

(viii) Supervision of operations

In order to ensure that the company is operating according to plan, and that the board and management mechanisms are appropriate and transparent, and that any risks are being limited, there needs to be adequate supervision. The Code recommends that supervision is carried out by the board of directors and its audit committee, the audit commission of the company, the control and audit service of the company, and the external auditor of the company. The Code prefers the audit committee to consist of independent directors only.

(ix) Dividends

Traditionally, dividends have been problematic in Russia and so the Code states that, if net profit is used to calculate the dividend, then this number must be the net profit figure that is reported in the company's accounts. Dividends should be paid in cash only and the company has to set a clear deadline for payment, which cannot exceed sixty days after the announcement. If announced dividends are delayed or not paid, then the board of directors has the right to reduce the director general's compensation and/or that of the managerial board members, or to dismiss them completely.

(x) Resolution of corporate conflicts

The company secretary is identified as the key person for determining and monitoring conflict between the company and its shareholders. Any response to shareholders must be based on the law and also the company can serve as an intermediary if there is a conflict between two shareholders.

It can be seen that the provisions of the Russian Code are quite far reaching. In some ways, the provisions largely relate to educating the Russian corporate sector so that they understand what good corporate governance actually is. Whilst some companies are already complying, others have been slower to comply and the Code's provisions are not legally binding. However, the companies may not wish to incur the disapproval of the government and many still rely heavily on political influence: for example, they may be denied the right to state tender or, alternatively, pension funds might be prohibited from investing in companies that do not comply.

Kostikov (2003) stated: 'Poor corporate governance in Russian companies makes them much less attractive as investment objects'. Initiatives to encourage more truly independent directors onto Russian boards are essential to help ensure improved corporate governance and to encourage investors. As Belikov (2004) stated: 'The challenge is to attract conservative portfolio investors who are willing to commit to long-term investments and who view good corporate governance as a vital part of an investment decision'. Legislation introduced in 2006 should help ensure that boards have more independent directors and hence that board committees have a higher proportion of independent directors. Bartha and Gillies (2006) believe that corporate governance is of great value to Russia:

> The adoption of a good corporate governance system—both at the macro legal-regulatory setting and at the micro level of business practices—can speed up and smooth the transition to a fully operational market economy. During mass privatization a decade ago the absence of the right structures, institutions and processes caused a major transformation effort to go awry. Now the appropriate framework, instruments and know-how are in place to generate and allocate capital effectively and efficiently. By developing a set of corporate governance practices and fostering a corporate governance culture, Russia is wisely pre-investing in its future.

In December 2011 the OECD and MICEX-RTS, the recently merged Russian stock exchange, launched a new work programme on corporate governance in the Russian Federation. This will consider the remaining challenges in the corporate governance framework; improving the understanding of Russia corporate governance practices; and facilitating ongoing reform efforts. The role of the stock exchange in setting corporate governance standards, disclosure, and transparency of listed companies, enforcement of insider trading, and market manipulation laws in Russia is also being considered.

Hungary

The third model, and arguably the one that produced the most successful results, involved selling majority control to an outside investor. This model was followed in Hungary and resulted in a high level of outside ownership and control. It is useful to mention various changes that occurred in Hungary in the late 1980s/early 1990s, as described in Pistor and Turkewitz (1996). A change in Hungarian law led, in the late 1980s, to a wave of manager-initiated organizational restructuring of enterprise assets and the right to form a limited liability company or joint stock company. Whilst the state retained ownership of a large proportion of these assets, state officials were unable to keep up with the pace of change and so were unable to keep up with the changes in the ownership structures. In 1989 the majority of state-owned companies were transferred to the State Property Agency (SPA), and over the next five years many of these were privatized. However, some of the assets were transferred to the State Holding Company (Av.Rt.). The state still retains significant holdings and influence, one way being through 'golden shares', which were issued to the state during the privatization process enabling the state to have control over key strategic issues. The World Bank–IMF ROSC 2003 report on corporate governance in Hungary identifies that ten of the fifty-six listed companies have issued a golden share that can only be held by the state.

Table 11.6 Key characteristics influencing Hungarian corporate governance

Feature	Key characteristic
Privatization method	Privatization via selling majority control to outside investor, often foreign
Predominant ownership structure	State; institutional outsiders (foreign)
Legal system	Civil law
Board structure	Dual
Important aspect	State influence but potential influence of foreign investor activism waiting to happen

For some time, Hungary did not have a published corporate governance code, although the Budapest Stock Exchange started to draft a corporate governance code in mid-2002. However, many areas relating to corporate governance were covered in the Companies Law and these areas are described later.

The World Bank–IMF ROSC 2003 report identified that, whilst Hungary had a robust legislative and regulatory framework to deal with corporate governance issues, there were shortcomings in the system, including the lack of a corporate governance code of best practice. The report identified the various sections of the Companies Act 1997 relating to corporate structure and governance.

(i) Board structure

Public companies should have a two-tier (dual) structure consisting of a board of directors (management board) and a supervisory board. The shareholders in general meeting usually appoint the directors of both boards and approve their remuneration. However, the company's charter may provide that the supervisory board appoint and set the remuneration of the management board.

The management board may comprise between three and eleven members, whilst the supervisory board can have as many as fifteen members, with employees appointing one-third of the supervisory board members.

(ii) Operation of the boards

The management board is responsible for the day-to-day running of the company, whilst the supervisory board exercises control over the management board on behalf of the shareholders. The management board's responsibilities include reporting on operational issues (such as the company's financial position) at the AGM and also quarterly to the supervisory board, and maintaining the books and records of the company.

Board meeting minutes are not required to be kept, but board members participate and report at the AGM. Both boards are accountable to the AGM and, in theory, to all shareholders; in practice, some directors appointed on the votes of large shareholders may effectively represent the interests of those large shareholders. Board members may seek expert opinions as appropriate.

(iii) Independence

There is no specific reference to independence, although the Companies Act does refer to the objectivity of board members so that close family members are not allowed to be members of the supervisory and management board at the same company. Board members may not be employees, except in their capacity as employee representatives on the supervisory board. Board members should disclose any conflicts of interest.

(iv) Disclosure

Hungary's disclosure of information relevant to investors was generally quite good. Disclosure requirements are contained in the Capital Markets Act 2002 and the Budapest Stock Exchange listing rules. The areas that companies must provide disclosure on include:

- the corporate objectives;
- major ownership and voting rights;
- the financial and operating results of the company;
- remuneration of board members;
- details of loans to board members;
- information relating to employees, such as the average number of employees employed.

Investors must have access to the company's annual report and many companies post this information on their website.

As mentioned earlier, the Budapest Stock Exchange began work on its Corporate Governance Recommendations in 2002, and the final document was published in 2004. The recommendations suggest applicable practices but are not mandatory for companies listed on the Stock Exchange. However, the publication of a declaration, whereby the corporate issuers provide information on their management practices in comparison with the contents of the recommendations, will be mandatory and confirmed in the Stock Exchange rules. If an issuer does not comply with a recommendation or applies it in a different manner, then an explanation should be provided, i.e. the 'comply or explain' approach.

The Budapest Stock Exchange has split the recommendations into corporate governance recommendations and recommendations on shareholders' meetings. The corporate governance recommendations are laid out in a three-column format, with the first column being the recommendations themselves, then the middle column, the relevant Hungarian legal regulations, and the final column, explanations and in-depth suggestions relating to each recommendation. The corporate governance recommendations are outlined below.

Corporate governance recommendations

(i) Competences of the board of directors and of the supervisory board

The recommendations emphasize that the most important role of the board is the overall stewardship of the company. The responsibilities of the board encompass:

- developing the strategy, supervision of business and financial plans, setting corporate objectives and overseeing corporate performance;

- ensuring the integrity of accounting reports;
- managing conflicts of interest and drafting a code of ethics;
- succession planning;
- risk management;
- mechanisms for nomination and remuneration of directors;
- guidelines for transparency and disclosure of corporate information, and timely communication with shareholders;
- continuous oversight of the effectiveness of corporate governance;
- communication with, and reporting to, the supervisory board.

The board should carry out its responsibilities with due diligence in the best interests of the company, having regard to the rights of shareholders and stakeholders, and also, as far as possible, in the best interests of stakeholders.

The supervisory board, on behalf of shareholders, monitors the activities of the board of directors and ensures its duties are carried out with due care. The supervisory board has a charter, which determines its mandate, and a work schedule.

Members of both boards should be notified well in advance of the meetings of the respective boards and of the agenda items, and all relevant information should be made available on a timely basis.

In terms of board membership, the board of directors and the supervisory board need to submit nominations for officers to the shareholders' meeting. The nominees should be competent and qualified, and have sufficient time to devote to their duties. The board of directors should contain an appropriate number of independent members to ensure that resolutions can be passed objectively in the interest of shareholders and not be subject to the influence of executive management or individual shareholders. Interestingly, the Code explains that the presence of a strategic investor is typical in Hungarian companies and so it is not considered a violation of the board's independence if a member of the board is delegated by one of the owners. The supervisory board members should be independent and not employees of the company, save for the employees' representatives.

In relation to the duties of the chairman and the CEO, these shall be outlined separately in the basic documents (such as articles of association or board charter).

In terms of remuneration, the board of directors should establish guidelines and rules relating to the performance review and remuneration of directors and executive management. These guidelines and rules should be approved by the shareholders' general meeting, taking into account the views of the supervisory board. The remuneration scheme should support the long-term strategic interests of the company (and hence the shareholders). For members of the supervisory board, a fixed remuneration is recommended.

Board committees, including remuneration, audit, and nomination committees, may be established and should be comprised of at least three members, the majority of whom are independent, and who are appropriately experienced and qualified to perform their duties. Committees, like the board of directors and the supervisory board, are entitled to consult with external advisors.

The board of directors should ensure that there is in place a reliable system of internal controls. Internal audit departments should be established and report regularly to the board of directors or supervisory board.

Succession planning is important in any business, so companies should identify potential successors to key figures in the company. The business should have appropriate coordination of corporate affairs to ensure appropriate and timely exchange of views between various parties.

(ii) Transparency and disclosure

There should be adequate and timely disclosure of information about the operations of the company and circumstances that may influence its share price. Information shall be made available to the public about the company's corporate strategy, its main business activities, business ethics, and its policies regarding other stakeholders. The company will disclose information on a range of issues, including:

- the background of directors and supervisory board members, the guidelines for the evaluation of their performance and the establishment of their remuneration;
- the risk management guidelines;
- the extent to which the company adopts the Hungarian corporate governance recommendations;
- its guidelines on insider trading.

It is also recommended that disclosures are made in English as well as the official language of the company.

(iii) Shareholders' rights and treatment of shareholders

All voting practices and treatment of shareholders should comply with laws, regulations and the company's formal documents (for example, articles of association). Shareholders should have the right to participate in key decisions about the company, via the shareholders' meeting, and should be notified of the time, location, and agenda of the shareholders' meeting. Minutes of the meeting should be made available to shareholders within thirty days of the meeting. An investor relations department should be established.

(iv) Role of stakeholders in corporate governance

The board of directors should respect the rights of all stakeholders and it is believed that shareholder interests are best served if the interests of other stakeholders are equally respected. The board shall strive to perform its duties in a socially responsible manner. It is recommended that companies publish a code of ethics, which defines the ethical guidelines of the company.

Recommendations on shareholders' meetings

The recommendations on shareholders' meetings are designed to establish principles to provide a basis for future shareholders' meetings, which support the validation of shareholders' interests, take into account the interests of potential investors, and facilitate the decision-making process. These recommendations are a supplement to the *Corporate Governance*

Recommendations and have three sections relating to the preliminary procedures prior to meetings, conducting the shareholders' meetings, and concluding the shareholders' meetings.

In 2007 and 2008 the Budapest Stock Exchange published updates of the *Corporate Governance Recommendations* to take into consideration European Commission recommendations on aspects of corporate governance and especially in relation to the remuneration of directors, and the role of non-executive directors and the supervisory board. The Hungarian Company Act 2006 has given legal force to the regulation of disclosure obligations regarding corporate governance, and companies are required to submit an annual comprehensive report on corporate governance to the company's AGM. Companies also have to indicate their compliance with specified sections of the *Corporate Governance Recommendations*, and the disclosure obligations may be quite detailed.

As can be seen from the earlier analysis, the Hungarian *Corporate Governance Recommendations* are quite comprehensive.

Earle *et al.* (2005) found that high-quality data available on companies listed on the Budapest Stock Exchange enabled them to undertake a study of ownership concentration and corporate performance. They found that the size of the largest block of shares increases profitability and efficiency but that the effects of the total block-holdings are much smaller. In other words: 'The marginal costs of concentration [of share ownership] may outweigh the benefits when the increased concentration involves "too many cooks"'.

More recently, Telegdy (2011) found that 'foreigners have an important role in the control structures of Hungarian corporations, which has partially resulted from their involvement in the privatization process, and partially it materialized through acquisitions of domestic companies and green field investments. The listed firms . . . tend to have one or multiple large blockholders, and only a small proportion of the stocks are widely held.'

Conclusions

In this chapter we have reviewed the three different approaches that were used in the privatization of state-owned enterprises in the former USSR. The effect of each of these approaches on the resultant ownership and control of privatized companies, and the implications for corporate governance developments have been discussed. In particular, it has been noted that the countries in CEE are keen to improve protection of minority shareholder rights, and to establish more confidence in their capital markets to attract foreign direct investment. All of the countries have already published corporate governance codes of best practice. In addition, the Czech Republic, Hungary, and Poland all joined the EU in 2004 and so we can expect to see their corporate governance developing in line with European Commission recommendations.

Summary

- Three main privatization methods were used to privatize state-owned enterprises in the former USSR: (i) the voucher privatization method was used in the Czech Republic and Russia, and enabled the public to own shares in privatized firms; (ii) management and employees were allowed to buy company assets, and this method was used in Poland; (iii) selling majority control to an outside investor was the method used in Hungary.

- The different privatization methods resulted in different ownership and control structures. In practice, the state retained considerable influence in many firms, either directly or indirectly.

- The four countries reviewed all have a dual board structure (supervisory board and management board).

- The Czech Republic has an ownership structure that includes predominantly the state and institutional outsiders (investment funds and banks). The IPFs can be quite influential.

- Poland has an ownership structure that includes predominantly institutional outsiders, the state, and individuals/families. The NIFs play an important role.

- Russia has an ownership structure that includes predominantly insiders (managers and workers), although outsiders are increasing. The Russian Corporate Governance Code is comprehensive at over 90 pages and includes sections on the company secretary and on dividends.

- Hungary has an ownership structure that includes predominantly the state and institutional outsiders (foreign investors). Whilst Hungary has many good practices, especially in the area of corporate disclosures, its corporate governance infrastructure could be improved in a number of ways and its comprehensive code of corporate governance should encourage this.

Example: VimpelCom, Russia

This is a good example of a Russian company that is recognized as having probably the best corporate governance amongst Russian companies.

VimpelCom is a leading provider of telecommunications services in Russia, with its 'Beeline' brand being well known and highly regarded in Russia. VimpelCom is a market leader and at the forefront of some of the latest technology, such as wireless Internet access and other services, mobile portals, etc.

VimpelCom was the first Russian company to list its shares on the New York Stock Exchange in 1996; it was included in the FT500 for the first time in 2008. VimpelCom's annual report is informative and includes a 'letter to shareholders', which reviews the company's financial performance and operations. The annual report emphasizes that its founders have inspired it with the values of 'transparency, strong corporate governance, quality, innovation and a pioneering spirit'. VimpelCom has consistently been the recipient of corporate governance and related awards—in the early 2000s it was awarded the 'Best Corporate Governance Award 2002' by the Russian Association for the Protection of Investor Rights. There has been recognition from overseas as well, with *Business Week* naming VimpelCom as number six in its list of the top 100 IT companies in the world for 2002. Its US$250 million 10.45 per cent bond issue was cited by *Euroweek* as third in the 'Best Corporate Deals in Emerging Europe'. More recently Vimpelcom was named the winner of the 'Best Corporate Governance Award' at the First Annual IR Magazine Russia Conference in 2004. Vimpelcom was also awarded the 'Grand Prix for Best Overall Investor Relations'. In February 2008 Beeline was acknowledged to be the 'Best Employer in Russian Telecommunications Sector' following the results of the HR-Brand Contest; in March 2008 VimpelCom's then Executive Vice-President, Nikolay Pryanishnikov, was included in the list of World's Young Leaders by the International Economic Forum.

In October 2008 VimpelCom received 'Best Corporate Governance', 'Best Annual Report', and 'Best IR' by the CEO awards from IR Magazine Russia. In November 2008 VimpelCom trademark 'Beeline' was rated as the Most Valuable Russian Brand for the fourth consecutive time by Interbrand Zintzmeyer & Lux AG with an estimated value of US$7.4 billion. In 2010 its Investor Relations Team received the 'Annual Investor Relations Excellence Award' from the Investor Protection Association in Russia for Best Investor Relation Function.

The company's website has a section devoted to corporate responsibility, with activities detailed under three headings: environment, community, and safety. For example, under the environment heading, it gives details of its involvement with the Asian Caucasus Leopard Rehabilitation Program as well as other activities.

The key to VimpelCom's success, in terms of its attractiveness to investors both domestically and overseas, is attributable to its openness and transparency, and to its regard for good corporate governance practices. VimpelCom is therefore an exemplary company in terms of having a good corporate governance structure that gives confidence to investors and helps restore confidence in the Russian market more generally.

 ## Mini case study   MOL, Hungary

This is an example of a Hungarian company that is recognized as having good corporate governance and sustainability policies, and excellent disclosure.

MOL Group is a leading integrated CEE oil and gas corporation with a market capitalization of over US$7.5 billion at the end of 2011. Its shares are listed on the Budapest, Luxembourg, and Warsaw Stock Exchanges, and its depository receipts are traded on London's International Order Book and OTC in the USA.

MOL is 'committed to maintaining and further improving the efficiency of its current portfolio, exploiting potential in its captive and new markets and to excellence in its social and environmental performance'. MOL's corporate governance practice meets the requirements of the regulations of the Budapest Stock Exchange, the recommendations of the Hungarian Financial Supervisory Authority, and the relevant regulations of the Capital Market Act. MOL has its own Corporate Governance Code, which contains the main corporate governance principles of the company and summarizes its approach to shareholders' rights, main governing bodies, remuneration, and ethical issues.

MOL's Board of Directors' key activities are focused on achieving increasing shareholder value with considerations given for other stakeholders' interest: improving efficiency and profitability, and ensuring transparency in corporate activities and sustainable operation. It also aims to ensure appropriate risk management, environmental protection, and conditions for safety at work. The majority of the board (eight of eleven members) are non-executive directors, with eight members qualifying as independent on the basis of its own set of criteria (based on New York Stock Exchange and EU recommendations) and the declaration of directors.

The board has three committees: the Corporate Governance and Remuneration Committee; the Finance and Risk Management Committee; and the Sustainable Development Committee. In 2010 these committees held, respectively, six meetings (85 per cent average attendance); five meetings (100 per cent attendance rate); and four meetings (100 per cent attendance rate).

(continued)

The Supervisory Board is responsible for monitoring and supervising the Board of Directors on behalf of the shareholders. In accordance with MOL's Articles of Association, the maximum number of members is nine (present membership is nine); by law one-third of the members should be representatives of the employees, accordingly three members of the MOL Supervisory Board are employee representatives with the other six external persons appointed by the shareholders, of whom five are independent.

There is an Audit Committee comprised of independent members of the Supervisory Board. In 2010 the Audit Committee held five meetings with an 87 per cent average attendance rate.

The MOL Policy on Corporate Governance also includes details of the remuneration of members of the Board of Directors and the Supervisory Board.

In 2011 MOL Group, the only CEE company to be in the running, qualified for the Sustainable Asset Management (SAM) Gold Class based on its performance in the field of corporate sustainability. The 2,500 largest global companies, based on the Dow Jones Stock Market Index, are invited to be independently assessed on three dimensions of sustainability: long-term economic, social, and environmental performance. The top 15 per cent of companies from fifty-eight business sectors are selected to appear in the SAM Yearbook. MOL Group was included in the Gold Class; to qualify for the SAM Gold Class, the SAM Sector Leader must achieve a minimum total score of 75 per cent. Peer group companies whose total scores are within 5 per cent of the SAM Sector Leader also enter the SAM Gold Class. Out of 113 global oil companies, 68 were examined in detail with 17 being selected to appear in the Yearbook of which 8 entered the Golden Class category. MOL state that 'According to SAM's assessment, the Corporate Governance practice of MOL is outstanding, and its result is above the industry average. The evaluation criteria consisted of several topics, e.g. board structure, corporate governance policies or transparency'.

Questions

The discussion questions to follow cover the key learning points of this chapter. Reading of some of the additional reference material will enhance the depth of the students' knowledge and understanding of these areas.

1. What do you think was the rationale behind the different privatization methods employed in various countries?
2. What effect did each of the privatization methods have on the ownership structure and control of privatized companies? In what ways may the ownership structures have changed over the years since privatization?
3. Which method of privatization do you think has resulted in the best structure in which to nurture good corporate governance?
4. What do you think a foreign investor would be looking for when it comes to investing in a country in CEE?
5. Critically discuss the role of NIFs and IPFs.
6. Do you think there is a role to be played by institutional investors, both domestic and foreign, in the corporate governance of privatized companies?

References

Aguilera, R.V., Kabbach-Castro, L. R., Lee, J. H. and You, J. (2012), 'Corporate Governance in Emerging Markets', in G. Morgan and R. Whitley (eds), *Capitalisms and Capitalism in the 21st Century*, Oxford University Press, Oxford. Available at SSRN: http://ssrn.com/abstract=1806525

Bartha, P. and Gillies, J. (2006), 'Corporate Governance in Russia: Is it Really Needed?', in C.A. Mallin (ed.), *Handbook on International Corporate Governance, Country Analyses*, Edward Elgar Publishing, Cheltenham, UK.

Belikov, I. (2004), *Corporate Governance in Russia: Who Will Pay For It and How Much?* Economic Reform Feature Service, Center for International Private Enterprise (Article adapted from a longer article originally appearing in Russian in the magazine *Rynok Tsennikh Bumag* (2004, No. 5).

Berglof, E. and Pajuste, A. (2003), 'Emerging Owners, Eclipsing Markets? Corporate Governance in Central and Eastern Europe', in P.K. Cornelius and B. Kogut (eds), *Corporate Governance and Capital Flows in a Global Economy*, Oxford University Press, Oxford.

Best Practices Committee at Corporate Governance Forum (2002), *Best Practices in Public Companies 2002*, Best Practices Committee at Corporate Governance Forum, Warsaw.

—— (2005), *Best Practices in Public Companies 2005*, Best Practices Committee at Corporate Governance Forum, Warsaw.

Boeri, T. and Perasso, G. (1998), 'Privatization and Corporate Governance: Some Lessons from the Experience of Transitional Economies', in M. Balling, E. Hennessy, and R. O'Brien (eds), *Corporate Governance, Financial Markets and Global Convergence*, Kluwer Academic Publishers, Dordrecht.

Budapest Stock Exchange (2004), *Corporate Governance Recommendations*, Budapest Stock Exchange, Budapest.

—— (2007), *Corporate Governance Recommendations*, Budapest Stock Exchange, Budapest.

—— (2008), *Corporate Governance Recommendations*, Budapest Stock Exchange, Budapest.

Cadbury, Sir Adrian (1992), *Report of the Committee on the Financial Aspects of Corporate Governance*, Gee & Co. Ltd, London.

Centre for European Policy Studies (1995), *Corporate Governance in Europe*, CEPS, Brussels.

Claessens, S., Djankov, S., and Pohl, G. (1997), 'Ownership and Corporate Governance: Evidence from the Czech Republic', World Bank Policy Research Working Paper, No. 1737.

Coffee, J.C. (1998), 'Inventing a Corporate Monitor for Transitional Economies', in K.J. Hopt, H. Kanda, M.J. Roe, E. Wymeersch, and S. Prigge (eds), *Comparative Corporate Governance, the State of the Art and Emerging Research*, Oxford University Press, Oxford.

—— (2002), 'Convergence and its Critics', in J.A. McCahery, P. Moerland, T. Raaijmakers, and L. Renneboog (eds), *Corporate Governance Regimes, Convergence and Diversity*, Oxford University Press, Oxford.

Co-ordination Council for Corporate Governance (2001), *The Russian Code of Corporate Conduct*, Federal Securities Commission, Moscow.

Czech Securities Commission (2004), *Corporate Governance Code based on the OECD Principles (2004)*, Czech Securities Commission, Prague.

Dzierzanowski, M. and Tamowicz, P. (2002), *The Corporate Governance Code for Polish Listed Companies*, Gdansk Institute for Market Economics/ Polish Corporate Governance Forum, Gdansk.

Earle, J.S., Kucsera, C., and Telegdy, A. (2005), 'Ownership Concentration and Corporate Performance on the Budapest Stock Exchange: Do Too Many Cooks Spoil the Goulash?', *Corporate Governance: An International Review*, Vol. 13, No. 2, March.

European Bank of Reconstruction and Development/ World Bank (1999), *Business Environment Survey*, EBRD, Brussels.

Frydman, R., Pistor, K., and Rapaczynski, A. (1996), 'Investing in Insider Dominated Firms: Russia', in R. Frydman, C.W. Gray, and A. Rapaczynski (eds), *Corporate Governance in Central Europe and Russia: Volume 1 Banks, Funds, and Foreign Investors*, CEU Press, Budapest.

Jandik, T. and Rennie, C.G. (2008), 'The Evolution of Corporate Governance and Firm Performance in Transition Economies: The Case of Sellier and Bellot in the Czech Republic', *European Financial Management*, Vol. 14, No. 4.

KCP (2001), *Revised Corporate Governance Code*, KCP/ Czech Securities Commission, Prague.

Kostikov, I. (2003), 'Governance in an Emerging Financial Market. The Case of Russia' in P.K. Cornelius and B. Kogut (eds), *Corporate Governance and Capital Flows in a Global Economy*, Oxford University Press, Oxford.

Kozarzewski, P. (2007), 'Corporate Governance Formation in Poland, Kyrgyzstan, Russia, and Ukraine', *Studies and Analyses No. 347*, available at SSRN: http://ssrn.com/abstract=1016064

OECD (1999), *Principles of Corporate Governance*, OECD, Paris.

—— (2004), *Principles of Corporate Governance*, OECD, Paris.

Pistor, K. (2000), 'Patterns of Legal Change: Shareholder and Creditor Rights in Transition Economies', EBRD, Working Paper No. 49.

—— and Turkewitz, J. (1996), 'Coping with Hydra—State Ownership after Privatization: A Comparative Study of the Czech Republic, Hungary and Russia', in R. Frydman, C.W. Gray, and A. Rapaczynski (eds), *Corporate Governance in Central Europe and Russia: Volume 2 Insiders and the State*, CEU Press, Budapest.

Rozlucki, W. (2003), 'Governance in an Emerging Financial Market, The Case of Poland', in P.K. Cornelius and B. Kogut (eds), *Corporate Governance and Capital Flows in a Global Economy*, Oxford University Press, Oxford.

Sprenger, C. (2002), 'Ownership and Corporate Governance in Russian Industry: A Survey', European Bank for Research and Development, Working Paper No. 70.

—— (2005), 'The Determinants of Ownership After Privatisation—The Case of Russia', EFA 2005 Moscow Meetings, August.

Telegdy A. (2011), 'Corporate Governance and the Structure of Ownership of Hungarian Corporations' in C.A. Mallin (ed.), *Handbook on International Corporate Governance, Country Analyses*, 2nd edition, Edward Elgar Publishing, Cheltenham.

Warsaw Stock Exchange (2002), *Code of Best Practice for WSE Listed Companies*, Warsaw Stock Exchange, Warsaw.

—— (2007), *Code of Best Practice for WSE Listed Companies*, Warsaw Stock Exchange, Warsaw.

—— (2010), *Code of Best Practice for WSE Listed Companies*, Warsaw Stock Exchange, Warsaw.

World Bank-IMF (2003), *Report on the Observance of Standards and Codes (ROSC) Corporate Governance Country Assessment, Hungary, February 2003*, drafted by O. Fremond and A. Berg, Corporate Governance Unit Private Sector Advisory Services, World Bank, Washington DC.

Useful websites

www.cipe.org The website of the Centre for International Private Enterprise has numerous articles of relevance to corporate governance.

www.corp-gov.org The website of Corporate Governance in Russia contains information about corporate governance in the Russian market.

www.ecgi.org The website of the European Corporate Governance Institute contains articles relating to corporate governance, and lists of corporate governance codes, guidelines, and principles.

www.iclg.ru The website of the Institute of Corporate Law and Corporate Governance has information about corporate governance developments in Russia.

 For further links to useful sources of information visit the Online Resource Centre
www.oxfordtextbooks.co.uk/orc/mallin4e/

 **FT Clippings**

FT: Investors wary over Rusal stand-off

By Catherine Belton in Moscow

March 14, 2012

A stand-off between two of the biggest shareholders in United Company Rusal is set to deepen investor concerns about the future of the world's biggest aluminium producer just as it seeks to weather a potentially prolonged dip in global aluminium markets.

This week's sudden resignation of Viktor Vekselberg, the Russian billionaire, as Rusal's chairman is raising new questions about the aggressive expansion strategy of its main owner, Oleg Deripaska. Mr Vekselberg, who said bad management had run Rusal into "deep crisis", notched up the rhetoric further on Wednesday, saying he was considering suing Rusal over its claims that he had failed to attend board meetings.

"In this situation, the interests of minority shareholders are not going to be in first place," said Sergei Ezimov, a fund manager at Wermuth Asset Management, a Moscow investment fund. Minority investors cannot say they were not warned. Rusal's initial public offering in Hong Kong in early 2010 was declared off limits to retail investors because of concerns over governance and the company's debt load.

Since then, shares have fallen 43 per cent below the offer price and the clash between the oligarchs sent them down a further 4 per cent on Wednesday.

The stand-off centres on disagreements over Mr Deripaska's $14bn acquisition of a 25 per cent stake in Norilsk Nickel, the world's biggest nickel miner, at the top of the market in 2008. After stocks crashed later that year, Mr Deripaska was forced to restructure nearly $17bn of debt, but he has consistently refused to sell the Norilsk stake.

For Mr Deripaska, the stake is part of a long running takeover war with rival metals tycoon Vladimir Potanin, who has combined with Norilsk's management to control the miner, leading to a web of lawsuits filed in jurisdictions from London to Siberia and the Caribbean.

But for financial investors, including Mr Vekselberg and many minority shareholders, the play looks increasingly risky, especially as aluminium prices remain depressed, while the company must still service $11bn in debt.

Mr Vekselberg, together with another of Rusal's main shareholders Mikhail Prokhorov, had backed accepting a $12.8bn offer from Norilsk last year to buy out 20 per cent from Rusal's 25 per cent stake in the nickel miner. The deal would have allowed Rusal to pay down its debt and start paying out dividends.

Mr Deripaska, who controls the Rusal board in partnership with another shareholder Glencore, the global commodities trader, however, rejected the offer as "gross corporate blackmail".

So far Mr Deripaska has staved off debt problems, paying down debt ahead of schedule last year and successfully refinancing $11.4bn of debt in October. He then won a 12-month "covenant holiday" from lender banks in January after aluminium prices dipped perilously close to covenant levels.

Aluminium prices have since recovered to $2,210 a tonne for three-month metal on the London Metal Exchange, just below the $2,224 base case Rusal set in its 2009 loan restructuring. But investors say all the restructuring has not removed worries about the debt burden.

"It is still a business which has liquidity constraints," said one western banker speaking on condition of anonymity. "The results aren't going to be great." Troika Dialog, the Moscow investment bank, expects Rusal to report full-year net income of $1.96bn when it releases results on Monday, nearly half what it reported last year The share slide and the disagreement over the Norilsk stake have exacerbated a clash in business styles between the two oligarchs. Mr Vekselberg, a financial investor, usually prefers to avoid conflict, while Mr Deripaska takes a strategic approach and appears to thrive on conflict.

"Oleg isn't [Mr Vekselberg's] favourite guy," said one associate of the two men. "He doesn't really prefer to be in a business when Deripaska is in charge." One person close to one of the shareholders claimed that the public blowout this week had been sparked by Mr Vekselberg's failure over the past six months to sell the 15.8 per cent Rusal stake he holds together with Len Blavatnik, via their Sual Partners Holding.

Mr Deripaska on Tuesday refused to say with which shareholder Mr Vekselberg had held talks, saying only that Mr Vekselberg had refused several proposals and had "always raised the price". Mr Vekselberg, however, via a spokesman, denied he had held any "official talks" over selling the stake.

"It looks like Vekselberg is behaving this way to try and get leverage over Deripaska so he can sell his stake. But the fact that the conflict has become public is not going to create positive sentiment around Rusal," Mr Ezimov said.

Mr Deripaska said he would advise Mr Vekselberg to sit on the stake for a while. "Rusal is a good company. It's in a difficult cycle right now but events that will influence the aluminium price—when the European and Asian markets rebalance—are still ahead. I would not advise any of the shareholders to sell or do something quick."

FT: Kazakhmys chairman to step down

By Helen Thomas in London

May 11, 2012

Vladimir Kim, the chairman of Kazakhmys and the copper miner's largest shareholder, will stand down to make way for an independent candidate, seven years after the company listed in London.

Mr Kim, speaking at the group's annual meeting on Friday, said he would stay on as a non-executive director of Kazakhmys and planned to remain as chairman while his replacement was found.

The change will bring Kazakhmys into line with the UK's guidelines on corporate governance.

"I feel that now is the right time to hand on the role to a new and independent chairman," said Mr Kim, adding that he

anticipated handing over the reins by the time of the next investor meeting.

Mr Kim added that he had no intention of reducing his 28 per cent stake in the miner.

One analyst said that he was comforted by Mr Kim's continuing presence at board level. "If you can't see these large owners and have the opportunity to speak to them once a year, they become invisible," he said.

Shares in Kazakhmys fell 1.55 per cent to 764p. Mr Kim was on Friday re-elected as a director of the company with the backing of more than 98 per cent of voting shareholders.

Kazakhmys, which listed in London in 2005, was among the first of a slew of companies from the former Soviet Union to pursue a full listing on the London Stock Exchange.

However, the miner—which is Kazakhstan's largest copper producer by volume and also mines gold, zinc and silver—has largely avoided the corporate governance headaches that have dogged some of its peers, such as Eurasian Natural Resources Corporation.

Investors have criticised some foreign-owned, London-listed miners, questioning their commitment to UK corporate governance norms and their interest in protecting minority owners.

ENRC, which listed in 2007 and in which Kazakhmys owns a 26 per cent stake, was last year engulfed in a corporate governance row after investors in the tightly held company voted against the re-election of two directors, including Sir Richard Sykes, the board's senior independent director.

The government of Kazakhstan has a 26 per cent stake in Kazakhmys, after a 2008 deal under which Mr Kim sold part of his stake to the authorities. The government's holding in both Kazakhmys and ENRC has long prompted speculation that the pair could combine to create a national champion.

Corporate Governance in the Asia-Pacific

Learning Objectives

- To understand the background to the development of corporate governance codes in the Asia-Pacific
- To be aware of the different ownership structures in the Asia-Pacific
- To be aware of the main differences in corporate governance codes in various countries in the Asia-Pacific
- To have a detailed knowledge of the corporate governance codes for a range of countries in the Asia-Pacific

Introduction

This chapter gives an overview of the development of corporate governance in the Asia-Pacific countries. The 1990s saw the meteoric rise and subsequent catastrophic collapse of many markets in the Asia-Pacific countries, in most of the so-called 'tiger economies'. Many investors, both local and overseas, had poured money into the stock markets to benefit from the vast gains that could be made. Equally, many investors lost large amounts when the markets crashed, when the bubble burst following on from Japan's prolonged recession in the early 1990s. By the late 1990s, it had spread to South Korea and several countries in the Asia-Pacific region. Following the crash, there was much soul-searching and questioning as to how and why this financial crisis could have happened. Many people expressed the view that the lack of transparency in companies' financial reports had been largely to blame, together with a lack of accountability of directors of companies. No one had really seemed to notice this situation, or if they had, they had not seemed to care about it, as long as the share prices were increasing and there were profits to be made from the stock market. However, once the markets crashed, it became a different story, and governments and stock exchanges sought to restore investor confidence in their countries by increasing transparency and accountability, and instituting better corporate governance.

In the context of the Asian countries with weak institutions and poor property rights (including protection of minority shareholders' rights), Claessens and Fan (2002) state that 'resulting forms of crony capitalism, i.e. combinations of weak corporate governance and government interference, not only lead to poor performance and risky financing patterns, but also are conductive to macro-economic crises'.

Following the financial downturn of the 1990s, many countries in South-East Asia, issued revised—and strengthened—corporate governance codes, and countries that previously had not had corporate governance codes introduced them.

The countries discussed in this chapter cover a range of ownership structures and influences that have impacted on the corporate governance structures. The countries discussed are:

- Japan, with the dominant shareholders being typically main banks of industrial groups or *keiretsu*;

- South Korea, with its *chaebol* representing the interests of dominant shareholders, often family groups;

- Malaysia, with families often being a dominant shareholder;

- Singapore, another country where families play a dominant role and which is emerging as one of the key players in financial markets in the region;

- China, where despite ongoing reforms the state still has significant influence in companies;

- Australia, which has a common law system and widespread institutional investor share ownership.

In a study of nine Asian countries (including Malaysia, South Korea, Japan, and Singapore but not China), Claessens *et al.* (2000) find that 'in all countries, voting rights frequently exceed cash flow rights via pyramid structures and cross-holdings'. This is indicative of the power that the dominant shareholders are able to build up. However, an encouraging and positive sign is that the countries examined in detail in this chapter have in common that they have felt the need to improve their corporate governance to provide greater transparency and enhance protection of minority shareholders' rights. Interestingly, Gilson (2008) states:

> While the absence of effective minority shareholder protection may in some circumstances explain the absence of corporations whose shares are widely held, it does not explain why we observe minority holdings at all, nor the special role of controlling-family shareholders in many countries. From the perspective of the product market, shareholder distribution, including family control, may play a role in facilitating the corporation's operation as a reputation bearer in markets where commercial exchange is supported by reputation rather than by formal enforcement.

Therefore where there is a weak legal environment and a lack of protection of minority shareholders, those firms that have regard for minority shareholders' rights may in this way be giving a positive signal to the market about their reputation.

Chen and Nowland (2010), in a study of family-owned companies in Asia, find that where 'the family group have a long record of successfully managing the company and where wealth is often created through undisclosable channels such as political connections, we find that too much monitoring is detrimental to company performance. This is because too much monitoring interferes with the ability of the family group to create wealth for all shareholders'.

Japan

Japan's economy developed very rapidly during the second half of the twentieth century. Particularly during the period 1985–9, there was a 'bubble economy', characterized by a sharp increase in share prices and the value of land; the early 1990s saw the bubble burst as share prices fell and land was devalued. As well as shareholders and landowners finding themselves losing vast fortunes, banks found that they had severe problems too. During the bubble period, the banks had lent large amounts of money against the value of land and, as the price of land fell, borrowers found themselves unable to make the repayments and the banks were left with large non-performing loans. The effect of the fall in share prices and land values spread through the Japanese economy, which became quite stagnant, and the effects spread to other countries' economies, precipitating a regional recession.

The Japanese government wished to restore confidence in the Japanese economy and in the stock market, and to attract foreign direct investment to help regenerate growth in companies. Improved corporate governance was seen as a very necessary step in this process.

Japan's corporate governance system is often likened to that of Germany because banks can play an influential role in companies in both countries. However, there are fundamental differences between the systems, driven partly by culture and partly by the Japanese shareholding structure with the influence of the *keiretsu* (broadly meaning 'associations of companies'). Charkham (1994) sums up three main concepts that affect Japanese attitudes towards corporate governance: obligation, family, and consensus. The first of these, obligation, is evidenced by the Japanese feeling of obligation to family, a company, or country; the second, family, is the strong feeling of being part of a 'family' whether this is a family per se, or a company; and the third concept, consensus, means that there is an emphasis on agreement rather than antagonism. These three concepts deeply influence the Japanese approach to corporate governance.

The *keiretsu* sprang out of the *zaibatsu*. Okumura (2002) states: 'Before World War II, when *zaibatsu* (giant pre-war conglomerates) dominated the Japanese economy, individuals or families governed companies as major stockholders. By contrast, after the war, by virtue of corporate capitalism, companies in the form of corporations became large stockowners, and companies became major stockholders of each other's stock.' The companies forming the *keiretsu* may be in different industries, forming a cluster often with a bank at the centre. Charkham (1994) states that 'banks are said to have encouraged the formation and development of groups of this kind, as a source of mutual strength and reciprocal help'. Indeed, banks themselves have a special relationship with the companies they lend to, particularly if they are the lead or main bank for a given company. Banks often buy shares in their customer companies to firm up the relationship between company and bank. However, they are limited to a 5 per cent holding in a given company but, in practice, the combination of the traditional bank relationship with its client and the shareholding mean that they can be influential, and often very helpful, if the company is in financial difficulties, viewing it as part of their obligation to the company to try to help it find a way out of its difficulties.

When compared to the German system, it should be noted that there is no automatic provision for employees to sit on the supervisory board. However, employees have traditionally come to expect that they will have lifelong employment with the same company—unfortunately, in times of economic downturn, this can no longer be guaranteed.

The Japan Corporate Governance Committee published its revised Corporate Governance Code in 2001 (hereafter, 'the Code'). The Code had six chapters, which contained a total of 14 principles. The Code had an interesting introduction, part of which stated 'a good company maximizes the profits of its shareholders by efficiently creating value, and in the process contributes to the creation of a more prosperous society by enriching the lives of its

Table 12.1 Key characteristics influencing Japanese corporate governance

Feature	Key characteristic
Main business form	Public limited company
Predominant ownership structure	*Keiretsu*; but institutional investor ownership is increasing
Legal system	Civil law
Board structure	Dual
Important aspect	Influence of *keiretsu*

employees and improving the welfare of its other stakeholders'. Hence the Code tried to take a balanced view of what a company is all about, and clearly the consideration of stakeholders is seen to be an important aspect. The foreword to the Code discussed and explained some of the basic tenets of corporate governance to help familiarize readers of the Code with areas including the role and function of the board of directors, the supervisory body, independent directors, incentive-based compensation, disclosure, and investor relations. Each of these areas are now looked at in more detail.

(i) Mission and role of the board of directors

This first chapter contained five principles relating to:

- the position and purpose of the board of directors;
- the function and powers of the board of directors;
- the organization of the board of directors;
- outside directors and their independence;
- the role of the leader of the board of directors.

The board should be comprised of outside directors (someone who has never been a full-time director, executive, or employee of the company)—preferably a majority—and inside directors (executives or employees of the company). Independent directors are outside directors who can make their decisions independently. The board of directors' role is seen as one of management supervision, including approving important strategic decisions, nominating candidates for director positions, appointment and removal of the chief executive officer (CEO), and general oversight of accounting and auditing. The board of directors may also be required to approve certain decisions made by the CEO.

(ii) Mission and role of the committees established within the board of directors

The board is recommended to establish various committees, including audit, compensation, and nominating committees. Each committee established should comprise at least three directors, with an outside director appointed as chair of each committee. The majority of directors on the audit committee should be independent directors, whilst the majority of directors on the other two committees should be outside directors, of whom at least one should be an independent director.

The roles of the various committees are broadly defined and cover the usual areas that one would expect for each of these committees.

(iii) Leadership responsibility of the CEO

The CEO's role is to formulate management strategies with the aim of maximizing corporate value in the long term. The CEO is supervised by the board of directors. The CEO may set up an executive management committee to assist him/her in conducting all aspects of the business. The CEO may not be a member of the committees listed above in (ii).

(iv) Addressing shareholder derivative litigation

A litigation committee, comprising a majority of independent directors, may be established to determine whether litigation action should be made against directors or executives against whom the company/shareholders may have a claim.

(v) Securing fairness and transparency for executive management

Two important areas were covered in this section of the Code: internal control and disclosure. The CEO should ensure that there is an effective corporate governance system with adequate internal control. The audit committee should evaluate the CEO's policies on internal audit and control. The CEO should prepare an annual report about the internal audit and control, which should preferably be audited by a certified public accountant.

Disclosure should be made by the CEO of any information that may influence share prices; also information should be disclosed to the various stakeholder groups as appropriate.

(vi) Reporting to the shareholders and communicating with investors

The shareholders' general meeting is seen as an opportunity for shareholders to listen to the reports of the directors and executives, and to obtain further information about the company through asking questions. Should the questions go unanswered in the general meeting, then the answer should be put on the company's website subsequent to the general meeting.

The company's executives are encouraged to meet analysts and others who can convey information to investors and shareholders about the company. Information should also be posted on the Internet to try to ensure equality of access to information amongst the various investors.

The Commercial Code in Japan provides for the appointment of statutory auditors to monitor the various aspects of the company's activities. However, in 2002 there was an extensive revision of the Commercial Code essentially providing companies with the option of adopting a 'US-style' corporate governance structure. The US-style structure would have a main board of directors to carry out the oversight function, and involve the establishment of audit, remuneration, and nomination committees, each with at least three members, a majority of whom should be non-executive. A board of corporate executive officers would also be appointed who would be in charge of the day-to-day business operations. Under the US-style structure, the board of statutory auditors would be abolished. It can be seen that the Japanese Corporate Governance Code's recommendations dovetailed with the revised Commercial Code.

In 2004 the Tokyo Stock Exchange issued the *Principles of Corporate Governance for Listed Companies*. In the preface, the purpose of the principles is described as being 'to provide a necessary common base for recognition, thereby enhancing corporate governance through the integration of voluntary activities by listed companies and demands by shareholders and investors'. The five principles are based around the Organisation for Economic Co-operation and Development (OECD) *Principles of Corporate Governance*.

The first principle relates to exercising various rights of shareholders, including the right to participate and vote in general meetings, voting on such issues as the election and dismissal of directors and auditors, and fundamental corporate changes; the basic right to share various profits such as dividends; and the special right to make derivative lawsuits and injunction of activities in contravention of laws, regulations, and other rules. The voting environment should be developed and improved so that shareholders can exercise their votes appropriately and participate in general meetings of shareholders.

The second principle relates to the equitable treatment of shareholders, including minority and foreign shareholders. To this end, there should be an adequate system to prohibit transactions through the abuse of officers, employees, and controlling shareholders, which are against the primary interests of the company or shareholders. There should be enhanced disclosure where it seems that such actions might occur, and there should be prohibition of special benefits to specified shareholders.

The third principle is the relationship with stakeholders in corporate governance. Whilst corporate governance should help to create corporate value and jobs, the fact that companies sustain and improve their strengths and enhance value over time is 'the result of the provision of company resources by all stakeholders', so the establishment of good relationships with stakeholders is important. To this end, companies should cultivate a corporate culture and internal systems, which respect the various stakeholder groups and ensure timely and accurate disclosure of information relating to them.

The fourth principle relates to disclosure and transparency. Companies should ensure timely and accurate disclosure on all material matters, including the financial state and performance of the company, and ownership distribution, through both quantitative and qualitative disclosures. The company should seek to ensure that investors can access information easily and that there is equal access to information. Internal systems should ensure the accuracy and timeliness of disclosure.

The final principle relates to the responsibilities of the board of directors, auditors, board of corporate auditors, and other relevant groups. Corporate governance should enhance the supervision of management by the aforementioned groups and ensure their accountability to shareholders. Systems should be developed, or enhanced, to ensure that these requirements can be met.

In 2009 the revised *Principles of Corporate Governance for Listed Companies* were published. The preface discussed the consideration of other stakeholders as well as shareholders:

> As the areas of corporate activity are expanding, corporations face a growing need to take into account the values of different cultures and societies. As such, enterprises will have to engage in their profit-pursuing activities with a greater awareness of their social responsibilities, with greater transparency and fairness in accordance with market principles, while accepting full accountability to the entire economic community as well as shareholders and investors.

The preface also makes the point that where there is a holding company with a group of companies, then it is important for corporate governance to be adopted across the group as a whole.

It is important to note that the legal framework in Japan, via the Commercial Code Revision on Boards (2003), provides for two corporate governance structures: a corporate auditors' system, consisting of general meetings with shareholders, the board of directors, representative directors, executive directors, corporate auditors, and the board of corporate auditors; and a committees system, where there are general meetings of the shareholders, the board of directors, and committees composed of members of the board of directors (nomination, audit, and compensation committees), representative executive officers, and executive officers. It is up to the company which system it chooses. In each case, the general meeting of shareholders is the decision-making body on matters of fundamental importance to the company. A key difference between the two structures is that companies with a committee system need to re-elect their directors annually through the general meeting of shareholders, because the board of directors has the authority regarding the definitive plan for the distribution of profit, whereas in the corporate auditors' system, this power lies with the general meetings of shareholders.

Charkham (2005) discusses the various changes that have taken place in the context of corporate governance in Japan and states:

> The important part the banks played has greatly diminished. In its place there are now better structured boards, more effective company auditors, and occasionally more active shareholders. An increase of interest, and, where appropriate, action on their part, might restore the balance that the banks' withdrawal from the scene has impaired.

Ahmadjian and Okumura (2011) also discuss the changes that have taken place in Japan in recent years:

> Over the last two decades, the debate on corporate governance has contrasted two extremes—whether to become 'like the US' or retain the post-war Japanese system of governance. Yet, as we noted earlier, retaining the 'traditional' post-war governance system is no longer an option, since it has been severely weakened by the demise of the role of the main bank, unwinding of cross-shareholdings, changes in accounting standards and increased investment by foreigners.

It is interesting to note that Japan is now using 'poison pills' much more to ward off hostile takeover bids (an undesirable development), whereas it does not have the huge problems associated with perceived excessive director remuneration, as its directors are not paid the vast multiples of the salary of the ordinary employees because this would be considered culturally unacceptable.

In 2008 the Asian Corporate Governance Association (ACGA) published its 'White Paper on Corporate Governance in Japan'. It states:

While a number of leading companies in Japan have made strides in corporate governance in recent years, we submit that the system of governance in most listed companies is not meeting the needs of stakeholders or the nation at large in three ways:

- By not providing for adequate supervision of corporate strategy;
- By protecting management from the discipline of the market, thus rendering the development of a healthy and efficient market in corporate control all but impossible;
- By failing to provide the returns that are vitally necessary to protect Japan's social safety net—its pension system.

It then advocates six areas for improvement: shareholders acting as owners, utilizing capital efficiently, independent supervision of management, pre-emption rights, poison pills and takeover defences, and shareholder meetings and voting.

South Korea

The downturn in the Japanese economy soon affected the Korean economy, which suffered similar consequences. Balino and Ubide (1999), amongst others, stated that poor corporate governance was an important contributory factor to the extent of the financial crisis in 1997. The poor corporate governance was characterized by a lack of transparency and disclosure, ineffective boards, and the activities of the *chaebols*.

The *chaebols* are large Korean conglomerates that wield considerable power through their cross-holdings of shares in various companies. The *chaebols* often constitute powerful family interests in Korea, and families may be able to exert more control in a particular company than their shareholdings on paper would merit. They often have little regard for the rights and interests of minority shareholders. However, in recent years, the People's Solidarity for Participatory Democracy (PSPD) has been established as an influential minority shareholder activist group that has campaigned for better corporate governance in a number of Korea's top companies. Jang and Kim (2002) emphasize the influence and power of families via the *chaebols*:

> Ownership by the controlling families in listed Korean chaebol companies has been only a fraction and their controlling power derives from their ownership through affiliated companies . . . personal stakes, particularly in listed companies, are minimized but control is maintained by an extensive matrix of circuitous cross-ownership among affiliated companies.

The Korean Committee on Corporate Governance was established in March 1999, with funding from the Korea Stock Exchange, the Korea Securities Dealers' Association, the Korea Listed Companies Association, and the Korea Investment Trust Companies Association. It reported six months later in September 1999, with a Code of Best Practice (hereinafter 'the Code'), which tries to take into account both internationally accepted corporate governance principles and also the 'unique managerial circumstances faced by Korean companies'. The purpose of the Code is stated as being to maximize corporate value by enhancing transparency and efficiency of corporations for the future. It is recognized that, in order to attract and retain both domestic and foreign investment, there needs to be more transparency and more regard to the rights of minority shareholders.

Table 12.2 Key characteristics influencing South Korean corporate governance

Feature	Key characteristic
Main business form	Public limited company
Predominant ownership structure	Controlling shareholder (family, corporate cross-holdings)
Legal system	Common law
Board structure	Unitary
Important aspect	Influence of *chaebol*

The Code applies to listed companies and other public companies but it is also advised that non-public companies follow the Code where practicable. The Code has five sections relating to shareholders, the board of directors, audit systems, stakeholders, and management monitoring by the market, which are looked at in more detail now.

(i) Shareholders

Shareholders possess basic rights, such as the right to attend and vote at general shareholder meetings, and to receive relevant information in a timely way, that should be protected. Shareholders shall be treated equitably: for example, shares of the same class shall have the same voting and other rights.

As well as rights, shareholders have responsibilities and so should try to exercise their voting rights. Controlling shareholders have the corresponding responsibilities when they exercise any influence toward the corporate management other than the exercise of voting rights.

(ii) Board of directors

The board of directors should make the corporation's key management policy decisions and shall supervise the activities of directors and management. Its activities should include:

- setting corporate goals and the strategies to achieve them;
- approving business plans and budgets;
- supervising risk management activities and associated controls;
- ensuring appropriate information disclosure.

Board meetings of the full board (inside and outside directors) should be held regularly, and at least once a quarter.

The board/directors should perform their duties faithfully in the best interests of the corporation and its shareholders; they shall also perform their social responsibilities and consider the interests of various stakeholders. The board shall observe the related statutes and the articles of incorporation when performing its duties, and shall ensure that all members of the corporation also observe them. If a director breaches the law or the company's articles of incorporation, or has neglected his/her duties, he/she may be liable for damages to the corporation.

The board may set up internal committees, such as audit, operation, and remuneration committees, comprised of directors with relevant expertise in the area. The remuneration of directors may be covered by a remuneration committee and should be related to an evaluation of their contribution to the company.

There should be outside directors who are 'capable of performing their duties independently from the management, controlling shareholders and the corporation'. The outside directors should comprise 25 per cent of the board (50 per cent for financial institutions and large-scale public corporations). It is recommended that there are also regular meetings between the outside directors only and the management to enable both to gain a fuller perspective of corporate management issues.

Directors should be appointed through a transparent process and it is recommended that a nomination committee be established, comprised one-half outside directors. There should be sufficient information disclosed about the director appointment nominees to enable shareholders to vote in an informed way.

(iii) Audit systems

Companies such as public corporations, government-invested institutions, and financial institutions, should establish an audit committee composed of at least three board members, of which at least two-thirds, including the audit committee chair, should be outside directors; at least one member should have professional auditing knowledge. When a company has an audit committee, it does not need to have an auditor as well (that is, an auditor appointed permanently in the company), but large firms (those with total assets of more than US$5.8 million) must have an annual accounting audit by an external firm.

The audit committee remit includes: evaluating the internal control system, evaluating the external auditors, reviewing the accuracy of the company's financial reports, and reviewing management's operations. The audit committee should be provided with sufficient information to enable it to perform its role properly, and should meet at least once a quarter, drafting appropriate detailed minutes, which shareholders are allowed to read.

The external audit shall be performed by those independent from stakeholders in the corporation, such as the management or controlling shareholder, and by those who specialize in auditing. External auditors should attend the company's general shareholder meeting and answer shareholders' questions on the audit report.

(iv) Stakeholders

The Code states that the rights of stakeholders, and appropriate means of redress for infringement of their rights, shall be protected. Companies need to take account of their social responsibilities too, such as consumer protection and environmental protection. Stakeholders may monitor management as appropriate (in the context of their particular stakeholder interest) and have access to relevant information to protect their rights.

There is no provision for employee representation as such (it is a unitary board system rather than dual), but the Act on Worker Participation and Promotion of Co-operation stipulates that employees and management have consultative meetings whereby the employees are informed of the company's plans, quarterly performance, personnel plans, etc.

(v) Management monitoring by the market

Corporations shall actively disclose matters of material importance to the decision-making of shareholders, creditors, and other interested parties. Anything that could lead to a change in corporate control, including takeovers, mergers, acquisitions, and business splits, should be carried out through a transparent and fair procedure. The board is entitled to defend against hostile takeovers but not to the detriment of the company's profits, to help maintain control for only some shareholders, or for management.

The company should explain in its annual report any differences between its corporate governance and the recommendations laid down in the Code. An interesting recommendation is that where there is a minimum of 20 per cent foreign ownership, then companies should make disclosures in both Korean and English languages for audit reports and 'material timely disclosures'.

Finally, and of some significance, is the recommendation that companies disclose detailed information on the share ownership status of controlling shareholders because 'the actual controlling shareholder of the corporation is one at the core of corporate governance'.

In 2003 an updated Code of Best Practices for Corporate Governance was issued. Retaining the same sections as previously, the impetus for the revised Code were the changes affecting corporate governance globally, including accounting frauds in the USA, and the reform of governance systems in many countries. Furthermore, it was recognized that investment risks associated with poor corporate governance remained as one of the main causes of the undervaluation of Korean stocks. The Code focused on the practical applications of its recommendations and attempted to take into account the unique managerial circumstances faced by Korean companies.

Black *et al.* (2005), in a study of firms' corporate governance practices in Korea, found that regulatory factors are very important, largely because Korean rules impose special governance requirements on large firms (as mentioned earlier). They found that industry factors, firm size, and firm risk are important, with larger firms and riskier firms being better governed.

Kim and Kim (2007) found that Korea has significantly improved its quality of corporate governance since the 1997 financial crisis. They state that:

> Most notable are improved corporate transparency, better alignment of managerial incentives to shareholder value, and more effective oversight by the board. A number of players also have emerged as key external monitors and enforcers of good governance. There remain, however, substantial differences between non-chaebol and chaebol affiliated firms and also across chaebol.

Aguilera *et al.* (2012), in a study of companies in emerging markets in the period 2000–8, found, in the context of South Korea, that whilst family ownership was gradually decreasing—implying that the traditional family-owned structure has weakened—this

> does not entail the collapse of the controlling power of families, particularly in business groups, as that would require not only that family control decreases but also that cross-shareholdings and pyramidal structures no longer exist. In fact, in 2009 the KFTC reports that internal ownership, which represents the sum of family direct shareholding and cross-shareholdings, of the top 10 business groups is still more than 50 per cent. Despite criticism for their lack of transparency and patriarchal management, *Chaebols* are continuing to

engage in the generation-to-generation transfer of ownership, with one-third of the top 50 family-owned businesses already having concluded the succession process.

Malaysia

Malaysia was one of the fastest growing of the tiger economies in the early 1990s. The government had introduced a succession of five-year plans with the aim of full industrialization in the twenty-first century. The government had also introduced the New Economic Policy (NEP) in 1970 to implement affirmative actions in favour of the Bumiputera (the indigenous Malay people). These types of affirmative action were designed to increase Bumiputera involvement in the corporate sector. The government also set up trusts to hold shares on behalf of the Bumiputera, and whether as companies, individuals, or trusts, they tend to be one of the largest shareholder groups in Malaysian companies. The corporate governance code in Malaysia concentrates on the principles and best practice of corporate governance, drawing largely on the UK corporate governance recommendations.

In Malaysia many of the listed companies are family-owned or controlled, with many companies having evolved from traditional family-owned enterprises. This means that the directors may not be responsive to minority shareholders' rights; better corporate governance would help to remedy this and ensure that minority shareholders' rights are protected. In addition, transparency should be improved to help restore investor confidence.

Malaysia established its High Level Finance Committee on Corporate Governance in 1998, following on from the drastic downturn of the Malaysian economy the previous year. The Committee reported in March 2000 with a detailed corporate governance code: the Malaysian Code of Corporate Governance (hereinafter 'the Code'). The Kuala Lumpur Stock Exchange adopted the Code's recommendations and, with effect from 2002, listed companies have had to include a statement of their compliance with the Code and explain any areas of the Code that they do not comply with (i.e. a 'comply or explain' mechanism).

The Code has four parts: first, broad principles of good corporate governance; secondly, best practices for companies, which gives more detail for each of the broad principles; thirdly, a section aimed at investors and auditors discussing their role in corporate governance; and fourthly, various explanatory notes are provided. As mentioned, the first part of the Code is

Table 12.3 Key characteristics influencing Malaysian corporate governance

Feature	Key characteristic
Main business form	Public limited company
Predominant ownership structure	Controlling shareholder (family, corporation, or trust nominee)
Legal system	Common law
Board structure	Unitary
Important aspect	Influence of Bumiputera shareholders

devoted to the principles of corporate governance, which cover directors, directors' remuneration, shareholders, and accountability and audit, whilst the second part essentially expands on the principles with examples of best practice, or guidelines as to how best to implement the principles. The principles held in the first part of the Code are looked at in more detail now.

(i) Directors

Every listed company should have an effective balanced board comprised of executive and non-executive directors. Independent non-executive directors should comprise at least one-third of the board. Where the company has a significant shareholder (a shareholder with the ability to exercise a majority of votes for the election of directors), the board should disclose annually whether it fairly reflects, through board representation, the investment of the minority of shareholders. There is a preference for the chairman and the CEO's roles to be separate to ensure that power is not centred in one individual. The roles can be combined but then the presence of an independent element on the board would be particularly important, and a decision to combine the roles would need to be publicly explained.

The board should have appropriate relevant information supplied in a timely fashion. Its responsibilities will include:

- the strategic direction of the company;
- ensuring proper management of the company;
- identifying risks and ensuring an appropriate risk management system;
- reviewing the overall effectiveness of the internal control systems of the company;
- succession planning and training of directors;
- the investor relations programme.

The board should meet regularly and disclose the attendance record of individual directors at board meetings.

The board should have access to a company secretary who should ensure that the board provides all appropriate information for corporate and statutory requirements. The board should also have access to independent professional advice as and when needed at the company's expense.

Directors should be appointed by a transparent nominations process by a nominating committee comprised exclusively of non-executive directors, a majority of these being independent. The nominating committee should review the mix of skills and experience on the board each year and identify any gaps that might need to be filled. The nominating committee should assess, on an annual basis, the effectiveness of the board, the committees of the board, and individual directors. Re-election should take place regularly (at least every three years). An important aspect is the emphasis on the importance of director training. The Code describes orientation and education of new directors as 'an integral element of the process of appointing new directors'.

(ii) Directors' remuneration

There should be a remuneration committee, comprised wholly or mainly of non-executive directors, to recommend the remuneration levels for the executive directors. Remuneration packages should reflect levels of both corporate and individual performance. The remuneration of non-executive directors should be decided by the board as a whole and should reflect each non-executive's experience and responsibilities in the company. The remuneration of each director should be disclosed in the company's annual report.

(iii) Accountability and audit

An audit committee should be established, comprised of at least three directors with the majority being independent. It should be chaired by an independent non-executive director. The audit committee's role includes:

- reviewing the year-end and quarterly financial statements of the company;
- considering the appointment of the external auditor, his/her fee, and the nature and scope of the audit;
- reviewing the scope, programme, and results of the internal audit.

The activities of the audit committee, the number of meetings held each year, and the attendance by individual directors should be disclosed. Internal audit should be independent of the activities they audit.

(iv) Shareholders

The board should ensure that there is an effective communications strategy between the board, management, shareholders, and stakeholders. There should be 'a dialogue based on the mutual understanding of objectives' between the company and its institutional investors. The annual general meeting (AGM) is a way to communicate with private investors and encourage their participation.

The third part of the Code is aimed at investors and auditors and their role in corporate governance. The role of institutional investors is emphasized: they should engage in constructive dialogue with companies, evaluate companies' corporate governance arrangements, and vote in a considered way at companies' AGMs. For their part, auditors should independently report to shareholders in accordance with statutory and professional requirements.

The Corporate Law Reform Committee was established in 2004 to lead a programme of corporate law reform in Malaysia. Corporate governance reforms are the focus of one of the working groups, which is looking at issues of corporate governance and shareholders' rights. A consultation document on engagement with shareholders was issued in February 2006, with comments invited for later in the spring. The review is seeking to find an appropriate balance between providing a framework for effective shareholder engagement and ensuring that this framework is cost efficient, flexible, and facilitative for business. The focus is on general meetings and associated issues such as voting.

In 2007 the revised *Malaysian Code on Corporate Governance* was issued. It states that

> The key amendments to the Code are aimed at strengthening the board of directors and audit committees, and ensuring that the board of directors and audit committees discharge their roles and responsibilities effectively. The amendments spell out the eligibility criteria for appointment of directors and the role of the nominating committee. On audit committees,

the amendments spell out the eligibility criteria for appointment as an audit committee member, the composition of audit committees, the frequency of meetings and the need for continuous training. In addition, internal audit functions are now required in all PLCs and the reporting line for internal auditors clarified.

Liew (2007) finds that Malaysia's corporate governance reforms have been modelled on the Anglo-American system to a large extent, but the majority of the interviewees in her research placed greater emphasis on the social aspect of corporate governance in contrast to the traditional notion of shareholder accountability.

In June 2009 the stock exchange in Malaysia, Bursa Malaysia, announced that it would be launching a new corporate governance index with the aim of encouraging greater transparency, more independence at board level and helping to deter related party transactions.

In 2011 the Securities Commission Malaysia published a Corporate Governance Blueprint setting out a broad-based approach to the corporate governance landscape going forward. Boards and shareholders should conduct business in a way that enhances the company's reputation for good governance and promote more internalization of the culture of good governance. The Blueprint 'seeks to enrich the governance process through promoting more extensive and proactive participation by a broader range of stakeholders'. The Blueprint details recent changes in Malaysia impacting on the corporate governance environment, these include that in 2010, the Capital Markets and Services Act 2007 was amended to include sections 317A and 320A which gave the Securities Commission Malaysia the power to act against directors of listed companies who cause wrongful loss to their company and against any person who misleads the public through falsely preparing or auditing the financial statements of companies; and also that Malaysia has committed to achieving full convergence with the International Financial Reporting Standards (IFRS) by January 2012.

The Corporate Governance Blueprint recognizes that Malaysia needs to embed corporate governance culture in listed companies and more generally within the corporate governance ecosystem, which it identifies as including shareholders, gatekeepers, and regulators as well as the board of directors. The Corporate Governance Blueprint has six chapters:

- Shareholder Rights advocates the empowerment of shareholders through a fair, efficient, and transparent voting process;
- Role of Institutional Investors exhorts institutional investors to take a leadership role in governance by exercising responsible ownership;
- Board's Role in Governance amplifies the role of boards as active and responsible fiduciaries;
- Disclosure and Transparency emphasizes the enhancement of disclosure standards and practices to promote informed decision-making by shareholders;
- Role of Gatekeepers and Influencers gives recognition to their critical role in fortifying self- and market discipline;
- Public and Private Enforcement reinforces the critical and complementary roles of public and private enforcement in maintaining market confidence.

In the following year the Malaysian Code on Corporate Governance (2012) was issued. This focuses on strengthening board structure and composition, recognizing the role of directors as active and responsible fiduciaries. It also encourages companies to have appropriate corporate disclosure policies and to make public their commitment to respecting shareholder rights. There are eight principles and twenty-six accompanying recommendations which focus on, amongst others, laying a strong foundation for the board and its committees to carry out their roles effectively, promote timely and balanced disclosure, safeguard the integrity of financial reporting, emphasize the importance of risk management and internal controls, and encourage shareholder participation in general meetings. The eight principles are as follows:

- Principle 1—Establish clear roles and responsibilities.
- Principle 2—Strengthen composition.
- Principle 3—Reinforce independence.
- Principle 4—Foster commitment.
- Principle 5—Uphold integrity in financial reporting.
- Principle 6—Recognize and manage risks.
- Principle 7—Ensure timely and high quality disclosure.
- Principle 8—Strengthen relationship between company and shareholders.

It is interesting to note that under Principle 1, Recommendation 1.4 states that, 'the board should ensure that the company's strategies promote sustainability'; and that Recommendation 1.6 states that, 'the board should ensure it is supported by a suitably qualified and competent company secretary'.

Salim (2011) discusses many of the issues that have affected corporate governance in Malaysia, identifying gaps between 'the law-in-books and the law-in-action'. Moreover he points out that the law operates within the environment of 'Malaysia's "syncretic" nature, her unique multi-racial setting as well as her corporate structure [which] has an impact on corporate practices'. He concludes that it requires the balancing of diverse stakeholder groups' interests and that 'the challenge for regulators is to identify who these stakeholder are, and to find the right balance to protect the interests of each. Also as corporate governance operates within a larger societal context, a true reform can only be achieved by including institutional and political reforms as part of the larger reform agenda'.

Singapore

Singapore is one of the leading financial centres in Asia, offering a broad range of financial services, including banking, insurance, investment banking, and treasury services. In just over four decades, it has established a thriving financial centre of international repute which attracts business on a global basis as well as from the wider Asia-Pacific region. The Singapore Exchange (SGX) has some 800 companies listed, about one-fifth of which are overseas companies.

Temasek Holdings is an investment company that was incorporated under the Singapore Companies Act in 1974 to hold and manage investments and assets previously held by the Singapore government. These were investments made since Singapore gained its independence in 1965. The aim was for Temasek to own and manage these investments on a commercial basis

Table 12.4 Key characteristics influencing Singaporean corporate governance

Feature	Key characteristic
Main business form	Public limited companies
Predominant ownership structure	Families; state
Legal system	Common law
Board structure	Unitary
Important aspect	Influence of State (for example, via Temasek Holdings)

whilst leaving the Ministry of Finance to focus on its core role of policymaking and regulations. Over the years Temasek has become an influential investor not just in the domestic market, where it has shares in many companies, but also internationally through its activities as a sovereign wealth fund.

The Code of Corporate Governance (hereafter 'the Code') was introduced in 2001 to promote a high standard of corporate governance amongst listed companies in Singapore. The Code has evolved over the years to try to ensure its relevance to a changing investor environment, and market developments with revisions being made in 2005 and most recently in May 2012. The most recent Code was drafted by the Corporate Governance Council, which was set up by the Monetary Authority of Singapore (MAS) in February 2010, to undertake a comprehensive review of the Code. The rationale being that 'strong corporate governance is critical to protecting the interest of the investing public, maintaining confidence in our listed companies and enhancing Singapore's global reputation as a trusted financial centre'.

The Code has several sections with key principles as now detailed.

Board matters

The Board's conduct of affairs

Principle 1—Every company should be headed by an effective Board to lead and control the company. The Board is collectively responsible for the long-term success of the company. The Board works with Management to achieve this objective and Management remains accountable to the Board.

Board composition and guidance

Principle 2—There should be a strong and independent element on the Board, which is able to exercise objective judgement on corporate affairs independently, in particular, from Management and 10% shareholders. No individual or small group of individuals should be allowed to dominate the Board's decision making.

Chairman and Chief Executive Officer

Principle 3—There should be a clear division of responsibilities between the leadership of the Board and the executives responsible for managing the company's business. No one individual should represent a considerable concentration of power.

Board membership

Principle 4—There should be a formal and transparent process for the appointment and re-appointment of directors to the Board.

Board performance

Principle 5—There should be a formal annual assessment of the effectiveness of the Board as a whole and its board committees and the contribution by each director to the effectiveness of the Board.

Access to information

Principle 6—In order to fulfil their responsibilities, directors should be provided with complete, adequate and timely information prior to board meetings and on an on-going basis so as to enable them to make informed decisions to discharge their duties and responsibilities.

Remuneration matters

Procedures for developing remuneration policies

Principle 7—There should be a formal and transparent procedure for developing policy on executive remuneration and for fixing the remuneration packages of individual directors. No director should be involved in deciding his own remuneration.

Level and mix of remuneration

Principle 8—The level and structure of remuneration should be aligned with the long-term interest and risk policies of the company, and should be appropriate to attract, retain and motivate (a) the directors to provide good stewardship of the company, and (b) key management personnel to successfully manage the company. However, companies should avoid paying more than is necessary for this purpose.

Disclosure of remuneration

Principle 9—Every company should provide clear disclosure of its remuneration policies, level and mix of remuneration, and the procedure for setting remuneration, in the company's Annual Report. It should provide disclosure in relation to its remuneration policies to enable investors to understand the link between remuneration paid to directors and key management personnel, and performance.

Accountability and audit

Accountability

Principle 10—The board should present a balanced and understandable assessment of the company's performance, position, and prospects.

Risk management and internal controls

Principle 11—The Board is responsible for the governance of risk. The Board should ensure that Management maintains a sound system of risk management and internal controls to safeguard shareholders' interests and the company's assets, and should determine the nature and extent of the significant risks which the Board is willing to take in achieving its strategic objectives.

Audit committee

Principle 12—The Board should establish an Audit Committee ("AC") with written terms of reference which clearly set out its authority and duties.

Internal audit

Principle 13—The company should establish an effective internal audit function that is adequately resourced and independent of the activities it audits.

Shareholder rights and responsibilities

Shareholder rights

Principle 14—Companies should treat all shareholders fairly and equitably, and should recognize, protect, and facilitate the exercise of shareholders' rights, and continually review and update such governance arrangements.

Communication with shareholders

Principle 15—Companies should actively engage their shareholders and put in place an investor relations policy to promote regular, effective and fair communication with shareholders.

Conduct of shareholder meetings

Principle 16—Companies should encourage greater shareholder participation at general meetings of shareholders, and allow shareholders the opportunity to communicate their views on various matters affecting the company.

The changes to the earlier Code are focused on the areas of director independence, board composition, director training, multiple directorships, alternate directors, remuneration practices and disclosures, risk management, and shareholder rights and roles.

In terms of disclosure of corporate governance arrangements, the Code states that the Listing Manual requires listed companies to describe in their company's annual reports their corporate governance practices with specific reference to the principles of the Code, as well as disclose and explain any deviation from any guideline of the Code. Companies should make a positive confirmation at the start of the corporate governance section of the company's annual report that they have adhered to the principles and guidelines of the Code, or specify each area of non-compliance.

At the end of the Code there is a statement on the role of shareholders in engaging with the companies in which they invest. The statement says that 'the objective of creating sustainable and financially sound enterprises that offer long-term value to shareholders is best served through a constructive relationship between shareholders and the Boards of companies. . . . By constructively engaging with the Board, shareholders can help to set the tone and expectation for governance of the company.' Shareholders are exhorted to attend the companies' AGMs and to vote their shares. The statement does not form part of the Code; it is aimed at enhancing the quality of engagement between shareholders and companies, so as to help drive higher standards of corporate governance and improve long-term returns to shareholders.

It is noteworthy that in 2010 the MAS issued Guidelines on Corporate Governance for Banks, Financial Holding Companies and Direct Insurers, which are incorporated in Singapore. These guidelines are based on the Corporate Governance Code with some additional recommendations for banks, financial holding companies, and insurers. The rationale given by MAS for these additional recommendations is that weak governance can undermine public confidence in financial institutions as well as the financial system and markets in which they operate.

In May 2012 the Corporate Governance Council released its Risk Governance Guidance for Listed Boards. The Guidance is

> intended to provide key information on risk governance to all Board members. This includes factors which the Board should collectively consider when overseeing the company's risk management framework and policies. The Guidance also spells out the Board's and Management's respective responsibilities in managing the company's risks. In particular, the Council hopes that the Guidance will assist the Board, as well as Management, of small to mid-capitalised listed companies in the risk governance of their companies.

China

The Peoples' Republic of China (PRC) has introduced a number of changes to develop its stock market. In the early 1990s, the Shanghai and Shenzhen Stock Exchanges were launched, with the aim of raising finance from domestic and foreign investors to provide listed companies with new funds. The 1990s saw many businesses move from being state-owned enterprises (SOEs) to joint stock companies, and then to companies listed on one of the stock exchanges. The PRC government wished to modernize its industry and other sectors, and to expand the economy, to move towards a socialist market economy.

However, many of the former SOEs were lumbering giants with outdated machinery, and employing far too many people to make them viable as commercially run businesses with the aim of increasing profits. They were used to receiving loans from the state-owned commercial banks, which the banks very often knew they had little chance of repaying, these being non-performing loans that, in turn, were a real drain on the resources of the state-owned banks. The SOEs were also subject to the influence of party members at a number of levels: as employees, as local government officials in the district in which they operate, and at national level. This situation is changing over time but the old influences still exist.

The situation was exacerbated by unfortunate incidents of corruption (which meant that the assets of the business were not safeguarded), and by a lack of transparency, disclosure, and accuracy of information. All in all, this was not a state of affairs that was going to build confidence in the stock market.

The government's desire to build a socialist market economy, to modernize, and to become part of the World Trade Organization all fuelled the move to try to improve shareholders' rights and protection of those rights, the insulation of company boards from inappropriate influence, and greater transparency and disclosure: in essence, the building of a corporate governance system. However, although many of the provisions are there on paper for an effective corporate governance system (as will be shown later), in practice, the state still owns large shareholdings in many companies (often more than half), minority shareholders' rights are sometimes ignored, and companies in the PRC are liable to have influence exerted over them from a number of different sources. Nonetheless, steps have been taken in the right direction and the government will be aware that if it wishes to attract foreign institutional investors, it will need to have a corporate governance system that protects minority rights, and encourages confidence in the corporate structure and operations, and companies will need to provide accurate and timely information. As On Kit Tam (1999) stated: 'The task of establishing functional and appropriate corporate governance arrangements [in China] is necessarily a long-term and continually changing one'.

In the PRC, corporate governance developments involve a number of regulatory bodies, including the China Securities Regulatory Commission (CSRC), the Ministry of Finance, the State Economic and Trade Commission, and the People's Bank of China, which is essentially the Central Bank of China.

A series of corporate scandals came to light in 2001, including that of Lantian Co. Ltd. Lantian Co. Ltd was the first publicly listed ecological agricultural company in China. However, investors grew suspicious of its high profit growth because its business could not have underpinned such growth. Subsequently, inaccuracies in its financial reporting came to light and it is estimated that Lantian overstated net profits by up to US$60 million. Scandals such as Lantian have helped fuel the drive for corporate governance reforms and, in January 2001, the CSRC issued a Code of Corporate Governance For Listed Companies in China (hereinafter 'the Code').

The Code is broadly based on the OECD *Principles of Corporate Governance*. The Code is aimed at listed companies and addresses 'the protection of investors' interests and rights, the basic behaviour rules and moral standards for directors, supervisors, managers, and other

Table 12.5 Key characteristics influencing Chinese corporate governance

Feature	Key characteristic
Main business form	State-owned enterprises, joint stock companies
Predominant ownership structures	State
Legal system	Civil law
Board structure	Dual
Important aspect	Influence of Communist Party

senior management members of listed companies'. The Code is seen as the yardstick by which a company is able to measure its corporate governance, and if there are deficiencies in the corporate governance of a company, then the securities supervision and regulatory authorities may instruct the company to correct its corporate governance to comply with the Code.

The Code contains seven main chapters dealing with: shareholders and shareholders' meetings; the listed company and its controlling shareholders; directors and the board of directors; the supervisors and the supervisory board; performance assessments and incentive and disciplinary systems; stakeholders; information disclosure and transparency. These are dealt with in turn now.

(i) Shareholders and shareholders' meetings

The Code states that the company should ensure that all shareholders are treated fairly, especially minority shareholders. Shareholders should have equal rights and, if their rights are infringed, then they should have redress through legal action. Directors, supervisors, and managers of companies will be liable to pay compensation if they breach laws and regulations.

Companies should establish communication channels with shareholders and shareholders should be informed of significant matters that affect the company. Shareholders should be notified in good time of a shareholders' meeting and agenda items should be given an appropriate amount of time in the meeting. Electronic communications may be used to help increase the number of shareholders participating. Shareholders may vote in person or may appoint a proxy to vote on their behalf. The role of institutional investors is specifically mentioned in the appointment of directors, remuneration, and other major decisions. In related party transactions, these transactions should, in principle, be at market value.

(ii) Listed company and its controlling shareholders

This section of the Code deals with a protocol for how the controlling shareholders should behave when an enterprise is being restructured or reorganized prior to listing. Certain aspects of the enterprise, such as its non-operational institutions and welfare institutions, will not be transferred to the listed company, but may continue to provide services to the listed company in the capacity of a separate company based on commercial principles. Reform of labour, personnel, and distribution systems may occur. However, the controlling shareholders should not act in a way that is detrimental to the listed company's or shareholders' legal rights and interests by adversely restructuring assets or otherwise taking advantage of their position.

The controlling shareholders initially nominate the candidates for directors and supervisors on the basis of their professional skills, knowledge, and experience. The shareholders' meeting or the board of directors will approve appointments as appropriate. The listed company should be able to act independently of the controlling shareholders, including its personnel, and also the financial and accounting management systems of the listed company should be independent from the controlling shareholders. Logically, the board of directors and supervisory committee should operate in an independent manner and indeed the Code states that 'a listed company's business shall be completely independent from that of its controlling shareholders'.

(iii) Directors and board of directors

In order to enable shareholders to make an informed choice as to which candidate to vote for in director elections, there should be detailed disclosure of information about the candidate. The emphasis is on appointments being made through a transparent process.

Directors should attend appropriate training sessions to familiarize themselves with their directorial duties and responsibilities. They should be suitably qualified with appropriate skills and knowledge. They should 'faithfully, honestly, and diligently perform their duties for the best interests of the company and all shareholders', and they should also devote adequate time to their role as director and to attending board meetings. The board of directors is accountable to shareholders and 'shall treat all shareholders equally and shall be concerned with the interests of stakeholders'.

The board of directors should meet periodically and have a pre-set agenda, with timely and clear information about the agenda items being sent to all the directors. If two or more independent directors feel that the information is unclear or inadequate, then they may apply to postpone the meeting or the discussion of the relevant agenda item. Minutes of the board meetings should be carefully maintained.

Independent directors should be independent of the company and its major shareholders, and should act in good faith and perform their duties diligently. They 'shall protect the overall interests of the company, and shall be especially concerned with protecting the interests of minority shareholders from being infringed'.

It is recommended that various committees of the board be established, such as a corporate strategy committee, a remuneration and appraisal committee, an audit committee, and a nomination committee. Independent directors should be in the majority on these committees and the audit, nomination, and remuneration/appraisal committees should be chaired by an independent director. In relation to the audit committee, at least one independent director should be an 'accounting professional'.

(iv) Supervisors and supervisory board

The supervisory board should comprise individuals with 'professional knowledge or work experience in such areas as law and accounting'. The supervisory board's members need to be able to supervise effectively the directors and managers and to examine knowledgeably the company's financial matters.

The supervisory board is accountable to shareholders and its duties include supervising corporate finance, overseeing the directors' and managers' performance, and protecting the company's and shareholders' legal rights and interests. The supervisory board's members should be provided with appropriate information to enable them to do their job effectively. The supervisory board's meetings should be minuted.

(v) Performance assessments and incentive and disciplinary systems

Directors, supervisors, and management's performance should be assessed through a fair and transparent procedure, with directors and management being evaluated by the board of directors or by the remuneration/appraisal committee. When any individual's performance is being reviewed, the director being discussed should leave the meeting. Independent directors and supervisors should be evaluated by a combination of self-assessment and peer review. The performance and compensation of the directors and supervisors should be reported to the shareholders' meeting.

The Code has an interesting provision in the context of the selection and appointment of management personnel, as it states 'no institution or individual shall interfere with a listed company's normal recruiting procedure for management personnel'. One problem with appointments in Chinese companies is that the state still wields a lot of influence and a mechanism is needed to isolate, as far as possible, the appointments process from the influence of political appointments. The Code seeks to make this an explicit point in the selection process.

Similarly, there is much demand from employees in Chinese companies, particularly at the higher levels where an awareness of Western practices is more apparent, to link compensation with performance. The Code states that the compensation for management personnel should be linked to both the company's performance and the individual's work performance.

(vi) Stakeholders

The section of the Code that deals with stakeholders states that, 'while maintaining the listed company's development and maximizing the benefits of shareholders, the company shall be concerned with the welfare, environmental protection and public interests of the community in which it resides, and shall pay attention to the company's social responsibilities'.

The Code also mentions that the company should respect the legal rights of the various stakeholder groups and provide them with information as appropriate. In particular, employees are encouraged to provide feedback on various issues that might affect them by direct communication with the board of directors, the supervisory board, and management personnel.

(vii) Information and disclosure and transparency

The importance of the provision of timely and accurate information is emphasized; as well as any mandatory disclosures, the company should disclose other information that may impact on the decisions of shareholders or stakeholders. The same access to information should be available to all shareholders.

There should be specific disclosures relating to the company's corporate governance (as already mentioned in the individual sections earlier), plus the company should make disclosure about its state of corporate governance and the reasons why it may differ from the Code. It should also mention any plans to improve its corporate governance.

The company should disclose information relating to the shareholding distribution in the company: for example, detail of shareholders who own 'a comparatively large percentage of the shares' (what level this might be is not specified in the Code), shareholders who can control the company by acting in concert (that is, acting together), and the shareholders who actually control the company.

In the summer of 2001 the CSRC produced 'Guidelines for Introducing Independent Directors to the Board of Directors of Listed Companies'. The Guidelines mandate all domestically listed companies to amend their articles as necessary to comply with the Guidelines and to appoint, by 30 June 2002, at least two independent directors to the board of directors; by 30 June 2003, at least one-third of the board should be independent directors.

Neoh (2003) stated there are at least two areas that must be addressed for the market to move away from short-termism and for good governance to take root. One is for investors to have a longer term time horizon and the second is for the system of management succession to be addressed, so that politics is separated from the enterprise. The legal system also needs to support important bankruptcy laws and company law reform.

In February 2006 China moved towards convergence with global standards with the release by the Ministry of Finance of thirty-nine standards based on IFRS, which, inter alia, aim to improve the quality of financial information and boost investor confidence. Given that transparency, disclosure, and accountability were at the heart of sound corporate governance, this was a most welcome development.

Tang (2008) details corporate and securities law reforms that have served to improve the corporate governance environment in China but he points out that unless enforcement capabilities are strengthened, the reforms may not be effective. From a different perspective, Clarke (2008) discusses some of the limitations in China:

> An important part of any solution to China's corporate governance problems, given its current set of administrative and legal institution[s], lies not in the state's actively beefing up those institutions, but simply in its relaxing its hostility to civil society institutions, and understanding that corporate governance is too important a matter to be left solely to the state.

The OECD-China Policy Dialogue on Corporate Governance Report (2011) looks at the institutional framework of corporate governance in China through the lens of the OECD *Principles of Corporate Governance*. The Report states 'that corporate governance has improved significantly since the Chinese stock market was created in 1990, with important achievements in establishing and developing the legal and regulatory framework'. It also states that

> the corporate governance framework in China is developing and adapting to the country's economic transformation. As market discipline is still evolving, the role played by the formal legal and regulatory framework remains essential for building an efficient and competitive capital market. Given China's concentrated ownership structure, potential conflicts of interest between majority and minority shareholders remain a core corporate governance issue. It is therefore very useful that the Report looks at the issues of equitable treatment of shareholders and mechanisms to prevent abusive related party transactions. The Report is also helpful in identifying mechanisms for shareholder redress. On a related topic, the Committee pointed to the challenges of coordinating the multiple roles played by state entities—as shareholders, regulators and managers.

It identified that priority areas for China may include curbing abusive related party transactions, enhancing the quality of boards, improving shareholder protection, and curbing market abuse. Also it might be useful to devote special attention to the all-important issue of how to improve effective implementation and enforcement.

Finally, Tam and Yu (2011) point out that 'corporate governance development in China is entering a new phase where effective corporate governance mechanisms and practices have become a necessary condition for the country's quest to achieve enduring prosperity through an open market economy that can compete globally'.

Australia

Whilst not suffering financial crisis in the same way as many countries in the region, Australia was nonetheless affected by the ripples from the various crises that occurred. It was, and is, vital for Australia's economic growth and well-being that the countries in the Asia-Pacific region are economically and financially sound, and politically stable. Australia therefore contributed to various International Monetary Fund initiatives to help Asia-Pacific Economic Co-operation (APEC) economies to recover from the crises and strengthen their economic and financial management.

In terms of its corporate governance, Australia has a common law system and, certainly at first glance, its corporate governance system seems to have developed along the lines of the Anglo-Saxon model, having features that would usually be typical of a UK unitary board structure. However, on closer inspection, Australia seems to have features of both an insider and an outsider system. Dignam and Galanis (2004) summarize the various features in Australia that might lead to doubt as to which corporate governance system it has, or indeed whether it is moving from one system and towards another. These features include the political system, which is socialist and so would usually be associated with an insider system, and yet the corporate governance system does not fit this proposition. Ownership of listed company shares is another interesting area because there are both dispersed shareholdings in listed companies and the presence of a significant non-institutional shareholder, or blockholder, in others. The former pattern of ownership is typical of an outsider system, whilst the latter is more commonly associated with an insider system.

Dignam and Galanis (2004) conclude their study by stating that the listed market in Australia is characterized by

significant blockholders engaged in private rent extraction; institutional investor powerlessness; a strong relationship between management and blockholders, which results in a weak market for corporate control; and a historical weakness in public and private securities regulation, which allows the creation and perpetuation of crucial blocks to information flow.

They feel that these characteristics make it more like an insider than an outsider system. Farrar (2005) also provides some interesting insights into corporate governance developments in Australia in his book about these developments in both Australia and New Zealand. Stapledon (2006) notes that

while many aspects of the corporate governance regime in Australia are similar to those in countries like the US and the UK, there are some features of the Australian regime that distinguish it; for example, the incidence and role of large blockholders. But, fundamentally, Australia has a relatively well-developed capital market, and its governance environment is generally reflective of shareholder supremacy.

Turning now to look in more detail at the regulatory and corporate governance systems in Australia, in this context, it is important to realize that Australia's present regulatory infrastructure is relatively young. The Australian Securities and Investments Commission (ASIC), an independent Australian government body, has regulated financial markets, securities, futures, and corporations since January 1991. The Australian Stock Exchange (ASX) was formed in 1987 through the amalgamation of six independent stock exchanges that formerly operated in the state capital cities. Each of those exchanges had a history of share trading dating back to the nineteenth century.

The Bosch Report on *Corporate Practice and Conduct* was first issued in 1991 with further issues in 1993 and 1995. It covered a range of corporate governance issues including:

- board structure and composition;
- appointment of non-executive directors;
- directors' remuneration;
- risk management;
- financial reporting and auditing;
- conflicts of interest;
- the role of the company secretary.

In many ways, it was the equivalent of the Cadbury Report in the UK.

A number of corporate governance codes and guidelines followed, including the Hilmer Report (1998), which had an emphasis on issues such as board composition, executive remuneration, and disclosure.

In 2003 the ASX Corporate Governance Council issued the *Principles of Good Corporate Governance and Best Practice Recommendations*. The introduction states

good corporate governance structures encourage companies to create value (through entrepreneurism, innovation, development and exploration) and provide accountability and control systems commensurate with the risks involved [and] demonstrably good corporate governance practices are increasingly important in determining the cost of capital in a global capital market. Australian companies must be equipped to compete globally and to maintain and promote investor confidence both in Australia and overseas.

Table 12.6 Key characteristics influencing Australian corporate governance

Feature	Key characteristic
Main business form	Public corporations
Predominant ownership structure	Institutional investors; non-institutional shareholders (corporate or family)
Legal system	Common law
Board structure	Unitary
Important aspect	More emphasis on shareholder rights in recent years; also board diversity

Ten core principles are identified: 'the essential corporate governance principles', which are now detailed in turn. Each of the principles has one or more recommendations associated with it that act as implementation guidance. The recommendations are not mandatory; rather, they are guidelines to help ensure the desired outcome.

(i) Lay solid foundations for management and oversight—recognize and publish the respective roles and responsibilities of board and management

The company should have in place a framework to enable the board to provide strategic guidance and effective oversight; the roles and responsibilities of board members and senior executives should be clarified (this will help with accountability), and no single individual should have too much power. One recommendation supports this principle—recommendation 1.1: to formalize and disclose the functions reserved to the board and those delegated to management.

(ii) Structure the board to add value—have a board of an effective composition, size, and commitment to discharge adequately its responsibilities and duties

The board should be structured so that it has an understanding of the current and future issues affecting the business, and can review and challenge the performance of management and exercise independent judgement. Five recommendations support this principle, which are that:

- the majority of the board should be independent directors;
- the chairperson should be an independent director;
- the roles of chairperson and CEO should not be exercised by the same individual;
- the board should establish a nomination committee;
- various information relating to the directors—including their skills, experience and expertise—and the names of the members of the nomination committee and their attendance at the meetings thereof, should be included in the corporate governance section of the company's annual report.

(iii) Promote ethical and responsible decision-making—actively promote ethical and responsible decision-making

The company should clarify the standards of ethical behaviour required of company directors and key executives, encourage the observance of standards, and publish its policy as regards board and employee trading in company securities and related products. Three recommendations support this principle, which include that there should be a code of conduct to guide the directors, the CEO, the chief financial officer (CFO) and any other key executives in relation to practices necessary to maintain confidence in the company's integrity, and the responsibility and accountability of individuals for reporting and investigating reports of unethical practices. There should also be disclosure of the policy concerning trading in company securities by directors, officers, and employees, and provision of information in relation to any departures from the aforesaid recommendations.

(iv) Safeguard integrity in financial reporting–have a structure to independently verify and safeguard the integrity of the company's financial reporting

Five recommendations support this principle. The CEO and the CFO (or their equivalents) should be required to state in writing to the board that the company's financial reports present a true and fair view, in all material respects, of the company's financial state and that the operational results are in accordance with relevant accounting standards. The board should establish an audit committee, which should consist of at least three members and these should comprise only non-executive directors of whom the majority are independent directors. The audit committee should be chaired by an independent chairperson who is not the chairperson of the board. The audit committee should have a formal charter. Information should be disclosed including the names and qualifications of those appointed to the audit committee, the number of meetings of the audit committee, and the names of those attending the meetings.

(v) Make timely and balanced disclosure–promote timely and balanced disclosure of all material matters concerning the company

Disclosures should be made in such a way that all investors have equal and timely access to information about the company, including its financial situation, performance, ownership, and governance. The concept of balance requires disclosure of both positive and negative information. Two recommendations support this principle: first, that written policies and procedures designed to ensure compliance with ASX Listing Rule disclosure requirements and to ensure accountability at a senior management level for that compliance be established; and secondly, certain information should be disclosed, including explanation from any departures.

(vi) Respect the rights of shareholders–respect the rights of shareholders and facilitate the effective exercise of those rights

A company should empower its shareholders by effective communication with them, enabling their access to balanced and comprehensible information, and facilitating their participation in general meetings. Two recommendations support this principle: first, the company should design and disclose a communications strategy to promote effective communication with shareholders and encourage effective participation at general meetings; and secondly, the company should request the external auditor to attend the AGM and to be available to answer shareholder questions about the conduct of the audit, and preparation and content of the auditor's report.

(vii) Recognize and manage risk–establish a sound system of risk oversight and management and internal control

The system should identify, assess, monitor, and manage risk, and inform investors of material changes to the company's risk profile. Three recommendations support this principle: the board or appropriate board committee should establish policies on risk oversight and management; the CEO and CFO (or equivalents) should state to the board in writing that they have made their statement about the integrity of the financial statements based on a sound system of risk management and internal control and compliance, and that that system is operating efficiently and effectively; and explanations should be provided of any departures from the aforesaid best practice recommendations.

(viii) Encourage enhanced performance–fairly review and actively encourage enhanced board and management effectiveness

Directors and key executives should have the knowledge and information to discharge their responsibilities effectively, and individual and collective performance should be regularly and fairly reviewed. There is one supporting recommendation, which is that there should be disclosure of the process for performance evaluation of the board, its committees and individual directors, and key executives.

(ix) Remunerate fairly and responsibly–ensure that the level and composition of remuneration is sufficient and reasonable and that its relationship to corporate and individual performance is defined

There are five recommendations relating to the principle:

- disclosure should be provided of the company's remuneration policies to enable investors to understand the costs and benefits of those policies, and the link between remuneration and corporate performance;
- the board should establish a remuneration committee;
- there should be a clear distinction between the structure of non-executive directors' remuneration and that of executives (non-executive directors should receive fees but not options or bonus payments);
- payment of equity-based executive remuneration should be made in accordance with thresholds set in plans approved by shareholders;
- there should be disclosure of various aspects, including the remuneration policies, and the names of the remuneration committee members and their attendance at meetings.

(x) Recognize the legitimate interests of stakeholders–recognize legal and other obligations to all legitimate stakeholders

There is recognition that, by better managing various stakeholder groups, value can be created. Companies therefore need to have commitment to appropriate practices to achieve this end. There is one recommendation supporting this principle, which is that companies should establish and disclose a code of conduct to guide compliance with legal and other obligations to legitimate stakeholders.

Under the ASX Listing Rules, companies are required to provide a statement in their annual report disclosing the extent to which they have followed the best practice recommendations. Where companies have not followed all the recommendations, they must identify the recommendations that have not been followed and give reasons for not following them, i.e. the 'if not, why not?' approach.

In October 2004 the Investment and Financial Services Association Limited (IFSA) in Australia published *Corporate Governance: A Guide for Fund Managers and Corporations*, which is commonly known as 'the IFSA Blue Book'. This was the fifth edition, the first one having been published in 1995. The IFSA's members manage investments on behalf of superannuation funds and retail clients, and the Blue Book is intended to guide the IFSA's members in monitoring the corporate governance of their investee companies, so that good governance can be encouraged to the benefit of shareholders and stakeholders.

The guidelines comprise two sections: one for fund managers and one for corporations. The section for fund managers encourages constructive communications and emphasizes the importance of voting and of having a corporate governance policy, which has a section on voting policy; fund managers should report back to the client on voting. In relation to corporations, the guidelines cover: the annual disclosures that a company should make in relation to corporate governance; the composition of the board of directors in terms of competency and independence; the number of permissible directorships an individual may hold; that the chairperson should be an independent director; key board committees and committees generally; the election of directors; performance evaluation; equity participation by non-executive directors; the respective roles of the board and management; board and executive remuneration policy and disclosure; company meetings; the disclosure of beneficial shareholder information; major corporate changes; the company code of ethics.

In August 2005 the Australian Council of Super Investors issued its revised Corporate Governance Guidelines. These Guidelines are for superannuation trustees in their monitoring of Australian listed companies. The guidelines reinforce the accountability of corporate boards and management teams to shareholders, and also emphasize the importance of having an ethical governance culture.

In addition to the above codes and guidelines, the Corporate Law Economic Reform Program (CLERP) has made a number of changes to Australia's corporate regulatory framework. Maintaining investor protection and confidence in the market is important, and issues such as director liability, disclosure, and shareholder participation have received attention.

In 2007 the ASX Corporate Governance Council issued its first revision of the *Principles of Good Corporate Governance and Best Practice Recommendations* (2003). This second edition is entitled *Corporate Governance Principles and Recommendations*. The ten Principles retain the same headings as detailed earlier, although there are some changes to the wording of the supporting recommendations.

In 2010 the ASX updated the *Changes to Corporate Governance Principles and Recommendations* in relation to diversity, remuneration, trading policies, and briefings. Regarding gender diversity, the ASX announced that a recommendation is now included that entities listed on the ASX disclose in their annual report their achievement against gender objectives set by their board, and the proportion of women on the board (in senior management and employed throughout the whole organization). The guidance commentary will also be changed to recommend that boards determine the appropriate committee for recommending strategies to address board diversity (considering diversity in succession planning, and having a charter that regularly reviews the proportion of women at all levels in the company); disclose the mix of skills and diversity they are looking for in their membership; and ensure that there is an accurate and not misleading impression of the relative participation of women and men in the workplace. In relation to remuneration, ASX-listed entities should establish a remuneration committee comprised of a majority of independent directors, chaired by an independent director, and with at least three members. At present the composition of a remuneration committee is reflected in guidance (rather than as a recommendation) with no obligation to disclose departures from this standard. Commentary will also be amended to indicate that the remuneration committee should have responsibility for reviewing and providing recommendations to the board on remuneration by gender. Regarding trading policies, the Principles and Recommendations will be changed to reflect the introduction of ASX Listing Rules requiring entities to adopt and disclose a company trading policy. Finally in relation to briefings, there will be new guidance for listed entities about the notification, accessibility, and record keeping of group briefings, which will strengthen the principle of respecting the rights of shareholders.

The changes took effect for the first financial year of listed entities beginning on or after 1 January 2011, with companies required to either adopt the new recommendations or explain in their annual report why they have not done so ('if not, why not?').

Hill (2012) provides an overview of the structure of corporate governance in Australia, highlighting that many elements of Australian corporate law differ markedly from the US system. She discusses a number of areas, including the effect of financial scandals on corporate law reform; the composition and structure of the board of directors, including board diversity; directors' duties; trends in executive compensation; shareholder activism; and shareholder rights and minority shareholder protection.

Conclusions

The financial downturn that affected countries in the Asia-Pacific in the 1990s came as a great shock. The so-called 'tiger economies' had seen their stock markets experience meteoric rises and then that golden situation was wiped out. This change in fortunes led to many questions as to how and why this could have happened, but also as to how they would be able to rebuild themselves and attract investment back into their stock markets. As we have seen, the lack of transparency and disclosure, the misuse of corporate assets by dominant shareholders, and the lack of protection for minority shareholders' interests, have all been seen as contributory factors to the demise, and as areas that need to be improved in order to rebuild economies and attract both domestic and overseas investment. The recent global financial crisis has also impacted on these countries but their improved corporate governance should help them to restore confidence more quickly.

The countries looked at in detail in this chapter have all strengthened their corporate governance codes. Without exception, the codes now recommend fuller disclosure and accountability, transparency of process, the appointment of independent directors, and recognition and protection of minority shareholders' rights. It is encouraging that these countries all seem to be moving in the right direction, and these changes should encourage more foreign direct investment and greater confidence in their stock markets.

Summary

- The financial downturn that occurred in the Asia-Pacific countries in the 1990s acted as a trigger for improved corporate governance structures to be developed. The subsequent global financial crisis led to renewed emphasis on disclosure and transparency, the role of the board and the appointment of independent directors, and better protection of minority shareholders' rights.

- The dominant form of ownership structure in many Asia-Pacific countries tends to be concentrated either in families or in cross-holdings. The state still exercises significant influence in a number of countries.

- In Japan the *keiretsu* (associations of companies with holdings of shares one in the other) are slowly beginning to loosen their grip on corporate ownership but are still very influential. New corporate governance provisions provide Japanese companies with more flexibility and encourage more disclosure and the appointment of independent directors.

- In Korea the *chaebol* (large conglomerates with extensive cross-holdings of shares) still wield enormous power. The corporate governance code emphasizes transparency and the protection of minority shareholders' rights.

- In Malaysia companies are largely family-owned or controlled. The Corporate Governance Blueprint and the revised Malaysian Corporate Governance Code emphasizes that Malaysia needs to embed corporate governance culture in listed companies and more generally within the corporate governance ecosystem, which it identifies as including shareholders, gatekeepers, and regulators, as well as the board of directors.

- In Singapore the Corporate Governance Code (2012) has made a number of changes to the earlier Code, these being focused on the areas of director independence, board composition, director training, multiple directorships, alternate directors, remuneration practices and disclosures, risk management, and shareholder rights and roles.

- China is a 'socialist market economy' and many of the state-owned enterprises have become joint stock companies with shares to be more widely held. Much of the corporate reporting in China remains quite opaque and greater reliable disclosure is generally required, although it has improved in recent years. However, the Corporate Governance Code's recommendations are encouraging and listed companies are required to appoint an appropriate number of independent directors. Furthermore, China has been working with the OECD to consider further development of its corporate governance.

- Australia has an interesting corporate governance system that has been strengthened in recent years to give more emphasis to shareholders' rights, to the ethical conduct of corporations, and to board diversity and executive remuneration.

Example: Kookmin Bank, South Korea

This is an example of a South Korean bank that is recognized both domestically and internationally as having good corporate governance.

Kookmin Bank (KB) is a well-established world-class retail bank. It has a good corporate governance structure as evidenced by the fact that, in addition to committees such as the audit committee, it has established a risk management committee and a compensation committee, which are comprised exclusively of outside directors. KB's Financial Group's Goal for Corporate Governance is enhancement of management transparency, securing independency of the board of directors, protection of shareholders' rights, and efficient operation of the auditing organization.

The confidence in KB's is evidenced by the fact that a substantial majority of its shares are in the hands of foreign ownership.

KB has a Code of Ethics that covers various aspects of the business. These aspects encompass the fundamental principles, including the objective of the bank ('maximization of shareholder values and customer satisfaction'), the bank management, the social responsibility of the bank, and work ethics for officers and employees of the bank. KB views itself as a 'good corporate citizen' with a role in helping to improve the community. KB's Sustainability Report 2010, classifies its efforts for sustainability management into three core topics of 'Changes, Value creation and Social contribution'; it also presents strategic issues related to those topics in a Q&A format.

KB participates in a number of global initiatives related to sustainability: United Nations Environment Program Finance Initiative (UNEP FI); UN Global Compact; Carbon Disclosure Project (CDP); Dow Jones Sustainability Index (DJSI) Asia Pacific and DJSI Korea; and Climate Change Business Forum.

KB received a number of major awards and recognition in 2011, including: 'Outstanding Corporation in Governance' (Korea Corporate Governance Association); 'Contribution Award', Korea True Journalist Awards (Korea Journalist Federation); 'Grand Award in Transparent Management' (Korea Accounting Society, The Joonang Daily); '2011 Forbes CEO Award' in the sustainability management category (The Jooang Daily Forbes); 'Grand Award in Financial Holding Company' at 2011 Korea Global Management Award (The Seoul Economic Daily, the Korea Management Evaluation Service); Named 21st 'CEO of the Year', the 21st Awards (New Industry Management Service); and 'Socially Responsible Corporation for Mutual Prosperity' (Chosun News Press).

 ### Mini case study   Singapore Airlines, Singapore

This is an example of a Singaporean company with an excellent reputation for its corporate governance.

Singapore Airlines was founded in 1972, evolving from a regional airline to one of the most respected travel brands around the world.

The Group's revenue was $14,525 million for the year ended 31 March 2011, and it achieved a net profit attributable to equity holders of $1,092 million.

Singapore Airlines has excellent disclosure of its corporate governance on its website. The board, which held four meetings in the financial year, currently comprises nine directors from diverse backgrounds with expertise in the finance, legal, industry, business, labour, and management fields. Seven of the nine directors are considered to be independent from management and from the company's substantial shareholder, Temasek Holdings; the remaining two are Mr Stephen Lee who is a member of Temasek's Advisory Panel and Mr Goh Choon Phong who is the CEO.

There is comprehensive information given about each of the directors, for example, academic and professional qualifications; the date of first appointment as a director; the date of last re-election as a

(continued)

director; board committees they serve on and their capacity (chair or member); current directorships in other listed companies; other major appointments; other appointments; and directorships/ appointments in the past three years.

Singapore Airlines Corporate Governance Report cross-references the various headings to the relevant principles in Singapore's Code of Corporate Governance, for example, Board Membership and Performance (Principles 4 and 5).

There are five board committees that have been formed to assist the board in the execution of its responsibilities, these are the Board Executive Committee, Board Audit Committee, Board Compensation and Industrial Relations Committee, Board Nominating Committee, and Board Safety and Risk Committee. These committees have written mandates and operating procedures, which are reviewed periodically.

Board Executive Committee (ExCo), comprised of Mr Stephen Lee (Chairman), Mr Chew Choon Seng (until 31 December 2010), Mr Goh Choon Phong (from 1 January 2011), Ms Euleen Goh and Mr James Koh. The ExCo oversees the execution by Management of the overall strategy, policies, directions and guidelines set by the Board for the SIA Group. The ExCo also reviews and makes recommendations to the Board on the annual operating and capital budgets and matters relating to the Group's wholly owned subsidiaries.

There is information about the remit and focus of each board committee, for example, leadership development and succession planning in the Company, remains a key focus for the Board Compensation and Industrial Relations Committee (BCIRC).

There is appropriate disclosure on the remuneration of directors, both in terms of the measures used and in relation to the amount of directors' fees. For example, in relation to short-term incentives which generally take the form of an annual profit-sharing bonus, payment of the variable bonus is based on employees achieving the target levels in the following: SIA Group's Return on Shareholders' Fund; SIA Company's Operating Profit Margin; and SIA Company's Passenger Load Factor. In relation to directors' fees for the financial year 2010/11, these amounted to $1,455,000 and were based on the following rates (in Singapore $):

Board Retainers Board Member 80,000

Chairman 160,000

Committee Retainers Chairman of Executive Committee and Audit Committee 50,000

Chairman of other Board Committees, 35,000

Member of Executive Committee and Audit Committee

Member of other Board Committees 20,000

Attendance Fees Home—City 5,000

In—Region 10,000

Out—Region 20,000

Teleconference—Normal hours 1,000

Teleconference—Odd hours 2,000

Furthermore, it was declared in the report that no employee of the Group who is an immediate family member of a director was paid a remuneration that exceeded $150,000 during the financial year ending 31 March 2011.

The Company was recognized as the Most Transparent Company—Transport/Storage/Communication Category by the Securities Investors Association of Singapore (SIAS) in 2010 for the ninth time since the inception of the 'SIAS Investors' Choice Award' in 2000. The company was also the winner of the 'Golden Circle Award' (an open category award for overall recognition of transparency excellence across all sectors) for the second consecutive year in 2010. In addition, the company won two awards in the IR Magazine South East Asia Awards 2010: for Singapore and Pan Asia, the best investor relations by a CEO.

Questions

The discussion questions to follow cover the key learning points of this chapter. Reading of some of the additional reference material will enhance the depth of the students' knowledge and understanding of these areas.

1. How might improving corporate governance help to restore investor confidence in countries in the Asia-Pacific region affected by financial collapse?

2. What are the defining features of the Japanese corporate governance system? Critically compare and contrast with the Korean corporate governance system.

3. How has corporate governance developed in China and what are the main obstacles to be overcome to improve effectively corporate governance?

4. Critically discuss corporate governance developments in Malaysia, comparing and contrasting them with those in Singapore.

5. Critically discuss the corporate governance system in Australia.

6. Critically discuss the impact of ownership structure on the development of corporate governance in the Asia-Pacific region.

References

Aguilera, R.V., Kabbach-Castro, L. R., Lee, J. H. and You, J. (2012), 'Corporate Governance in Emerging Markets', *Capitalisms and Capitalism in the 21st Century*, G. Morgan and R. Whitley, (eds), Oxford University Press, Oxford. Available at SSRN: **http://ssrn.com/abstract=1806525**

Ahmadjian, C L. and Okumura, A. (2011), 'Corporate Governance in Japan', in C.A. Mallin (ed.), *Handbook on International Corporate Governance, Country Analyses*, 2nd edition, Edward Elgar Publishing, Cheltenham, UK.

Allen, J., Connors, M., and Krutikov, A., (2008), *White Paper on Corporate Governance in Japan*, ACGA, Hong Kong.

Australian Council of Super Investors Inc. (2005), *Corporate Governance Guidelines: A Guide for Superannuation Trustees to Monitor Listed Australian Companies*, ACSI, Melbourne.

ASX Corporate Governance Council (2003), *Principles of Good Corporate Governance and Best Practice Recommendations*, ASX, Sydney.

—— (2007), *Corporate Governance Principles and Recommendations*, ASX, Sydney.

——(2010), *Corporate Governance Principles and Recommendations*, ASX, Sydney.

Balino, T.J.T. and Ubide, A. (1999), 'The Korean Financial Crisis of 1997—A Strategy of Financial Sector Reform', International Monetary Fund Working Paper No. WP/99/28.

Black, B.S., Jang, H., and Kim, W. (2005), 'Predicting Firms' Corporate Governance Choices: Evidence from Korea', *Journal of Corporate Finance*, Vol. 12, No. 3, pp. 660–91.

Bosch (1995), *Corporate Practice and Conduct*, Woodslane Pty Ltd, Australia.

Charkham, J. (1994), *Keeping Good Company: A Study of Corporate Governance in Five Countries*, Clarendon Press, Oxford.

—— (2005), *Keeping Better Company: Corporate Governance Ten Years On*, Oxford University Press, Oxford.

Chen E-T. and Nowland J. (2010), 'Optimal Board Monitoring in Family-Owned Companies: Evidence from Asia', *Corporate Governance: An International Review*, 18(1), pp. 3–17.

CSRC (2001), *Code of Corporate Governance for Listed Companies in China*, CSRC, State Economic Trade Commission, Beijing.

—— (2001), *Guidelines for Introducing Independent Directors to the Board of Directors of Listed Companies*, CSRC, State Economic Trade Commission, Beijing.

Claessens, S., Djankov, S. and Lang, L.H.P. (2000), 'The Separation of Ownership and Control in East Asian Corporations', *Journal of Financial Economics*, Vol. 58.

Claessens, S. and Fan, J.P.H. (2002) 'Corporate Governance in Asia: A Survey', *International Review of Finance*, Vol. 3, Issue 2.

Clarke, D.C. (2008), 'The Role of Non-Legal Institutions in Chinese Corporate Governance', in H. Kanda, K.S. Kim, and C.J. Milhaupt (eds), *Transforming Corporate Governance in East Asia*, Routledge, London.

Corporate Governance Blueprint (2011), Securities Commission Malaysia, Kuala Lumpur.

Corporate Governance Council (2012), *Code of Corporate Governance*, MAS.

——(2012), *Risk Governance Guidance for Listed Boards*, MAS.

Dignam, A.J. and Galanis, M. (2004), 'Australia Inside/Out: The Corporate Governance System of the Australian Listed Market', *Melbourne University Law Review*, Vol. 28, No. 3, December.

Farrar, J. (2005), *Corporate Governance in Australia and New Zealand*, Oxford University Press, Oxford.

Finance Committee on Corporate Governance (2000), *Malaysian Code on Corporate Governance*, Ministry of Finance, Kuala Lumpur.

Gilson, R.J. (2008), 'Controlling-family Shareholders in Asia: Anchoring Relational Exchange', in H. Kanda, K-S. Kim and C.J. Milhaupt (eds), *Transforming Corporate Governance in East Asia*, Routledge, London.

Hill, J.G. (2012), 'The Architecture of Corporate Governance in Australia: Corporate Governance—National Report: Australia' in K. J. Hopt (ed.), *Comparative Corporate Governance* (forthcoming, 2012, Cambridge University Press). Available at SSRN: **http://ssrn.com/abstract=1657810**

Hilmer, F.A. (1998), *Strictly Boardroom: Enhancing Governance to Improve Company Performance*, Report of the Independent Working Party into Corporate Governance, 2nd edn, Information Australia, Sydney.

IFSA (2004), *Corporate Governance: A Guide for Fund Managers and Corporations*, IFSA, Sydney.

Jang, H. and Kim, J. (2002), 'Nascent Stages of Corporate Governance in an Emerging Market: Regulatory Change, Shareholder Activism and Samsung Electronics', *Corporate Governance: An International Review*, Vol. 10, No. 2.

Japan Corporate Governance Committee (2001), *Revised Corporate Governance Principles*, Japan Corporate Governance Forum, Tokyo.

Kim, E.H. and Kim, W. (2007), 'Corporate Governance in Korea: A Decade after the Financial Crisis' (December 2007), University of Texas Law, Law and Econ Research Paper No. 123, available at SSRN: **http://ssrn.com/abstract=1084066**

Korean Committee on Corporate Governance (1999) *Code of Best Practice for Corporate Governance*, Korean Committee on Corporate Governance, Seoul.

——(2003) *Code of Best Practice for Corporate Governance*, Korean Committee on Corporate Governance, Seoul.

Liew, P. (2007), 'Corporate Governance Reforms in Malaysia: The Key Leading Players' Perspectives', *Corporate Governance: An International Review*, Vol. 15, No. 5.

Malaysian Code on Corporate Governance (2012), Ministry of Finance, Kuala Lumpur.

Monetary Authority of Singapore (2010), *Guidelines on Corporate Governance for Banks, Financial Holding Companies and Direct Insurers which are incorporated in Singapore*, MAS.

Ministry of Justice (2003), *Commercial Code Revision on Boards (April 2003)*, Tokyo.

Neoh, A. (2003), 'Corporate Governance in Mainland China: Where Do We Go from Here?' in P.K. Cornelius and B. Kogut (eds), *Corporate Governance and Capital Flows in a Global Economy*, Oxford University Press, Oxford.

OECD-China Policy Dialogue on Corporate Governance (2011), *Governance of Listed Companies in China Self-Assessment by the China Securities Regulatory Commission*, OECD, Paris.

Okumura, H. (2002), 'Corporate Governance in Japan', in H. Shibuya, M. Maruyama, and M. Yasaka (eds), *Japanese Economy and Society under Pax-Americana*, University of Tokyo Press, Tokyo.

Salim M.R. (2011), 'Corporate Governance in Malaysia: the Macro and Micro Issues', in C.A. Mallin (ed.), *Handbook on International Corporate Governance, Country Analyses*, 2nd edition, Edward Elgar Publishing, Cheltenham, UK.

Stapledon, G. (2006), 'The Development of Corporate Governance in Australia', in C.A. Mallin (ed.), *Handbook on International Corporate Governance, Country Analyses*, Edward Elgar Publishing, Cheltenham, UK.

Tam, O.K. (1999), *The Development of Corporate Governance in China*, Edward Elgar, Cheltenham.

—— and Yu, C.P. (2011), 'China's corporate governance development', in C.A. Mallin (ed.), *Handbook on International Corporate Governance, Country*

Analyses, 2nd edition, Edward Elgar Publishing, Cheltenham, UK.

Tang, X. (2008), 'Protecting Minority Shareholders in China: A Task for Both Legislation and Enforcement', in H. Kanda, K.-S. Kim, and C.J. Milhaupt (eds), *Transforming Corporate Governance in East Asia*, Routledge, London.

Tokyo Stock Exchange (2004), *Principles of Corporate Governance for Listed Companies*, Tokyo Stock Exchange, Tokyo.

——(2009), *Principles of Corporate Governance for Listed Companies*, Tokyo Stock Exchange, Tokyo.

Useful websites

www.acsi.org.au The website of the Australian Council of Superannuation Investors, a not-for-profit organization, which provides independent research and education services to superannuation funds in relation to the corporate governance practices of investee companies.

www.adbi.org The website of the Asian Development Bank Institute, which contains information and articles about corporate governance developments in the Asia-Pacific region.

www.asa.asn.au The website of the Australian Shareholders' Association, which has a range of material relevant to investors.

www.asx.com.au The website of the Australian Stock Exchange, which contains information relating to corporate governance, companies, and investors.

www.csrc.gov.cn The website of the China Securities Regulatory Commission has information about corporate governance developments in China.

www.jcgf.org The website of the Japan Corporate Governance Forum has information about corporate governance issues in Japan.

www.maicsa.org.my The website of the Chartered Secretaries Malaysia has details of a series of good governance guides.

www.mas.gov.sg/ The website of the Monetary Authority of Singapore, including the Corporate Governance Code 2012.

www.sc.com.my The website of the Securities Commission in Malaysia has a range of material relating to corporate governance issues in Malaysia, including the Corporate Governance Blueprint.

 For further links to useful sources of information visit the Online Resource Centre **www.oxfordtextbooks.co.uk/orc/mallin4e/**

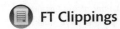 **FT Clippings**

FT: Auditor quits Chinese group Boshiwa

By Robert Cookson in Hong Kong

March 15, 2012

Deloitte has resigned as auditor of Boshiwa International, a Chinese maker of children's apparel that has licences for brands including Harry Potter and Manchester United, over corporate governance concerns.

Shares in Boshiwa plunged 36 per cent in Hong Kong on Thursday on the news before being suspended from trading.

Boshiwa is one of dozens of Chinese companies whose auditors have resigned in recent years amid concerns about corporate governance. In its resignation letter, Deloitte said it was unable to complete its audit of Boshiwa because the company's management had not provided enough financial information.

Deloitte said that it had "concerns about matters pervasive to the financial statements", including the existence and commercial substance of recorded prepayments amounting to Rbm392m ($62m) to a supplier of the group. In a filing to the Hong Kong stock exchange, Boshiwa said it expected to be unable to publish its annual results as planned by the end of the month, which would put it in breach of stock exchange rules.

Boshiwa raised $321m in September 2010 through an initial public offering in Hong Kong arranged by UBS, Credit Suisse, and Bocom International. At the time, Chinese consumer stocks were strongly in favour with investors so the shares sold at the top of the price range.

Since listing, however, Boshiwa's shares have lost more than two-thirds of their value. Investors have grown more cautious about Chinese companies because of fears of a slowdown in the mainland economy as well as concerns about corporate governance.

Dozens of Chinese groups listed in the US, the UK and Hong Kong have been accused of fraud or accounting discrcpancies over the past two years, often by shortsellers hoping to profit from declines in their shares.

Last year, Deloitte quit as auditor of Longtop after accusing the company of "very serious defects", including faking its bank statements. The software group, which raised $210m in 2007 via a New York IPO organised by Deutsche Bank and Goldman Sachs, delisted from the New York Stock Exchange last August.

Deloitte also last year resigned as auditor of Real Gold Mining, saying that the Chinese gold miner had failed to disclose material information involving related parties. Real Gold's Hong Kong-listed shares have been suspended since May.

Boshiwa said it was "disappointed" with Deloitte's decision to resign and would appoint a new auditor in due course. The company added that it is considering establishing a special committee to investigate the circumstances.

FT: Japan insider deal ruling raises questions

By Michiyo Nakamoto and Brooke Masters

March 26, 2012

Last week, Japanese regulators recommended their first ever fine of an established bank in connection with insider dealing.

However, the size of the proposed penalty for Chuo Mitsui Asset Trust and Banking—Y50,000 ($600)—was laughable in comparison with the punishments routinely handed down in other major financial centres. It also raised more questions than it answered about Japan's ability to stop what is rumoured to be rampant leaking of insider information during the sales activity of investment banks.

"The question this case raises is, 'Is this all they could do?'" says Junzaburo Kiuchi, a partner at law firm Freshfields, in Tokyo.

In recent years, the US has used wiretaps, dawn raids and other aggressive tactics to fight insider dealing. Serial insider trader Raj Rajaratnam, founder of the Galleon hedge fund, was recently ordered to pay $156.6m in civil and criminal penalties and sentenced to 11 years in jail.

"Insider trading prosecutions have always had a particular allure for US authorities. Even in a market dominated by institutional investors, the idea of a 'fair playing field' is politically potent and has real courtroom appeal," says Daniel Richman, a Columbia University law professor.

The UK Financial Services Authority has spent the past seven years building its enforcement division into a "credible deterrent" in an effort to squash suspicious trading ahead of merger announcements. It recently handed down a record combined £7.2m penalty to David Einhorn and his Greenlight Capital hedge fund management company.

Even Japanese courts have been tougher in the past—in 2007, Yoshiaki Murakami, a former investment manager, was fined Y1.15bn as part of a criminal case about improper trading in shares of Nippon Broadcasting System.

The Chuo Mitsui case emerged after the Securities and Exchange Surveillance Commission spent more than a year of investigation into allegations of insider trading ahead of new share issues. It was triggered by widespread complaints among investors that shares in companies preparing to issue new shares regularly fell ahead of the announcement.

The SESC said a Chuo Mitsui fund manager had received material non-public information about a pending share offer from Inpex, an oil developer, from a sales officer at one of the investment banks that was serving as lead underwriter. According to the SESC's findings, the fund manager used the information to trade on behalf of a foreign fund it was managing and obtained profits of more than Y14m.

The SESC expressed serious concern that an employee of an investment bank would provide insider information in the course of their job selling equities.

The breach of trust between the investment bank and the issuing company "has hurt Japan's securities industry substantially", an SESC official said.

Nevertheless, the SESC did not recommend penalties for either the fund, which made the profits, or the sales official at the bank who tipped Chuo Mitsui. Under Japanese law, Chuo Mitsui's penalty was based on the Y50,000 fee that the bank made on the trade, rather than the profit made by the fund.

The Japanese Financial Services Agency is studying the SESC's recommendation and is expected to make a decision shortly. In addition to fining Chuo Mitsui, the FSA could also choose to impose an "administrative guidance" penalty on the underwriter for failing to keep strict control of inside information, according to an SESC official.

"In that respect, it might have been a breach of the law and if that is the case, it could be a cause for penalty," the official says.

The case highlights differences between the way different countries approach the problem of tippers who do not trade themselves. Under Japanese law, tippers can only be fined if a criminal charge is filed, something that is unlikely in a case with a fine of this size, according to outside lawyers.

But the UK and US both view tipping as a violation even if the tipper does not directly profit and they take a broader view of the profits used to calculate the fine. The UK recently brought two cases against the broker who talked to Mr Einhorn and a Credit Suisse credit trader who invited hedge fund managers to "play charades" to identify the issuer of a pending bond.

Some in Japan fear the Chuo Mitsui case could be a black eye for the securities industry. The findings highlight a breach of the so-called Chinese wall that is supposed to exist between the investment banking division and the equity sales division and it also gives the impression that Japanese regulations are weak.

"I think the impact [of this case] on the market is immense," says Nobutoshi Yamauchi, a lawyer with Jones Day in Tokyo. "People outside Japan may think that the Japanese system doesn't have the framework to deal with compliance." Some predict that global markets will gradually erode the cross-border differences.

"The level of penalty needed for deterrence and proportionality can vary from jurisdiction to jurisdiction, [but] it is likely that in the current political climate the world will converge across tougher penalties—whatever the demands of proportionality," says Carlos Conceicao, UK partner at Clifford Chance.

. . .

A minefield of interpretation At its core, the definition of insider trading is the same world over. Somebody with privileged access to information about a deal or a company's results uses their advantage to buy or sell securities and either reaps a profit or avoids a loss.

However, national quirks around the definition of what counts as inside information and who can be punished for trading on it can make enforcement a minefield.

In the US, which has led the pack on tough enforcement, the courts have taken a quite narrow view of what counts as inside information. There, it is only illegal if the information has been obtained in violation of a legal duty to keep it quiet. Both the leaker and the trader can be punished.

However, the UK, the European Union and Hong Kong take much more expansive laws. In general, people who are given material nonpublic information have a duty not to trade on it. The UK also has a category of "unintentional" market abuse for parties who may not have realised they were facilitating or committing improper trading. In recent weeks, UK authorities have also cracked down on two brokers who passed on inside information without trading on it themselves.

Japan has a particularly narrow approach, limiting enforcement to the actual trader. Tipsters are immune from fines if they do not trade, although they could in theory be subject to criminal enforcement in serious cases.

13

Corporate Governance in South Africa, Egypt, India, and Brazil

Learning Objectives

- To understand the background to the development of corporate governance codes in a range of countries globally
- To be aware of the different ownership structures in a global context
- To be aware of the main differences in corporate governance codes in various countries in a global context
- To have a detailed knowledge of the corporate governance codes for a sample of countries in a global context

Introduction

In this chapter, corporate governance developments in a sample of countries in a global context are examined. The countries are diverse in their cultural and legal backgrounds, ownership structures, and corporate governance structures. Nonetheless, we can see that certain core principles, seen in earlier chapters, are evident in the corporate governance codes of these countries. These core principles will help build or restore confidence in stock markets, help ensure more transparency and disclosure, enhance protection of minority shareholders' rights, and help ensure that the company is managed in the interests of shareholders and stakeholders, as appropriate.

Of course, as well as the existence of a corporate governance code, the firm-level corporate governance is very important: that is, to what extent a firm itself actually has good governance. Klapper and Love (2002) undertook a study of firm-level governance in fourteen emerging market countries, including South Africa, India, and Brazil. They find that 'firm-level corporate governance provisions matter more in countries with weak legal environments' and their results 'suggest that firms can partially compensate for ineffective laws and enforcement by establishing good corporate governance and credible investor protection'. Hence, a firm with good corporate governance in a country with a generally weaker corporate governance will stand out from the crowd and be able to obtain capital at a lower cost, and generally be more attractive to investors.

Each of the selected countries has interesting characteristics that make it a good choice to include in this penultimate chapter to illustrate that corporate governance is relevant to all countries, whatever their ownership structure and whatever their stage of development.

South Africa has a well-developed corporate governance code. In fact, its revised code published in 2009 is the most comprehensive in the world, and leading edge in terms of its outlook and recommendations. Egypt was one of the pioneers of corporate governance in the Middle East and North Africa (MENA) countries, introducing a corporate governance code in 2005 based on the Organisation for Economic Co-operation and Development (OECD) Principles of Corporate Governance. India's corporate governance code aims to differentiate between mandatory recommendations and non-mandatory, whilst recognizing that both categories of recommendations will result in the most effective corporate governance system. Brazil is trying to encourage compliance with its corporate governance code but the progress seems quite slow, with controlling groups still exercising disproportionate influence.

South Africa

South Africa has had a troubled and turbulent past. In the latter half of the twentieth century there was considerable social unrest and inequality exacerbated by the policy of apartheid (racial segregation). Extensive legislation was introduced in the 1990s, which led to social and political transformation; this included the Employment Equity Act (No. 55 of 1998) and the National Environmental Management Act (No. 107 of 1998).

In 1992 a Committee on Corporate Governance was established in South Africa. Chaired by Mervyn King, the Committee produced the *King Report on Corporate Governance* (the 'King I') late in 1994. The King I contained some of the most far-reaching recommendations at that time. Some eight years later, the King Report II (hereinafter 'King II') was published in 2002. Between the dates of the two reports (1994–2002), there was extensive legislation as mentioned above, and the King II needed to take account of these developments. In common with its earlier version, the King II is one of the most comprehensive and most innovative reports published to date anywhere in the world. It takes an 'inclusive' approach, in other words, the company should not develop its strategies and carry out its operations without considering the wider community, including employees, customers, and suppliers. An interesting cultural aspect is mentioned in the context of labour relations and people management, which is the tradition of consultation practised by African chiefs; clearly, consultation is part and parcel of the African psyche and so a company should take this into account in its relationship with employees and people generally.

As well as addressing what might be perceived as the traditional areas of corporate governance, such as the role and function of boards of directors, and internal audit, the King II pays significant attention to integrated sustainability reporting, including stakeholder relations, ethical practices, and social and transformation issues. The whole report is a comprehensive 354 pages, which includes detailed appendices covering areas such as board self-evaluation and developing a code of ethics. In addition, the appendices include details about the *United Nations Global Compact* and the *Global Sullivan Principles*.

The King II identifies what can be regarded as seven characteristics of good corporate governance: discipline, transparency, independence, Accountability, Responsibility, fairness, and social responsibility. Discipline in the context of proper and appropriate behaviour, includes acceptance of good governance, at senior management level. Transparency is the extent to which, and how easily, investors can know the true picture of what is happening in the company. Independence is the existence of appropriate mechanisms to ensure that there

Table 13.1 Key characteristics influencing South African corporate governance

Feature	Key characteristic
Main business form	Public limited company
Predominant ownership structure	Institutional investors
Legal system	Common law
Board structure	Unitary
Important aspect	Inclusive approach

are no conflicts of interest at board/management level. Decision-makers in the company must be accountable for their decisions and actions, and there should be mechanisms to ensure this accountability. Management have a responsibility for their actions and should correct inappropriate actions. Fairness should exist in the consideration of the rights of various parties with an interest in the company. Finally, social responsibility is characteristic of a good corporate citizen, and companies should give a high priority to ethical standards.

The King II contains the Code of Corporate Practices and Conduct (hereinafter 'the Code'), which contains principles in a number of areas, now discussed in turn.

(i) Boards and directors

This section of the Code covers board best practice, the responsibilities of the directors, and director remuneration. The board is viewed as 'the focal point of the corporate governance system' and so the constitution of the board, and the operation of the board and its sub-committees are of fundamental importance. The Code recommends that the board should preferably comprise a majority of non-executive directors, with sufficient of these being independent to enable shareowner interests, including minority interests, to be protected.

The roles of chair and chief executive officer (CEO) should be separate, and it is recommended that the chair is an independent non-executive director.

There should be an audit committee and a remuneration committee, and other committees as appropriate for the particular company and its operations. In relation to director remuneration, there should be a transparent process to develop policy in this area and companies should form a remuneration, or similar, committee to make recommendations on directors' pay to the board. This committee, comprised wholly or mainly of independent non-executive directors, should also be chaired by an independent non-executive director.

(ii) Risk management

The board has responsibility for the overall risk management process, with management being accountable to the board for the actual day-to-day risk management. It is the board's responsibility to form an opinion on the effectiveness of the risk management process.

It stands to reason that the board should identify areas where the business may be particularly vulnerable, and utilize accepted risk management internal controls and frameworks to ensure that such risks are appropriately monitored. A board committee may be established, possibly as a dedicated risk management committee, to help the board with reviewing risk management issues. The Code points out that risk management, rather than perhaps being viewed as only a negative process, may also give rise to opportunities to create competitive advantage.

(iii) Internal audit

Companies should establish an internal audit function with a reporting line directly between the head of internal audit and the CEO. However, if a company does not establish an internal audit function, then it must disclose this in its annual report together with details as to why it has not done so and, in its absence, also how assurance in internal controls can be made.

Internal audit should have a plan that delineates its scope and function. The audit committee should approve the internal audit work agenda, and internal audit should report at all audit committee meetings. In addition, internal audit should liaise with the external auditors.

(iv) Integrated sustainability reporting

The Code states that each company should report every year 'on the nature and extent of its social, transformation, ethical, safety, health and environmental management policies and practices'. The board, therefore, is reporting both on the policies it has in place, and on the implementation of those policies and the resultant changes and benefits.

The company's integrity is seen as something that should be company-wide, and which should also involve the stakeholders in terms of developing appropriate standards of ethical behaviour for the company. The company should disclose the extent of its compliance with its code of ethics. Similarly, companies should think twice before doing business with those who do not seem so committed to integrity.

(v) Accounting and auditing

An audit committee should be established, comprising a majority of independent non-executive directors, the majority of whom are 'financially literate'. It should be chaired by an independent non-executive director. There should be written terms of reference, and the company should disclose in its annual report if the audit committee has adopted formal terms of reference and whether these have been complied with. The audit committee prepares a recommendation for the appointment of the external auditors, in addition to their other duties.

(vi) Relations with shareowners

There is encouragement for companies to have a meaningful dialogue with institutional investors. Companies should ensure adequate information is provided in advance to all shareowners about annual general meeting (AGM) agenda items, and there should be reasonable time for discussion of items. The results of decisions made at AGMs should be made available to shareowners to enable particularly those who could not attend to be aware of the outcomes.

(vii) Communications

There is an emphasis on the company providing a balanced view of the company's position to stakeholders. Reporting should be clear and include non-financial as well as financial matters.

Companies listed on the Johannesburg Securities Exchange and all public sector entities are expected to abide by the recommendations of the Code on a 'comply or explain' basis. Directors therefore need to provide a statement in the annual report about compliance with the Code or give reasons for non-compliance.

The Code of Corporate Governance Principles for South Africa 2009 was launched in September 2009, and is generally known as 'King III'. The report was driven by the new Companies Act in South Africa and also by changes in international governance trends. As with King I and II, the code is an exemplar of good governance practice and focuses on the importance of reporting annually on 'how a company has both positively and negatively affected the economic life of the community in which it operated during the year under review; and how the company intends to enhance those positive aspects and eradicate or ameliorate the negative aspects on the economic life of the community in which it will operate in the year ahead'.

The philosophy of King III revolves around leadership, sustainability, and corporate citizenship. Sustainability has been integrated as a major aspect of performance and reporting to enable stakeholders to better assess the value of a company. King III utilizes an 'apply or explain' basis; that is, companies should apply the principles or explain why they have not done so. There are nine chapters some with the same titles as King II but others being different to reflect the changes mentioned above. The nine chapters are:

- boards and directors;
- corporate citizenship: leadership, integrity and responsibility;
- audit committees;
- risk management;
- internal audit;
- integrated sustainability reporting;
- compliance with laws, regulations, rules and standards;
- managing stakeholder relationships;
- fundamental and affected transactions (such as mergers, acquisitions and amalgamations) and business rescue.

King III became effective from 1 March 2010.

In 2011 the Committee on Responsible Investing by Institutional Investors in South Africa issued the Code for Responsible Investing in South Africa (CRISA). South Africa is only the second country next to the UK to formally encourage institutional investors to integrate into their investment decisions sustainability issues such as environmental, social, and governance (ESG) matters (see Chapters 6 and 7 for more detail). CRISA provides the investor community with the guidance needed to give effect to King III as well as the UN Principles for Responsible Investment.

There are five principles as follows:

- Principle 1—An institutional investor should incorporate sustainability considerations, including ESG, into its investment analysis and investment activities as part of the delivery of superior risk-adjusted returns to the ultimate beneficiaries.

- Principle 2—An institutional investor should demonstrate its acceptance of ownership responsibilities in its investment arrangements and investment activities.

- Principle 3—Where appropriate, institutional investors should consider a collaborative approach to promote acceptance and implementation of the principles of CRISA, and other codes and standards applicable to institutional investors.

- Principle 4—An institutional investor should recognize the circumstances and relationships that hold a potential for conflicts of interest and should proactively manage these when they occur.

- Principle 5—Institutional investors should be transparent about the content of their policies, how the policies are implemented, and how CRISA is applied to enable stakeholders to make informed assessments.

CRISA uses the 'apply or explain' approach and requires institutional investors to fully and publicly disclose to stakeholders, at least once a year, to what extent CRISA has been applied. If an institutional investor has not fully applied one of the Principles of the CRISA, the reasons should be disclosed.

Ntim *et al.* (2012), using a sample of 169 South African listed firms from 2002 to 2007, find that 'disclosing good corporate governance practices on both shareholders and stakeholders impacts positively on firm value, with the latter evidence providing new explicit support for the resource dependence theory. However, we provide additional new evidence, which suggests that disclosing shareholder corporate governance practices contributes significantly more to firm value than stakeholder ones.'

Egypt

During the early 1990s, the Egyptian government began a programme of economic reform, including the privatization of some of the state-owned companies which led to the private sector becoming a major player in the economy. Given this background, there is still a diverse range of corporate ownership in Egypt, including state ownership, dispersed ownership, and companies owned by families or individuals. Egypt was one of the pioneers of corporate governance in the MENA countries, introducing a corporate governance code in 2005 based on the OECD Principles of Corporate Governance. The Egyptian Institute of Directors and the Hawkamah Institute of Corporate Governance have done much to raise awareness of corporate governance in Egypt and the MENA countries respectively.

The Egyptian Code of Corporate Governance (hereafter 'the Code') was issued in October 2005. It applies on a voluntary basis to companies listed on the Cairo and Alexandra Stock Exchange (CASE), to financial institutions (including banks and insurance companies) in the form of joint stock companies even if not listed on CASE, and to companies that obtain major financing from the banking sector. The Code's preface makes the insightful point that 'implementing corporate governance in the right manner is not only limited to respecting a set

Table 13.2 Key characteristics influencing Egyptian corporate governance

Feature	Key characteristic
Main business form	Joint stock company
Predominant ownership structure	State; institutional and individual investors
Legal system	Civil law
Board structure	Unitary
Important aspect	Shariah law (for example, in Islamic financial institutions)

of rules and interpreting it literally in a restricted manner, but it is also a culture and a way of managing the relationship between owners of the company, its directors, and its stakeholders'.

The Code covers:

- the scope of implementation;
- the general assembly (including that generally small shareholders should not be excluded from the general assembly by virtue of the small size of their shareholding);
- the board of directors (including separation of the roles of chairman and managing director, appointment of non-executive directors, the formation of key board committees, the appointment of a company secretary, risk management, and voting;
- the internal audit department;
- the external auditor;
- the audit committee;
- disclosure of social policies (including disclosure of policies relating to social, environmental, occupational health and safety areas);
- avoiding conflict of interest;
- corporate governance rules for other corporations.

In 2006 the *Code of Corporate Governance for the Public Enterprise Sector* was issued in response to the OECD *Guidelines on the Corporate Governance of State-Owned Enterprises* (2005). The principles are divided into six areas: ensuring the existence of an effective regulatory and legal framework for the public enterprise sector; the state acting as the owner; equitable treatment of shareholders (owners); relationships with stakeholders; transparency and disclosure; and responsibilities of the board of directors of public enterprises.

In 2011 the *Code of Corporate Governance for Listed Companies* was issued. The Egyptian Institute of Directors, in cooperation with different entities, has reviewed the Code of Corporate Governance published in October 2005 in order to update it based on the latest Egyptian and international experiences.

Dahawy (2008), in an analysis of the financial statements and websites of the thirty enterprises that make up the CASE 30—which consists of the most active companies in CASE— finds that, in line with previous research from other developing nations, the level of disclosure in Egypt is low. He states that

> some of the non conformity might be due to lack of knowledge about the needs and benefits of corporate governance. The main recommendation of this study is for the Egyptian

government to keep the fast pace of change and to focus mainly on training and education to explain to all stakeholders the means and benefits of disclosures in general, and disclosures related to corporate governance in particular.

Pierce (2008, 2012) provides interesting insights into the development of corporate governance in the MENA and Gulf countries, highlighting key features and developments in these various regions. Furthermore, the OECD (2011, 2012) has issued several papers including a discussion of corporate governance frameworks in the MENA and arrangements for state ownership in the MENA.

Of course the MENA countries must also consider the impact of Shariah laws, for example in banks and financial institutions. Grais and Pellegrin (2006) review the issues and options facing current arrangements for ensuring Shariah compliance by Islamic financial services. They suggest 'a framework that draws on internal and external arrangements to the firm and emphasizes market discipline . . . this framework would enhance public understanding of the requirements of Shariah and lead to more effective options available to stakeholders to achieve improvements in Islamic financial services'. Safieddine (2009) adopts a theory building approach to highlighting variations of agency theory in the unique and complex context of Islamic banks, mainly stemming from the need to comply with Shariah, and the separation of cash flow and control rights for a category of investors. He finds that Islamic banks should improve governance practices currently in place whilst policymakers need to be aware of the need to tailor the regulations to safeguard the interests of all investors without violating the principles of Shariah.

Finally, Abedifar et al. (2012) consider risks in Islamic banking, using a sample of 553 banks from 24 countries between 1999 and 2009. They find that small Islamic banks that are leveraged or based in countries with predominantly Muslim populations have lower credit risk than conventional banks. In terms of insolvency risk, small Islamic banks also appear more stable.

India

Following on from a period of economic downturn and social unrest in 1990–1, the Indian government introduced a programme of reforms to open up the economy and encourage greater reliance on market mechanisms and less reliance on government. Further reforms were aimed at making the public sector more efficient and divestment of government holdings was initiated. There were also reforms to the banking sector to bring it into line with international norms, and to the securities market, with the Securities and Exchange Board of India (SEBI) becoming the regulator of the securities market.

The securities market was transformed as disclosure requirements were brought in to help protect shareholders' interests. Kar (2001) mentions how 'foreign portfolio investment was permitted in India since 1992 and foreign institutional investors also began to play an important role in the institutionalisation of the market'. All of the reforms mentioned led to a much-improved environment in which corporate governance was able to develop.

India has a range of business forms, including public limited companies (which are listed on the stock exchange), domestic private companies, and foreign companies. Ownership data is difficult to find because the number of studies carried out in this area is few, however it is clear that, as the economy has opened up, so the institutional investors are increasing their share of the market.

Table 13.3 Key characteristics influencing Indian corporate governance

Feature	Key characteristic
Main business form	Public limited company
Predominant ownership structure	Corporate bodies; families; but institutional investors' ownership increasing
Legal system	Common law
Board structure	Unitary
Important aspect	Some aspects of the Code are mandatory recommendations

The Confederation of Indian Industry (CII) published *Desirable Corporate Governance in India—A Code* in 1998 and a number of forward-looking companies took its recommendations on board. However, many companies still had poor governance practices, which led to concerns about their financial reporting practices, their accountability, and ultimately to losses being suffered by investors, and the resultant loss of confidence that this caused.

SEBI formally established the Committee on Corporate Governance in May 1999, chaired by Shri Kumar Mangalam Birla. The *Report of the Kumar Mangalam Birla Committee on Corporate Governance* (hereinafter 'the Report') was published in 2000.

The Report emphasizes the importance of corporate governance to future growth of the capital market and the economy. Three key aspects underlying corporate governance are defined as accountability, transparency, and equality of treatment for all stakeholders. The impact of corporate governance on both shareholders and stakeholders is mentioned, although the corporate objective is seen as one of maximizing shareholder value, and indeed the Committee views the fundamental objective of corporate governance as 'enhancement of shareholder value, keeping in view the interests of other stakeholders'. The Committee feels that companies should see the Code as 'a way of life'. The recommendations apply to all listed private and public sector companies, and are split into mandatory requirements (ones that the Committee sees as essential for effective corporate governance) enforceable via the listing rules, and non-mandatory (but nonetheless recommended as best practice). The main areas covered by the Code are now discussed in more detail.

(i) Board of directors

This section of the Code covers the composition of the board, and independent directors. The board provides leadership and strategic guidance for the company and is at all times accountable to the shareholders. The Code recommends that not less than 50 per cent of the board is comprised of non-executive directors; where there is a non-executive chairman, then at least one-third of the board should comprise independent directors, but where there is an executive chairman, at least half of the board should be independent. The latter recommendation is mandatory.

(ii) Nominee directors

The Indian system allows for nominee directors to be put forward by financial or investment institutions to safeguard their investment in the company. The Code decided to allow this practice to continue, but stated that such nominees should have the same responsibility as other directors and be accountable to the shareholders generally.

(iii) Chairman of the board

Whilst recognizing that the roles of chairman and CEO are different, the Code recognizes that the roles may be combined and performed by one individual in some instances.

(iv) Audit committee

There are a number of mandatory recommendations in the Code in relation to audit committees, including the recommendation that a qualified and independent audit committee is established to help to enhance confidence in the company's disclosures. The committee should comprise a minimum three members, all of whom are non-executive, with a majority being independent; it should be chaired by an independent director. At least one director should have appropriate financial knowledge. The audit committee is empowered to seek external advice as appropriate, and, interestingly, to seek information from any employee.

(v) Remuneration committee

A remuneration committee should be established to make recommendations on executive directors' remuneration. The committee should be comprised of at least three non-executive directors, and chaired by an independent director. A mandatory requirement is that there should be disclosures in the annual report relating to 'all elements of remuneration package of all the directors, i.e. salary, benefits, bonuses, stock options, pension, etc.' together with 'details of fixed component and performance-linked incentives, along with performance criteria'. Finally, another mandatory requirement is that the board of directors should decide the remuneration of the non-executive directors.

(vi) Board procedures

There are two mandatory requirements in relation to board meetings. First, that they should be held at least four times a year with a maximum of four months between any two meetings. Secondly, that a director should not be involved in more than ten committees or act as chairman of more than five committees across all companies of which he/she is a director.

(vii) Management

The role of the management of the company (chief executive, executive directors, and key management personnel) in ensuring the smooth running of the day-to-day activities of the company is emphasized. A mandatory recommendation is that there should be disclosure in the annual report—either as part of the directors' report, or as a 'management discussion and analysis' report—about the company's position, its outlook, performance, and other relevant areas of interest to shareholders. There should also be disclosure of any material financial/commercial transactions in which management has a personal interest that may have a potential conflict with the interest of the company.

(viii) Shareholders

Shareholders are entitled to be able to participate effectively in the AGM. Therefore, in support of this aim, it is a mandatory recommendation that, on the appointment of new, or reappointment of existing, directors, the shareholders are provided with relevant information about the director(s). Similarly, companies are mandated to disclose certain information, including their quarterly results and presentations, to company analysts, which may be made available via the Internet.

The growing influence of institutional investors is recognized, along with the fact that they have a responsibility to exercise their votes.

(ix) Manner of implementation

There are mandatory recommendations that a company should have a separate section on corporate governance in its annual report, including a detailed compliance report. Non-compliance with any mandatory recommendations should be highlighted, as should the level of compliance with non-mandatory recommendations. A company should obtain a certificate from its auditors in relation to compliance with the mandatory recommendations and it should be attached to the directors' report, which is sent each year to all the shareholders, and to the stock exchange.

The Indian Code is clearly rather complex having as it does a series of mandatory and non-mandatory recommendations. The feasibility of this approach will lie in a number of areas: first, the extent to which companies are willing to implement the recommendations; secondly, the growing influence of shareholders and how effectively they can exercise their voice; and thirdly, the approach taken by the stock exchange in India in terms of enforcing compliance.

Chakrabarti (2005) provides an interesting review of the evolution of corporate governance in India and highlights the fact that, whilst India has good corporate governance codes/guidelines, there is poor adoption of the recommendations in many companies. Subsequently, Chakrabati *et al*. (2008) state that:

> While on paper the country's legal system provides some of the best investor protection in the world, the reality is different with slow, over-burdened courts and widespread corruption. Consequently, ownership remains highly concentrated and family business groups continue to be the dominant business model. There is significant pyramiding and tunneling among Indian business groups and, notwithstanding copious reporting requirements, widespread earnings management. However, most of India's corporate governance shortcomings are no worse than in other Asian countries and its banking sector has one of the lowest proportions of non-performing assets, signifying that corporate fraud and tunneling are not out of control.

Balasubramanian *et al.* (2008) provide an overview of Indian corporate governance practices, based primarily on responses to a 2006 survey of 370 Indian public companies. They find that:

> Compliance with legal norms is reasonably high in most areas, but not complete. We identify areas where Indian corporate governance is relatively strong and weak, and areas where regulation might usefully be either relaxed or strengthened. On the whole, Indian corporate governance rules appear appropriate for larger companies, but could use some strengthening in the area of related party transactions, and some relaxation for smaller companies. Executive compensation is low by US standards and is not currently a problem area. We also examine whether there is a cross-sectional relationship between measures of governance and measures of firm performance and find evidence of a positive relationship for an overall governance index and for an index covering shareholder rights.

In December 2009 the Corporate Governance–Voluntary Guidelines 2009, were introduced for voluntary adoption by the corporate sector. The Guidelines took into account the recommendations the CII made in February 2009 to propose ways in which corporate governance could be further improved. The Guidelines have six sections:

(i) Board of directors

Appointment of directors–covering appointments to the board; separation of offices of chairman and CEO; nomination committee; and the number of companies in which an individual may become a director (where an individual is a managing director or full-time director in a public company, then the maximum number of companies in which the individual can serve as a non-executive or independent director is seven).

Independent directors–covering attributes for independent directors; tenure for independent directors; and independent directors to have the option and freedom to meet company management periodically.

Remuneration of directors–covering remuneration (guiding principles linking corporate and individual performance; remuneration of non-executive directors; structure of compensation to non-executive directors; remuneration of independent directors); remuneration committees.

(ii) Responsibilities of the board

Covering training of directors; enabling quality decision-making; risk management; evaluation of performance of the board of directors, committees thereof and of individual directors; board to place systems to ensure compliance with laws.

(iii) Audit committee of board

Covering audit committee constitution; audit committee enabling powers; audit committee role and responsibilities.

(iv) Auditors

Covering appointment of auditors; certificate of independence; rotation of audit partners and firms; need for clarity on information to be sought by auditor and/or provided by the company to the auditor; appointment of internal auditor.

(v) Secretarial audit

A competent professional may carry out a secretarial audit to help confirm that the board processes and compliance mechanisms of the company are robust.

(vi) Institution of mechanism for whistleblowing

Employees should be able to report concerns about unethical behavior, suspected fraud, or violation of the company's code of ethics and be provided with adequate safeguards against victimization.

In 2011 the National Voluntary Guidelines on Social, Environmental and Economical Responsibilities of Business were issued by the Ministry of Corporate Affairs. The Guidelines are a refinement of the Corporate Social Responsibility Voluntary Guidelines 2009, released by the Ministry of Corporate Affairs in December 2009. In the foreword to the Guidelines, it emphasizes that nowadays businesses have to take responsibility for the ways their operations impact society and the natural environment. There are nine principles, namely, that businesses should:

- conduct and govern themselves with ethics, transparency, and accountability;
- provide goods and services that are safe and contribute to sustainability throughout their life cycle;
- promote the wellbeing of all employees;
- respect the interests of, and be responsive towards all stakeholders, especially those who are disadvantaged, vulnerable and marginalized;
- respect and promote human rights;
- respect, protect, and make efforts to restore the environment;
- when engaged in influencing public and regulatory policy, do so in a responsible manner;
- support inclusive growth and equitable development;
- engage with, and provide value to, their customers and consumers in a responsible manner.

Afsharipour (2009) examines recent corporate governance reforms in India and posits that

the Indian experience demonstrates that traditional theories predicting convergence, or a lack thereof, fail to fully capture the trajectory of actual corporate governance reforms. India's reform efforts demonstrate that while corporate governance rules may converge on a formal level with Anglo-American corporate governance norms, local characteristics tend to prevent reforms from being more than merely formal. India's inability to effectively implement and enforce its extensive new rules corroborates the argument that comprehensive convergence is limited, and that the transmission of ideas from one system to another is highly complex and difficult, requiring political, social and institutional changes that cannot be made easily.

Furthermore Varottil (2010) discusses whether a US/UK concept of independent directors is appropriate, or effective, in an Indian context. He states:

> a transplantation of the concept [of independent directors] to a country such as India without placing emphasis on local corporate structures and associated factors is likely to produce unintended results and outcomes that are less than desirable. This Article finds that due to the concentrated ownership structures in Indian companies, it is the minority shareholders who require the protection of corporate governance norms from actions of the controlling shareholders. Board independence, in the form it originated, does not provide a solution to this problem.

Brazil

The economies of various countries in South America were also affected adversely by the world economic downturn in the 1990s. As with many other countries around the globe, this led to a demand for more transparency and accountability, and the need to restore and build confidence in the stock market.

Many businesses in South America are dominated by a controlling group, often representing family interests. This pattern can be seen in Brazil, Mexico, and Chile, for example. In this section, we will look in more detail at the corporate governance of Brazil.

As with most South American countries, in Brazil, the protection of minority interests has traditionally been a weak area, with minority shareholders lacking both access to information and the means to take appropriate action. In the past companies have often issued preferred shares as a means of raising capital. Although preferred shares carry a dividend, they do not usually have voting rights except in certain specific circumstances. Therefore holders of preferred shares are often in a weak position and are vulnerable to the whims of controlling shareholders.

The São Paulo Stock Exchange (BOVESPA) has introduced a new index: the ICG (Index of Shares under Special Corporate Governance Registration). Companies can register at different levels: Level 1 and Level 2. Level 1 requirements include 'compliance with disclosure

Table 13.4 Key characteristics influencing Brazilian corporate governance

Feature	Key characteristic
Main business form	Public limited company
Predominant ownership structure	Controlling owner (corporations or individuals)
Legal system	Civil law
Board structure	Dual
Important aspect	Fiscal councils

regulations for transactions involving shares issued by the company's controlling share-holders or directors' and 'disclosure of shareholder agreements and stock option programs'.

The Brazilian Institute of Corporate Governance (BICG) published a *Code of Best Practice of Corporate Governance* in 2001 (hereafter 'the Code'). The BICG was established as a civil not-for-profit association to act as a leading forum for corporate governance in Brazil. The Code identifies transparency, accountability, and fairness as the 'pillars' of corporate governance. The Code is very helpful in identifying some of the key features of Brazilian companies, such as the fact that the majority have controlling owners. It also recommends that family-controlled businesses should establish a family council 'to settle family issues and keep them apart from the governance of the company'.

The corporate governance structure is essentially a two-tier, or dual, structure because Brazilian companies have a board of directors and also a fiscal council. The fiscal council is elected by, and accountable to, the owners. The Code states that the fiscal council 'is created because the minorities and the owners of non-voting stock have no influence and little information. The fiscal council is a partial remedy to this. It has access to information and can express its opinion in the annual general meeting'. Its access to information is quite extensive because copies of board of directors' meeting minutes, financial statements, and other information are available to its members. They may also have access to the independent auditors.

The Comissao de Valores Mobiliarios (CVM) is the Securities and Exchange Commission of Brazil, and in June 2002 the CVM issued recommendations on corporate governance. The Code covers four main areas: transparency of ownership and control, and shareholder meetings; structure and responsibilities of the board of directors; minority shareholder protection; and accounting and auditing. It is interesting that there is a specific section dedicated to minority shareholder protection. Each of the main areas of the Code are now detailed in turn.

(i) Transparency of ownership and control, shareholder meetings

All shareholders should be provided with full information about agenda items to be discussed at the general shareholders' meeting. The meeting should be arranged on a date/time that will not preclude attendance by shareholders; where there are complex agenda items, then the company should give at least 30 days' notice of the meeting.

A list of shareholders, together with the amount of their shareholdings, should be available on request by shareholders. There should be clear regulations laid down about the process for voting on general meeting agenda items.

(ii) Structure and responsibilities of the board of directors

The board of directors should safeguard the assets of the business whilst ensuring that the company's goals and objectives are met. There is an emphasis on maximizing return on investment.

The roles of chair and CEO should not be carried out by the same person. The board should comprise five to ten directors, at least two of whom should have appropriate experience of finance/accounting practices. There are three categories of director: internal, being officers or employees of the company; external, being those who do not work in the company but are not classed as independent; and independent directors. The

Code states that 'as many board members as possible should be independent of company management'.

Board subcommittees may be set up to focus on certain aspects, for example, an audit committee. Board members are entitled to appropriate information to enable them to fulfil their function and also to take external advice as necessary.

An interesting recommendation is that holders of preferred shares should be entitled to nominate and elect a representative to the board of directors. This would give holders of preferred shares a voice and would be particularly helpful where there is a group of controlling shareholders who might otherwise not consider the views of holders of preferred shares.

(iii) Minority shareholder protection

Recent changes to legislation have instructed Brazilian public companies not to issue more than 50 per cent of their capital as preferred shares. Preferred shares (as in the UK) have limited voting rights, usually to vote only on issues that directly affect them rather than on all general meeting agenda issues. This part of the Code recommends that there should be no voting restrictions for preferred shares in relation to decisions being made on a number of areas, including alteration of the company's activities, and mergers/spin-offs, as these areas impact on all shareholders.

There is a specific recommendation that, if dividends are not paid to shares with the right to fixed or guaranteed dividends, then those shares immediately acquire the right to vote; also, if the company does not pay dividends for three years, then any non-voting shares will acquire the right to vote. These are particularly important recommendations in situations where controlling shareholders may try to deprive minority shareholders of their right to the company's cash flows in the form of dividends.

There are a number of recommendations that relate to utilizing the idea of 'tag-along', including that, if there is a change in control, then both controlling shareholders and minority shareholders should be paid the same price for their shares. Disagreements between either the company and its shareholders, or the controlling shareholders and the minority shareholders, may be solved by arbitration.

(iv) Accounting and auditing

Quarterly financial statements should be published, along with details of the factors that have affected business performance over the quarter.

This section of the Code also contains recommendations in relation to the fiscal board, which should have between three and five members. The Code states:

> Holders of preferred shares and holders of common shares, excluding shareholders in the controlling group, should have the right to elect an equal number of members as the controlling group. The controlling group should renounce the right to elect the last member (third or fifth member), who should be elected by the majority of share capital, in a shareholders' meeting at which each share represents one vote, regardless of its type or sort, including controlling shares.

The Code emphasizes that all appropriate information should be made available to members of the fiscal board so that their 'supervisory capacity shall be the broadest possible'.

An audit committee should be established, comprising board members with knowledge of finance, and there should be at least one member representing minority shareholders. The audit committee will oversee the relationship with the auditor; the fiscal board and the audit committee should meet with the auditors.

The Code recommends that the board should either prohibit or restrict the amount of non-audit services provided to the company by the company's auditor in order to try to ensure that the auditor retains independence.

The CVM requires that public companies include in their annual report the level to which they comply with the recommendations, utilizing a 'comply or explain' approach.

In 2004 the BICG published an updated and enlarged edition of the *Code of Best Practice of Corporate Governance*. The Code aims to provide guidelines to all types of company—ranging from publicly or privately held corporations to non-governmental organizations—with the aim of increasing company value, improving corporate performance, facilitating access to capital at lower costs and contributing to the long-term survival of the company.

The Code has six sections: ownership, the board of directors, management, independent auditing, the fiscal council, and conduct and conflicts of interest.

(i) Ownership

A number of points are covered under this section, including:

- that every shareholder is a company owner, commensurate with his/her respective share in the company's capital;
- the 'one share, one vote' concept is advocated;
- there is discussion of the general assembly and the powers it has;
- a minimum of 30 days' notice of the AGM of the company should be given;
- the agenda and documentation for the AGM should be circulated to all shareholders well in advance of the meeting itself;
- the responsibilities of the family council are outlined, such as differentiating between family and company interests, preserving family values, succession planning, and establishing criteria to appoint members to the board of directors.

(ii) Board of directors

This section includes the recommendations that every organization should have a board of directors, of between five and nine members, elected by its owners. It should also take into account other stakeholders, corporate objectives, and corporate sustainability. An advisory board is recommended, particularly in certain companies such as family companies and private companies. The mission of the board is to protect and add value to the company, and maximize the return on investment. The responsibilities of the board are detailed, together with the recommendation that there are internal regulations laid down for the activities of the board. The roles of chair and CEO should be split. Board committees, including an audit committee, may be set up and the latter should be made up preferably of independent directors; criteria for independent directors are discussed as are director qualifications. There should be an annual formal performance evaluation of the board and of individual directors; directors' compensation should reflect their experience and the time and effort they put in. Succession planning should be in place, and there should be induction training for new directors and continuing education thereafter. Risk management should be undertaken, and the company's policies on social, environmental, occupational, and health safety practices should be disclosed at least annually.

(iii) Management

The CEO is accountable to the board of directors; the CEO and corporate officers are accountable for a transparent relationship with stakeholders. There should be adequate disclosure, which should be clear and well balanced, and the annual report should include mention of the company's corporate governance practices, shareholdings, and compensation of directors, and be prepared in accordance with international accounting standards. There should be a system of internal controls, a code of conduct, an appropriate structure for management compensation, and access to information for the directors and fiscal council.

(iv) Independent auditing

Every organization should have an independent auditor who should express clearly their opinion on the financial statements. The board of directors and/or the audit committee should establish a work plan and the fees of the independent auditors. The independent auditors should report issues of concern to the audit committee, or in its absence, to the board, and the independence of auditors is discussed in relation to the length of their contract and to the provision of non-audit services.

(v) The Fiscal Council

The Fiscal Council is described in the Code as 'an essential part of the Brazilian companies' governance system', although it is, however, non-mandatory. Its purpose is to oversee the actions of the companies' administrative bodies and to give its opinion on certain matters to the owners. It acts as a tool 'designed to add value to the company, since it works as an independent control for the owners of the company'. The controlling and minority shareholders should discuss the composition of the fiscal council prior to its election, at the assembly meeting, in order to ensure an appropriate mix of professional backgrounds.

(vi) Conduct and conflicts of interest

Each organization should have a code of conduct, covering such areas as conflicts of interest, discrimination in the workplace, political activities, community relations, company share-trading policies, loans between related parties, and lawsuits/arbitration, which is followed by everyone in the company.

There are four basic principles of the Code: transparency, fairness, accountability, and corporate responsibility. With regard to the last principle, the Code states:

> corporate responsibility is a broader view of corporate strategy, contemplating all kinds of relations with the community where the company operates. The 'social role' of the company should include the creation of wealth and job opportunities, work force skills and diversity, promotion of scientific advancements through technology, and improved standards of living through educational, cultural, social, and environmental initiatives. This principle should include preferred treatment of local people and resources.

In 2009 a revised *Code of Best Practice of Corporate Governance* was issued. It retains the same six sections as its predecessor but seeks to implement more robust corporate governance practices in the light of changes both in Brazil (for example, the capital market revival, a large number of companies going public, the diffuse share ownership in some companies, mergers and acquisitions, etc.) and internationally (the global financial downturn).

Black *et al.* (2008) provide an overview of corporate governance practices in Brazilian companies and they identify areas where Brazilian corporate governance is relatively strong and weak. They state:

> Board independence is an area of weakness: The boards of most Brazilian private firms are comprised entirely or almost entirely of insiders or representatives of the controlling family or group. Many firms have zero independent directors. At the same time, minority shareholders have legal rights to representation on the boards of many firms, and this representation is reasonably common. Financial disclosure lags behind world standards. Only a minority of firms provide a statement of cash flows or consolidated financial statements. However, many provide English language financial statements, and an English language version of their website. Audit committees are uncommon, but many Brazilian firms use an alternate approach to ensuring financial statement accuracy—establishing a fiscal board. A minority of firms provide takeout rights to minority shareholders on a sale of control. Controlling shareholders often use shareholders agreements to ensure control.

Chavez and Silva (2009) study the reaction of stock prices to the announcement by thirty-one Brazilian companies of their intent to list on one of the special governance exchanges. Their analysis shows that the companies choosing to list in these segments experienced an increase in both the value and the liquidity of their shares. They conclude that 'in countries where governance legislation is weak and the progress of reform is slow, stock markets can play a key role in helping companies differentiate themselves through exchange-defined governance codes'.

Black *et al.* (2011) state that 'a central issue in corporate governance research is the extent to which "good" governance practices are universal (one size mostly fits all) or instead depend on country and firm characteristics.' They conduct a case study of Brazil, surveying Brazilian firms' governance practices, and then extending prior studies of India, Korea, and Russia, and comparing those countries to Brazil, to assess which aspects of governance matter in which countries, and for which types of firms. They find that their '"multi-country" results suggest that country characteristics strongly influence both which aspects of governance predict firm market value, and at which firms that association is found. They support a flexible approach to governance, with ample room for firm choice'.

Leal (2011) states 'corporate governance is discussed intensively and new regulations and self-regulations are brought about constantly. New laws and regulations impose greater disclosure, convergence to international accounting standards, and better protection to minority shareholders'. However, he identifies that there are still improvements to be made, for example, making the board process more formal and independent; reducing the dominance of controlling shareholders over boards; improving the use of committees; increasing the amount of board evaluations; and improving participation in general assemblies.

Conclusions

In this chapter, the corporate governance of three very different countries has been discussed. We have seen that South Africa, India, and Brazil have different cultural influences, legal systems, and corporate governance structures (the first two have a unitary board system, the last a two-tier board system). However, there appears to be a certain commonality of approach to their corporate governance codes, with an emphasis on transparency and accountability, and the desire to enhance the protection of minority shareholders' rights. There is an emphasis on the importance of having a balanced board with an appropriate proportion of independent directors, and also recognition that a company cannot operate in isolation but should consider the interests of its various stakeholder groups.

These countries, diverse as they are in many respects, illustrate that corporate governance is relevant and valuable to countries around the globe. Over time, it is to be expected that corporate governance will improve, as countries seek to attract international investment and maintain investor confidence.

Summary

- The financial downturn that occurred in many countries in the 1990s has had an impact in driving forward corporate governance globally. Countries are seeking to improve their corporate governance to help restore confidence in the markets by increasing transparency and disclosure, and ensuring better protection of minority shareholders' rights.

- South Africa arguably has the most comprehensive corporate governance code in the world. The Code takes an inclusive approach, paying significant attention to integrated sustainability reporting, including stakeholder relations, ethical practices, and social and transformation issues. King III uses an 'apply or explain' basis, that is companies should apply the principles or explain why they have not done so.

- Egypt was one of the first MENA countries to develop its corporate governance. It went through a period of economic reform and privatization in the early 1990s which led to a range of ownership structures. In 2011 the 'Arab Spring' saw much turmoil and an uprising in the country. Shariah law is to be considered, for example, in Islamic banking and financial institutions.

- India has a unitary board system. The corporate governance code splits recommendations into mandatory and non-mandatory recommendations. Both are desirable but the mandatory recommendations are seen as core to effective corporate governance.

- Brazil is fairly typical of South American countries, with controlling groups and a lack of effective mechanisms for minority shareholders' protection of rights. Brazil has a two-tier structure, with a fiscal board acting as a balance to the board of directors.

Example: MindTree, India

This is an example of a company in India which has good corporate governance and corporate social responsibility. It has been the recipient of several corporate governance awards/rankings.

MindTree Limited is a mid-sized international information technology (IT) consulting and implementation company which was started up in 1999 and went public in December 2006 listing on the Bombay Stock Exchange. It has operating in two units—IT and production engineering services—and has been heavily involved in the development of Bluetooth technology.

MindTree has comprehensive disclosure of its corporate governance and sustainability policies. In its annual report for 2010/11, details of the board members and the various committees are given. There are eleven board members comprising six independent non-executive directors, two non-executive directors and three executive directors (including the CEO and managing director). The executive chairman resigned at the end of March 2011 and was replaced by a non-executive chairman. There are five committees: audit, investor grievances, compensation, strategic initiatives, and administrative.

Details of directors' compensation (remuneration) are disclosed, including fixed salary, bonus, sitting fees and commission (the latter being a sum not exceeding 1 per cent per annum of the net profits). The number of directorships held by directors in other Indian public companies is disclosed, together with the number of committees they chair, or are a member of, in other Indian companies.

MindTree had an integrity policy guided by its CLASS values: Caring, Learning, Achieving, Sharing and Socially Responsible. The MindTree Foundation supports three broad initiatives: supporting differently abled and physically challenged people, with specific focus on assistive technologies; improving and enhancing the quality and development of primary education; and Mindshare, which is a programme that allows MindTree Minds (employees) to interact with people outside their normal course of life.

MindTree has received a number of awards relating to its corporate governance, its corporate social responsibility, and its business activities. These include the 'NASSCOM IT User Award 2012' under Social Media Adoption in an Enterprise category for its intranet application, 'PeopleHub'; the 'Best Corporate Governance, India, 2012' by *World Finance* magazine; and Krishnakumar Natarajan, the MD and CEO, received the Bloomberg UTV, 'CEO of the Year' under Emerging Companies category in 2011. Furthermore, MindTree was ranked third in India in the 'Best overall for Corporate Governance' category in the Asiamoney Corporate Governance Poll, 2011; ranked nineteenth in the list of top twenty-five best employers in India; and ranked second amongst the IT companies by AON Hewitt Best Employers' Survey 2011.

Mini case study   SABMiller, South Africa

SabMiller has both a South African and a UK listing. It has good corporate governance and disclosure practices, and displays a good awareness of stakeholders' interests.

In 2002 SAB Plc, a company with brewing interests dating back to the 1880s, acquired Miller Brewing, and the company became known as SABMiller Plc. SABMiller Plc is the world's leading brewer in developing markets.

(continued)

SABMiller views corporate governance as a 'process through which its shareholders may derive assurance that, in protecting and adding value to SABMiller's financial and human investment, the group is being managed ethically, according to prudently determined risk parameters'.

The board of directors, according to the annual report 2011, consists of eighteen members: the chairman; nine independent non-executive directors (including the senior independent director); five non-executive directors who are not considered to be independent; and three executive directors (the chief executive, the chief financial officer, and the deputy chief financial officer). The company has an audit committee, nomination committee, remuneration committee, corporate accountability and risk assurance committee (CARAC), disclosure committee, and executive committee. SABMiller gives comprehensive disclosure of the function/role of each of the key board committees, including the CARAC (established in 2001) with the main objective being 'to assist the board in the discharge of its duties relating to corporate accountability and associated risk and opportunities in terms of direction, assurance and reporting for the group. The committee also provides independent and objective oversight'.

The company aims to engage in appropriate dialogue with institutional investors and encourages its shareholders to attend AGMs and ask questions as appropriate.

SABMiller provides good disclosure of its company values, which 'guide us in our relations with all those who have a direct interest in the business—our stakeholders—and inform the Guiding Principles which govern those relationships'. The company values include respecting the rights and dignity of individuals, being a responsible corporate citizen, and respecting the values and cultures of the communities in which they operate.

SABMiller has been named 'Best Company to Work for' in South Africa, and is seeking to encourage diversity in its workforce globally. The company published information on its website relating to its policies on, and measurement of, environmental impacts and social impacts. Environmental measures include the efficient use of water and CO_2 emissions, whilst social impacts relating to the workforce include accident rates and days allocated to training.

SABMiller won the 'Relevance and Materiality' category of the Corporate Register Global Reporting Awards in March 2011. This award, which is voted for by Corporate Register's 7,000 users, is recognition of SABMiller's excellent reporting and communication of its approach to sustainable development.

Questions

The discussion questions to follow cover the key learning points of this chapter. Reading of some of the additional reference material will enhance the depth of the students' knowledge and understanding of these areas.

1. Critically discuss the potential advantages and disadvantages of an 'inclusive' approach to corporate governance.

2. What might be the complexities of developing corporate governance in the MENA countries?

3. Critically discuss the problems that minority shareholders may face in the presence of controlling shareholders.

4. What might be the advantages or disadvantages of a corporate governance code that splits recommendations into mandatory and non-mandatory?

5. What commonalities seem to be emerging in various corporate governance codes?

6. Critically discuss the drivers to corporate governance reform in a global context.

References

Abedifar, P., Molyneux, P., and Tarazi, A. (2012), *Risk in Islamic Banking*, available at SSRN: http://ssrn.com/abstract=1663406 or http://dx.doi.org/10.2139/ssrn.1663406

Afsharipour, A. (2009), 'Corporate Governance Convergence: Lessons from the Indian Experience', *Northwestern Journal of International Law & Business*, Vol. 29, No. 2.

Balasubramanian, B.N., Black, B.S., and Khanna, V.S. (2008), 'Firm-level Corporate Governance in Emerging Markets: A Case Study of India', ECGI–Law Working Paper; 2nd Annual Conference on Empirical Legal Studies Paper; University of Michigan Law and Economics, Olin Working Paper 08-011; University of Texas Law, Law and Econ Research Paper No. 87, available at SSRN: http://ssrn.com/abstract=992529

Black, B.S., De Carvalho, A.G., and Gorga, E. (2008), 'The Corporate Governance of Privately Controlled Brazilian Firms', University of Texas Law, Law and Econ Research Paper No. 109; Cornell Legal Studies Research Paper No. 08-014; ECGI–Finance Working Paper No. 206/2008, available at SSRN: http://ssrn.com/abstract=1003059

——— (2011), 'What Matters and for Which Firms for Corporate Governance in Emerging Markets? Evidence from Brazil (and Other BRIK Countries)', *Journal of Corporate Finance*, http://dx.doi.org/10.1016/j.jcorpfin.2011.10.001

BICG (2001), *Code of Best Practice of Corporate Governance*, BICG, São Paulo.

—— (2004), *Code of Best Practice of Corporate Governance*, BICG, São Paulo.

—— (2009), *Code of Best Practice of Corporate Governance*, BICG, São Paulo.

Chakrabarti, R. (2005), *Corporate Governance in India—Evolution and Challenges*, available at SSRN: http://ssrn.com/abstract=649857

—— Megginson W., and K. Yadav (2008) 'Corporate Governance in India', *Journal of Applied Corporate Finance*, Vol. 20, No. 1, Winter.

Chavez, G.A. and Silva, A.C. (2009), 'Brazil's Experiment with Corporate Governance', *Journal of Applied Corporate Finance*, Vol. 21, No. 1, Winter.

Comissao de Valores Mobiliarios (2002), *CVM Recommendations on Corporate Governance*, CVM, Rio de Janeiro.

Committee on Responsible Investing by Institutional Investors in South Africa (2011), *Code for Responsible Investing in South Africa 2011*, Institute of Directors in Southern Africa, Johannesburg.

CII (1998), Desirable *Corporate Governance in India—A Code*, CII, Delhi.

Dahawy, K. (2008), *Developing Nations and Corporate Governance: The Story of Egypt*, available at http://www.ifc.org/ifcext/cgf.nsf/AttachmentsByTitle/PaperKhaledDahawy/$FILE/Dahawy_Kahled4.pdf

Egyptian Institute of Directors (2005), Guide to Corporate Governance Principles in Egypt, EIoD, Egypt.

—— (2006), *Code of Corporate Governance for the Public Enterprise Sector*, EIoD/Ministry of Investment, Egypt.

—— (2011), *Code of Corporate Governance for Listed Companies*, Egyptian Institute of Directors/Ministry of Investment, Egypt.

Grais, W. and Pellegrin M. (2006), 'Corporate Governance and Shariah Compliance in Institutions Offering Islamic Financial Services', *World Bank Policy Research Working Paper No. 4054*. Available at SSRN: http://ssrn.com/abstract=940711

Kar, P. (2001), 'Corporate Governance in India', *Corporate Governance in Asia: A Comparative Perspective*, OECD, Paris.

King, M. (1994), *King Report on Corporate Governance* (King I), Institute of Directors, Johannesburg.

—— (2002), *King Report on Corporate Governance* (King II), Institute of Directors, Johannesburg.

—— (2009), *King Report on Corporate Governance* (King III), Institute of Directors, Johannesburg.

Klapper, L.F. and Love, I. (2002), 'Corporate Governance, Investor Protection, and Performance in Emerging Markets', World Bank Policy Research Working Paper 2818, World Bank, Washington, DC.

Kumar Mangalam Birla (2000), *Report of the Kumar Mangalam Birla Committee on Corporate Governance*, Securities and Exchange Board of India, Delhi.

Leal, R.C. (2011), 'The Emergence of a Serious Contender: Corporate Governance in Brazil', in C.A. Mallin (ed.), *Handbook on International Corporate Governance, Country Analyses*, 2nd edition, Edward Elgar Publishing, Cheltenham, UK.

Ministry of Corporate Affairs (2009), *Corporate Governance—Voluntary Guidelines 2009*, Ministry of Corporate Affairs, Government of India.

—— (2011), *National Voluntary Guidelines on Social, Environmental and Economical Responsibilities of Business*, Ministry of Corporate Affairs, Government of India.

Ntim, C. G., Opong, K. K., and Danbolt, J. (2012), 'The Relative Value Relevance of Shareholder Versus Stakeholder Corporate Governance Disclosure Policy

Reforms in South Africa', *Corporate Governance: An International Review*, Vol. 20, Issue 1, pp. 84–105.

OECD (2005), *Guidelines on the Corporate Governance of State-Owned Enterprises*, OECD, Paris.

——(2011), *Survey on Corporate Governance Frameworks in the Middle East and North Africa*, OECD, Paris.

——(2012), Towards New Arrangements for State Ownership in the Middle East and North Africa, OECD, Paris.

Pierce, C. (2008), *Corporate Governance in the Middle East and North Africa*, published in association with Hawkamah, the Institute for Corporate Governance and Mudara Institute of Directors, GMB Publishing Ltd, London.

——(2012), *Corporate Governance in the Gulf*, Global Governance Services Ltd, Kent.

Safieddine A. (2009), 'Islamic Financial Institutions and Corporate Governance: New Insights for Agency Theory', *Corporate Governance: An International Review*, Volume 17, Issue 2, pages 142–158.

Varottil, U. (2010), 'Evolution and Effectiveness of Independent Directors in Indian Corporate Governance', *Hastings Business Law Journal*, Vol. 6, No. 2, p. 281.

Useful websites

www.aaoifi.com The website for the Accounting and Auditing Organization for Islamic Financial Institutions, which prepares accounting, auditing, governance, ethics, and Shari'a standards for Islamic financial institutions and the industry.

www.cii.in The Confederation of Indian Industry website has information about corporate governance issues in India.

www.ecgi.org The website of the European Corporate Governance Institute contains codes from around the world.

http://econ.worldbank.org The World Bank website has comprehensive information about various corporate governance issues and reports.

www.eiod.org The website of the Egyptian Institute of Directors has information about corporate governance developments in Egypt.

www.hawkamah.org The website of the Hawkamah Institute for Corporate Governance has details of developments in corporate governance affecting the MENA region.

www.ibgc.org.br The website of the Institute of Brazilian Corporate Governance has information about various corporate governance issues in Brazil.

www.ifsb.org The website of the Islamic Financial Services Board, which contains information about various aspects relating to developments in standard-setting in Islamic financial services.

www.iodsa.co.za The website of the Institute of Directors Southern Africa, various governance publications can be accessed here.

www.jse.co.za The website of the JSE Securities Exchange South Africa contains useful information relating to South Africa.

www.nfcgindia.org The website of the National Foundation for Corporate Governance, which has the goal of promoting better corporate governance practices in India, has details on corporate governance initiatives.

www.sebi.gov.in The website of the Securities and Exchange Board of India has information about various issues in India.

 For further links to useful sources of information visit the Online Resource Centre **www.oxfordtextbooks.co.uk/orc/mallin4e/**

 FT Clippings

FT: TCI fund clashes with Indian deference

By James Crabtree in Mumbai

March 15, 2012

The Children's Investment Fund is an unusually vocal investor. But in India, a country unused to even a modicum of shareholder activism, its latest move was unprecedented.

This week TCI launched an aggressive and public attack on the management of Coal India, the state-backed energy group with a market capitalisation of $43bn, accusing its directors of bowing to government meddling to the detriment of minority shareholders, of which TCI is the largest. The fund controls close to 2 per cent of Coal India.

Such dramatic moves have become something of a habit for the fund, which has about $8bn of assets under management, although its chances of success in a country known for opaque and unresponsive corporate governance remain doubtful.

Nonetheless India's first genuine shareholder revolt raises a host of awkward questions, both for a corporate sector with a reputation for paying scant attention to investor concerns and a cash-strapped government long-used to manipulating state-backed enterprises for its own ends.

"This is the first action of this type I have seen in India in nearly thirty years," says Raamdeo Agrawal, managing director of Motilala Oswal, a leading Mumbai-based brokerage. "It will be warmly welcomed by investors, while clearly for the government it is a PR disaster." India's minority shareholders are typically a respectful and cautious bunch, with annual general meetings that border on the sycophantic and any worries addressed quietly behind closed doors—if at all.

Foreign investors, meanwhile, have become accustomed to feeling trampled underfoot by both state-backed companies and India's powerful "promoter" tycoons alike.

The country's large state-backed enterprises can be especially uncooperative, often acting in ways that suit political expediency rather than shareholders interests—something TCI illustrated by releasing a letter from a senior government bureaucrat requesting Coal India to reverse a recent coal price increase.

TCI, led by chief executive Chris Hohn, thinks it can change this through a mixture of public pressure and legal threats: its founders have launched a website to lobby for coal price increases and higher dividends, and it is threatening to sue Coal India's board directors.

It has some legal backing. India's powerful Supreme Court has ruled that government bodies are not allowed to mandate prices, while the nation's Companies Act allows for appeals to a body called the Company Law Board if 100 shareholders demand it.

Awkwardly, however, legal analysts say the result of such an appeal may only be an investigation or the appointment of a new director by the government itself—a tricky prospect in an already state-dominated enterprise.

Coal India has so far refused to comment on the issue, but a speedy change of heart from the company seems unlikely, not least because its management and board directors are stacked with former civil servants loyal to their political masters.

TCI's move is likely to cause some concern in New Delhi, however. The government badly needs support from international investors to help it address a deteriorating budget deficit through further state divestments, having met barely half of its target to raise $8bn through such sales in this financial year.

Nonetheless, providing cheap fuel to the nation's struggling power sector is an even higher political priority. Analysts say the government is highly unlikely to voluntarily give up its ability to use groups like Coal India for politically convenient ends.

David Cornell, managing director at Ocean Dial Advisors, a Mumbai-based investment manager, says: "This sort of shareholder activism is unheard of in India because everyone knows it is like pushing water uphill.

"These companies are tools for use as the government pleases, and sadly this isn't going to change quickly. So if you invest in a public sector company here, you get what you deserve." Other analysts are more sympathetic towards TCI's move, arguing that even if ultimately unsuccessful it could

embolden other shareholders to speak out in public, or at least to begin to demand more accountability from the management of groups in which they invest.

Many feel corporate India is ripe for the beginnings of a cultural shift towards greater shareholder activism, in the form of complaints against political interference in other state-backed companies, or more generally in the numerous other cases in which minority shareholders feel poorly treated.

Sandeep Parekh, founder of Finsec Law Advisors, a Mumbai-based financial sector law firm, says: "I think this can be substantial nuisance value and also it could have a disproportionately large impact on the independent directors, many of whom are quite distinguished people. But it contributes to the wider war for improved corporate governance significantly, even if ends up having limited impact on the battle at hand."

14 Conclusions

This chapter is a useful point to review the main themes that have been covered in this book and to sum up developments that have occurred in corporate governance in recent years. We have seen that various corporate collapses and financial scandals have been the impetus for many companies to improve their corporate governance. The loss of confidence produced by corporate failures can be truly devastating, reverberating not just in the country where the collapse occurs but around the globe. We are all too aware of the consequences of Enron, Royal Ahold, and Parmalat; their effects have been felt across the world and, in some cases, their fallout continues. In the previous edition of this book, I wrote 'Yet that does not seem to stop new scandals from occurring and one thing we can be sure of is that there will be more, and maybe bigger, scandals in the future'. The last few years have seen new corporate scandals and collapses around the world, including Olympus Corporation in Japan, China Forestry in China, and Securency in Australia and, of course, the meltdown of the whole financial system, which resulted in many banks having to be bailed out by their governments and austerity measures being introduced in a number of countries. In the UK, the Royal Bank of Scotland has continued to be one of the high-profile, headline-hitting cases, largely because of the excessive remuneration packages paid to its directors and the perceived overly generous 'rewards for failure'. Therefore, corporate governance has a heavy load on its shoulders if it is to be effective in trying to stop more financial scandals and collapses in the future. It may be that it can only, at best, partially succeed, but then it will still have been a worthwhile investment because investor confidence will be higher, corporations will be in better shape, investors will be more active and involved, and the views and interests of stakeholder groups will be given more consideration.

As we have seen, corporate governance is concerned with both the internal aspects of the company, such as internal control and board structure, and the external aspects, such as the company's relationship with its shareholders and other stakeholders. Corporate governance is also seen as an essential mechanism to help the company attain its corporate objectives, and monitoring performance is a key element in achieving the objectives. Corporate governance is fundamental to well-managed companies and to ensuring that they operate at optimum efficiency.

Interestingly, despite the recognition that one model of corporate governance cannot be applied to all companies in all countries, there does seem to be convergence on certain common core principles, usually based around the Organisation for Economic Co-operation and Development's (OECD's) *Principles of Corporate Governance* (1999) and their subsequent revision in 2004, and often influenced by the Cadbury Report (1992) recommendations. However, the growing influence of other organizations has also been noted, with the World Bank and OECD providing the impetus for the Global Corporate Governance Forum; the

Commonwealth Association for Corporate Governance promoting corporate governance in various countries; and the International Corporate Governance Network (ICGN) proving an influential group that has issued its own guidelines and reports on a number of corporate governance issues, ranging from global corporate governance principles, to executive remuneration, to barriers to cross-border voting. The ICGN's recent programme has included work on updating its global corporate governance principles, guidance on model contract terms for asset owners and their managers, and guidance on political lobbying and donations.

Corporate governance is indeed truly international. As mentioned previously, a corporate collapse in one country can have knock-on effects around the globe, the fallout rippling like waves in a pool. The impact of Enron, for example, has been felt across the world, not least because of the Sarbanes–Oxley Act, which the US legislature has decreed applies to all companies listed on a US stock exchange, including non-US firms that have a US listing. The Dodd-Frank Wall Street Reform has introduced the 'say on pay' in the USA, whilst the EU has introduced reforms that impact on the corporate governance of Member States. Notable amongst the EU reforms are proposals to strengthen shareholders' rights, and relating to executive remuneration, including a proposal to make the 'say on pay' binding, rather than advisory, in Member States. The EU is also considering introducing a quota system to ensure board diversity in terms of gender by specifying a certain quota of females on boards. Practically every month, a new corporate governance code, or revision to an existing one, is produced somewhere in the globe with the aim of increasing transparency, disclosure, or accountability. Some codes are being revised in the light of lessons learnt from recent scandals, collapses, and the global financial crisis to try to ensure that corporate governance develops and is better placed to enable organizations to cope with the changing world around them.

Corporate governance is just as applicable to a family-owned business as to one with a diverse shareholder base, and just as applicable to a public limited company as to a state-owned enterprise. EcoDa has produced corporate governance guidelines for unlisted companies, highlighting the value of corporate governance to unlisted enterprises many of which are owned and controlled by single individuals or coalitions of company insiders (for example, a family). Corporate governance is also beneficial to some of the newer types of investor such as sovereign wealth funds and private equity, and yet can also offer a lot to non-governmental organizations, the public sector, non-profit organizations, and charities. Whatever the form of business organization, a good corporate governance structure can help ensure the longevity of the organization by means of appropriate internal controls, management structures, performance measures, succession plans, and full consideration of shareholder and wider stakeholder interests. The role of independent non-executive directors is a crucial one in helping ensure that good governance is present, both in form and in substance.

We have seen too that the legal and ownership structures, whilst influencing the corporate governance structure, in no way negate the necessity for such a structure to be in place. Legal systems based on common law tend to give greater protection of shareholders' rights, including minority shareholders' rights, whereas legal systems based on civil law tend to give less protection. This has influenced the way that ownership structures have developed, with common law system countries tending to have more public companies with widely dispersed share ownership, and civil law system countries tending to have more ownership by families or blockholders. In each system, however, a strong case can be made for the benefits of good corporate governance.

The growing trend in a number of countries for institutional investors to be a dominant shareholder group has had an impact on the development of corporate governance in those countries, such as the UK and the USA. The role that institutional investors can play in corporate governance is significant, although they have been criticized for not being active enough, not really caring about the companies in which they invest, not trying to change things for the better, and, in short, not acting as owners. However, there now seems to be a change of mindset, partly spurred on by the institutional investors themselves, partly by governments, and partly by the ultimate beneficiaries whom they represent. Institutional investors are coming under increasing pressure to be more activist in corporate governance matters, and to be proactive in their rights and responsibilities as shareholders. The advent of the first Stewardship Code occurred in the UK in 2010, formalizing what is expected of institutional investors. There have been some highly visible changes, including more institutional investors being prepared to vote against management; for example, on executive directors' remuneration packages, the latter spurred on by high levels of discontent at excessive executive director remuneration, and the willingness to express dissent at this through the 'say on pay'. The level of voting overall by institutional investors is also increasing, albeit slowly, as they recognize that the vote is an asset of share ownership with an economic value and that they should therefore exercise their votes. Institutional investors are gradually exercising their 'voice' more effectively by constructive dialogue with management, by voting, and by focus lists, to name but a few ways. Equally, institutional investors are themselves now coming under more scrutiny and there seems to be a desire to 'round the circle', to have more transparency and disclosure from institutional investors, and more accountability to their ultimate beneficiaries (ordinary men and women who have an interest in what institutional investors are doing). The ultimate beneficiaries may be contributing to a pension scheme, or may already be retirees, or may simply be investing into the market. Whatever their interest, the institutional investors are wielding large amounts of power by virtue of millions of individuals who essentially are the roots from which the tree of institutional investment grows. Institutional investors should be acting as owners and they should also themselves be more accountable to the suppliers of their funds, the investors and policyholders whom they ultimately represent. There is also now an increasing emphasis on the role and responsibilities of the trustees of pension funds, with more emphasis being placed on trustees being appointed with appropriate experience and the facility to undertake training specifically related to their role.

With the change in 2000 to the UK Pensions Act, pension fund trustees had to state their policy on social, environmental, and ethical issues. There seems now to be a growing awareness of these issues and companies themselves will have to consider their stance on corporate social responsibility issues more fully with the growing recognition that a company cannot act in isolation from its wider stakeholder groups—including employees, customers, suppliers, and the local community—but must take account of their interests too.

In terms of board composition, the question of board diversity has gained a lot of attention in the last few years; more countries are introducing a quota system with the aim of increasing female representation on the board of directors. Where countries have not introduced a formal quota system, there is nonetheless often a proactive approach to in-creasing the number of females on the board through voluntary means (including appro-priate mentoring); recruitment consultants being encouraged to put forward more women to companies when short-listing for directorships; and an explanation of the potential ben-efits of board diversity to help change the mindset of boards which remain 'traditional' in their composition.

Many of the 'hot issues' of corporate governance will no doubt continue as the most de-bated issues for some time to come. These issues include:

- directors' remuneration;
- directors' performance;
- board evaluation;
- the role and independence of non-executive directors;
- board diversity;
- succession planning;
- the internal governance of institutional shareholders;
- the role of pension fund trustees;
- the social responsibilities of companies.

At the same time, in both developed and developing markets, there will continue to be a focus on improving corporate governance, especially in relation to transparency and disclosure, for without that, one cannot determine how well a company is performing, whether it is acting in a socially responsible way, and whether it is being run and managed appropriately. There is an old saying that 'knowledge is power' and shareholders must have knowledge about companies to enable them to fulfil their role as owners. Part of that role is to try to ensure that companies perform to their best capabilities, and the evidence increasingly points to the fact that good corporate governance and corporate performance are linked. This is yet another reason why corporate governance will continue to have a high profile across the globe.

Corporate governance and corporate social responsibility can be seen as areas that can help to make lives better: not just the corporate lives, the directors, managers, and share-holders, but the lives of the various stakeholder groups too. Society at large may, in the longer term, become better off in a holistic sense, not only commercially but in terms of overall well-being. Charkham (1994) summed this up with his usual intuitive insight when he said it is

> vital to keep a system of corporate governance under review. It is as important to a nation as any other crucial part of its institutional framework, because on it depends a good portion of the nation's prosperity; it contributes to its social cohesion in a way too little recognized. A proper framework for the exercise of power is an economic necessity, a political requirement, and a moral imperative.

Corporate governance therefore seems likely to continue its high-profile growth and will no doubt evolve to meet new challenges to be faced in the future, some of which we are already aware of, some hinted at, and some as yet unknown. However, corporate governance structures and frameworks can only do so much. We may well ask why we have had so many corporate governance developments over the years in terms of regulation, self-regulation, codes of best practice, guidelines and so on, and yet still suffered financial scandal and collapse on such a scale. Part of the answer lies in the fact that at the root of so many problems has been a lack of ethical behaviour by the individuals involved in positions of power and influence in companies. They have displayed a lack of consideration for others who would be affected by their actions, and all too often a consummate greed for money, power, or both. A lack of independent directors who have been willing to stand up to powerful, often charismatic, individuals has meant that millions of ordinary people have lost out, often in a way that a multi-millionaire director would find difficult to understand, as companies have underperformed and, when the full facts have emerged, have been the object of damaging scandals resulting in significant financial losses for shareholders with the concomitant implications for stakeholders. As Morck (2008) highlighted, behavioural issues are important in corporate governance, and maybe it is these issues that need to be more fully addressed in future corporate governance debates.

Ultimately, it is individual integrity and then the board as a collective of individuals acting with integrity that will help shape ethical corporate behaviour in the future. And it is ethical corporate behaviour that will determine the effectiveness of corporate governance and thereby the future of many corporations and livelihoods, both directly in the company and in the wider society. Some may question the value of corporate governance but the world is clearly a much better place with it than without it.

References

Cadbury, Sir Adrian (1992), *Report of the Committee on the Financial Aspects of Corporate Governance*, Gee & Co. Ltd, London.

Charkham, J. (1994), *Keeping Good Company: A Study of Corporate Governance in Five Countries*, Oxford University Press, Oxford.

Dodd-Frank Wall Street Reform and Consumer Protection Act (2010), USA Congress, Washington DC.

European Confederation of Directors' Associations (2010), *ecoDa Corporate Governance Guidance and Principles for Unlisted Companies in Europe*, European Confederation of Directors' Associations, Brussels.

Financial Reporting Council (2010), *The UK Stewardship Code*, FRC, London.

Morck R. (2008) 'Behavioral Finance in Corporate Governance: Economics and Ethics of the Devil's Advocate', *Journal of Management and Governance*, Vol. 12, No. 2, pp. 179–200.

OECD (1999), *Principles of Corporate Governance*, OECD, Paris.

——(2004), *Principles of Corporate Governance*, OECD, Paris.

Sarbanes–Oxley Act (2002), US Legislature, Washington, DC.

 For further links to useful sources of information visit the Online Resource Centre **www.oxfordtextbooks.co.uk/orc/mallin4e/**

Index